RICHARD STRAUSS

AND HIS WORLD

Richard Strauss
AND HIS WORLD

EDITED BY BRYAN GILLIAM

PRINCETON UNIVERSITY PRESS

Copyright © 1992 by Princeton University Press
Published by Princeton University Press, 41 William Street,
Princeton, New Jersey

ALL RIGHTS RESERVED

Library of Congress Cataloging-in-Publication Data

Richard Strauss and his world / edited by Bryan Gilliam.
p. cm.
Includes bibliographical references and index.
ISBN 0-691-09146-3—ISBN 0-691-02762-5 (pck.)
1. Strauss, Richard. 1864–1949.
2. Strauss, Richard. 1864–1949—Criticism and interpretation.
I. Gilliam, Bryan Randolph.
ML410.S93R44 1992 780'.92—dc20 [B] 92-15748

This book has been composed in Baskerville
by Don Giller

Princeton University Press books are printed on acid-free paper,
and meet the guidelines for permanence and durability of
the Committee on Production Guidelines for Book Longevity of
the Council on Library Resources
Printed in the United States of America

10 9 8 7 6 5 4 3 2 1

10 9 8 7 6 5 4 3 2 1
(Pbk.)

Designed by Laury A. Egan

Contents

CONTENTS

PART III
MEMOIRS

PART IV
CRITICISM AND RECEPTION

Preface and Acknowledgments

As we approach the end of the century, attention to Strauss and his music has experienced exponential growth. The famous tone poems, as well as *Salome, Elektra,* and *Der Rosenkavalier,* remain fixtures to any musical season, but the past decade has also witnessed unprecedented interest in lesser-known works, as evinced by various Strauss festivals and recording projects. Growing scholarly interest in Strauss's music has been more recent, but it is no less real. 1989 and 1990 saw back-to-back Strauss conferences in Leipzig and at Duke University in Durham, North Carolina, respectively. And a major Strauss festival—unprecedented in scope by American standards—is planned for this year at Bard College (Annandale-on-Hudson, New York). Beyond the musical offerings is included a panel discussion, "Modernism, Romanticism, and Postmodernism: Politics and Aesthetics in the Twentieth Century (The Case of Richard Strauss)."

For decades Strauss remained at the periphery of the musicological discourse, somehow lost between the Brahms-Wagner polemic of the late nineteenth century and the Schoenberg-Stravinsky dialectic of the twentieth. Glenn Gould, indeed, stood out as an iconoclast in the early 1960s when he suggested that Strauss and Schoenberg were the two greatest composers of the century. Gould was convinced that Strauss's greatness would ultimately become evident once "the time-style equation which clutters most judgment of his work" was dissolved.[1] But that equation, which sees progress in music in harmonic terms and views musical style as an inevitable, evolutionary process, has been the long-standing legacy of the post-Schoenbergian era; only recently has it begun to erode. Current scholarly interest in Strauss is one result of this paradigm shift, but it is part of a broader picture: an effort among various contemporary scholars to grapple with the problems of musical modernism.

Dahlhaus, in his book *Nineteenth-Century Music,* was among the first to try, but he succeeded more in pointing to important issues than finding solutions. He described *Don Juan* as the "dawning of 'musical modernism,'" (decrying the term *late romanticism* as a "terminological blunder of the first order") but failed to develop the issue much further.[2] Yet, in raising the issue, Dahlhaus has galvanized present and

· vii ·

future research, for once we disregard the "time-style equation," once we look beyond the tonal-atonal axis as the sole defining factor in twentieth-century modernism, a whole range of other issues emerge: historicism, fragmentation, the desacralization of art, and the like. Surely one of the most fascinating paradoxes of Strauss is that he was a composer immersed in Wagner's musical style and technique, yet his philosophy of art was far removed from that world. In short, he exploited Wagner's "sacred apparatus," his "sacred language," in order to demythologize the philosophy that gave us that very language. James Hepokoski, for one, suggests that

> this aspect of Strauss, which we may regard as the principal challenge of his work, was not lost on those of his critics who continued to uphold the Schopenhauerian-Wagnerian belief in a music that transcends the merely phenomenal. For any true believer—Mahler, Schoenberg, Bloch, Adorno, and others—the all too easy link between Strauss and the acceptance of the everyday experience poisoned the composer's *oeuvre* and tilted dangerously at the seriousness of music itself: as one of the defenders of the faith, Bloch would refer to Strauss as "the master of the superficial."[3]

In this vein Strauss's D-minor *Burleske* (1886)—not *Don Juan*—might well be considered his first modern work, for it is one of the earliest pieces to use the historical canon as a source for parody. Fully aware of the Brahms-Wagner polemic, Strauss delights in burlesquing Brahms (the D-minor and B♭-major piano concerti) and Wagner (*Die Walküre* and *Tristan*), sometimes in arresting juxtapositions. In doing so, Strauss seeks to forge a new relationship between composer, performer, and audience, for without the audience's knowledge of works from recent history the sense of parody would collapse.

Ariadne auf Naxos likewise exploits an established canon as a source of parody. Its juxtaposition and fragmentation of elements foreshadow certain works that would not emerge until the 1920s. Preoccupation with the time-style equation has obscured compelling similarities between *Ariadne* and Schoenberg's *Pierrot Lunaire*, both of which were composed in 1912 and both of which set the world of commedia dell' arte against unfamiliar landscapes. Stravinsky's *Pulcinella* (1920), which adapts music attributed to Pergolesi, is often cited as an early example of neoclassicism, but preliminary *Ariadne* sketches, which include fragments from Pergolesi and Corelli, demonstrate Strauss's historicism nearly a decade earlier. But the historicist aspects of *Ariadne* go beyond the exploration of the baroque, for the opera succeeds in juxtaposing the styles of Mozart, Schubert, and nineteenth-century bel canto.

The concept of Strauss as early modernist is an important theme throughout the essays in Part I of this volume. Leon Botstein addresses the issue head-on, contradicting various clichés about Strauss's music, the most important one being the supposed stylistic about-face after *Elektra*. Botstein, rather, finds a remarkable artistic coherency throughout Strauss's creative life. One such consistent trait is explored by Derrick Puffett, who examines the phenomenon of pitch specificity in Strauss's work—a phenomenon of "tonal symbolism" or "key association" whereby certain themes are inseparable from their tonal settings. These "pitch-specific motives," especially when quoted in different harmonic contexts, often create a sense of fragmentation.

Dahlhaus claimed *Don Juan* as the dawn of musical modernism, but Hepokoski locates these roots in the composer's first tone poem, *Macbeth*. And whereas Dahlhaus falls short of explaining *Don Juan*'s modernistic traits (describing only a certain "breakaway mood") Hepokoski delves into the issue of Strauss's "structural deformations," where structural paradigm and narrative strategy coexist in intricate relationships. Michael P. Steinberg's essay shifts the emphasis to Strauss and the 1930s. Rather than revisit the well-known chronology of Strauss's vicissitudinary relationship with the National Socialist regime, Steinberg looks to ideological currents internal to the composer's musico-dramatic conceptions—specifically *Friedenstag* (1936) and *Daphne* (1937). My own study focuses entirely on the latter opera, *Daphne,* discussing the textual and musical genesis of the final scene: Daphne's transformation. Timothy Jackson, likewise, explores late Strauss, offering a new hypothesis concerning the makeup of the so-called *Four Last Songs*. His exhaustive source study suggests that these four orchestral songs are incomplete as they now stand, and he makes a convincing argument for the inclusion of the earlier *Ruhe, meine Seele!* which was orchestrated directly after *Im Abendrot*. The early song exhibits strong textual and motivic connections with the later ones, especially *Im Abendrot*.

Strauss was a prodigious correspondent, and over the past decades numerous volumes of correspondence have been published, but relatively little has appeared in English. The letters of Part II present, now in translation, two pictures of Strauss—young and old. The letters to his boyhood friend, composer and theorist Ludwig Thuille, are important to understanding Strauss during his formative years. Highly opinionated, even brash at times, Strauss was clearly still under the influence of his conservative father, Franz, but one detects the emerging artistic individual as well. His correspondence from the 1930s with post-Hofmannsthal librettist Joseph Gregor reveals Strauss the seasoned master of the operatic stage, an almost overbearing artistic personality when compared to the minimally gifted Gregor. These letters offer an important context for Steinberg's and my own essays, both of which explore Strauss's artistic relationship with Gregor.

Part III offers memoirs of the composer from various periods of his creative life. The Alfred Kalisch memoir (1908) represents the earliest English-language biographical sketch of the composer. Percy Grainger was a great admirer of Strauss, and he even made piano arrangements of some of his works. The decade that separates these two essays produced some of Strauss's best-known works: *Elektra, Der Rosenkavalier, Ariadne auf Naxos,* and *Eine Alpensinfonie.* Willi Schuh and Rudolf Hartmann each offer an appreciation of a composer at the end of a long life of composing: the former, an eightieth-birthday tribute that attempts to sum up the significance of the composer; and the latter, a moving account of a visit with Strauss eight days before he died. Both appear in English for the first time. Important critical reviews of Strauss and his music, also for the first time in English, constitute Part IV; these include essays by Guido Adler, Theodor Adorno, Paul Bekker, Robert Hirschfeld, Max Kalbeck, Julius Korngold, Karl Kraus, Rudolf Louis, and Gustav Schoenaich.

.

This volume endured a remarkably rapid production schedule, and without the assistance and cooperation of many individuals it never would have appeared. The idea for a Strauss festival began with Leon Botstein, founder of the Bard Music Festival, and many of his ideas found their way into this book. I am greatly indebted to Susan Gillespie, who translated a large amount of difficult German prose into lucid English in a short amount of time. Her important contribution to this volume cannot be overstated. I would like to thank the staff at Princeton University Press for their esprit de corps, especially Elizabeth Powers for her encouragement and optimism throughout the process and Lauren Oppenheim, whose tireless dedication to this project was central to its success. I am deeply grateful to the Richard Strauss–Archiv in Garmisch for permission to quote excerpts from primary sources. As this book went to press Alice Strauss, the composer's daughter-in-law, passed away. A large portion of her life was dedicated to the creation and maintainance of this archive, which is now in the capable hands of her son Richard. He and his wife, Gabrielle, have been most helpful. Thanks go as well to the Houghton Library at Harvard University for permission to cite Strauss sketch material. I am also indebted to Hans Schneider Verlag (Tutzing) and Atlantis Verlag (Zurich) for their permission to cite selections in translation for Parts II and III. At Duke I would like to thank my colleague R. Larry Todd, editor of *Mendelssohn and His World* (Princeton, 1991), for his helpful advice, J. Michael Cooper both for his diligent proofreading and for compiling the index, and Isabelle Bélance-Zank.

BRYAN GILLIAM

17 APRIL 1992

NOTES

1. Unpublished letter of 13 December 1961 to Leonard Bernstein (National Library of Canada, Glenn Gould Collection).

2. Carl Dahlhaus, *Nineteenth-Century Music,* trans. J. Bradford Robinson (Berkeley and Los Angeles: University of California Press, 1989), pp. 330 and 334.

3. James Hepokoski, "Fiery-Pulsed Libertine or Domestic Hero? *Don Juan* Reinvestigated," in *Richard Strauss: New Perspectives on the Composer and His Work,* ed. Bryan Gilliam (Durham, N.C.: Duke University Press, 1992).

PART I

ESSAYS

The Enigmas of Richard Strauss:

A Revisionist View

LEON BOTSTEIN

I am ultimately now the only composer who has humor and wit and a marked parodistic talent. Yes, I feel downright the calling to be the Offenbach of the twentieth century . . . Starting with *Der Rosenkavalier* is our way: its success proves it, and it is also this genre (sentimentality and parody are the sensibilities to which my talent responds strongest and most fruitfully) that I happen to be keenest on.
—RICHARD STRAUSS TO HUGO VON HOFMANNSTHAL, 5 JUNE 1916[1]

I have often thought about those of our subjects—*Rosenkavalier, Ariadne, Frau ohne Schatten*—which are about purification, about a Goethe-like atmosphere, and for which your profound understanding has pleased me indefinitely . . . But at the same time other sides of your productive nature are being less made use of, I mean the massive, grandiose, wholly compelling qualities that distinguish you from all living composers and give you a singular and incomparable position . . . But that other element, which you also command, that mastery of the dark and savage side—which I intentionally refused to nourish—remains nonetheless one of your most valuable gifts.
—HUGO VON HOFMANNSTHAL TO RICHARD STRAUSS, 8 MARCH 1912[2]

The Man and the Artist

Few composers have remained as resistant to penetrating historical characterization and biographical analysis as Richard Strauss. There was something elusive and opaque about Strauss's personality and his aesthetic credo. Nevertheless, since his death there has been a remarkable degree of agreement among historians and critics about the basic shape of Strauss's career and his place in the history of twentieth-century music. The explanatory hypothesis that has sufficed until now argues that Strauss was a late-nineteenth-century figure who lived on, in the words of Robert P. Morgan (writing in 1991), as if "in a time warp" into the twentieth century. In this view, all of

· 3 ·

Strauss's music produced after 1908 (when Strauss finished *Elektra*) is, as Morgan has put it, curiously "unhistorical."[3] Apparently, until *Elektra*, Strauss worked in synchrony with progressive movements in the history of music and culture during the late nineteenth century and at the fin de siècle. However, after *Elektra*, Strauss made what in 1962 Norman Del Mar called "an abrupt volte-face."[4]

In the wake of postmodernist developments, perhaps the moment has come to reconsider this standard view. The place to begin is with a reconsideration of the nature and significance of Strauss's entire oeuvre as well as its relationship to biographical and historical circumstances. Among the consequences of such a reevaluation might be a revision in the critical estimate of Strauss's works. For example, *Elektra*, *Salome*, and *Der Rosenkavalier* are still regarded as Strauss's greatest operatic achievements. It may turn out that, at a minimum, the three operas that deal with love and marriage—*Die Frau ohne Schatten* (1919), *Intermezzo* (1924), and *Die ägyptische Helena* (1928)—are no less deserving of admiration and attention.

Any attempt at a radical reassessment of Strauss's work and his place in history is complicated by the enigmas presented by Strauss himself. Perhaps the most blatant enigma about Richard Strauss stems from the perceived incongruities between the man and his work. Few composers have demonstrated such prodigious and wide-ranging musical facility so early in their careers and so consistently afterward. In terms of Strauss's mature work—*Elektra* and *Der Rosenkavalier*, for example—one can argue convincingly that not since Mozart has so subtle, wise, and affectionately differentiated a characterization of diverse aspects of the human condition been represented through music on the operatic stage. The virtuosity evident in Strauss's musical settings of poetic and dramatic texts and the startling beauty of his writing for the female voice are rarely contested.[5]

Yet, as Strauss's contemporaries Fritz Busch and Romain Rolland observed (not to speak of Gustav and Alma Mahler), it was truly baffling that so seemingly crude, insensitive, and ordinary a man could write such compelling music.[6] Strauss defied any reasonable expectation of the artistic personality. His avoidance of behavior that might give the appearance of being anything out of the ordinary, particularly an artist, was meticulous and intentional. Writing to Hugo von Hofmannsthal in response to the notion of giving the figure of the Composer a large role in the revised *Ariadne*, Strauss commented that in drama and novels the characterizations of artists, "particularly composers," inspired in him "an inborn antipathy."[7] Given the dependency on fictional characterization of the image of the artist within everyday life during the nineteenth century, it can be assumed that Strauss's antipathy to the artistic personality was not limited to the stage or to books.

On the other hand, Strauss's prose writings and correspondence reveal a sharp, ironic, somewhat self-deprecatory, and shrewd intellect. The picture of the old Strauss reading Goethe mirrors how oversimplified the judgments of some of his detractors were. Fritz Busch, like Arnold Schoenberg, may have been baffled but he was not fooled.[8] Busch observed:

> To solve the riddle of Strauss's nature, which although in possession of one of the most astounding talents at the same time was not permeated and possessed by it like other great artists; it was as if Strauss was really just wearing talent like a suit that one can take off; to solve that riddle neither I nor anybody else has succeeded. His strong material tendencies made him a marked representative of capitalism and a decided enemy of social change, a man without any taste for self-sacrifice. His needs, down to the philistine delight in his world-famous skat playing at which he seldom was defeated, seemed at times more important to him than his music. That this self-presentation nevertheless was deceiving one could see at quiet and intimate gatherings, for example when the conversation turned to his favorite composer, Mozart.[9]

Despite Norman Del Mar's assertions, Strauss was not really the object of contempt on the part of Hofmannsthal just because of some apparent lack of culture *(Bildung)*.[10] In a moment of anger, Hofmannsthal accused Strauss of almost "rhythmic" lapses into *Kulturlosigkeit* [loss of culture], from which Strauss would then manage to free himself. Hofmannsthal identified Strauss's egotism (defined as placing himself above all ideas and institutions) as the cause.[11] But Hofmannsthal never doubted Strauss's capacity for culture, only his willful and periodic retreat from it. As Charles Osborne has argued, the oft-repeated notion that the meaning of the libretto of *Die Frau ohne Schatten*, which Strauss (without cynicism or irony) regarded as his finest opera, eluded Strauss to the detriment of the final artistic result is implausible.[12]

By any reasonable comparison (with Mahler, Stravinsky, and Schoenberg, for example) Strauss's formal education, in nonmusical terms, was sophisticated.[13] In the early 1890s he read Schopenhauer closely.[14] Later in life he cited Burckhardt and Nietzsche with ease.[15] Strauss's critique of literary texts was consistently incisive. He may have played the fool, the simpleton, and the bourgeois. For one of the finest masters of stylistic appropriation and imitation in music, Strauss seems to have been, in life as well as in art, the consummate wearer of masks. The skat-playing Bavarian musician with vulgar tastes, (as Strauss disarmingly once described himself to Hofmannsthal) was one such mask. Strauss identified personally with the image of the good, solid man of the people, practically uncorrupted by the superficial polish of culture.[16] Beneath this overt allegiance to a Wagnerian or Rousseau-like ideology was a keen, critical, well-educated, and refined, if somewhat laconic, Strauss.

Strauss can be credited for possessing a self-confidence sufficient for humor and self-criticism. Despite Pauline Strauss's sense of the superiority of her family background, Richard Strauss, certainly in contrast to Gustav Mahler, was secure in his vocation and his social and national identity. That security enabled him to sustain a lifelong insularity from truly intimate friendships and privacy. It also permitted Strauss alternately to contain and display what Hofmannsthal perceptively deemed a "truly artistic and anarchic nature."[17] In this sense, Strauss was shrewder than Romain Rolland, who sarcastically wondered, in response to *Die ägyptische Helena*, why Strauss, "who so well realizes an inaptitude for great subjects of thought, let himself be caught by them again."[18] The facade Strauss successfully sought for himself convinced his overconfident French friend: it permitted him the solitude to think and work.

Strauss's biographers and admirers, both German and English (particularly Krause and Del Mar), much less Strauss's detractors, have not been able to resolve the dissonances between Strauss the man and his music. They have resorted to ad hominem arguments about both the personality and his work.[19] The difficulty that Richard Strauss posed as a personality was compounded in part by the opacity of the materials he left. Only clues remain. Beneath the masks Strauss wore lay a great deal of self-understanding, most of which was left implied rather than asserted. In contrast, for example, the letters of Mozart, the accounts of Beethoven, and the ample source material on Wagner have permitted biographers to generate revealing symmetries and relationships between personality and work.[20] We still understand too little about Richard Strauss to identify and clarify the biographical sources, intentions, and meanings associated with his work.

Despite his penchant for self-quotation as a composer, Strauss was not a composer who used music as an instrument for powerful autobiographical reflection and declaration. By way of contrast, one thinks of Wagner or Mahler. Even though Strauss's *Intermezzo* is embarrassingly candid in terms of its personal details, here again Strauss's use of masks comes to the fore. *Ein Heldenleben,* the *Symphonia Domestica,* and *Intermezzo* may be directly illustrative of Strauss's life, but they are neither intimate nor revelatory. The extreme use of realism about personal life (e.g., the *Symphonia Domestica*) itself becomes a mask. The Sixth Symphony of Gustav Mahler (written at the same time as Strauss's *Domestica*) and Wagner's *Tristan und Isolde* suggest to the listener more about their composers than perhaps all of Strauss's explicitly autobiographical works combined tell us about Strauss.[21] The closest Strauss came to autobiographical revelation through music may be found in the characterizations of the Dyer and his wife in *Die Frau ohne Schatten.*

Central to the enigma of Strauss's personality and the difficulty in reconciling it with his greatness as an artist was Strauss's conduct during the Nazi era. Although efforts have been made to compare his case to that of Wilhelm Furtwängler, Strauss's enthusiastic acceptance of an official position with the regime does not compare well even with Furtwängler's initial efforts to help Jewish colleagues and his halting attempts to remain independent.[22] There was a terrifying consistency in Strauss's relationship to politics throughout his life. His attitude to Kaiser Wilhelm, his negative reaction to Hofmannsthal's being drafted in 1914, and his passive but still unshakably firm German chauvinism all were comparable in their thoughtlessness. Strauss's political allegiances mirrored a single-minded focus on himself. At the same time, Strauss possessed a thoroughgoing contempt for politics and politicians and all manner of official authority. He was, as an egotist, as Hofmannsthal noted with acuity, actually an anarchist.

In order to justify the uninterrupted pursuit of his comfort and craft, servile pandering to politicians became a necessary and justifiable mask. The apolitical dimension of Strauss, unlike that of Furtwängler, took shape in his not taking any politics or ideology seriously. For example, Strauss never fell into the war-mongering enthusiasm of the early days of World War I, even though he assumed that the Germans were superior in all ways and should and would win.[23] Cynicism (even about Christianity and most German patriots) and a pessimism about social organizations revealed at one and the same time a contempt for the political, articulated as snobbishness.

This allowed Strauss to disavow responsibility for the consequences of the political realities around him. The same individual could lose patience with Stefan Zweig's doubts about working together, express disdain for the Nazis, then grovel to Hitler, assent to Nazi aesthetic policies, limit his anti-Semitism, and justify his own passivity and collaboration without feeling a shred of moral doubt and culpability. If Furtwängler remained anguished and shaken by external criticism,

Strauss responded reflexively, without struggle, and remained impervious to criticism. Unlike Hans Pfitzner, Strauss found the Nazis' antimodernism as merely a convenient turn of events rather than the triumph of hotly contested truths.[24]

One solution to the enigma presented by the clash between the man and his art was offered by Theodor Adorno, whose two essays on Strauss remain challenging and perceptive indictments. Adorno was one of the first to suggest (albeit with sarcasm) that Strauss would turn out, perhaps tragically, to be more important in the history of music than most observers during the mid–twentieth century were willing to concede. But he possessed the theoretical framework to reconcile Strauss's personality with his work.[25] Since Adorno's conception of Strauss's aesthetics and musical language relegated them to the position of a regressive historical and ethical force, Strauss's self-irony, consummate command of musical craft, and capacity to wear masks fit neatly into the perception that the beautiful surfaces of his music were mirages and mirrors of corrupt alienation. Strauss's neoromantic surface, his concessions (in contrast to Mahler) to the tastes of the audience in terms of continuity and melodic clarity, and his illustrative manipulation of emotions through a clichéd musical rhetoric all were evidence of the evil of the historical moment and society in which he flourished. Strauss vindicated the argument contained in Adorno's and Horkheimer's *The Dialectic of Enlightenment.* The seemingly rational and beautiful in culture became the handmaiden of oppression, commercial exploitation, domination, and false consciousness in late-capitalist bourgeois society. Strauss manipulated the potential of freedom within the aesthetic realm by spinning a seductive surface that was at once virtuosic and yet alluring.

For Adorno the matter was clear: there was no enigma. Art and personality meshed coherently. Strauss's aesthetics, his self-awareness, his technical prowess, and his ordinariness made him the ideal collaborator and spokesperson for a culture within which the unequaled barbarism of the twentieth century could flourish. Strauss represented the disfiguring of a philosophic ideal of culture and civilization as autonomous instruments of freedom.[26]

Barring an acceptance of Adorno's standpoint (which included, predictably, the acknowledgment of Strauss's originality during the late 1880s, particularly in *Don Juan*), the enigma remains. Adorno, for example, accepted as part of his analysis the familiar narrative of the decline in Strauss's creative work after *Elektra.* Likewise, he adopted the explanatory paradigm in which, in terms of musical aesthetics, the high point of Strauss's career in the positive sense was *Elektra.* For

Adorno, Strauss devoted the rest of his career to "consonances" that stood in contrast with *Elektra*'s "dissonances." Strauss refused to make the progress imperative within history that demanded that such distinctions be "abolished." Instead, particularly at the very end of his career, Strauss wrote music that "arouses nausea; music that has been debased to a delicacy and comes to self-consciousness with revulsion."[27]

Rereading Adorno's 1964 indictment reminds us that some reconciliation of the artist and the man still eludes us. The most plausible explanation rests with Strauss's single-minded allegiance to a definition of the craft of music as a simple vocation in the ordinary sense. Ironic distance, detachment, and the refuge behind masks that Strauss displayed in his mature years enabled him to act as if he were isolating the musical realm as mere work and pursuing it as a financial necessity and an item of mundane self-interest. That Strauss as a young man demonstrated a different sort of commitment and vulnerability is evident from his letters to his parents, his early relationship to Ludwig Thuille, and what little we know of his intense romance with Dora Weis Wihan.[28] But the Strauss that dates from his marriage to Pauline de Ahna is the man we have come to know: the elusive, businesslike, greedy, card-playing, conceited bourgeois whose humor, insight, warmth, and subtlety were disorienting dissonances. In light of his behavior during the Nazi era, the best explanation may be that as a man Richard Strauss was an early exemplar of a widespread late-twentieth-century phenomenon: the cultivation of a disavowal of resonsibility for one's community based on a seemingly legitimate historical pessimism and cynical realism. The result is a peculiar mixture of brilliance, conventional respectability, egotism, a self-justified disregard bordering on fatalism, and hopelessness that finally is little more than thoughtless complicity with radical evil.

Strauss's Career: Its Stages and Aesthetic Logic

The second enigma regarding Richard Strauss emerges from the unsuccessful search for some underlying coherence between the man and his music. What explains the three apparently radical shifts in Strauss's musical style?

The conventional assumption shared by music historians (and, for that matter, art historians) who employ a biographical strategy is that the corpus of an artist's work must possess either an inner unity or some consistency in its relationship to the causal factors that inspire the artist to produce. The simple fact that the same person has produced all the work makes this quest for coherence reasonable. Adorno, for example, found a coherence by integrating Strauss's personality and career within a theory of history and an interpretation of late-capitalist society. Few Strauss scholars, however, have shared so clear a philosophical construct of the late nineteenth and early twentieth centuries.

Therefore traditional methods of biographical periodization and analysis have dominated the Strauss literature. The division of a career into discrete periods becomes justified by some stylistic analysis of the artistic work itself. In the case of Beethoven, the designations "early," "middle," and "late" are presumably internally justified by the music. Once identifiable shifts in technique or genre are located, linkages between the stages can be adduced, replete with "transition" works, so that a unified portrait can emerge, more often than not in the form of a triptych. Even in the case of a composer who died at age thirty-one, Franz Schubert, the interpretive convention is strong enough to justify talk of a "late" period, even though, from a biographical or psychological standpoint, that notion might seem odd at best.

In the standard scholarly account, in Strauss's case, there was an early period, which ended in the mid-1880s. In this period Strauss wrote most of his chamber music, the two symphonies, and several concerti. Strauss, under the influence of his anti-Wagnerian father, worked comfortably in a neo-Schumannesque and pseudo-Brahmsian mode. As his enthusiastic correspondence with Ludwig Thuille from this period reveals, Strauss responded with intense revulsion at Wagner's orchestration and expressive rhetoric. Beethoven, Spohr, and Auber, as well as earlier masters, commanded his admiration.[29] Mozart in particular (and interestingly, although to a lesser extent, Haydn) was singled out for admiration by the young Strauss.

Ironically, Strauss's relationship to his father, a distinguished professional musician, has an important parallel in W. A. Mozart's relationship to Leopold Mozart. In both cases the aesthetic judgment of the father was a crucial force in terms of imitation and accommodation. It also served as a psychological impetus for subsequent innovation and rebellion.

The father was replaced, in Strauss's case, with a fatherlike figure, Alexander Ritter (1833–96), a fanatical Wagner adherent.[30] Strauss turned away steadily from the neo-Brahmsian direction favored by another mentor, Hans von Bülow, and became converted, so to speak, to the cause of neo-Wagnerianism. From the mid-1880s on Strauss would remain steadfast in his admiration for Wagner. According to the convention, the second period of Strauss's work begins around 1885 with his new style, evident first in the *Burleske* and *Aus Italien*. The genres of symphony, quartet, concerto, and sonata were gradually set aside in favor of the tone poem and opera as Strauss embraced the Wagnerian alliance of poetry, drama, and music.

Strauss later took a dim view of the music from his first period. Therefore it is not surprising that only those works (e.g., the Wind Serenade, Op. 7, from 1881) that, so to speak, prefigure "second-period" Strauss remained within the active repertoire. Continuities between the early and later work, such as thematic structure and juxtaposition (e.g., in the Second Symphony in F minor, itself a powerful and underperformed work) and the use of ironic reminiscences of classical models (e.g., in the *Burleske*) traditionally have been overlooked.

The second period includes the great tone poems of the 1880s and 1890s. It also encompasses the first four operas. In this standard narrative of Strauss's career, the second period ends with *Salome* (1905) and *Elektra* (1908). The second period might well be called Strauss's modernist and progressive phase. Both the apostles of twentieth-century modernism and their opponents have embraced this period of Strauss's work. *Don Juan* and *Elektra* in particular are cited as models of musical innovation. In both works observers have located a modernist approach to harmony (i.e., the extension of tonal practice and use of dissonances), the employment of extremes in sonorities from the orchestra, an outstanding virtuosity in thematic invention, rhythmic elaboration, formal development, and dramatic characterization through musical means.

This was the Richard Strauss who became both wildly famous and notorious throughout Europe and America in his own time. He was identified by the public and the critical community as a leading, if not radical, modern. As one journalist wrote in 1907, Strauss's *Salome*, Mahler's Sixth Symphony, Reger's *Sinfonietta*, and Schilling's *Moloch* were the signposts of German musical modernism. But it was ultimately Strauss whose works, even in the eyes of detractors, were the "musical quintessence" of modernity; the "burning reflection, in music of culture as it is today." Strauss's music "accompanies the spiritual concerns of our era."[31] This was the Strauss with whom Gustav Mahler felt a kinship. In the fifteen years between 1890 and 1905 Strauss assumed a visible public role as conductor and organizer on behalf of his modernist contemporaries. The apogee of this period for Strauss, even in the eyes of his contemporaries, was *Elektra*, which was subsequently incorporated into the canon of twentieth-century modernism.[32]

It is at this point that the enigma in Strauss's development as a composer begins. Reconciling the first two periods, despite their stylistic contrasts, is relatively easy. However, as Bryan Gilliam has observed, Strauss's career has been regarded through the prism of a polemical paradigm of the evolution of twentieth-century music. *Elektra* fits the paradigm. However, after 1908 the paradigmatic historical logic points directly at Schoenberg and his followers as the appropriate path and destination for twentieth-century aesthetic development.[33] In this paradigm, modernism's progressive direction rendered the strategies of late romanticism obsolete by the end of the first decade of the twentieth century. The scholarly extension of this essentially Schoenbergian paradigm in recent years has broadened the range of "true" twentieth-century progressive modernism to account for a wider range of music than Schoenberg and Adorno might have tolerated.[34] In this redefined periodization of the twentieth century, Stravinsky, French and Russian neoclassicism, Varèse and his followers, minimalism, as well as the Second Viennese School and its post–World War II successors are incorporated as appropriately coincident with the "true" development of the twentieth century.

Within this paradigm Strauss's work after *Elektra* represents a backward turn. With *Elektra* (1908), Strauss had exhausted the nineteenth century. Although he pointed a way to the future in that work, he is said to have lacked the will or desire to take it. He turned his back on both present and future. His next work, *Der Rosenkavalier* (1910), may have been a singular success, but it marked the beginning of a retreat, a concession to popular taste and commercialism. However, even critics not sympathetic to what they regard as Strauss's "new" style in *Der Rosenkavalier* have admitted consistently to that work's striking effectiveness if not greatness. Nevertheless, with *Elektra* the second period ends, and with it Strauss's greatest creative moment as well as his centrality to the twentieth century.

There is, however, a more convincing revisionist argument. *Der Rosenkavalier* was, as Strauss and Hofmannsthal consistently argued, a breakthrough. It was a model and the beginning of an innovative period, one filled with evident linkages to Strauss's second period. There is a profound continuity between *Elektra* and *Der Rosenkavalier*. The use of extended tonal blocks and contrasts to delineate character and action, the line of experimentation regarding the setting of dialogue, the use of the orchestra with voice, the vocal ensemble writing, the structure of beginings and endings, not to speak of specific thematic resemblances, can be identified. The linking of *Elektra* and *Der Rosenkavalier* is consistent with the view that with *Der Rosenkavalier* an innovative, rather than a regressive, third period in Strauss's work begins.

The conventional narrative of Strauss's career—particularly among his staunch admirers—views the third period as one of uneven and weakening inspiration. Despite (and for some, on account of it) the continued collaboration with Hofmannsthal, the originality of *Elektra*, and the success of *Der Rosenkavalier* are never again equaled.[35] In fact, this almost wistful critical condescension has become standard. Most scholarly accounts begin with the search for difficulties and shortcomings; and for nuggets of greatness in the either minor or flawed works from 1911 on, particularly those written in the 1920s and 1930s.[36] Prior aesthetic valuation has consistently preceded scholarly investigation and has been its driving premise.

It will be argued that the third period, from 1910 to 1941, is Strauss's most singular and significant. Far from being aesthetically anachronistic, Strauss's next opera, *Ariadne*, was his most innovative and daring in form and design. The subsequent works, from *Die Frau ohne Schatten* to *Die Liebe der Danae* (including *Friedenstag, Daphne,* and the neglected orchestral and choral works from the 1920s and 1930s), are the center and apogee of Strauss as a modernist and innovator.[37] Their importance as parts of the repertoire will increase substantially in the decades ahead as a result of their visionary dimensions and the importance of this era in Strauss's work to late-twentieth-century music and theater. In the years ahead perhaps *Elektra*, not *Die ägyptische Helena,* will seem somewhat dated, flawed, and less alluring.

Owing to Strauss's longevity, there was a fourth and final stage in his creative work. Late Strauss is hailed by many as a parallel to late Verdi. The so-called Indian summer begins, for many, with *Capriccio* in 1941. For others it coincided with the fall of Nazi Germany in 1945. Few dispute that Strauss produced a series of stunning works, including *Metamorphosen*, the Oboe Concerto, and the *Four Last Songs*. The eloquence and craftsmanship of these works, anachronistic as the surface style may appear, and the dignified venerability of the composer in his last years have helped earn the late Strauss near-universal admiration reminiscent of the reception of the works from the second period.

It is no accident that the works from the 1930s and early 1940s have suffered by comparison. Understandably, Strauss's collaboration with the Nazis still creates considerable unease when one seeks to evaluate the merits of *Capriccio*, for example, which was completed in August 1941, two months after the invasion of the Soviet Union and six months before the infamous 1942 Wannsee Conference. The association of Strauss's musical rhetoric of the 1930s and 1940s with Nazi aesthetics and cultural politics cannot (and should not) be set aside easily. The fact that the last of Strauss's works to gain universal acceptance (again, with reservations) was *Arabella,* completed (although not produced) before the Nazi seizure of power in 1933, is no coincidence.

Running parallel with this fact is the other coincidence: the fact that the concert and critical community miraculously has accepted Strauss's works written after 1945. Despite the greatness of the late Strauss works, the convenient political parallelism in critical reception may not dovetail with a dispassionate analysis of the merits of the case.[38] In any event, the neglect of the works from the 1920s cannot be justified on such evident cultural political grounds, even though Karl Kraus's critique is a brilliant effort to do so.[39]

There are, then, four periods from which to fashion a coherent artistic biography. What late Strauss suggests, along with a revision of the critical assessment of the works between 1911 and 1928, is that there is in Strauss—as in Verdi, Beethoven, Haydn, and Brahms—a continuous evolution in technique and aesthetic ambition rather than a set of discontinuous breaks. There may have been neither a radical shift in direction nor a decline in artistic quality between 1910 and 1941. Each period has its masterpieces. Furthermore, the work from 1919 to 1928 represents the Straussian equivalent of great middle-period Beethoven, midcareer Verdi (his works from the late 1850s to the mid 1870s, including *Un Ballo in Maschera, Don Carlos,* and the *Messa da Requiem*), and the Wagner of the late 1850s and 1860s (*Tristan und Isolde* and *Die Meistersinger*).

Strauss, Modernism, and the Twentieth Century

The third enigma regarding Richard Strauss concerns his place in twentieth-century music and the significance of his work for the present and future. The first attack on the standard modernist paradigm was made by Glenn Gould in the early 1960s in two famous articles, the first of which was entitled "An Argument for Richard Strauss." It appeared in 1962, several years before the English translation of Adorno's second long essay on Strauss.[40] Gould was writing during the heyday of postwar modernism, in an era dominated by serialism and experimentalism. Stockhausen, Babbitt, and Boulez had become synonymous with musical modernism. Gould's penchant for debunking conventional wisdom led him to argue the merits of Strauss. Gould was attracted by Strauss's artistic evolution and the peculiarities in the critical reception of Strauss's music. The idea that

there was a great late period made a comparison with Beethoven alluring. But Gould's contribution was, curiously enough, the rehabilitation of the very early work as well as the late work.[41] Gould's claim
that Strauss was the "greatest man of music of our time" rested on
his reevaluation of Strauss's early chamber music, the symphonies, and
the concerti (e.g., the Violin Concerto, Op. 8). It also was based on
the similarities between late Strauss and late Beethoven. Gould was
convinced that Strauss had achieved "the transfiguring light of ultimate philosophic repose" characteristic of late Beethoven. Gould went
only so far in his revisionism. He shared the commonplace dismissive view of Strauss's works written between 1912 (including *Ariadne*)
and 1941 (i.e., *Capriccio*). Gould based his praise of Strauss on the
consistency of Strauss's musical vocabulary, the ease of his craftsmanship, and his ability for both simulated and genuine "ecstasy."[42] Gould
used Strauss as a foil against the conceits of his own time; as an undifferentiated symbol of the continued vitality of tonality and
neoromanticism. As to Strauss's place in music history, Gould wrote,
"I do not for one minute suggest that with all my admiration for Richard Strauss, I could possibly imagine that the future of music will
somehow be influenced in any actual stylistic sense by his works." After hedging this claim with a set of rhetorical questions about what
it means to be influenced or to influence others, Gould concluded,
"certainly Richard Strauss had very little to do with the twentieth century as we know it."[43]

One of the surprises about historical periodization and the history
of our own century is that in some decisive sense twentieth-century
composers today are influenced by Strauss, not only in terms of style
but in the conception of the relationship of music to theater, narrative, and language. Indeed, the last quarter of the twentieth century
has experienced a Strauss revival, in part because audiences and composers have begun to rethink the character of twentieth-century musical aesthetics in ways that make midcareer Strauss very much a part
of it. Strauss may emerge as less a transition figure than a forerun-
ner. A convincing account of twentieth-century aesthetic history might
place Richard Strauss (and not Arnold Schoenberg) in the center of
"the twentieth century as we know it."

A key to such a reconfiguration of Strauss's place in the twentieth
century is a reevaluation of the work from 1910 to 1941. In turn,
crucial to that reevaluation is a reformulation of Strauss's career development. The externally most "modern" works (e.g., *Elektra*) need
to be integrated into a larger compositional and stylistic framework.
The work after 1910 has to be considered not as flawed by compari-

son or weak in inspiration but exemplary and innovative. If the peak of Strauss's work can be located between *Die Frau ohne Schatten* and *Die Liebe der Danae,* then Strauss's second period becomes less unusual; it gains significance as prelude to the third period. The last stage retains its distinction. Furthermore, the definition of twentieth-century modernism becomes less narrow. A differentiated image of the nature of twentieth-century innovation—away from a single-minded concern for tonality as a category—based in part on an examination of Strauss's third period, can make his work an integral part of twentieth-century aesthetic developments.

Indeed, the work from 1912 until 1941 was not regressive but innovative in ways both comparable to and divergent from the paths taken by Schoenberg and Stravinsky. At stake here is not merely a matter of labels or concerns about the use of the term *modernist.* Rather, the challenge is to rethink what happened to the nineteenth-century traditions of concert music in the twentieth century, in terms not only of musical texts but of how works were heard, seen, and played by audiences in the theater, concert halls, and at home, particularly by means of recordings.

However, in this mix of textual analysis and reception history, Adorno's challenge regarding the connections between Strauss's musical project and the political horrors of the mid–twentieth century remains. The conception and appropriation of music, whether viewed as a self-consciously discrete realm of culture or not, need to be understood in connection to the propagation of and tolerance for inhumanity in the twentieth century.

The most compelling model for a revisionist analysis of Strauss is Arnold Schoenberg's brilliant 1947 essay on Brahms, entitled "Brahms the Progressive."[44] Schoenberg consciously sought to undercut the conventional idea of Brahms as a conservative. He painstakingly identified the technical aspects of Brahms's compositional manner and linked them and the innovations they contained, by family resemblances, not only to the work of classical masters but to the project and strategies of modernist composers—that is, Schoenberg and his followers. Brahms was turned on his head, so to speak, from being the last exponent of the classical tradition (as Heinrich Schenker argued) to being at one and the same time the first modernist composer, the father of modernist aesthetics. In turn, Richard Wagner appeared as a more regressive figure. Wagner's use of repetition and his conception of musical narration, expressiveness, and drama—his view of the nature and aesthetics of music—appeared as a relic of late romanticism incompatible with the twentieth century task of redeeming the "purely" musical through a reworking of preromantic musical procedures.[45]

The comparable argument for Strauss would have to show that Strauss prefigured the aesthetics of postmodernism; that beneath the surface of seemingly stylistically regressive music aspects of aesthetic innovation, which have become hallmarks of a new movement, were apparent. In line with Glenn Gould's 1962 speculations, one would be saying that contemporary composers are now exploring the sort of thing that Strauss attempted—a Straussian project—whether they are aware of it or not. Schoenberg, like the Wagner in Schoenberg's account, despite the fact that Schoenberg (like Wagner) during his lifetime took on the explicit mantle of the modern and progressive, might then appear dated and emblematic of a tradition that a new generation needs to overcome.

Furthermore, if one were to approach the catalog of Strauss's work not from a historical and chronological perspective—sequentially as alternating responses to Brahms and Wagner—but methodologically in retrospect (as Schoenberg did in 1947 with Brahms), starting with the range of issues that preoccupy composers and painters at the end of the twentieth century, one might come to a set of novel conclusions.

Following the Schoenberg-Brahms strategy, one immediately places at the center of Strauss's achievement the three operas written between 1917 and 1928: *Die Frau ohne Schatten, Intermezzo,* and *Die ägyptische Helena*. Intimately linked to those three works are two major operas: the 1912 and 1916 versions of *Ariadne auf Naxos* and *Die Liebe der Danae,* Op. 83, written with Joseph Gregor and completed in 1940, a work whose composition can be considered the end of Strauss's third and middle period.[46] *Intermezzo* and *Die ägyptische Helena* in particular show a marked economy, technical command, restraint, and refinement in technique. *Ariadne* is, as Hofmannsthal suggested, as integrated and tightly constructed a musical and poetic achievement as *Elektra* or *Salome*.[47]

These five works are, arguably, innovative in several distinct ways that have particular relevance to late twentieth-century aesthetics:

1. As Hofmannsthal suggested to Strauss, following the success of *Der Rosenkavalier,* a new direction was being set by the two of them in contradistinction to the tradition of Puccini (*verismo*), the neo-Wagnerian dramatic tradition (e.g., Franz Schmidt's *Notre Dame*), and other forms of modernism. Although Strauss referred in 1928 to the works of Schoenberg and Krenek as "goat dung" and in 1912 sought to pillory the idea of the "modern" as an aesthetic mantle, both

Hofmannsthal and Strauss played, ironically, on the word *modern*.[48]

Strauss, despite overt references to Wagnerian and Mozartian models, was as intent as Schoenberg in shaking the shadow of the past. As Richard Specht observed, Strauss's ambition was to find a way to place music at the center of dramatic continuity in a manner distinct from Wagner.[49] The crucial aspect in Strauss's modernism was his concept of style. Unlike Schoenberg, Strauss as a composer was self-consciously pessimistic, if not cynical, about aesthetic progress. Awareness of modernity, in the sense of knowing one's historical place, was tantamount to using the past against itself. This becomes apparent in Strauss's handling of Couperin and Mozart in the 1923 *Tanzsuite* and the 1930 version of *Idomeneo*.

Strauss was the first composer to deconstruct the conventional historical narrative (in the sense of the German historical tradition, from Ranke and Burckhardt to Wilhelm Dilthey) in which style in the arts was evidence of a spiritually unique and unified discrete historical period. Strauss's keen eye for style in painting, as testified to by Romain Rolland, and his fondness for visiting museums[50] mirrored an intense interest in the essence of musical style in the past.[51] Unlike Brahms, his interest was not allied to the traditions of historical periodization and description; to any effort to re-create or document the past "wie es eigentlich gewesen." Strauss, given his historical pessimism, sought in the past distinctive stylistic elements that could be appropriated by him entirely for antihistorical purposes. At the same time, almost tongue in cheek, he used the external surface recognizability of aspects of historical style—the initial expectation, if not illusion, on the part of the hearer that the past was indeed being evoked—as part of his technique of creation. The past would be transformed without being entirely submerged.

This sort of stylistic extraction and appropriation would become a characteristic of the late twentieth century. Schoenberg's aesthetic ideology, evident from the 1911 phrase "emancipation of the dissonance" to his last writings, was more akin to a nineteenth-century philosophy of history, in which a teleology of historical progress could be identified through the sequence of distinct historical epochs. Strauss, beginning with *Der Rosenkavalier*, helped to invent a new twentieth-century form of self-critical historicism. What distinguished the Straussian form of historicism from mid-nineteenth-century historicism (against which fin-de-siècle modernism consciously struggled, particularly in architecture and painting) was the fragmentation in the use of the past and the irony associated with Strauss's (and Hofmannsthal's) approach to historical appropriation. In the name of the modern, fragments of the past had to be brought back, suggestively, and reordered and integrated anew.

Beginning with *Der Rosenkavalier,* Strauss's pattern of interjection and withdrawal of evident hallmarks of earlier surface styles was cast within a seamless dramatic continuity. In contrast, when Gustav Mahler utilized evident fragments he betrayed a self-conscious recognition of that element as artifact and remnant and kept it distinct. Mahler did not use the illusion of the historical to forge a style or to give shape to formal structure and unity. In *Der Rosenkavalier,* Strauss and Hofmannsthal did. As Hofmannsthal noted in 1913, "[*Der Rosenkavalier*] readmitted quasi-stealthily a seemingly remote stylistic method—the set numbers. From then on it was an inner necessity for me to explore to the end the set numbers and the formal and spiritual possibilities that they contain. Therefore the choice of a subject of almost contrapunctual severity; therefore the stylizing of emotion. And to make this possible, palatable, and true in a higher sense, the creation of an archaistic frame was added."[52]

What differentiated Strauss's post-1910 strategy from French postwar neoclassicism was its disregard for consistency as a dimension of historical appropriation. In *Pulcinella,* for example, Stravinsky played off one single, coherent historical allusion. In 1920s neoclassicism, the use of historical models carried with it an almost faithful respect for the historical model's procedural integrity; not so in the case of Strauss and Hofmannsthal. Strauss combined the presentation of a recognizable historicist surface with a more thoroughgoing distortion as well as the integration of fragments from disparate periods. A mélange of noncontiguous or overlapping historical sources was used, not only in musical terms but with the sets, the language, and the characters on the stage (e.g., the biblical Joseph in Veronese style in *Josephslegende*). What emerged from this juxtaposition of incongruent stylistic moments and selective self-quotations (the use of one's own work as history) was distinctly Straussian. The Mozartian and the Wagnerian, for example, in clearly recognizable ways coexisted side by side in the works of Strauss's middle years.

In *Der Rosenkavalier* and in later work, discontinuous stylistic citations and allusions (e.g., evocations of *Rheingold* at the end of *Die ägyptische Helena*) are used to form not a fragmented organism (as in Mahler) but an integrated, suggestive (vis-à-vis the audience), highly personalized narrative style. This partial and yet complete transformation of appropriated historical remnants, which become constituent elements of an identifiable personal musical vocabulary, was Strauss's contribution to the twentieth-century redefinition of artistic originality. Musical originality becomes defined in Strauss as the creative acknowledgment and free utilization of one's own self-conscious place in a historical continuum in a way that the audience—bred on a musical canon—can follow clearly. Originality does not derive from novelty in the sense of a rejection, transcendence, camouflage, or selective imitation of the past but rather as the result of an irreverent surrender to the past, one that dismembers any coherent sense of history.

What this new technique permitted was a flexible vocabulary that Strauss used to represent, through music, the complexities in mood, thought, and personality of his characters; to extend the psychological and narrative possibilities inherent in the idea of the Wagnerian leitmotif. Strauss, using appropriated styles and fragments could engender allusions beyond those set up or made possible internally by the thematic elements and tonal structure specific to any given work.

2. The technique of the appropriation of the past and the transformation of the past into usable remnants—as fragments of distinct styles—influenced Strauss's view of dramatic form. Hofmannsthal and Strauss certainly were right when they protested that the original version of *Ariadne* was far ahead of its time. As Hofmannsthal wrote Strauss during their work on the ballet *Josephslegende:*

> What heightens my sense of responsibilty to a painful degree is the idea that I might have confused you with the refinements of the unrepeatable experiment that is *Ariadne;* also that once again I might have created confusion in your mind with an absolutely secondary detail, that is the plan to perform this biblical subject in a Veronesian costume or something of that kind . . . I have only mentioned it to postulate a desire for a splendid costume and at the same time to escape the dry archeological exactness . . . The conception of *Ariadne* demanded from you to *partially* mask your music, to treat it as a quotation, and you solved this demand with wonderful tact . . . My dear Dr. Strauss, you do understand me, don't you?—and you do not consider me so arrogant as to assume the right to tie you down on your own works . . . but here it is a question of *style,* of a conscious choice among the inner possibilities.[53]

The use of a Molière play rewritten with very little of its authentic seventeenth-century character intact, accompanied by a distorted but imitative musical accompaniment and followed by an opera in which *commedia dell'arte* and an ambivalently serious *Tristan*-like nineteenth-century music drama of love are presented in one evening, all within the explicit context of theater as paid entertainment for a staged historicized group of patrons and the modern public is nothing if not courageously experimental. Even the 1916 version of *Ariadne* is a prefiguring of postmodernist dramatic aesthetics in painting, photography, architecture, film, and music.[54]

The 1912 *Ariadne* was also an attempt to elevate the comic and the parodistic to a polemic about modernity itself. What Hofmannsthal and Strauss shared was a pessimistic historical self-consciousness. That in turn led to a direct attack on clichés regarding the autonomy of art and the quasi-religious and philosophical importance of the art work, particularly the idea that art has the capacity to exert ethical and political force as Wagner and even Schoenberg (e.g., in *Moses und Aron* and the later works) hoped. Hofmannsthal and Strauss sought only to preserve and extend an aesthetic and cultural heritage, whether that did or did not have ramifications outside of the realm of art. For Hofmannsthal (but not Strauss), that cultural project was a political project directed at some idea of renewal; a transformation of life without mundane politics.[55]

Strauss's and Hofmannsthal's innovations in *Ariadne* and after are also a direct commentary on their remarkably affectionate conception of the relations between the audience and the composer and playwright. If in the post–World War I period Schoenberg and Alban Berg took the opportunity with the Society for Private Performances to express their hostility and contempt for the audience and the commerce of music and the theater, Strauss and Hofmannsthal, with no less a measure of conviction, took the opposite stance. Both were aware of changes that had taken place in the musical audience since the late eighteenth century. Hofmannsthal was conscious of his own limitations as a musical listener. He and Strauss, unlike Wagner or Schoenberg, never blamed the contemporary public as lacking in the capacity for response. Critics, directors, singers, and performers came under attack.

The premise of Strauss and Hofmannsthal was that one's public must be and could be reached. Strauss's critique of Hofmannsthal's drafts (as the latter knew) was rooted in his sense of what made for effective theater and what could be comprehended.[56] Only in the case of the 1912 *Ariadne* did they speculate that they had unexpectedly anticipated the future. Even though their use of stylistic juxtapositions and their laying bare the illusions of the theatrical in *Ariadne* paid exaggerated respect to the audience's powers of discernment, their consistent ambition was to reach a broad public—what Hofmannsthal termed the "average listener," not the self-styled connoisseur.[57] Art, ultimately, was not a secret language.

3. After *Elektra* and particularly after World War I, Richard Strauss recognized one unique condition of twentieth-century modernity: the impossibility of sustaining either the comic or the tragic in their inherited modes without a dimension of distance, self-criticism, and doubt. The simultaneous presentation, undercutting, and gradual withdrawal of the sentimental in music is perhaps Strauss's profoundest contribution. Using an extended lyrical and dramatic line, Strauss, in the middle-period operas, paralleled an effect comparable to the undercutting of the sentimental achieved quite differently by Gustav Mahler. With a nearly Kierkegaard-like insight, Strauss, in the three marriage operas and in *Ariadne*, resisted the self-delusive embrace of sentimentality, dramatic closure, or moral certainty. In the mundane, ordinary, and intimate there was sufficient ambiguity and poignancy for serious art. *Intermezzo* displayed this directly. In *Die ägyptische Helena* the mythological and historical are rendered ordinary, in contrast to Wagner. Over the span of two acts, the heroic characters turn out to be human, recognizable, and subject to empathy on the part of every unexceptional modern observer. Magic and the divine—spells and potions included—are powerless against the human, defined conventionally. As Hofmannsthal's reading of *Elektra* suggested, Orestes and Chrysothemis triumph over their sister, the divine heroic instrument.

Strauss sought to reveal the profundity inherent in the mundane. From the standpoint of the audience, in contrast to most of Wagner after *Lohengrin*, the embrace of the real and the flawed human experience is underscored, rather than any idealization of the heroic. Menelaeus must love Helen without illusions in full recognition of the past for which she accepts responsibility. The implicit critique of the Lohengrin-Elsa relationship in *Die ägyptische Helena* is striking. In *Die Frau ohne Schatten* the Empress seeks humanity. With humanity comes sacrifice and pain. Choice is the risk that forces the human being to act in the highest sense. The hesitant rather than the heroic comes to the fore. Barak and his wife are not idealized. In *Intermezzo*, the resolution at the end is evidently only partial and temporary.

In his collaboration with Hofmannsthal, Strauss developed the capacity to illustrate affectionate, clear-eyed recognitions, tinged with pessimism, bittersweet irony, and nostalgia. This subtle musical narrative virtuosity demanded that he communicate with the sentiments of his audience and with the experiences of their daily lives. Therefore, the appropriation of style and its imitation, all cast within a clear tonal framework, was a necessary component for the new project.

Works as disparate as the music dramas of Wagner, Busoni's *Doktor*

Faustus, Debussy's *Pelléas et Mélisande,* Alban Berg's *Wozzeck,* and Schoenberg's *Erwartung* and *Moses und Aron* all are, in narrative and style, part of a different and seemingly more ambitious tradition crucial to twentieth-century modernism. In these works the aesthetic surface becomes the ethical instrument. The experience of art becomes implicitly didactic. Through surface modernist originality, aestheticized ethics eschew compromise with reigning tastes. The intent of art becomes confrontational and therefore ultimately redemptive.

These modernist conceits and ambitions were abandoned by Strauss and Hofmannsthal. It was no accident that Hofmannsthal invoked part 2 of Goethe's *Faust* and the late work of Palladio to Strauss in 1912 as ideal models. Irony, ornament, and detachment in Strauss do not undercut wisdom; they are its instruments—a fact that eluded Rolland, who missed the point of *Die Frau ohne Schatten,* whose power "as the last romantic opera" rested not only in its fanciful mix of disparate elements but in its effort to use symbolism in the tradition of Mozart's *Die Zauberflöte* as a direct appeal to the audience.[58] The use of tonality and historical surfaces broadened this appeal by making the use of association and memory on the part of the audience of contemporaries possible.

4. In terms of technique, in order to achieve these ends, Strauss let his fascination with the relationship of speech to music dominate his work from 1912 on. Strauss had always been a literary composer. From the days of the first tone poems (many of which have literary origins) to *Daphne,* observers repeatedly described how Strauss sketched musical equivalents to words as he was reading. Strauss needed words to write music. One needs to consider as evidence not only the massive output of songs but also the substantial choral compositions. In all, Strauss set the works of at least seventy-four different authors, not including the writers of his opera libretti. Specific language inspired both musical forms and thematic equivalents. As he wrote Hofmannsthal in 1911, "Maybe you know my predilection for hymns in Schiller's manner and flourishes à la Rückert. They inspire me to formal orgies and these have to substitute where the inner action leaves you cold. An animated rhetoric can drug me sufficiently to let me write music through a passage of no interest. The interplay of forms: the formal garden has to come into its rights here."[59]

Musical structure paralleled the literary dimensions in midcareer Strauss (and in *Capriccio* as well). The most important case in point is *Die ägyptische Helena,* which began in Strauss's mind as an operetta and then was envisaged as a singspiel with a great deal of dialogue.

The end result, owing to Hofmannsthal's poetic text, was a cleanly delineated and restrained lyric and dramatic opera.

The thematic contrasts and tonal organization in the later Strauss operas correspond not only to what is being said but how it is being said. As Strauss explained to Hofmannsthal, a self-conscious sense of style stimulated by language prevailed in ways that developed further the Wagnerian innovations in the relationship between text and music. As Specht observed in *Die Frau ohne Schatten,* this strategy is particularly striking and effective.

As the preface (in both versions) to *Intermezzo* and the foreword to *Capriccio* explain, Strauss sought ways to enhance the comprehensibility and impact of speech in opera.[60] The use of large, purely orchestral sections in *Die Frau* and *Intermezzo* was Strauss's way of furthering, by separating music alone from music with text, the special qualities of the musical depiction of the literary. Strauss's innovations during the middle period in the use of recitative as a musical illustration of emotion and psyche far outdistanced the Wagnerian achievement Strauss so admired.

This midcareer interest extended in opera what Strauss in the 1880s and 1890s, during the second phase of his career, had achieved in the genre of orchestral music. In the tone poems he perfected a language of musical illustration that played with the illusion of realism. In the later work Strauss echoed this penchant with representations of card shuffling, falcons, and Arabs. These illustrative effects (however musical), his thematic materials, and the total form became governed by the deeper demands of poetic text. Strauss was not embarrassed by the musical illustration. His point was that by telling a story in music, the emotional and psychic impact of that story would transcend any parallel effort to represent reality in visual or literary terms. The mix of concrete illustration, symbolic allusion, and music-dependent association engendered by creating stylistic remembrances and similarities extended the narrative power of music.

But the story that inspired the musical had to remain comprehensible (and visible) in its original linguistic sense. It was no coincidence that on his deathbed Strauss reportedly told his daughter-in-law, the late Alice Strauss, that death was as he imagined it in *Death and Transfiguration.* Music, in fact, was more adequate to the real, defined linguistically, than language. It could speak where language could not.

Whether used autonomously or with a text, music could transmit a meaning that could be either retranslated or coordinated with a parallel in language. This, curiously, was precisely the way in which the majority of the audience in Strauss's lifetime listened to music. Much to Schoenberg's dismay, the twentieth-century public employed parallel linguistic commentaries in order to comprehend musical continuities.[61] Strauss's need for a text was reflective of his fascination for, if not addiction to, the way words work. Strauss's position on the relation of text to music and his actual use of music with texts after 1911 therefore diverged from the position Schoenberg put forward in a 1912 essay, "The Relationship to the Text." In Schoenberg's account, music achieved its unique ends by eschewing overt parallels with how a text sounded or with what it seemed to say.[62]

5. Strauss's use of style in music and music in narration point to yet another innovative aspect of his musical strategy after *Elektra*. What words and music have in common, in Strauss's view, is their capacity to engender the visual. The notion that mental images, whether of death or of something concretely man-made, can be conjured by musical means connects the power of music to the psychological capacity for visualization through language. Visualization by the hearer (and its subsequent description in language) becomes an integral part of the proper response to music. This does not mean that Strauss subordinated the musical to the visual.

But it explains Strauss's intense allegiance to the operatic genre. In *Capriccio* this lifelong engagement with how the verbal, the musical, and the visual relate to one another gains its most explicit expression. As has been noted already, Strauss maintained a lifelong fascination with painting and an obsessive concern with the way his operas looked. During the First World War Strauss was most concerned that, owing to politics, one would not be able to see the treasures in the French and English galleries. Among his motivations to go to England after 1945 was the desire to visit the National Gallery once more.

Strauss's interest in music as illustration and in the process of visualization through music explains why his tastes in painting were limited to particular historical styles; to the baroque and most of all to the rococo. The debate regarding the connections and divisions among the musical, linguistic, theatrical, and visual was pronounced in these historical eras. These periods in art history offered Strauss relief from the residues of romanticism and the overworked and tired language of the nineteenth-century aesthetic debate (e.g., Schopenhauer, Hanslick, and Wagner). Strauss's interest in Vernet's painting (documented by Rolland) mirrored his interest in the eighteenth century's conception of the relationship of viewer to canvas. As Michael Fried has suggested brilliantly, within the traditions of realist representation in the seventeenth and eighteenth centuries the sense that the viewer is an observer was crucial. The conscious manipulation and rejection of the eye of the beholder and the depiction of absorption influenced the character of the art itself. All these aspects of this period of French painting are theatrical and tie directly to the operatic tradition. They raise theoretical issues regarding the function of painting.[63] Painting that did not engage these issues and did not play with realist composition in the strict sense was of little interest to Strauss. Rolland observed, "everything which has a tendency to heroism, all painting which is tragic or in the spirit of Corneille, leaves him tired or bored."[64]

The dynamic between viewer and canvas explored in the late seventeenth, eighteenth, and early nineteenth centuries was analagous for Strauss to his project as an illustrative composer and related directly to the form of the opera; to the problems posed by historical depiction; the use of style; and the dynamic between composer and audience. It is this connection between the visual, the theatrical, and the musical and the desire to maintain the tension between the viewer and the canvas (i.e., the operatic experience) that explain not only Strauss's allegiance to a tradition of realist painting but his resistance to certain innovations in musical modernism. The abandonment of tonality or its substitution by other systems and the experimentation with radical rhythmic displacement and discontinuity would make the creation of powerful visual and narrative tension with the viewer and audience impossible. Strauss's so-called stylistic conservatism and his constant references to past models was, in fact, a necessary means to sustain novel possibilities within a tradition of realism. Part of that tradition was the self-conscious awareness of how illusions of realism were spun out in differentiated relationships with the audience.

After 1910 the preservation and possible renewal of the possibilities for subtle communication through instrumental music and opera demanded an engagement with the power of realist strategies within music. Strauss's allegiance to a musical language that possessed a long historic tradition was a statement that argued the parallels between language and visual realism on the one hand and the inherited musical tradition and realistic linguistic representation and meaning on the other. Strauss needs to be understood as an innovative master of new techniques of musical realism.

Strauss's apparent aesthetic "conservatism" derived as well from his notion of the role that music played in culture as a whole. Through its explicit confrontation with the expectations of the audience, twentieth-century modernism threatened, for Strauss, any possible link between civility and art; between music and what Strauss regarded as culture. As he argued in a letter from 1945 regarding the future of the curriculum in the German humanistic *Gymnasium,* the cultivation of serious musical literacy for the lay person was essential for ordinary literacy and therefore any definition of culture. Music was not something to be acquired as a supplement to ordinary literacy. It enabled the individual to gain the full understanding and insight usually associated exclusively with writing and for which the written word, no doubt, was indispensable. Strauss quoted with admiration the ironic observation made by the Austrian satirical writer Friedrich Kürnberger in 1848: "He who is not in a position to read a musical score does not know how to read in any sense of the word."[65]

Strauss's musical project, particularly during his middle years, was in his view in the service of basic literacy and culture. To alter the grammar of music, in the sense of Schoenberg, seemed as senseless as altering the rules of language. Such a project would render any hope of communication with people impossible. The language of music was not an arbitrary instrument of art. Art was not the province of individualist appropriation and alteration. In contrast to Schoenberg's claims in his 1911 *Harmonielehre,* for Strauss the composer was subject to normative constraints much the way a writer naturally seemed to be. The challenge was to adapt a mundane, everyday vehicle—the rules of language that were used in life thoughtlessly, routinely, and unartistically—and transform them for perceptibly higher purposes.

The reason Strauss was attracted to myth after 1912 as a vehicle for music was that in myth, mundane communication and aesthetic transformation might be more readily reconciled. At a time when modernism seemed to be challenging the basic rules of musical communication, an alternative strategy to reach the heights of the artistic using a normative musical language needed to be found. The requirements of myth, as Hofmannsthal developed them in poetic and dramatic language, were adaptable to subtle illustration and a differentiated musical parallelism with language. The use of allegory, metaphor, and indirection became indispensable as musical techniques. Myth was a bridge between the imaginative and the real. Myth could preserve the surface and virtues of realism without conceding its limitations. Likewise, the use of realistic situations and conversations in *Intermezzo* and *Capriccio* enabled the narrowly mundane to be transfigured much the way Beckett and Pinter transformed seemingly banal diction and speech through an ascetic reemployment and invention.

After 1919 Strauss was quite conscious of innovations in musical realism. The opening to *Die Liebe der Danae* reflects Strauss's awareness of Kurt Weill's work of the late 1920s and early 1930s, as a comparison of the opening of *Die Liebe der Danae* with the musical rhetoric and use of chorus in *Mahagonny* might suggest. Despite Strauss's overt lack of interest in film, the narrative techniques of musical illustration and their relationship to the literary and visual give the later operas their filmic quality. As in a film, Strauss plays with memory and narration, with sequences of distinct moments—set numbers—all woven, from start to finish, into an economical form determined by a literary narrative line.[66]

These dimensions of Strauss's achievement after *Elektra* may justify a reassessment of his career and work as well as Strauss's significance to contemporary aesthetic movements. Although the passage of time has diminished the discomfort associated with Strauss's behavior during the Third Reich and has dimmed the memory of his less attractive sides, Strauss will continue to present a specific enigma that cannot be forgotten. That enigma concerns the notion of art and culture and the conception of the relationship of art and audience cultivated by Strauss. In this sense no reconsideration of Strauss's work, and certainly no revival of his less-appreciated works from the 1920s and 1930s, can dispense with the issues of how art and politics are connected. The ugly facts remain, and our growing susceptibility to the greatness and beauty of Strauss's work should at one and the same time inspire and disturb us. In an era in which surface realism has returned as an aesthetic strategy, the weakness of Strauss's behavior is a warning. The actual relationships in one's own time of the aesthetic to the ethical and the political, even in the realm of music, can be denied, avoided, or misrepresented only at the peril of humanity.

NOTES

1. *Richard Strauss–Hugo von Hofmannsthal: Briefwechsel*, ed. Willi Schuh (Zurich: Atlantis, 1978), p. 344.

2. Ibid., pp. 170–71.

3. Robert P. Morgan, *Twentieth-Century Music: A History of Musical Style in Modern Europe and America* (New York: Norton, 1991), p. 35.

4. Norman Del Mar, *Richard Strauss: A Critical Commentary on His Life and Works* (London: Barrie and Rockliff, 1969), vol. 1, p. 2.

5. In contrast to Wagner, Strauss, like Mozart, relied extensively on the female character as protagonist and vehicle. The extent to which the female characters are subtly delineated and the men less so (with the possible ex-

ception of Ochs, Barak, Mandryka, and Storch [Strauss])—one thinks of Herod, Orestes, Aegisthus, Bacchus, Menelaeus, and Jupiter—constitutes a significant biographical clue. Only in *Feuersnot* and perhaps *Capriccio* do the male figures truly dominate or hold their own in the narrative and music.

6. See *Richard Strauss and Romain Rolland: Correspondence,* ed. Rollo Myers (Berkeley and Los Angeles: University of California Press, 1968), pp. 126, 140–41; Fritz Busch, *Aus dem Leben eines Musikers* (Frankfurt: Fischer, 1948/ 1982), pp.168–69; and the letter from Gustav Mahler to Alma Mahler dated January 1907 in Alma Mahler, *Gustav Mahler: Memories and Letters,* ed. Donald Mitchell (New York: Viking, 1969), p. 282. See also Herta Blaukopf, "Rivalität und Freundschaft," in *Gustav Mahler–Richard Strauss: Briefwechsel 1888–1911* (Munich: Piper, 1980), pp. 129ff.

7. *Strauss-Hofmannsthal: Briefwechsel,* p. 237.

8. See Arnold Schoenberg, "On Strauss and Furtwängler," in H. H. Stuckenschmidt, *Schoenberg: His Life, Work, and World* (New York: Schirmer Books, 1978), p. 544.

9. Busch, p. 168.

10. Del Mar, vol. 2, p. 438.

11. *Strauss-Hofmannsthal: Briefwechsel,* p. 418.

12. Richard Strauss, *Betrachtungen und Erinnerungen,* ed. Willi Schuh (Zurich: Atlantis, 1981), pp. 244–46; Del Mar, vol. 2, pp. 214–15; and Charles Osborne, *The Complete Operas of Richard Strauss* (London: Michael O'Mara, 1988), pp. 111–12.

13. See Willi Schuh, *Richard Strauss Jugend und frühe Meisterjahre Lebenschronik 1864–1898* (Zurich: Atlantis, 1976), p. 69.

14. *Richard Strauss–Ludwig Thuille: Ein Briefwechsel,* ed. Franz Trenner (Tutzing: Schneider, 1980), p. 128.

15. *Strauss-Hofmannsthal: Briefwechsel,* pp. 128 and 249.

16. Ibid., p. 294.

17. Ibid., p. 154.

18. *Strauss and Rolland: Correspondence,* p. 165.

19. Despite the virtues of Del Mar's crucial three-volume study, it is marred by arrogantly asserted aesthetic judgments about much of Strauss's music. In contrast, Ernst Krause's biography, in its first three editions (1955–1964), presents a curious mix of adulation and old-fashioned chauvinism, with official East German ideological explanations tacked on, which have the effect of denigrating much of Strauss's midcareer works, particularly from the 1920s. See Ernst Krause, *Richard Strauss: The Man and His Work,* trans. John Coombs (London: Collett's, 1964).

20. See, for example, Maynard Solomon, *Beethoven* (New York: Schirmer Books, 1977). The speculations and commercialized romanticizations of the personalities of Mozart and also Schubert are, in contrast to the matter of Strauss, cases of willful distortions of evidence.

21. See Norman Del Mar, *Mahler's Sixth Symphony: A Study* (London: Eulenberg, 1980).

22. See Michael Meyer, *The Politics of Music in the Third Reich* (New York:

Peter Lang, 1991) for the most recent English-language account of this issue.

23. *Strauss-Hofmannsthal: Briefwechsel*, pp. 293 and 298.

24. This contrast is evident in the wealth of pro-Pfitzner literature that appeared in Germany after 1933. See in particular Walter Abendroth, *Hans Pfitzner* (Munich: Langen-Müller, 1935); and Erich Valentin, *Hans Pfitzner: Werk und Gestalt eines Deutschen* (Regensburg: Bosse, 1939).

25. See Theodor Adorno, "Richard Strauss. Born June 11, 1864," trans. Samuel and Shierry Weber, in *Perspectives of New Music* 1 (1965): 14–32; and 2 (1966): 113–29, esp. p. 127.

26. See Adorno, "Über den Fetischcharakter in der Musik und die Regression des Hörens" (1938), in *Dissonanzen* (Göttingen: Wardenhoeck and Ruprecht, 1963), pp. 9–45; and Theodor Adorno and Max Horkheimer, *Dialektik der Aufklärung* (Frankfurt: Fischer, 1969; reprint, 1988), pp. 128–76.

27. Adorno, "Richard Strauss," p. 126.

28. See Richard Strauss, *Briefe an die Eltern 1882–1906*, ed. Willi Schuh (Zurich: Atlantis, 1954); and Kurt Wilhelm, *Richard Strauss: Persönlich* (Munich: Kindler, 1984), p. 34; also Schuh, pp. 95–97 and 166f.

29. See *Strauss-Thuille: Ein Briefwechsel*, pp. 41–42, 46–50, and 67.

30. When Strauss agreed to become the nominal editor-in-chief of a series of small musical monographs entitled *Die Musik: Sammlung illustrierter Einzeldarstellungen*, published by Marquardt in Berlin, Strauss arranged for his friend and colleague the composer Siegmund von Hausegger to write a volume on Ritter. It remains the best source on Ritter's career and music. See Siegmund von Hausegger, *Alexander Ritter* (Berlin, 1907).

31. Max Hehemann, "Die Musik unsrer Tage," in *Monographien moderner Musiker* (Leipzig: C. F. Kahnt, 1907), vol. 2, pp. 2–3.

32. See, for example, Hermann Bahr's account of the premiere of *Elektra* in Hermann Bahr, *Essays* (Leipzig: Insel, 1912), pp. 71f.

33. Bryan Gilliam, *Richard Strauss's "Elektra"* (Oxford: Oxford University Press, 1991), pp. ix–x.

34. See, for example, Adorno's postwar *Philosophie der neuen Musik* (Frankfurt: Fischer, 1976 [1949]) and compare it with Morgan's 1991 textbook cited in n. 3.

35. See, for example, Del Mar's account in vol. 2 of his study.

36. The worst offender is Del Mar. But see also Karen Forsyth, *"Ariadne auf Naxos" by Hugo von Hofmannsthal and Richard Strauss: Its Genesis and Meaning* (Oxford: Oxford University Press, 1982).

37. One nonoperatic work that has been entirely neglected, for example, is the *Panathenänzug*, Op. 74, for piano (left hand alone) and orchestra, from 1927.

38. This point is made in a recent study of *Friedenstag* and *Daphne*. See Kenneth Birkin, *Friedenstag and Daphne: An Interpretive Study of the Literary and Dramatic Sources of Two Operas by Richard Strauss* (New York: Garland, 1989), p. 1. But Birkin also accepts the idea that these works are "inherently weak." Strauss scholarship has yet to unpack the premises of its own critical assessments.

39. See the Kraus selections from the 1920s in this volume.

40. The second is called "Strauss and the Electronic Future," from 1964; Gould also wrote notes for his recording of *Enoch Arden;* see Tim Page, ed., *The Glenn Gould Reader* (New York: Knopf, 1984), pp. 84–99.

41. Gould recorded the Five Piano Pieces, Op. 3; the B-minor Sonata, Op. 5; *Enoch Arden;* and the *Stimmungsbilder,* Op. 9.

42. See Geoffrey Payzant, *Glenn Gould: Music and Mind* (Toronto: Van Nostrand, 1978), p. 155.

43. See Page, ed., pp. 86 and 91.

44. In Arnold Schoenberg, *Style and Idea,* ed. Leonard Stein (London: Faber, 1975), p. 398–441.

45. See Walter Frisch's brilliant extension of Schoenberg's insights in the analysis of Brahms in *Brahms and the Principle of Developing Variation* (Berkeley and Los Angeles: University of California Press, 1984).

46. This periodization is not meant to slight the virtues of *Capriccio.* The divisions used here reflect not only biographical considerations but reception history. *Capriccio* has enjoyed more careful and positive attention. It shares in the virtues associated with Strauss's works from the 1920s and 1930s.

47. *Strauss-Hofmannsthal: Briefwechsel,* p. 204.

48. See ibid., pp. 183, 266, and 625.

49. Richard Specht, *Richard Strauss und sein Werk* (Leipzig: E. P. Tal, 1921), vol. 2, pp. 369–74.

50. Around the time of *Elektra* Strauss considered composing an instrumental work (*Vier Frauengestalten der National Gallery*) consisting of four musical portraits based upon paintings he had seen in London's National Gallery. See Gilliam, *Elektra,* pp. 183–84.

51. One needs to remember only the Italian aria, which appears in the first act of *Der Rosenkavalier,* and its presentation and reprise. It is significant to contrast Strauss's near-obsession with style after 1910 as a category with Schoenberg's consistent denigration of the notion of style and the persistent contrast between style and "idea." Schoenberg's insistence may have been motivated by his awareness of Strauss's concern with the issue of style.

52. *Strauss-Hofmannsthal: Briefwechsel,* p. 213.

53. Ibid., p. 205. Perhaps it should be underscored that Hofmannsthal and Strauss, by their emphasis on the category of style as a constructive instrument in modern aesthetics, directly challenged the Schoenbergian paradigm. Strauss attacked the fundamental theoretical construct that made style the moral equivalent of superficiality and idea the basis of a link between ethics and art. That this distinction was crucial to the conceits of twentieth-century modernism can be seen in the fact that Charles Ives, independently of Schoenberg, reached similar conclusions. Ives contrased "substance" with "matter" (and "repose"), distinctions parallel to idea and style. Not suprisingly, Ives had little regard for Strauss's talent and his music, which for him were all about manner and not substance. See Charles E. Ives, "Essay before a Sonata," in *Three Classics in the Aesthetics of Music* (New York: Dover, n.d.), pp. 155–79.

54. One thinks of the techniques and work of artists David Salle, Cindy

Sherman, and Sigmar Polke, and architects working in a variety of postmodernist manners, such as Robert Venturi, Philip Johnson, and Michael Graves. In music, one thinks of the work of John Corigliano; David del Tredici also comes to mind.

55. See Michael Steinberg, *The Meaning of the Salzburg Festival: Austria as Theater and Ideology, 1890–1938* (Ithaca: Cornell University Press, 1990).

56. Strauss was more blunt about audience expectations in his later correspondence with collaborator Joseph Gregor. During their work on *Daphne,* Strauss constantly reminded Gregor to write theater and not literature: "The whole thing [libretto] in its current form . . . would not draw a hundred people to the theater" (letter of 25 September 1935). See p. 240 of the Strauss-Gregor correspondence in this volume.

57. Hofmannsthal wrote Strauss, "the essence of poetical meaning comes to be understood gradually, very gradually . . . and takes decades to spread," in *Strauss-Hofmannsthal: Briefwechsel*, p. 139.

58. *Strauss and Rolland: Correspondence*, p. 100. Again, one can contrast Schoenberg and Strauss. The latter embraced ornament and decoration as musical techniques. The former, following the example of Adolf Loos, distinguished ornament from essence, paralleling Loos's separation of structure and materials from facade decoration. The honest presentation of structure and materials was an ethical credo of architectural modernism. See Adolf Loos, "Ornament und Vergrechen," in *Trotzdem* (Vienna: Prachner, 1931; reprint, 1982).

59. *Strauss-Hofmannsthal: Briefwechsel*, p. 124.

60. See the foreword in the vocal score of *Capriccio* published by Schott (Boosey and Hawkes) in 1942 and the *Intermezzo* prefaces in the Strauss *Betrachtungen*, pp. 135–39 and 140–49.

61. The concert guides of Hermann Kretszchmar and the innumerable histories of music and works that began to appear in the 1880s and books such as *Spemanns goldenes Buch der Musik eine Hauskunde für Jedermann* (Stuttgart: Spemann, 1916) are examples of this phenomenon.

62. First published in Franz Marc and Wassily Kandinsky's *Die Blaue Reiter Almanach* in 1912 and reprinted in Schoenberg's *Style and Idea*, pp. 141–44.

63. Claude Joseph Vernet (1714–89). See Michael Fried, *Absorption and Theatricality: Painting and the Beholder in the Age of Diderot* (Berkeley and Los Angeles: University of California Press, 1980).

64. *Strauss and Rolland: Correspondence*, p. 130.

65. Franz Grasberger, ed., *Die Welt um Richard Strauss in Briefen* (Tutzing: Schneider, 1967), p. 441.

66. See Gilliam's discussion of *Intermezzo*'s filmic aspects in "Strauss's *Intermezzo*: Innovation and Tradition," in *Richard Strauss: New Perspectives on the Composer and His Work*, ed. Bryan Gilliam (Durham, N.C.: Duke University Press, 1992). On 1 January 1917, when Hermann Bahr was working on the *Intermezzo* text, Strauss urged him to write scenes that would be "almost just cinematic pictures" (*fast nur Kinobilder*). Strauss ultimately wrote the libretto himself.

Daphne's Transformation

BRYAN GILLIAM

During the summer of 1949, a short documentary film about Strauss—*Ein Leben für die Musik* [A life for music]—was made. A memorable moment in the film features Strauss, shortly before his death, sitting at the piano in his Garmisch studio. Asked to play an excerpt from one of his works, the eighty-five-year-old composer chose a portion of the transformation scene from *Daphne* (1937)—the part beginning in F♯ major (six bars after fig. 250). That moment may have been the last time Strauss played the piano.[1] Given the choice of a lifetime of works, Strauss's selection might seem arbitrary or, at best, curious. But the composer's choice surely came as no surprise to members of his family, for he played the transformation music from *Daphne* almost exclusively during the last year of his life. It offered comfort to Strauss and his wife during a period of physical and emotional pain.[2] This famous passage, with its soaring melodies, seemingly effortless contrapuntal interplay of returning motives, skillful harmonic pacing, and mastery of orchestral sound that is at once rich and refined, may well be the most compelling finale of any late Strauss opera.

Daphne dates from the 1930s, one of the bleakest periods in Strauss's career: it began without his treasured librettist, Hugo von Hofmannsthal, who died in 1929; Hitler rose to power four years later; the composer lost his next librettist, Stefan Zweig, to Nazi politics (their *Schweigsame Frau* was banned in 1935 after four performances); that same year Strauss fell out of favor with the government and was forced to resign his post as head of the *Reichsmusikkammer;* and in 1938 Austria was annexed into the Third Reich. Strauss and his family lived part of the time in Vienna, where the safety of his Jewish daughter-in-law and two grandsons could no longer be taken for granted. The end of the decade saw Germany on the brink of war, and after a *Festkonzert* in Vienna (1939) celebrating Strauss's seventy-fifth birthday, the normally reserved, taciturn composer stood in the corridor of the *Musikvereinsaal* mumbling with tears in his eyes: "Now everything is finished! Everything is past!"[3] But, paradoxically, this unsettling period also represented one of the most prolific periods for Strauss the opera composer. The years 1932 through 1940 saw no fewer than five new operas: *Arabella* (1932), *Die schweigsame Frau* (1935), *Friedenstag* (1936), *Daphne* (1937), and *Die Liebe der Danae* (1940).

The leading collaborator for Strauss opera during this period was Joseph Gregor, the composer's librettist for three of these operas (*Friedenstag, Daphne,* and *Die Liebe der Danae*) and second only to Hofmannsthal in terms of output.[4] Gregor, a theater historian who fancied himself a poet, was neither a Hofmannsthal nor even a Zweig, but he was Strauss's only alternative during a time when the septuagenarian preferred composing opera to searching for yet another collaborator. The story of Gregor's emergence as Strauss's librettist in the wake of Zweig's departure has been often told.[5] And the published Strauss-Zweig and Strauss-Gregor correspondences, as well as the unpublished letters between Gregor and Zweig, offer abundant detail for anyone interested in this unique relationship in which Zweig, for a time, served as Gregor's silent partner.[6]

Daphne is Gregor's only original libretto, and it is arguably his best. Zweig had originated the idea for *Friedenstag;* he devised the original scenario and, after stepping down as Strauss's official collaborator, helped Gregor extensively in the shaping and drafting of the opera text until at least as late as November 1935.[7] Gregor finished the final portion of the libretto by the end of December. The genesis of the libretto for *Die Liebe der Danae* is more complicated. In April 1920, Hofmannsthal submitted a three-act sketch, *Danae oder die Vernunftheirat* [Danae, or the marriage of convenience], to Strauss, who believed that after *Die Frau ohne Schatten* his "tragic vein [was] more or less exhausted."[8] Strauss savored certain details of the sketch but had doubts about the overall plot, which contained an abundance of transformations and processions. Furthermore, the composer was becoming increasingly preoccupied with his *opera domestica, Intermezzo,* which would be his next published work. In short, *Danae* was soon forgotten. Hofmannsthal's sketch reappeared in 1933 in the literary magazine *Corona,* which Willi Schuh brought to Strauss's attention. Having composed *Friedenstag* and *Daphne,* the composer again found his tragic vein depleted, and in 1936 he asked the faithful Gregor to forge a libretto from Hofmannsthal's fragment. A year earlier Gregor had shown Strauss his own version of *Danae,* along with five other proposals, and was hurt at the composer's failure to recall.[9]

The meeting in which Gregor had shown Strauss ideas for possible libretti took place in Berchtesgaden on 7 July 1935. *Daphne* was one of the six proposals. Gregor described the meeting as follows:

> On 7 July I met Richard Strauss at a spa in the Alps, not in Garmisch. While the fog of a rainy afternoon flowed, he read the six pages, the drafts based on ideas that I had already mentioned. I still remember, with great precision, that he did not read any of the pages more than approximately two minutes, and he did not read any a second time. Rather he had already put three drafts aside, drafts that he indicated to me had dramatic themes that would interest him. Thus, in a short quarter of an hour, the working program for the next four years was established.[10]

Exactly what the "sechs Blätter" were is unclear, and the situation is further muddled by the fact that Strauss did not remember reading a *Danae* draft at the meeting. However, if we follow the logic of Gregor's account, the four-year "Arbeitsprogramm" probably included *Friedenstag*, *Daphne*, and *Die Liebe der Danae*.

Gregor's enthusiasm for collaborating with Strauss was hardly matched by the composer, still unable to accept the termination of his relationship with Zweig, even four months after the Berchtesgaden meeting with his successor. No doubt Gregor saw himself as part of a legacy, as the end of a line that included such literary luminaries as Wolzogen, Wilde, Hofmannsthal, and Zweig. After his first trip to Garmisch in late October 1935 Gregor was ecstatic, and he reported to Zweig that Strauss was delighted with *Daphne*, which was still only a sketch: "S[trauss] at first wanted to make a number of changes, but suddenly said: 'No, leave it the way it is. It is too great a work of art.' You can well believe that the music of *Salome* and *Elektra* was in my ears."[11] *Daphne*, of course, probably went through more textual changes than any other opera by Strauss.[12]

Genesis of the *Daphne* Text: A Summary

In *Richard Strauss: Der Meister der Oper*, Gregor surveys the evolution of the *Daphne* libretto, but his account should be approached with caution. He not only omits vital dates but fails to acknowledge Zweig's involvement with the libretto. Nor does he mention Strauss's reliance on others for dramaturgical ideas, and he fails to provide the full extent and context of Strauss's criticisms concerning the various drafts.[13] The catalyst for the *Daphne* libretto, Gregor explains, was a lithograph of Apollo and Daphne by Theodor Chasseriau. What inspired him was the depiction of Apollo as an ardent, romantic god in contrast to that of Daphne in all her naive, childlike innocence. On a train ride on the summer solstice of 1935, he apparently wrote the original scenario:

> DAPHNE. One-act tragedy with dances and choruses.—Wonderful Greek landscape. People, identical with nature and with the gods!—The old Peneios is at the same time the river and the singing fisherman who lives at the river. Gäa is his wife and at the same time the beautiful green earth at the Peneios. Their daughter Daphne of deep innocence. . . . Playing with the waves at the Peneios are choruses of nymphs. Two suitors: the cowherd Apollo, wise, baritonal, surrounded by his maiden priestesses, and the young tenorlike shepherd Leukippos, Daphne remains puzzled even when the cowherd shows her his lightning. . . . Leukippos, pursued with jealousy by Apollo, has the idea to dress up as a girl. This totally changes Daphne's conception and she treats him as a girlfriend. Through this mistake [of identity] he achieves the goal of his desire. Now Daphne is completely dismayed [at Leukippos's deception] and reveals everything to the cowherd!—Apollo reacts in both a godly and a mortal way and kills Leukippos, Peneios asks Zeus to transform the people back to their original state. Zeus responds and, amid the play of the water nymphs and in front of the flames of the cremation of Leukippos, the Daphne tree grows upward.[14]

This scenario is probably what Strauss saw on 7 July 1935. Gregor expanded it into a full-scale libretto over the ensuing weeks, finishing it by the end of August. It would be the first of three versions written over the course of two years (summer 1935 through summer 1937).[15] A chief dramaturgical flaw of the original libretto is its failure to differentiate between major and minor characters. Daphne herself plays a decidedly secondary part in Gregor's first version, despite the fact that she is the title role. Her only major speech (a lament over the death of Leukippos) occurs toward the end of the opera. But this focus placed on the end of the work was part of Gregor's original plan, for the highlight of the piece was to be Daphne's transformation into a laurel tree—while a chorus sings:

Herrlich geliebter Baum!	Splendid, beloved tree!
Wie zu Zweigen sich wandeln	How your slender limbs
Die schlanken Glieder!	Are transformed into branches!

Wie um zarte Finger es	How the green leaves sprout
Grünt und grünt!	Around your tender fingers!
Deine Augen aber	Your eyes, however,
Erstrahlen neu	Shine anew
Im Sterne der Blüte!	In the stars of your blossoms!
Glücklicher bist du, O Baum,	You are happier, O tree,
Denn du wächst empor,	For you grow upward
Ohne Leiden und Reue	Without suffering or regret,
Und erneuerst dich	You renew yourself
Ohne Hass, ohne Liebe	Without hate, without love—
Ewiglich!	Eternally!
Glücklicher bist du, O Baum,	You are happier, O tree,
Denn deine Arme halten	For your arms hold
Eine Welt froher Wesen,	A world of happy creatures—
Die breiten Goldammern,	The stout yellowhammers,
Die schmetternde Drossel	The warbling thrush,
Und die summende Bienen,	And the buzzing bees.
Dein Fuss aber haftet	Your foot, however, grips
Fester auf Erden	The earth more strongly,
Als das wandelbare	Than the changeable
Geschlecht der Menschen.	Species of man.[16]

This choral finale marked the climax of the opera, but it did not end the work. After the chorus Gregor offers the following stage directions: "Everyone slowly exits, first Zeus, then Apollo with Hermes, and finally the chorus. Peneios and Gäa slowly follow and gaze at the large, new tree, which—filling up the middle of the stage—stands out blooming in the moonlight."

PENEIOS	PENEIOS
Sieh—Mutter!	See—Mother!
Den herrlichen Baum!	The splendid tree!
GÄA	GÄA
So kindlich ist der Mann:	This man is such a child.
Als ich ihm morgens	This morning when I reminded him
Gemahnte des Feigenbaums,	Of the fig tree,
Des liebenden Ernährers	The loving bearer of fruit,
Achtete er dessen gering.	He thought little of it.
Götter rief er und Götter	He called for gods and gods
kamen	came,

Götter raubten ihm seine Tochter,	Gods robbed him of his daughter
Voll von Eifersucht.	Full of jealousy.
Aber Abende,	But in the evening,
Eines Baumes gewahr	Aware only of a tree,
Preist er sich glücklich,	He calls himself happy,
Voll des Vergessens.	Filled with forgetfulness.
PENEIOS	PENEIOS
Dieser aber ist viel schöner	But this tree is much more beautiful
Als der alte Feigenbaum!	Than the old fig tree!
Du wirst ihn nähren,	You will nourish it,
Ich will sein warten	I want to maintain it
Und in seinem Schatten	And in its shadow
Wollen wir ausruhn.	We will take our rest.
GÄA	GÄA
Ja, und wir wollen die Tochter bitten	Yes, and we will ask our daughter
Dass sie uns beschütze vor den Strahlen	To protect us from the rays
Phoibos Apollons.	Of Phoebus Apollo.

It is difficult to comprehend the purpose of this final exchange between Daphne's mother and father: the earthbound, skeptical Gäa and the visionary Peneios. If Gregor intended ironic or even lighthearted contrast following the chorus, the humor falls flat. The Earth Mother may get the last word, but Gregor's heavy hand creates outright sarcasm instead of irony. This ill-timed exchange seriously undercuts the intended magic of the transformation chorus.

Zweig read through Gregor's libretto, and, in a lengthy letter (3 September 1935), he made a host of comments, the final scene itself prompting numerous criticisms. In the first place, Zweig did not like the chorus singing during the transformation: "I would represent the gradual process of this miracle in individual voices, so that the viewer witnesses it, so that one may see the growing of the tree before his eyes."[17] In short, only when the laurel tree has been fully transformed should the chorus sing, praising the miracle that has just taken place.

Not surprisingly, Zweig criticized the prosaic exchange between Peneios and Gäa following the chorus: "You let this mythological play end in a psychological dialogue and thus neglect a great dramaturgical and musical possibility."[18] After the chorus Zweig suggests:

While both parents stand before the tree, the sky becomes lit up with stars, and out of the dark of the grove the parents present their offering in front of the transformed tree, because Daphne has become, through her transformation, a guardian of pure love, a shrine of reverence and piousness. The two [Peneios and Gäa] call to Daphne and touch her leaves with their hands, etc. In short, a sphere of holiness, reverence, and contentment ends the work in an elevated spirit. A great myth is created and, at the same time, a wonderful, touching and transfigured picture. Along with this I can really hear Strauss's music in its spiritual vein as at the end of the first act of *Die Frau ohne Schatten,* and I believe it would be a welcome to him, with the sounds of a celeste, to return the work to eternity.[19]

Zweig criticized the overall text with such diplomacy that, despite the negative remarks, Gregor believed his general reaction to be quite positive. Indeed, he even included Zweig's criticisms when he mailed the libretto to Strauss. The composer's initial reaction was noncommittal; at best he could only say that he liked the text "pretty well."[20] After rereading the text, he became more critical: "Lots of words, schoolmaster banalities, no concentration on one focus; no gripping human conflict"; these candid comments from Strauss to Zweig sum up the composer's feelings about the libretto.[21] Work on *Die Frau ohne Schatten* had taught Strauss the difficulties of composing music for obscure literary characters, figures without empathetic human qualities that produce "a breath of academic chill (what my wife very rightly calls 'note spinning') which no bellows can ever kindle into a real fire."[22]

Concentrated revision of the *Daphne* text during the remainder of the fall and early winter produced a second version (*Daphne* II), which Gregor completed around mid-January 1936; Strauss received the final portion of the manuscript on the seventeenth. The idea of a choral finale was retained, but certain changes were made—some along the lines of Zweig's suggestions from September 1935. The transformation, for example, occurs before the chorus sings. As the stage darkens, Gregor suggests that the music should articulate the beginning of the transformation. Gäa, lost in a dense fog, exclaims: "Daughter, where are you?" and once the transformation occurs there are off-stage choruses. After the fog clears, a full moon illuminates the scene, and Peneios and Gäa sing a less sarcastic dialogue. Thereafter the chorus is directed to enter the stage in ten male-female pairs, each singing a couplet as they enter:

DAS ERSTE PAAR	FIRST PAIR
Sei du Beschützer	Be the protector
Unsere Liebe!	Of our love!
DAS ZWEITE PAAR	SECOND PAIR
Dein holder Schatten	May your gentle shade
Erquicke uns!	Refresh us!
DAS DRITTE PAAR	THIRD PAIR
Dein Blätterrauschen	May your rustling leaves
Singe uns Träume! . . .	Sing dreams to us! . . .

Once assembled in front of the laurel tree, they sing a revised final chorus:

ALLE	ALL
Gesegneter Baum,	Blessed tree
Hoch über die Menschen	High above mankind
Ragst du empor!	You loom upward!
Viel näher lebst du	You live much nearer
Den reineren Sphären,	To the purer spheres,
Beständiger bist du	You are more lasting
Und grösser dein Glück.	And your happiness greater.
Du bist das Sinnbild	You are the emblem
Der allumfassenden,	Of all-embracing,
Der ewgen Natur—	Eternal nature—
Sei uns das Zeichen	Be for us the sign
Neuer, herrlicher,	Of new, splendid
Unendlicher Liebe!	Unending love!

Strauss still found the revised libretto too wordy. Urging his librettist toward concision, Strauss himself made some cuts.[23] Galvanized by his suggested deletions and other comments, Gregor trimmed a good dozen pages by early March, but it was still too long for the composer.[24] Further, the more Strauss read through the manuscript, the more confusing he found the treatment of the main characters: from what motivations do Apollo, Leukippos, and Daphne act, from the Apollo-Daphne love scene through the death of Leukippos? Strauss confessed that without grasping each character's motivating force he simply could not compose.

Frustrated, Strauss discussed his misgivings with Lothar Wallerstein, senior producer at the Vienna State Opera.[25] Strauss valued Wallerstein's theatrical instincts, and would later turn to him for advice during work on *Die Liebe der Danae* and *Capriccio*. Their discussion made it clear that *Daphne* II should probably be scrapped. Strauss urged Gregor to get in touch as soon as possible with Wallerstein, who would relay the composer's observations: "I have thoroughly discussed the work with [Wallerstein] and have explained exactly what I want—namely, something almost entirely new!"[26]

A few weeks later Strauss also consulted Clemens Krauss, conductor and future *Capriccio* collaborator, who made further suggestions that were ultimately forwarded to Gregor. In short, fundamental changes were necessary, enough to require the librettist to write a third version (*Daphne* III). But this second overhaul of the libretto did not seriously affect the choral finale of the work, for during spring 1936, Strauss was preoccupied with the relationships between Daphne, Apollo, and Leukippos. Strauss could not begin composing in earnest until he fully understood these characters, and he hoped that *Daphne* III would bring them into sharper focus.

Gregor sent Strauss a copy of this version on 16 April 1936; now Strauss could begin composing. The text featured an entirely reshaped opening aria for Daphne, an inserted scene between Daphne and Gäa toward the beginning, an abridged Dionysian festival, and an added monologue toward the end for Apollo. The ending, although essentially the same in overall structure, was retouched in one important way: Gregor decided to do away with the dialogue between Peneios and Gäa; the old fig tree goes unmentioned. Instead, Peneios sings ("in a priestly manner") a tribute to the transformed tree:

Dich grüsse ich,	I greet you
Daphne, Tochter!	Daphne, daughter!
Nicht zu den Höhen	Never more shall I travel
Will ich mehr schweifen,	To the heights,
Nicht mehr die Götter	Never more wait for
Hinieden erwarten:	The gods here below.
Ich empfing sie durch dich!	I received them through you!
Priesterlich dien ich	As a priest I serve
Dem ewigen Bruder	The eternal brother
Phoibos Apollon,	Phoebus Apollo,
Löse das Reis	I break off a sprig
Von dir, O Tochter,	From you, O daughter,
Winde den Kranz! . . .	Weave the wreath, . . .

No longer the childish dreamer chided by his wife, Peneios, now a priestly character, recognizes the spiritual significance of this miraculous transformation. Gäa, bitter toward Apollo and the rest of the gods in the second version, is now equally moved by the transformation:

Geliebter Baum!	Beloved tree!
Ich will dich nähren.	I want to nourish you.
Ich will dein warten,	I want to care for you
Und in deinem Schatten	And in your shade
Ausruhn dereinst.	Take my rest one day.

As in the previous version, the ten mixed pairs enter the stage and—once gathered—praise the laurel tree, although a few lines of the final chorus were changed.[27]

With the final version of text in hand, Strauss began composing, and *Daphne* went unmentioned in his letters for months. The only extant evidence of his work on *Daphne* consists of two terse reports to Gregor ("in the meantime I remain working on *Daphne*" and "*Daphne* strides forward") on 2 September and 17 October 1936, respectively. By early spring 1937, Strauss had evidently gotten as far as the final scene. There he reached a serious creative impasse, and the trouble, not surprisingly, lay with Gregor's text. Strauss was interested, above all, in the magic of Daphne's transformation, while Gregor only offered stiff pageantry. On 9 May, without informing Gregor, Strauss again consulted Clemens Krauss, who later described their meeting: "Strauss said to me: 'Just read through it once, I can't get on with the ending.' I told him quite simply that the idea of bringing people onto the stage to sing to the [Daphne] tree after the transformation was absurd."[28]

A few days after their meeting Strauss broke the news to Gregor:

Clemens Krauss was here on Sunday, and we are in agreement that after Apollo's final monologue no other human being should be on stage except Daphne, no Peneios, no solo voices—no chorus—in short, no oratorio: all of that would only have a weakening effect. By the end of Apollo's final monologue Daphne rises from Leukippos's corpse, stares at [Apollo] in amazement, and, as Apollo departs, wants to follow him. However, after a few steps, she suddenly remains standing as if rooted, and now in the moonlight, but still fully visible, the miracle of transformation is slowly worked upon her: *only with the orchestra alone!* During the transformation Daphne still speaks, at most a few words, which dissolve into wordless melody! Perhaps not even that! In any case, right at the end, when the tree is fully transformed, she sings—as a voice of nature—eight more bars of the laurel motive![29]

This letter epitomizes the working relationship between Strauss and Gregor, for what the composer offered his librettist was less a suggestion than an ultimatum. Significantly, the decision resulted from a discussion held without Gregor's knowledge. Gregor tried to put the best face on it in his published account of the genesis of *Daphne,* and even declared that the revised ending was "one of the most musical inspirations of [Strauss's] genius." But, in fact, he was deeply angered by the composer's suggestion. In an unpublished letter to Zweig, Gregor complained of Strauss's "artistic egotism" and described the great pains he took to try to convince the composer that the opera should end with voices.[30]

The idea of a choral ending was important to Gregor for two reasons. To begin with, he envisioned *Friedenstag* and *Daphne* as a double bill—a pair of one-act operas, each ending in a chorus.[31] Strauss's revision upset that symmetry, loosening the connection between the two works. But on a more personal level, the choral finale represented practically the last thing in the libretto that Gregor could call his own. His original draft is barely recognizable in this third version—now with solo ending—while most of the cuts, additions, and rewritings were the product of either the friendly advice of Zweig or the unsolicited suggestions of Krauss and Wallerstein.

Still, Gregor agreed with Zweig that one should be grateful that the libretto, in whatever shape or form, would ultimately be set to music and that the opera would be premiered soon thereafter. Thus, in late spring 1937, Gregor—by now used to swallowing his pride—visited the composer in Garmisch, and there he revised the ending. This Garmisch revision differs only slightly from the printed text, which is a bit more concise:

"Garmisch" Version, p. 34:	Printed Version, p. 48:
STIMME DER DAPHNE	DAPHNE
Ich komme, ich komme	Ich komme—ich komme
Grünende Brüder	Grünende Brüder . . .
Süß durchströmt mich	Süß durchströmt mich
Der Erde Saft!	Der Erde Saft!
Tausendfach feilt sich	Dir entgegen—
Mein ganzes Wesen	In Blättern und Zweigen
In Blättern und Zweigen	Keuschetes Licht!
Dir entgegen	
Keuschetes Licht!	

(Hier bricht der Strahl des Mondes durch und beleuchtet den Wipfel des Lorbeerbaumes.)

(Daphne unsichtbar, an ihrer Stelle erhebt sich der Baum.)

[STIMME DER DAPHNE]
Apollo . . . Brüder
Nimm . . . mein . . . Gezweige . . .

STIMME DER DAPHNE
Apollo! Brüder!
Nimm . . . mein . . . Gezweige . . .

(So wie sich das Licht über den ganzen Baum gebreitet hat, fällt der Vorhang.)

(Mondlicht hat sich über den ganzen Baum gebreitet. Daphnes Stimme tönt aus seinem Geäst weiter.)
Der Vorhang fällt langsam.

DAPHNE'S VOICE
I am coming, I am coming,
Growing brother!
Sweetly the earth's sap
Runs through me!
My entire being
Spreads into leaves and boughs
A thousandfold
Toward you
Chaste light!

DAPHNE
I am coming, I am coming
Growing brother . . .
Sweetly the earth's sap
Runs through me!
Toward you—
Into leaves and branches
Chaste light!

(Here the moonbeam breaks through and illuminates the top of the laurel tree.)

(Daphne invisible; in her place the tree rises.)

DAPHNE'S VOICE
Apollo . . . Brother
Take . . . my . . . branches . . .
[etc.]

DAPHNE'S VOICE
Apollo! Brother!
Take . . . my . . . branches . . .
[etc.]

(When the light drifts over the entire tree, the curtain falls.)

(The moonlight has spread itself over the entire tree. Daphne's voice fades out farther from her branches.)
The curtain closes slowly.

Genesis of the Transformation Music

Sketches for Daphne's transformation are found in three of thirteen extant sketchbooks for the opera. These are located at the Richard Strauss–Archiv in Garmisch (RSA), the Bavarian State Library in

Munich (BSL), and the Houghton Library at Harvard University (HL). (Franz Trenner's numbering of the RSA sketchbooks [e.g., TR. 95] is adopted throughout this study. See Trenner's *Die Skizzenbücher von Richard Strauss–Archiv in Garmisch* [Tutzing: Schneider, 1977].) Strauss's most intensive compositional work on *Daphne* took place in April–May 1936 and fall 1937. The last page of the *Particell* is dated 9 November 1937, and the full score was finished on Christmas Eve. Strauss did a limited amount of sketching shortly after receiving *Daphne* II on 17 January 1936. Eleven days later, Gregor wrote Zweig that Strauss had begun composing.[32] But he did not get very far; January optimism soon gave way to February disappointment. Strauss would have to wait until the spring before he could begin extensive composition, for his early attempts at setting the text seemed continually to expose weaknesses in the libretto. A sketchbook given to Karl Böhm, conductor of the *Daphne* premiere and the work's dedicatee, documents Strauss's work from that brief January period. In it the composer succeeds in sketching descriptive themes or thematic fragments ("Daphne," "Peneios," "Leukippos," "the tree," etc.) as well as some fragmentary passages corresponding to sections at the beginning of the opera. Strauss would, of course, later draw on much of the material composed in the Böhm sketchbook. There are no extensive continuity sketches, with the exception of a draft (toward the end of the sketchbook) for Daphne's opening monologue. It was sketched after January—probably from spring 1936—for the version of the text is taken from *Daphne* III.

The critical period for the composition of the transformation was, of course, around late April or early May 1937. Strauss had been composing steadily for about a year, but as he approached the final scene of the opera he could go no farther. For the first time in three decades, since his work on *Elektra,* Strauss reached a serious creative block toward the end of an opera. There are, indeed, a number of compelling parallels between *Elektra* and *Daphne* that shed light on his ultimate solution for the finale of the later opera.

Daphne was Strauss's first one-act mythological opera since *Elektra,* and in late April or early May 1937, when Strauss once again found himself struggling with an operatic ending, the earlier work might well have come to mind. In both cases Strauss decided to give the primary musico-dramatic burden to the orchestra. Three days after his meeting (9 May 1937) with Krauss, Strauss decided to jettison "oratorio" and once again embrace tone poem. During the transformation, Daphne's voice would hover above an orchestral continuum. Once transformed, her wordless melody would literally join the orchestra (representing eternal nature), in imitation with the oboe. Furthermore, this miniature tone poem—Strauss called it "[ein] langes Orchesterstück"[33]—featured a structural parallel to *Elektra*, for it, too, focuses a harmonic tension first presented in an expository monologue (Daphne's): that between G and F♯ major.[34] Through G major, Strauss depicts Daphne in all her bucolic simplicity; the movement down a semitone ultimately signifies her magical transformation into a laurel tree.

The overall layout of Daphne's monologue aria is as follows:

PART	KEY	REHEARSAL NUMBER	TEXT
1	G	three bars after fig. 17	"O bleib geliebter Tag!"
	(F♯)	five bars before fig. 18	"du läßt mich leben mit meinem Brüder . . ."
2	modulatory	six bars after fig. 21	"Wenn du mich verläßt . . ."
3	modulatory	fig. 23	"Warum lieber Vater . . ."
4	F♯	five bars after fig. 26	"O wie gerne bleib ich bei dir . . ."
	(G)	four bars before fig. 28	". . . und so mein Brüder."

In this opening monologue for Daphne, Strauss creates a compelling musical symmetry. The two outer sections serve as tonally stable bookends, while the two inner sections are not only modulatory but often break down into accompanied recitative with the orchestra commenting on Daphne's declamatory phrases with important referential motives. Each of these outer bookends features a brief incursion of the other key (in both instances with a reference to her brothers, the trees), providing a vital sense of unity to an aria that ends a semitone lower than it began.

Early on in their collaborative work on *Daphne* Strauss and Gregor agreed that not only should the opera be paired with *Friedenstag* but the two works should be musically linked. *Friedenstag*, the intended second half of the double bill, had already been composed, and as Strauss initially reached the unrevised choral finale of *Daphne* he entertained the notion of setting it in C major to match the tonality of the final chorus of the earlier work.[35] Tr. 95 (RSA), a preliminary *Daphne* sketchbook, contains a four-page continuity sketch for this final chorus (Example 1). The sketch reveals the composer's original C-major plan, but it also demonstrates his struggle to come up with a felicitous ending.

Example 1. Continuity sketch for the final chorus of *Daphne* in sketchbook Tr. 95 (fols. 5–6v)

Example 1, cont.

Atop the first page Strauss labels the sketch "Anbetung des Baumes" [Adoration of the tree]. At the foot of the page he offers his own candid assessment: "Not very good! Especially for Peneios as priest!" His negative verdict quite likely referred as much to his own musical sketch as to Gregor's text. But why the reference to Peneios at all? The chorus should sing at this moment in the drama; Peneios's priestly monologue has already occurred. Strauss may have toyed with the idea of having Peneios participate with the chorus in some way, and he might have even entertained the thought of Peneios singing instead of the chorus. The list of contents on the inside front cover of Tr. 95 makes no mention of a "Schlusschor" but rather of a "Schlussgesang des Peneios."

C major is, after all, not only the key of the *Friedenstag* finale but that for Peneios throughout the opera (see fig. 23, eight bars before fig. 86, etc.). Strauss might have even decided to forge a double link, but whatever the case, the annotation ("Schlussgesang Fis dur") in the upper left corner of fol. 5 suggests the composer's ultimate doubts about a C-major *Daphne* finale as well as his decision to transpose it to F♯ major, the key symbolizing the transformed laurel tree.[36] By emphasizing F♯, he achieves two objectives: first, he deemphasizes the priestly Peneios—properly shifting the focus to the transformed Daphne—and, second, creates a tonal relationship to the second bookend of Daphne's opening monologue.

A glance at this brief continuity sketch brings to mind Strauss's aforementioned confession to Hofmannsthal that unconvincing, two-dimensional characters produce an "academic chill" in the musical setting. This repetitive musical fragment, with its constant reiterations of a single turn-figure, is a prime candidate for what Strauss's wife described as "note spinning." And although he originally thought he might make use of this material—writing *gut* in the upper right corner—Strauss later on cancels that designation. Instead of being reworked in some way in the revised finale, the sketch is essentially scrapped.

Strauss's ultimate finale, of course, represents more than a mere reference to F♯, a tonal allusion to the laurel tree; his central interest has shifted from the adoration of the transformed tree to the transformation process itself. He suggests this process by revisiting the G–F♯ relationship of the monologue. In the monologue these two relatively stable tonal areas (bucolic simplicity and the magical laurel tree) were separated by two modulatory sections. By the final scene, the transformation itself, we are already approaching the magical world of F♯; any references to G are more a memory of who Daphne once was. The use of half-step relationships to suggest different worlds has a rich tradition in Strauss's music. One need only think of the opposing worlds of Octavian (E) and the Marschallin (E♭) in act 1 of *Der Rosenkavalier* or, in *Ariadne auf Naxos,* the banal, everyday Prologue (C) versus the sublime ending of the opera (D♭), and there are numerous other examples.

But the keys of G and F♯ themselves have a tradition as topical harmonies in the Straussian repertoire. G major—the simple, idyllic key— is generally presented in a transparent texture, often featuring woodwinds (especially oboe). James Hepokoski discusses the G-major Idyll (introduced by oboe) from *Don Juan* at great length and even looks to the opening theme from the *Siegfried Idyll* as a possible model for melodic shape.[37] The beginning of the slow section of *Symphonia Domestica* (fig. 49), where husband and wife experience idyllic domestic bliss at sundown, is not only introduced by the oboe but accompanied only by woodwinds. Indeed, the G-major opening of *Daphne* (again, featuring the oboe) is likewise scored solely for woodwinds. On the other hand, Strauss usually uses F♯ major to suggest magical, or even dreamlike, states; the orchestration is generally fuller than in G-major passages. Don Quixote's dream of knightly adventures at the end of the third variation of the tone poem; the magical, *Märchen*-like presentation of the rose in act 2 of *Der Rosenkavalier;* the Empress's act 1 entrance in *Die Frau ohne Schatten* where she, indeed, suggests transformation ("Perhaps I shall dream myself back into the body of a bird or a young white gazelle!") are all cast in F♯ major.

In the Böhm sketchbook we see, among other things, Strauss's concern for these two symbolic tonal areas (Examples 2a and 2b). The nine-bar passage, labeled "Der Baum," has already been mentioned (see n. 35), and on the next folio we see a brief G-major sketch labeled "Daphne." Her opening monologue begins on the very next folio. The transformation music makes up the final 218 measures of the opera. Labeled "Daphnes Verwandlung" in the score, it is the only scene in this one-act work to receive a specific designation. Strauss divides the scene into two roughly equal parts: part 1 consists of the transformation process ("Ich komme, ich komme, grünende Brüder . . .") and, once transformed (part 2), the tree stands tall beneath the moonlight. Part 1 thus represents Daphne's transition from human voice into a voice of nature, represented by the orchestra; once transformed she becomes part of the instrumental realm. In short, these two parts suggest, first, a process of constant and gradual change and, second, the contemplation, even glorification, of that change. In musical terms it means a chromatic,

Example 2a. Sketch for F♯-major "Der Baum" passage in the Böhm sketchbook (fol. 11)

Example 2b. Sketch for G-major "Daphne" passage in the Böhm sketchbook (fol. 12)

harmonically restless first half (beginning and ending on the dominant of F♯), followed by a second part firmly grounded in F♯ major:

Daphne's Transformation

PART	KEY	REHEARSAL NUMBER	TEXT
1	modulatory ("V/F♯")	fig. 238	"Ich komme, ich komme . . ."
2	F♯	six bars after fig. 250	(Daphne sings wordless melody.)

Strauss achieves this sense of restless chromaticism by recalling the sequential, half-step motive from the Apollo-Daphne love scene (Example 3)—a motive first heard just before she sinks into Apollo's arms. The only other important referential theme during part 1 is one of the Apollo motives

which Strauss alludes to quite subtly at first with various adumbrations of the rhythm, such as

and

At the moment when Daphne actually becomes invisible, singing "Apollo!" (fig. 243), we finally hear the Apollo motive in its proper intervallic and rhythmic form.

The climax of part 1, however, is the return of the Daphne motive (see Example 2b) five bars after fig. 249.[38] This motive, presented in augmentation, sets Daphne's final words as a mortal being's; the climactic moment represents an incursion of G major as we are about

Example 3. Chromatic motive from the Apollo-Daphne love scene (eight bars before fig. 127)

to enter the stable realm of F♯ major in part 2. It is no doubt reminiscent of the earlier intrusion of G major in the last part of her opening monologue (four bars before fig. 28), but at the end we realize its full significance. With the progression of the G^6_4 down a half-step to the $C\sharp^7$, a sustained five-bar preparation for part 2, Daphne's process of transformation is finally complete. That final clash between G and F♯, culminating in the latter, suggests that she has now completely left the realm of mortality (Example 4).

Example 4. G–F♯ clash representing the completion of Daphne's transformation (five bars after fig. 249)

Example 4, cont.

Preliminary sketches for transformation part 1 are in HL and BSL, and they illustrate how Strauss conceived it as a primarily orchestral passage. There are four compositional layers: 1) textless continuity sketch (on two staves and in pencil); 2) initial placement of unset text (mostly between those staves and in pencil); 3) revised text placement (pencil); and 4) rare instances of additional text with musical setting added (in ink). Daphne sings intentionally disconnected, fragmentary phrases that seem to grow out of the instrumental continuum, and, indeed, the sketches reveal how much her vocal line is the product of motivic material worked out in the orchestra. Referring to earlier Strauss operas such as *Elektra*, Paul Bekker described the voice as the "final . . . translation of the instrumental action," but his observation applies just as easily to the later *Daphne*. Thus, Strauss's chief task in sketching Daphne's part is not the determination of her vocal line (that will ultimately come from the orchestra) but rather the placement of her part within this orchestral continuum. Strauss did not deal with the issue of placement until the "instrumental

Example 5a. Sketch for part 1 of Daphne's transformation in the Houghton Library sketchbook (fols. 24v–25). In his sketchbooks Strauss frequently omitted the dots when notating dotted rhythms; this convention has been preserved here.

action" was firmly established. This fact surely explains why no text appears in any measure of this continuity draft that is scratched out (such as measures 13–16 of Example 5a) or is somehow questionable in the composer's mind. The text "Apollo! Brüder! Nimm . . . mein Gezweige," for example, appears nowhere in HL because Strauss was

Example 5b. Final version of Daphne's transformation (two bars before fig. 240)

simply not satisfied with the passage. Only after resketching the passage (on pp. 43 and 42, respectively, of BSL) does he add that text. But, as Example 5a shows, he is somewhat indecisive about the placement of text (i.e., Daphne's vocal line) even after the orchestral continuum has been established, albeit at a preliminary stage. Her four

süß— durch - strömt— mich der Er-

242

de Saft! Dir___ ent-ge - gen–

Example 5b, cont.

opening lines should read: "Ich komme, ich komme / grünende Brüder / süß durchströmmt mich / der Erde Saft!" Beginning at the fourth bar of the example, he tries to fit in the first two phrases of this text, but we see another attempt in measure 16 and thereafter. But by then, Strauss also makes a couple of tries at working in the third and fourth phrases of the text (see measures 19, etc.). Example 5b shows Strauss's final decision.

The only significant exception—where Strauss actually sets some of Daphne's text—underscores the importance of that G-major incursion at the end of part 1, when she sings, "Menschen, Freunde, nehmt mich als Zeichen unsterblicher Liebe" (see Example 4). These final lines represent the only instance of vocal independence in part 1 and, as the sketches show, the composer (using a pen) squeezes text and its musical setting into the preexistent penciled continuity sketch (see Example 6). Strauss may well have already decided on the musical setting for at least part of those lines."[39]

The only extant sketches for part 2 of the transformation are in BSL, and they are in three layers of various lengths. The first layer

Example 6. Sketch for part 1 of Daphne's transformation in the Houghton Library sketchbook (fol. 30)

represents an entire pass through the scene with all the scratch-outs and *ossias* that one might expect in a first attempt. Despite their various differences, all three layers indicate that with the shift to F♯ major, Strauss decided to make a motivic reference to the F♯ modulation in Daphne's opening monologue by recalling the head motive of "O wie gerne" (five bars after fig. 26); each layer begins with that thematic gesture (see Example 7).

The differences between the second and third layers in the first eight bars are minimal, but the first layer is another matter. Here we see a composer trying to bring back no fewer than six thematic ideas within the span of the first eight bars alone ("O wie gerne," the Daphne motive, "blieb ich bei dir," the laurel motive, the love motive, and the Apollo motive, respectively). While the dizzying return of various motives in the *Elektra* finale may have been appropriate for the cathartic, emotional explosion following the deaths of Klytämnestra and Aegisthus, and Agamemnon, such a busy linear display is hardly in keeping with Daphne's peaceful transition from mortal to an eternal being—where humans and gods are at one with nature. Furthermore, Strauss's emphasis (in the first layer) on motivic return undermines the sense of periodicity for which he was clearly aiming, as evinced in the second and third layers. Here we see how Strauss divides the eight-bar period into two clear 4 + 4 phrases, articulating the beginning of each phrase with the ♩ ♩ figure.

The first layer covers some eleven pages of sketches in BSL, and much of it did not make it to the final version—especially its frequent reliance on the tense, chromatic, sequential figure that plays such a

Example 7. Sketches for part 2 of Daphne's transformation in the Bavarian State Library sketchbook (pp. 12, 30, and 32)

prominent role in part 1 of the transformation. The final score indicates that Strauss ultimately wished to leave behind the motive of sexual tension between Apollo and Daphne in part 1; once transformed as a tree she rises above that world. However, one thing is clear from this earliest known layer of sketching for part 2: Strauss knew well how he should end the opera. Daphne would become part of the orchestra in wordless melody, which would fuse together the laurel tree and Daphne motives—the new and old Daphne, respectively.

In the printed score Daphne sings in imitation with the oboe (see Example 8), but in this early sketch it is not apparent how extensive Strauss intended the imitation to be (see Example 9). Perhaps the composer's annotation ("only [a] high accompanying [instrumental] voice") suggests imitation in a voice the same register as the soprano's, but one could also take the term "accompanying" at face value as well.

Example 8. Fusion of Daphne's voice with the orchestra (printed score, five bars after fig. 257)

There is no doubt that Strauss intends an imitative instrumental voice after Daphne begins singing the laurel theme in augmentation.

Of course Strauss's letter to Gregor of 12 May 1937 (see p. 268) already suggested that Daphne should sing "as a voice of nature" in wordless melody eight bars of the laurel motive, but a later source, still predating Example 9, offers more detailed verbal instructions as to how the opera should end. These are marginal annotations in Strauss's hand, written on the last page of Gregor's revised text.[40]

Example 9. Sketch for part 2 of Daphne's transformation in the Bavarian State
Library sketchbook (pp. 21–22)

Beneath the librettist's final stage directions ("as the light spreads
above the entire tree, the curtain falls") Strauss writes: "During the
last sounding sixteen final bars one hears only Daphne's voice from
the treetop singing without words the Daphne and laurel theme!"[41]

·

Transformation, transfiguration, metamorphosis: these are all related
concepts that weave their way throughout Strauss's music—from the
tone poems of the 1880s and 1890s through the operas of the twentieth century. Transformation was, of course, a theme dear to the
heart of Hofmannsthal, and it played a role in one form or another
in nearly every Strauss-Hofmannsthal collaboration. Baron Ochs may
brag to Octavian (disguised as Mariandl) that he is "holy Jupiter in
his thousand manifestations," but Octavian himself is the one who
takes on various transformations throughout the opera: as adolescent
lover, chambermaid, rose cavalier, and—by the end—a wiser young
man. Through the love of Ariadne, Bacchus is transformed into a god;
but Ariadne, by forgetting the unfaithful Theseus, is herself transformed. Unlike Daphne, the Empress of *Die Frau ohne Schatten* desires
mortality, she wants to bear children, and through an act of humanity (that of self-sacrifice) she is transformed into a mortal being.
Strauss's and Hofmannsthal's mutual fascination with this theme was
central to their long-standing collaboration.

But the composer of Daphne's transformation could no longer rely
on Hofmannsthal at this crucial moment in the work. Instead, Strauss
had Gregor, whose leaden verse only burdened the composer's inspi-

ration. The 12 May 1937 letter to his librettist reveals a composer inspired by the magic of Daphne's transformation, but it also shows a man who ultimately realized that he could only compose it successfully on his own terms. The revised ending was not merely a matter of discarding the idea of "oratorio." By rejecting the choral finale and embracing the instrumental realm, he both eliminated Gregor's pedantic text and found a deeper, more personal mode of expression. In composing his "long orchestral piece," Strauss looked back not only to the symphonic finale of *Elektra* but to the days of his tone poems. Indeed, in a return to a tone poem of sorts, Strauss would explore the phenomenon of transformation one last time with the *Metamorphosen* of 1945.

Daphne's transformation, the crowning glory of the opera, is one of the finest final curtains in all of Strauss's stage works. Ernst Krause, who attended the *Daphne* premiere (15 October 1938), rightfully asks:

> Where else among Strauss's works is there a sound picture to compare with the chroma of the tranquility of nature during Daphne's transformation into the laurel tree? The manner in which this metamorphosis occurs in tenderly veiled music in F♯ major, the sound growing from that of a woodwind ensemble until the whole foliage of the tree seems to spread itself out, shimmering gently in the divided strings, harp and other instruments, finally to be taken up by the soprano, now freely vocalizing coloratura passages like a bird—all this creates the effect of a great "marriage of nature."[42]

The success of *Daphne*—far greater than that of *Friedenstag* or *Die Liebe der Danae*—owes much to the expressive power of its ending.[43] Seeing the eighty-five-year-old Strauss on film performing Daphne's *Verwandlungsmusik* at the piano only a few months before his death, one realizes that this final scene itself represents a kind of transformation: it explores a realm of personal expression more profound than anything Gregor originally intended.

NOTES

1. Kurt Wilhelm, *Richard Strauss Persönlich* (Munich: Kindler, 1984), p. 420.

2. Personal communication with the late Alice Strauss, the composer's daughter-in-law.

3. Otto Strasser, *Und dafür wird man noch bezahlt* (Vienna, 1974), p. 182.

4. Hofmannsthal's operatic libretti numbered five: *Der Rosenkavalier, Ariadne auf Naxos, Die Frau ohne Schatten, Die ägyptische Helena,* and *Arabella.*

5. See, for example, Kenneth Birkin, "Strauss, Zweig, and Gregor: Unpublished Letters," *Music and Letters* 56 (April 1975): 180–95; Edward Lowinsky's preface to *A Confidential Matter: The Letters of Richard Strauss and Stefan Zweig, 1931–1935*, ed. Willi Schuh, trans. Max Knight (Berkeley and Los Angeles: University of California Press, 1977), pp. xi–xxxi; and Bryan Gilliam, "Stefan Zweig's Contribution to Strauss Opera after *Die schweigsame Frau:* New Evidence," in *Stefan Zweig: Yesterday's European Today* (Albany: SUNY Press, 1983), pp. 217–26.

6. In addition to the Strauss-Zweig letters cited here, there is *Richard Strauss und Joseph Gregor: Briefwechsel (1934–1949)*, ed. Roland Tenschert (Salzburg: Otto Müller, 1955). The unpublished letters from Zweig to Gregor are housed at the Archive of the Vienna Philharmonic; the unpublished correspondence from Gregor to Zweig may be found at the Reed Library of Fredonia State University College (SUNY), henceforth RLF. As this volume went to press I learned that the Zweig-Gregor letters have been recently published in New Zealand. See *Stefan Zweig–Joseph Gregor: Correspondence, 1921–1938*, ed. Kenneth Birkin (Dunedin: Department of German, University of Otago, 1991).

7. See Gilliam, "Stefan Zweig's Contribution," p. 222.

8. Letter of 5 June 1916 in *The Correspondence between Richard Strauss and Hugo von Hofmannsthal*, ed. Hanns Hammelmann and Ewald Osers (Cambridge: Cambridge University Press, 1980), p. 250.

9. On 20 July 1936 Gregor wrote Strauss: "It saddens me that you no longer remember the sketch of the work [*Danae*] that I handed to you at Berchtesgaden." See Birkin, "Strauss, Zweig, and Gregor," p. 191.

10. Joseph Gregor, *Richard Strauss: Der Meister der Oper* (Munich: Piper, 1939), pp. 246–47.

11. Unpublished letter to Zweig (31 July [1935]), RLF. I am grateful to Joanna Schweik at the Reed Library for letting me examine these letters in March 1981.

12. The genesis of the *Daphne* text is discussed at length in two dissertations: Kenneth Birkin, *Friedenstag and Daphne: The Literary and Dramatic Sources of the Two Operas* (Ph.D. dissertation, University of Birmingham, 1983); and Bryan Gilliam, *Richard Strauss's Daphne: Opera and Symphonic Continuity* (Ph.D. dissertation, Harvard University, 1984). The latter work examines musical as well as textual sources for *Daphne*. Birkin's dissertation was published in 1989 by Garland (*Outstanding Dissertations in Music from British Universities*, ed. John Caldwell).

13. To be fair to Gregor, Nazi censorship would have prevented any mention of Zweig in his book on Strauss.

14. Gregor, pp. 245–46.

15. The third version was actually completed by April 1936, but the ending of this version was revised in May or June 1937.

16. I am very grateful to Susan Gillespie for her assistance in translating the Gregor excerpts.

17. Unpublished letter to Gregor (3 September 1935), Vienna Philharmonic Archive (henceforth VPA).

18. Ibid.

19. Ibid.

20. Letter to Gregor (15 September 1935) in Tenschert, p. 33.

21. Letters to Gregor (25 and 29 September 1935) in ibid., pp. 33–34; and letter to Zweig (31 October 1935) in *A Confidential Matter*, p. 104.

22. Strauss-Hofmannsthal, *Correspondence*, p. 258.

23. See, for example, letter to Gregor (29 February 1936) in Tenschert, p. 51.

24. "Everything is still too long around the midpoint . . . you still always get intoxicated with your own verses." See letter to Gregor (4 March 1939) in ibid., p. 51.

25. Strauss and Wallerstein were in Milan in conjunction with a production of *Arabella*.

26. Letter to Gregor (12 March 1936) in Tenschert, pp. 57–58.

27. Gregor replaced the lines "You are the emblem / Of the all-embracing / Eternal Nature" (*Daphne* II) with "Even above Dionysos / And Phoebus Apollo" (*Daphne* III).

28. Norman Del Mar, *Richard Strauss: A Critical Commentary on His Life and Works*, vol. 3 (London: Chilton, 1972), p. 111.

29. Letter to Gregor (12 May 1937) in Tenschert, pp. 83–84.

30. Unpublished letter to Zweig (28 May 1937), RLF.

31. The first recorded suggestion by Gregor that the operas should form a pair was in February 1936: "The *Friedenstag* [Day of peace] expresses the highest human idea, as *Daphne* sings of the peace of nature. Both works naturally belong together entirely." See letter to Strauss (17 February 1936) in Tenschert, p. 50.

32. Unpublished letter to Zweig (28 January 1936), RLF.

33. Strauss's description comes from a marginal annotation beside Daphne's final lines ("Ich komme, ich komme," etc.) on the last page of the autograph libretto, which appears in facsimile in Ernst Krause, *Richard Strauss: The Man and His Work*, trans. John Coombs (Boston: Crescendo, 1969), following p. 368. This document is discussed briefly on pp. 61–62.

34. The final scene of *Elektra* brings to a head a harmonic tension first presented in Elektra's expository monologue: the conflict between C and E major.

35. Here, again, we possibly find a parallel to *Elektra* where—in a preliminary sketchbook—Strauss closed the opera in an entirely different key (E♭ minor rather than the ultimate C major). It may well be that, in both *Elektra* and *Daphne*, Strauss made the changes of key in order to conform with tonal events in the respective opening monologues.

36. We see evidence of Strauss's decision that F♯ major should signify the laurel tree as early as the Böhm sketchbook. On fol. 11 he composes a nine-bar F♯-major passage labeled "Der Baum."

37. James A. Hepokoski, "Fiery-Pulsed Libertine or Domestic Hero? Strauss's *Don Juan* Reinvestigated," in *Richard Strauss: New Perspectives on the Composer and His Work*, ed. Bryan Gilliam (Durham, N.C.: Duke University Press, 1992).

38. Strauss hinted at the motive as early as fig. 245 ("Wind"), above an $F\sharp^6_4$ sonority.

39. Beneath the last system of this passage is a curious annotation by Strauss: "from here onward F♯-major melody: chorus and single voices." Why does the composer refer to a chorus and solo voices at this stage in the composition? Strauss could possibly be referring to the F♯-major melody of an earlier sketch for chorus and voices. The early sketch in Tr. 95 (see Example 1) was to be transposed to F♯ major; there may have been further sketching in a missing source. But it is equally possible that this sketch in the HL sketchbook predates Strauss's decision to change the ending. In the original finale for *Daphne* III Gregor writes: "Suddenly it becomes dark. The music begins to depict the growth of the Daphne tree." Example 6 could very well be that music, a self-sufficient instrumental passage ultimately destined for Daphne's solo voice rather than for multiple voices.

40. This copy of the text, now lost, is discussed in detail in Gilliam, *Richard Strauss's "Daphne,"* pp. 161–67. This page, however, is preserved in facsimile in various secondary sources.

41. See facsimile in Krause, following p. 368.

42. Ibid., p. 372.

43. Indeed, the transformation scene has been both performed and recorded as a separate concert number.

Structure and Program in *Macbeth:*

A Proposed Reading of Strauss's

First Symphonic Poem

JAMES HEPOKOSKI

On 24 August 1888 Richard Strauss wrote to Hans von Bülow of the "ever increasing contradiction between the musical-poetic content that I want to convey a[nd] the ternary sonata form that has come down to us from the classical composers." Adopting Lisztian argumentation, Strauss went on to insist that a composer who grasps the musical problems of the current moment should strive to create idiosyncratic structures that spring from "the inspiration by a poetical idea, whether or not it be introduced as a programme. I consider it a legitimate artistic method to create a correspondingly new form for every new subject." In the same letter Strauss referred to his newly composed symphonic poem, *Macbeth,* a preliminary version of which he had completed by 9 January 1888, but whose concluding sections he had subjected to a massive revision, at least partially on von Bülow's advice, by 8 February. The result was now "the exact expression of my artistic thinking and feeling, a[nd] in style the most independent and purposeful work I have yet done."[1] In sum, Strauss wished von Bülow to know that he regarded *Macbeth* as something of a modernist manifesto that challenged its intended listeners to confront three issues head-on: perceiving the piece's architectural newness (or, as I prefer to call it, its structure's "deformational character");[2] recalling the content of Shakespeare's *Macbeth* and accepting it, in some sense, as a significantly determining poetic idea; and actively using that recollection of the play to function as the dominant framework of understanding to account both for the piece's color or tone and for its structural-deformational character.

In actual hermeneutic practice, trying to accomplish all this responsibly is difficult business. The methodological ramifications of symphonic-poem interpretation are notoriously thorny, and I have reviewed elsewhere the complexities involved in accepting Strauss's triple challenge.[3] It must suffice here to point out that of his eight symphonic poems composed between 1887 and 1903 it is this earliest and most neglected one, *Macbeth*, whose programmatic outline has proven to be the least clear. In the printed score Strauss provided a paratext that comprises no more than the title and two thematic labels, "Macbeth" and "Lady Macbeth" (the latter along with a brief quotation from the play), for the two contrasting themes (measures 6 and 64) of what is surely to be heard as a sonata exposition. In other words, although the composer verbally identified two of the characters (themes), the subsequent action and denouement is unaccompanied by any composer-sanctioned verbal text, even though at times it gives the impression of being both dramatically stylized and narratively illustrative (with marches, fortissimo catastrophes, trumpet fanfares, and so on).[4] That its musical structure has also confounded most commentators has only added to the image of the work's obscurities.

The main lines of *Macbeth* interpretation were laid down by Germanic writers from 1892 to about 1930—and here, too, none of these reading-traditions, so far as we currently know, was either endorsed or rejected by Strauss. The first to grapple with the score was Heinrich Reimann, who provided a six-page poetic interpretation of the tone poem in the printed program booklet for the Berlin Philharmonic premiere of the "final version" on 29 February 1892.[5] However one might assess its current value and relevance (as will emerge, I find it remarkably persuasive), Reimann's reading seems to have made little lasting impact on the principal writers on *Macbeth* in subsequent years. These writers included, most notably, Arthur Seidl (1896), Ernst Otto Nodnagel (1902), Hermann Teibler (1908), Otto Klauwell (1910), Max Steinitzer (1911), Richard Specht (1921), Hermann W. von Waltershausen (1921), and Reinhold Muschler (1924).[6] All were impressed with Strauss's vivid representation of "the madness of the most horrifying ferocity," as Seidl put it: "[Strauss] strives to paint in [musical] tones the wild demonism of this fearful character; to this end no color is too harsh for him, no expressive nuance too acrid" (p. 23). Seidl judged *Macbeth*, along with the immediately subsequent *Don Juan*, to be an uncompromisingly "extreme" work, a "bold Columbus-voyage" that sought to explore the "modern" question of the limits of "music's expressive capability" (pp. 20–22). Over two decades later the Viennese Specht went further: *Macbeth* was "a work built from

blood and iron" (p. 169), a pointed allusion to the work's expressive
compatibility with the atmosphere of naked power-politics in
Bismarckian Germany.[7] Still, most of the commentators shied away
from confronting directly the formal traditions to which the musical
structure was alluding, and, apart from Specht, each of those who
dealt with the musical architecture at all skirted the issue by hearing
the work as cast into an ad hoc structure unrelatable to the well-es-
tablished *Formenlehre* traditions.

Among the early twentieth-century commentaries we may discern an
influential Teibler-Klauwell-Muschler line of analysis, which understood
Macbeth as divided into two halves that overrode any claim to meaningful intersection with "ternary" sonata form. In this scheme the first
half, usually considered as measures 1–259, is broadly concerned with
the exposition of the characters and with Macbeth's fearful resolution
to murder the king. Thus Teibler referred to the first half as
"Entschluss" ("Decision," p. 68) and considered the actual moment
of decision to be the climactic *fff* outburst at measures 242ff. The
second half ("Tat" [Deed], Teibler, p. 68) encompasses measures 324–
558, and the murder of King Duncan is located at the *molto agitato*
measures 427ff., a prolonged $^{\flat 6}_{4}$ chord over a G bass (the so-called
C-minor $^{6}_{4}$ chord). Connecting the two halves is a B♭, marchlike interlude (although in $^{3}_{4}$ time, *Moderato maestoso*, measures 260–323),
which, given the "Entschluss-Tat" format assumed to govern the outer
halves, has generally been taken to represent the processional arrival
of King Duncan at Macbeth's castle.

In a more thorough discussion of the work Richard Specht adopted
aspects of this interpretive line but began to merge them—although
not too clearly—with some conventions of sonata-praxis. He thus referred to the whole work's "symphonic form forged with a giant hammer" (p. 174). This seems to imply the presence of a separate exposition (surely measures 1–122, although Specht was not explicit on
this point), and he seems to have considered the remainder of the
piece as constituting a huge development, itself subdivided into two
halves (labeled as "Vorsatz" [Premeditation] and "Tat" [Deed], measures 123–259 and 324–558) linked by the usual "king's procession"
Zwischenspiel (measures 260–323). Moreover, according to Specht the
second section of the development (the "Deed") "simultaneously contains the reprise within itself," but in ways that Specht chose not to
specify (pp. 176–77). This somewhat obscure argument appears to
have filtered into English-language criticism with Gerald Abraham's
A Hundred Years of Music (1938), and the most recent commentators,
such as Norman Del Mar and Michael Kennedy, have gone several

steps further in blocking out the musical architecture to suggest that *Macbeth* is "one movement of extended sonata form, in which the lengthy development [at least measures 123–323] incorporates two self-contained episodes."[8]

To date, though, no commentary has convincingly merged a proposed musical structure with the specifics of the presumed poetic idea that generates it. Clearly, the chief discomfort of Teibler's influential "Entschluss-Tat" program is that King Duncan is murdered too late in the score—in measures 427–33 of the total 558 measures. (And, for that matter, Macbeth himself is usually considered to have been brought to ruin by measure 516. Discussing Macbeth's *Coriolan*-like "dramatic collapse" is one of the main points of John Williamson's recent study of several portions of the work.)[9] This reading omits everything from the play's act 2, scene 2 (Duncan's murder) to its off-stage events in the final scene, act 5, scene 8 (Macbeth's death). Adherents of this reading are consequently obliged to conclude that Strauss was unconcerned with most of the events of the play's final three acts—with the gruesomely mounting consequences of the murder, with Macbeth's growing anxiety and guilt, and so on, all of which constitutes the play's real core. At best, this reading seems clumsily proportioned. The common strategy to parry this problem has been to assert that Strauss's first symphonic poem, unlike its immediate successors, is not closely concerned with narrative detail. An early form of this strategy emerged in Klauwell, who argued that the play and its characters are represented in the music in only a general and "purely psychological" way (p. 230).[10] In manifold variants, that strategy has echoed through the decades, down to Williamson's evident satisfaction that, apart from a few more or less standard associations, "*Macbeth* emerges from the primitive hermeneutics of the programme note relatively intact."[11]

My own view is that in confronting this elusive work the tradition of *Macbeth* interpretation took a wrong turn early on from which it has been unable to recover fully and which has also hindered our perception of the piece's poetic and formal structure. This wrong turn, fully developed in Teibler by 1908 in a prominent member of Schlesinger's widely distributed *Meisterführer* series, is the assertion that the "Deed"— the assassination—is to be located at measure 427. But if we shift the regicide to the earlier fortissimo climax at measures 242–54, as, in fact, the far less widely read Reimann and Nodnagel had maintained in 1892 and 1902,[12] and if we follow the consequences of this relocation within a more sophisticated concept of sonata-deformational practice as it seems to have been grasped by late nineteenth-century composers, a more measured and convincing understanding of the piece and its compositional choices is made possible.

In what follows I outline the framework for a surface reading of the symphonic poem that both accounts for more of the play and hopes, even within the context of a brief overview in which many salient details must be passed over, to confront the problem of the piece's architecture more squarely than have prior analyses. As a personalized reading it will seek to merge poetic idea and processual structure; but as a mere proposal it can make no claim to objective solution, nor is it intended to. The essence of a symphonic poem as a genre lies in our individual efforts to imbricate the given musical text and the implications of a poetic paratext, and the procedure involved is clearly that of a historically informed, dialogical hermeneutics, not that of objective knowledge. For better or worse, this is an exegetical situation with which we shall have to make our peace.[13]

Emblem (measures 1–5)

Set off from the exposition proper by a fermata in measure 5, the opening measures of *Macbeth* sound in crescendo the open-fifth dominant (A–E) of the D minor to come. Surely among Strauss's models for such an initial sonority were two other D-minor pieces: the first movement of Beethoven's Ninth Symphony (open-fifth dominant)—with which this music has an especially clear connection—and Wagner's Overture to *The Flying Dutchman* (open-fifth tonic). As in the canonic models the "overtone-generated" *Klang* is immediately overlaid with an open-fifth melodic motive, here one with a fanfarelike, annunciatory character. The tradition has labeled this motive in a variety of ways: "Macbeth's aspiring, ambitious temperament" (Reimann, p. 11); "listen!" [Hört!] or "victory cry" (Teibler, pp. 62, 71); "warlike atmosphere" or "war cry" (Specht, pp. 174–75; Muschler, p. 285); "kingliness" (Del Mar 1.55). In view of how the motive is used later in the work, my preference is to agree with Del Mar (and indirectly with Reimann), but to label it "throne/power" (Example 1; in all instances an indication in brackets will signify that it is mine, not Strauss's).[14] Here at the outset Strauss presents the motive as a plot-defining emblem, the sign under which the narrative to follow will be played.

[measures 1–5: "throne/power"]

Example 1.

Exposition (measures 6–122)

As a whole, the D-minor/F-major [*sic*] exposition is broadly patterned after the influential model provided in *The Flying Dutchman:* the representation of two radically contrasting characters, masculine and feminine, in two self-standing blocks separated by minimal (or no) transitional material. Wagner himself wrote of these reductive exposition-types as dominated by the principle of *Wechsel* (succession or alternation). Somewhat frequently encountered in post-Wagnerian symphonic composition, such expositions are particularly apt for illustrative or quasi-illustrative purposes, and according to the Wagnerian formula the characters were to be thrown into genuine plot-motion with the onset of the development.[15]

The most notable aspect of the exposition's principal group, the dark, D-minor block that Strauss explicitly labels "Macbeth," is that it is subdivided into two differing, but complementary, passages—measures 6–19 and 20–63. The former would seem to be a thumbnail sketch of Macbeth as we first meet him in his capacity as a grimly determined, loyal soldier to the king. Hence the pitiless, marchlike steps that seem to invade and conquer both registral and tonal space; hence the jackboot quality and wide span of the theme itself, whose first four measures occupy nearly two and a half octaves; hence the four succeeding measures' broad sweeps, which imperiously stride into and secure such far-flung foreign regions as E♭ (measures 12–13) before turning back to return to D minor (Example 2).

Strauss explicitly associates D minor here with Macbeth: it is his normal tonal identity. Within the production and reception conventions of traditional sonata practice (and especially within music that invites the listener to project archetypally heroic, tragic, or romancelike contents upon its musical processes) such oppressive, minor-mode tonics may be said normally to aspire to be "redeemed" (Wagner's *erlöst*) into the major mode. In this formulaic redemption narrative the usual

[measures 6–13: "Macbeth"]

Example 2.

tonal shift to the mediant major (or other major-mode area) for the second portion of the exposition typically represents a temporary or only potential redemptive space that must be brought into the more conclusive tonic major in the recapitulation.[16] From this sonata-generic perspective (and also considering the chain of musical events to come in this work) we may suggest that Macbeth's "tragic flaw," implicit here at the beginning, is to be understood within the musical process as discontentment with his D-minor identity, which he longs to supplant with a more stable, positive major mode.

Of the major-mode candidates D major is obviously the distant goal, and more will be said about it later. But for the moment Strauss unsettles Macbeth's D minor with something different. Put in the most succinct terms, Macbeth's D-minor "$\frac{5}{3}$ identity" tends to shift to a "$\frac{6}{3}$ identity." In measure 7, for instance, we may perceive the $\frac{5}{3}$ and the $\frac{6}{3}$ clashing up against each other (a dissonance heightened further by a simultaneous 4–3 suspension).[17] And when this initial passage drives toward a cadence in D minor in measures 17–19 (Example 3), the expected D-minor $\frac{5}{3}$ is undermined by a D-minor $\frac{6}{3}$ sonority before it is repacked down, fortissimo and in tremolo, to the normal constituents of the $\frac{5}{3}$ chord (measure 19, beats 2–4; note, however, that at this "corrective" point the D-bass momentarily drops out, and F is the lowest-sounding pitch).

This 5–6 shift is a common feature of tonal practice, and the relevant point to observe about it here is that nineteenth-century composers sometimes sought to exploit its potential harmonic ambiguities. On the one hand, from a contrapuntal perspective, a $\frac{6}{3}$ above a fixed

[measures 17–19]

Example 3.

or established bass—here, D—is often best considered to be an alternate, less stable expression of that bass's $\frac{5}{3}$ sonority (as in Brahms's First Piano Concerto, which opens with a $\frac{6}{3}$ above D, but is nonetheless best considered to begin "in D minor"). On the other hand, one can scarcely deny the simultaneous historical existence of a strong production and reception convention oriented in concepts of "roots and inversions" that would describe the same sonority as a B♭^{6} chord. In the context of the *Macbeth* passage at hand, measures 6–19, such a description would appear shortsighted from a current perspective;[18] and yet this aspect of the $\frac{6}{3}$ ambiguity seems incontestable when Strauss actually supplies the presumed root, B♭, to establish the tonic of much of this piece's extended developmental-space section (measures 123–323). In terms of its related poetic idea, though, the harmonic point seems clear enough: from the beginning the grimly D-minor Macbeth craves to be someone other than who he is, and we first see this "tragic flaw" (also identifiable as one facet of his ambition, as so much in *Macbeth*) in the shifts toward $\frac{6}{3}$—or "B♭"—space. (A temporary escape from a minor tonic onto a sometimes wistful, "if-only," or Arcadian "VI-space," of course, is a standard feature of the poetics of common tonal practice.)

The second portion of the primary theme (measures 20–63) introduces a new figure in the bass (Example 4, measure 20) that is reiterated at differing pitch levels. Significantly, its first three levels arpeggiate a D-major triad, D, F♯, and A (measures 20 and 25; measure 29; and measure 32). This figure—which the twentieth-century tradition has erratically labeled the "hero's cruel desire for deeds" mixed with "tormenting doubt" (Teibler, p. 64), the "evil principle in humankind" (Muschler, p. 285), instability (Del Mar, p. 56), and so on—is perhaps better considered Strauss's illustration of the witches' threefold prophecy to Macbeth (act 1, scene 3). The sinuous, chromatic bass line (touching "Macbeth's tonic" at its root, then crazing it) followed by the eldritch G♮–G♯ cross-relation between the upper voices and the bass in measure 24—and the whole shot through with tremolo strings shivering on a frozen "Macbeth chord" (D minor, measures 20–23)—would seem sufficient to evoke a topos of the uncanny, weird, or supernatural. (Curiously, in 1892 Reimann [p. 11] seems to have regarded this passage not as the "prophecy" itself but as Macbeth's disturbed reaction to that prophecy. As in the play, of course, the "fact" of the prophecy, whether really present, re-membered, or only imagined, immediately transmutes into and is thus synonomous with Macbeth's dark ambition to assume the throne.) Moreover, the first statements of the motive immediately enkindle the "throne/power" emblem in the trumpet (initially on F♯, measure 28). The process is repeated at intensified pitch levels and elaborations until the end of the section, in which Macbeth collects himself to re-assert his D minor in a potent, expanded cadence, while echoes of "throne/power" and "prophecy/troubled ambition" still swirl about him (measures 44–56, with codetta, measures 56–63).

[measures 20–25: "prophecy/troubled ambition"]

Example 4.

Dutchman-like, the scene shifts without transition to "Lady Macbeth" (measures 64–122), the second-theme area, at the head of which Strauss also had printed the five and a half lines from act 1, scene 5 beginning, "Hie thee hither, / That I may pour my spirits in thine ear." All commentators have recognized this section as a representa-tion of her seductive leading of Macbeth to resolve to kill King Duncan. Strauss constructed it from essentially two musical ideas (Ex-amples 5a and 5b). The smooth, undulate contours of the first (which might strike us as a distorted, flickering variant of the Gutrune mo-tive from *Götterdämmerung*) have invariably been identified with Lady Macbeth and her persuasive powers (Teibler, p. 66, "Über-redungsthema"). The more aggressive second would seem to be her "urging to commit murder," and it is characterized by a triple state-ment of a single chord. In syncopated quarters, each prodded onward by a grace note (measure 83), the motive seems intended to suggest

Example 5a.

Example 5b.

a spur or goad—the "urging" proper; in the immediately subsequent, more rapid triplet in the lower voices (measure 84) it may suggest the violence of the "death blow" itself (Specht, p. 175: "It cries out as if to say, 'Mord im Schlaf!' [Murder in his sleep]"; similarly, for Muschler, p. 285, this is the "wish and will to power" [see n. 7]). The whole second-theme passage shifts abruptly—or obsessively—between these contrasting ideas and brings them to a *stringendo* climax (her now-explicit mention of the "death blow" to come?) on a distant Eb-minor chord.

Perhaps the subtlest aspect of the second-theme area is Strauss's treatment of its tonality. The most common subordinate key for a D-minor exposition is F major, which in fact is the locally governing key here, one for which the composer continues to provide a one-flat signature. But for most of the passage's acoustic surface Strauss constructs Lady Macbeth as operating outside of this generically normal tonic; she often insinuates and persuades, that is, on and around a $\begin{smallmatrix}\#6\\\#3\end{smallmatrix}$ sonority above a prolonged A, *sul ponticello* and tremolo

(F$\sharp^6$, measures 64–70, 99–105). The tonal point of that "F$\sharp$-ness," though, is not to express itself; rather, its point is its oblique, often half-step slippage (via a C$\sharp$–D shift) onto the "redemptive" D-major sonority: Lady Macbeth touches all too effectively, that is, on her husband's dissatisfaction with himself. (Such is the case, for example, with the prevailing D sonority in measures 71–73 and 81–82. Similarly, the first statements of the agitato "urging" occur on a D^6 sonority, in measures 83 and 87.) Midway through this process Strauss moves onto D major's dark dominant, A minor (measure 91), then slides up a diminished triad in the bass to attain the E♭-minor "death blow" proposal mentioned above.

But all this disturbed, off-tonic activity is put aside at the end, as the composer finally permits her F$\sharp$ "persuasion" theme (now articulated *calmato* on an unstable F$\sharp$-major sonority, whose root is sounded in measure 106) to sink down a half-step and settle onto the "normal" F major in measure 109 (Example 6).[19] The poetic point could scarcely be clearer. As Lady Macbeth relaxes, *molto tranquillo,* onto the governing subordinate key of the sonata exposition, so too she takes on the proper role of traditional or decorous outward appearances. The emergence of F major at the exposition's end—an effect as brilliant as it is chilling—is poetically equivalent to her donning of the mask of social propriety, and it also furnishes the gateway through which Macbeth can move into his "tragic flaw" key, B♭ major. The grisly action of the drama may now ensue.

[measures 106–10]

Example 6.

Developmental Space: Two Episodes
(measures 123–259 and 260–323)

In mid- and late nineteenth-century sonata practice, particularly among "progressive" composers, a palpable danger in filling out the developmental space (the obligatory middle zone of "ternary" sonata form) was that of producing a merely academic, blustery *Durchführung*. One solution that helped to sidestep this lapse into formula was to treat the developmental space as a set of more or less new, contrasting episodes (which may be inset with some developmental passages). Two episodes seem to have been the norm, and Strauss surely knew of this solution from some of Liszt's symphonic poems (*Tasso* provided a rudimentary example) and from Wagner's *Siegfried Idyll*.[20] He would adopt the deformation in *Macbeth, Don Juan,* and *Death and Transfiguration* and expand it further in such works as *Till Eulenspiegel* and *Also sprach Zarathustra.* In *Macbeth* both developmental episodes are controlled locally by B♭ major. As mentioned above, this is to be considered a pseudoredemptive space for the D-minor protagonist, merely a promising way station on the path to the anticipated, more permanent corrective of D major. Moreover, as frequently happens within Straussian tone poems, the two episodes correspond roughly to a symphony's "lyrical movement" (slow movement) and "characteristic movement" (or scherzo). Thus the overarching structure of *Macbeth* as a whole suggests a multimovement form within a single movement, with the recapitulatory space representing the finale.

The first developmental episode begins with a new, lyrical idea (Example 7a) that the post-Reimann interpretive tradition, somewhat wonderingly, has insisted is a "love theme" between Macbeth and Lady Macbeth—something superfluous with regard to the drama at hand, as several have remarked. (Thus Klauwell, pp. 232–33, claimed feebly that Strauss adopted it not for programmatic or narrative reasons but only to provide needed musical contrast, "from the [purely] musical standpoint," apparently considered in the abstract.) Reimann, on the other hand, had insisted that the passage represents even more seductive persuasion on Lady Macbeth's part. This could well be the case, but it also seems possible that the short-winded theme is meant to evoke the couple's joint plan now set into action, glossed over with lyrical outward appearances and pushed ahead inexorably toward the murder. Throughout the first episode Strauss intercuts this idea with several of the previously heard motives in something of a nervous, angular collage that builds in successive waves of intensity and resolution. (Examples 2, 4, and 5 are thus simultaneously treated to a programmatic development at various tonal levels.) By measure 152 a new idea is released (on B♭) that seems linked to the notion of "attainment"—the sense that the plot can succeed; that Macbeth will in fact rule (Example 7b; its motivic sources may lie in the exposition's Macbeth zone, measures 53–54, or even earlier).

[measures 123–28: "the plan in action/further persuasion"]

Example 7a.

[measures 152–54: "attainment"]

Example 7b.

All the motives surge forward to the moment of the assassination of Duncan, measures 242–54. Here Strauss graphically expands the triple-stroke "death blow" into three held $\textit{fff}$ gestures separated by vast pauses and fermatas marked *lunga:* D° (measures 242–45, Macbeth's D minor now precipitated into diminished-sonority crisis), $A\flat^6$ (measures 246–49), and $E^7_{\sharp5}$–C^7–$F^9_{\flat7}$ (measures 250–54). While sounding these strenuous chordal "shocks," the composer emphatically reintroduces a fourfold, *marcatissimo* statement of the "throne/power" motive—for indeed, it is the kingship that is at stake here. The fortissimo cymbal crash in measure 252 (on $V^9_7/B\flat$) probably represents the actual moment of the king's death.[21] In the immediately subsequent string presentation of "attainment," measures 252 to 259, marked *wild* and scurrying frenetically about in sixteenth notes (all continuing to express $V^7/B\flat$), we are probably to envision Macbeth's and Lady Macbeth's agitated, hasty exits from the murder scene.

In the reading offered here the ensuing second episode, the $\frac{3}{4}$ B♭ march (which was surely a source passage for many of the characteristic sounds that would appeal to the young Edward Elgar), stands not for Duncan's processional arrival, as the Teibler-Klauwell-Muschler tradition would have it, but rather, following the earlier commentaries of Reimann (p. 14) and Nodnagel (p. 75), for Macbeth's own coronation after the assassination. This new reading accounts both for the imposing presence of the "throne/power" motive, of which this epi-sode is manifestly an expanded variant, and for the complementary appearance of "Lady Macbeth" (striding by the new king's side). Per-haps the most splendid passage of the entire score occurs at the end of this episode: the full-blown, climactic embrace (also pre-Elgarian) of the "attainment" motive, measures 308–23, with the poetic sense of the leading characters' heads perversely swimming in the ecstasy of victory. As Banquo put it in the play, but far more forebodingly, "Thou hast it now: king, Cawdor, Glamis, all, / As the weird women promised" (act 3, scene 1).

Recapitulatory Space: Distorted (measures 324–535)

Within modernist works whose architecture is idiosyncratic, as it is here, the presence or absence of a quasi-symmetrical recapitulation is the key factor that serves retroactively to define the genre, deformational structure, and poetic content of the whole. In works with doubly divided, episodic developmental spaces, by the end of the second episode the piece's "sonata" character has been substantially weakened, and is perhaps barely present at all. Up to this point the listeners to such structures have been presented only with a linear chain of contrasting events, which may instead be heard as rondo-like—or only as arbitrarily successive. The recapitulatory space thus bears the heaviest structural and expressive burden, that of concep-tually binding a loosely episodic piece together. The central problem facing a "progressive" composer (and particularly a composer of a sym-phonic poem) is how to keep the implicit narrative moving forward in an obligatory zone that, if one adhered to the *Formenlehre* tradi-tions, lapsed all too readily into a stereotyped expression of static, spa-tial symmetry.

Ultimately, the method of sonata-deformational symphonic-poem composition was to use the unavoidable, de facto connotations of the literal recapitulation—an expression of Enlightenment-forged ideals of symmetrical balance and harmonic resolution—as a ground, or set of reified expectations, on which to superpose an individualized figure that corresponded to the desired narrative. More concretely: in this narrative the newly crowned Macbeth's concern is to solidify his reign, to restore stability and confidence, and, presumably, to exorcise those gloomy (D-minor) discontents that in the exposition had stamped his preregal character. The symphonic analogue would be to create a stable, generally symmetrical recapitulation that confidently secures D major and sustains it through a redemptive conclusion. A successful (or a traditional) recapitulation would serve as the sign of a successful reign—the *lieto fine* for which the work's protagonist yearns.

But the central point of this reprise is that this is precisely what does not happen. Pointedly marking the passage's opening *Tempo primo, allegro un poco maestoso* and returning here to the original D-minor "Macbeth" idea, Strauss repeatedly sets out to establish a symmetrical recapitulation in a series of multiple beginnings (the "Macbeth" strides in measures 324, 331, 338, 341, 343, 345, 347, 350, 352, and so on, several of which are derailed off the tonic). Each is likely to impress us as a false or unsuccessful start, as if what should have been a normal or relatively frictionless process has disintegrated into something surpassingly difficult. (For Reimann, p. 14, this is one sign of "the beginning of Macbeth's madness.") At measures 354–55 the three propelling motives of Macbeth's intrigue, "throne/power," "death blow," and "prophecy/troubled ambition," flash out fortissimo. Together they trigger the onset of a dissonant, tonally unstable phantasmagoria whose central effect is to undermine recapitulatory symmetry. In short, we are confronted with an image of the unattainability of the symmetrical reprise, even though such a reprise persists as the conceptual category under which we are to register its actual acoustic events.

Thus the intrigue and murder represented in the first two portions of the "ternary" sonata deformation lead not to symmetrical resolutions and balances but only to more crimes. As in the play, each crime opens the gateway to another. In this way the recapitulatory threads that ought to bind the whole together become progressively unraveled. It is worth observing that the "prophecy" section of the exposition is not included here: as a past, one-time event, it is clearly not needed, although motivic memories of it continue to linger. Similarly, Strauss suppresses (around measures 369–72) the "Lady Macbeth" subordinate theme of persuasion, although her insistent "urging" toward inescapable new crimes is brought back in the passage beginning at measure 373 (initially here governed by B♭, the "tragic flaw" sonority). All this mounts obsessively on varying pitch levels to ever-more-violent "death blows" (measures 403, 405, 427–32, 473, 479), intermixed with stretches of massive exhaustion, anxiety, and guilt (for instance, the quieter measures 433–68, dominated ironically by a weary, pain-ridden "attainment" figure; see n. 4).

Were specific events supposed to be depicted in all this? Clearly the twentieth-century commentators thought not, although since the tradition of wrongly locating Duncan's murder had by now taken firm root (as had, in some circles, a deep skepticism regarding the narrative claims of "program music"), it is not difficult to understand why they were so baffled at this point. But in 1892 Reimann thought so, and he read Banquo's ghost and the spectral "show of Eight Kings" (along with the murders provoking and associated with these things?) into measures 324–435—he even quoted act 4, scene 1: "Thy crown does sear mine eye-balls. . . . Now, I see, 'tis true; / For the blood-bolter'd Banquo smiles upon me, / And points at them for his"—and followed this by reading the climactic battle of "Birnam wood [coming] to Dunsinane" into measures 469–516. Perhaps for many of us this level of specificity is not needed: the implication of mere further crimes and crises may suffice. In any event, toward the end of this recapitulatory space Macbeth's failed attempt desperately to clasp his "redemptive" D major (measures 481ff., preceded by two bars of powerful dominant harmony) is particularly graphic in suggesting the hero in extremis, and it ushers in one of the most strained, dissonant passages of the score.

Finally, we should observe that the whole recapitulatory space may be considered a monstrously distorted expansion of the "Macbeth" portion of the exposition's primary theme (measures 6–63). The reprise begins in measure 324 with the music of measure 6 but soon decays into the nightmare world of "developmental" consequences. Notwithstanding a few notable variants, the reprise rejoins the music of the exposition over a hundred bars later, at measure 497 (marked *tempo I⁰ Allegro, un poco maestoso*). This music corresponds to the exposition's measure 38, that is, to Macbeth's regrasping of "his own" D minor after the witches' prophecy and his subsequent driving toward a firm cadence in that key (measures 38–63). In other words the outer portions of the exposition's "Macbeth" themes enclose nearly the entire recapitulatory space: the image presented is that of an originally single identity split down the middle, or cracked in half, by the consequences of its actions.[22] In the reprise, however, this move at measure 497 to restore the exposition's powerful D-minor cadence veers off in measures 509–16 to the hammer strokes of Macbeth's own death (analyzed by Williamson, as mentioned earlier). Here the promise of D minor is violently wrenched and ultimately subdued to a pianissimo cadence on A minor. Strauss extends this A minor into a reflective passage of aftermath (measures 516–36)[23] that emptily swirls together the main motives of the drama and then, inflecting the tonicized A minor into an A-major dominant chord, drops downward to a pizzicato cadence in D minor to seal off the recapitulatory space (measures 535–36).[24]

Coda (measures 536–558)

In the never-performed preliminary version of *Macbeth* the work had concluded with a lengthy "triumphal march in D major of Macduff," an ending that, according to Strauss (recalling the incident several decades later), von Bülow had derided as "nonsense": "It was all very well for an Egmont overture to conclude with a triumphal march of Egmont, but a symphonic poem *Macbeth* could never finish with the triumph of Macduff."[25] In the revised ending we are presented instead with only a few bars of D major: a ***ppp*** brass and woodwind fanfare (Example 8). If we assume Strauss's later words to be definitive, this fanfare is to be associated in some way with Macduff. Contrarily, however, with the exception of Reimann (who in 1892 did conjure up Macduff here)[26] the early stages of the twentieth-century interpretive tradition uniformly considered this a last glimpse of the now-dead Macbeth as hero. Nodnagel's suggestion that it refers to "Macbeth the conqueror" (p. 75) is characteristic, as is Teibler's claim that here "the Hero has entered into eternal peace" (p. 73) or Klauwell's reference to "the heroic in the character of Macbeth."[27] It appears to be only comparatively recently—that is, after the publication of Strauss's anecdote—that commentators have once again interpreted the passage to be "the triumph of Macduff and the coronation of Malcolm in a joyous Scotland freed from tyranny" (Del Mar, p. 60).

[measures 538–39: "Macduff's fanfare"]

Example 8.

The advantage of the Macduff interpretation—apart from the evidence of Strauss's later remarks—is that when Macbeth's long-desired, redemptive D major finally surfaces with relative stability, not only does it belong, ironically, to someone else but it is also separated, in a coda, from the essential structure of the Macbeth-narrative—that is, from the arduous processes of what has been an extraordinarily strained sonata deformation. That a snare drum accompanies the fanfare *hinter der Scene* also adds a nice touch of literal, physical separation from the orchestral apparatus that we are to understand has been narrating Macbeth's story. But this D major is short-lived. At the end of a subsequent passage of elegiac valediction (measures 544–51) the mode darkens back to minor. And Strauss brings this grim tale of sound and fury to a *molto stringendo*, smoldering close in D minor, in which the "tragic-flaw" $^{6-5}_{3-3}$ nexus, the heart of Macbeth's drama, is given the last word.

NOTES

1. Willi Schuh and Franz Trenner, eds., *Hans von Bülow and Richard Strauss: Correspondence*, trans. Anthony Gishford (London: Boosey and Hawkes, 1955), pp. 82–83. Even in its preliminary January 1888 version, Strauss had considered *Macbeth* to mark the point at which he had "set out upon a completely new path" [einen ganz neuen Weg betreten], as he explained to his uncle, Carl Hörburger on 11 January 1888: see Willi Schuh, *Richard Strauss: A Chronicle of the Early Years: 1864–1898*, trans. Mary Whittall (Cambridge: Cambridge University Press, 1982), p. 142.

The (compositionally revised) February 1888 version of *Macbeth* received its premiere in Weimar on 13 October 1890. Strauss subsequently revised the orchestration and added a few bars here and there (most notably an extra four bars of sixteenth-note scurrying, measures 255–58, before the B♭, *Moderato maestoso* march in the center of the work) to produce a "final version" published by Aibl in 1891 and first performed in Berlin on 29 February 1892. (This version itself was then subjected to minor retouchings.) It is this final version—the only version ever performed after 1891—that I shall discuss in this essay: it agrees in all structural essentials with the February 1888 score to which Strauss referred in his letter to von Bülow.

The best treatment of the complicated history of this work is to be found in Scott Warfield's forthcoming dissertation, "The Genesis of Richard Strauss's *Macbeth*" (University of North Carolina). I am grateful to Mr. Warfield for sharing some of the information in this dissertation with me, for providing me with a copy of the important, but little-known, Reimann program for the work (see n. 5), and for reading an early version of this essay. For some of the minor alterations from the February 1888 version to the final version, one may also consult John Williamson, "Strauss and 'Macbeth': The Realisation of the Poetic Idea," *Soundings* 13 (1985): 3–21.

2. For the concept of structural "deformation" see my "Fiery-Pulsed Libertine or Domestic Hero? Strauss's *Don Juan* Reinvestigated," in *Richard Strauss: New Perspectives on the Composer and His Work*, ed. Bryan Gilliam (Durham, N.C.: Duke University Press, 1992); and chapter 1 of *Sibelius: Symphony No. 5* (Cambridge: Cambridge University Press, forthcoming).

3. Such a triple challenge lies at the heart of the symphonic poem as a genre, and it may be considered to be its defining feature, one intended to be offered by the artwork's producer and reciprocally accepted by its receiver. Lacking these conditions, the artwork's symphonic-poem status collapses into

that of a different, unintended genre—perhaps that of the abstract overture or symphonic movement. See "Fiery-Pulsed Libertine."

4. The work's intended audiences would have been unaware that in an early continuity draft Strauss also referred to both a "pain melody" and a "first Macbeth theme": "aus gedehnter Schmerzensmelodie mit Steigerung auf den Schluß des 1. Macbeththemas, fällt ab lang auf den Orgelpunkt A, dann / Beckenschläge." This line is transcribed in Franz Trenner, *Die Skizzenbücher von Richard Strauss* (Tutzing: Schneider, 1977), p. 1, and it is discussed at some length and placed in a musical context by Warfield in "The Genesis." The precise identity of Strauss's "Schmerzensmelodie" is unclear. To judge from the word's placement in the draft (ca. measure 438 of the final version), it may be what I call "attainment" (the consequences of which have certainly turned painful for Macbeth by the time of the recapitulation; but the problem is that by this point in the score every melody has become a "Schmerzensmelodie"). The "first Macbeth theme" is simply the equivalent of measures 6–19, which Strauss at this early point seems to have planned to bring back largely in toto. See n. 22.

5. Since Strauss conducted *Macbeth* on that concert, Reimann's is the document that has the closest physical proximity to the composer. Yet at present, as suggested above, there is no evidence to suggest either that Strauss approved of it or that any portion of it—once past the obvious "Macbeth" and "Lady Macbeth" sections—is traceable to him. Particularly since Strauss never sought to have it reprinted or distributed elsewhere, Warfield doubts that the composer was involved with it in any way ("The Genesis"). This may indeed be the case, and we may be content to regard it here as merely an early, independent, and thoughtful intersection with the score. Although not formally "authorized," that is, it remains a provocative reading to be taken seriously. (See also n. 26.)

6. Seidl, "Richard Strauß: Eine Charakterskizze" (1896), in *Straußiana: Aufsätze zur Richard Strauß-Frage aus drei Jahrzehnten* (Regensburg: Bosse, 1914), pp. 11–66; Nodnagel, *Jenseits von Wagner und Liszt: Profile und Perspektiven* (Königsberg: Ostpreußischen Druckerei, 1902), pp. 74–75; Teibler, "Macbeth," in Herwath Walden, ed., *Richard Strauss: Symphonien und Tondichtungen* (*Meisterführer* no. 6, Berlin: Schlesinger [1908]), pp. 61–73; Steinitzer, *Richard Strauss* (Berlin and Leipzig: Schuster and Loeffler, 1911), pp. 230–32; Richard Specht, *Richard Strauss und sein Werk* (Leipzig: E. P. Tal, 1921), vol. 1, pp. 167–80; Waltershausen, *Richard Strauss: Ein Versuch* (Munich: Drei Masken, 1921), p. 49; Muschler, *Richard Strauss* (Hildesheim: Borgmeyer [1924]), pp. 281–88. Subsequent references to or quotations from these works will be made directly within the text.

7. Specht refers here to one of the period's catchphrases, stemming from Bismarck's famous "Eisen und Blut" speech on 30 September 1862 to the Prussian Budget Commission: "The great issues of the age are not decided by speeches and majority decisions—that was the great error of 1848 and 1849—but by blood and iron." See, e.g., Michael Hughes, *Nationalism and So-*

ciety: Germany 1800–1945 (London: Edward Arnold, 1988), pp. 114–15. Cf. Muschler's Nietzschean reference in 1924 to the combination in *Macbeth* of "dark passion [and] the cruel will to power" (p. 281).

8. Kennedy (and Robert Bailey), "Richard Strauss," in *The New Grove: Turn of the Century Masters* (1980) (New York: Norton, 1985), p. 218. Cf. Abraham, *A Hundred Years of Music* (New York: Knopf, 1938), p. 246; Del Mar, *Richard Strauss: A Critical Commentary on His Life and Works,* vol. 1 (1962) (Ithaca: Cornell University Press, 1986), pp. 55–60; Kennedy, *Richard Strauss* (London: Dent, 1976), pp. 128–29. Opinions seem to differ about where the recapitulation begins. Kennedy appears to imply that it occurs at measure 324; for Del Mar it occurs later—perhaps either at the D-major passage at measure 481 or around measure 497, a crucial seam at which some expositional music is rejoined. (It might be added that the most recent, full-length German treatment of the tone poem, Bernhold Schmid, "Richard Strauss' *Macbeth,*" *Musik in Bayern,* vol. 35 [Tutzing: Schneider, 1987], pp. 25–53, seems pointedly to avoid confronting the issue of the work's sonata character.)

9. Williamson, pp. 3–21.

10. An even more extreme statement along these lines may be found in Ernest Newman, *Richard Strauss* (London: John Lane [1921]), pp. 65–66: "Strauss makes no attempt whatever to cover the whole ground of Shakespeare's drama; no other character is introduced but Lady Macbeth— and she is really kept in the background of the picture—and absolutely nothing 'happens,' not even the murder of the king. The whole drama is enacted in the soul of Macbeth; apart from the comparatively few bars that depict his wife, the score is entirely concerned with the internal conflict of the three main elements of his character—his ambitious pride, his irresolution, and his love for Lady Macbeth. There is nothing here that is not pure 'stuff for music,' as Wagner would have said."

11. Williamson, p. 13. For another recent declaration on behalf of the supposed secondary quality of the program see Schmid, "Richard Strauss' *Macbeth,*" p. 37, who views it as "nur ein Ausgangspunkt, ein Hilfsmittel. Die fertige Komposition benötigt kein Programm, um verstanden zu werden," etc.

12. Reimann, p. 13: "Die unselige That geschieht, Duncan erliegt dem mörderischen Streiche. Fünf gewaltige Accorde im *ff* des ganzen Orchesters [measures 242–52] bezeichnen augenscheinlich die Katastrophe." Nodnagel, p. 75: "Endlich hat die Steigerung ihren Höhepunkt erreicht, einige furchtbare Akkordschläge des ganzen Orchesters, in die der ganze Blechbläserchor mit furchtbarer Energie die Fanfare des Ehrgeizes viermal hineinschmettert, sowie ein klirrender Beckenschlag deuten auf Macbeths grausiges Verbrechen hin."

I should add that this interpretation has also been proposed recently—and apparently without an awareness of Nodnagel's remarks from 1902—in an unpublished paper by Hon-Lun Yang, "From Symphony to Symphonic Poem," (M.A. thesis, Washington University in St. Louis, 1989), p. 89. I am grateful to the author for sharing a copy of this paper with me, and it could well be that it was her relocation of the moment of the regicide, along with her pursuit of some of its consequences, that provided an initial impulse for my own rethinking of *Macbeth*.

13. Hepokoski, "Fiery-Pulsed Libertine."

14. It may be useful to stress that nearly all such labels are inferable only in retrospect, after the entire work has been analyzed, absorbed, and considered synoptically. "First hearings" of a symphonic poem—that is, those unaware of the future consequences of a musical idea—typically tell us little or nothing about the nature of its representational procedures.

15. See, e.g., Thomas S. Grey, "Wagner, the Overture, and the Aesthetics of Musical Form," *19th-Century Music* 12 (1988): 3–22.

16. From a Schenkerian perspective, of course, the new tonicization at this expositional point also initiates a broader arpeggiation that is typically completed toward the close of the development (that is, a i–III motion in the exposition characteristically finds its goal with the usual V at the end of the development, whereupon a harmonic interruption ensues). This consideration, which itself deals with formulaic and rather obvious matters, is not our primary concern here, although we should notice that at the conclusion of what I call the "developmental space" of *Macbeth* the usual dominant is pointedly lacking. We find here instead the strong articulation of VI, B♭ major, whereupon we "rebegin" in D minor, measure 324. Note, though, the recovery of the lacking V in the powerful dominant utterances toward the end of the recapitulatory space, measures 479–80 (*appassionato*) and, of course, in measures 504–9 and 516–35.

17. This dissonance—a minor $\frac{5}{3}$ with an added $\hat{6}$ (a simultaneous sounding of a $\frac{5}{3}$ and a $\frac{6}{3}$ position above the bass)—would prove to be one of the most characteristic Straussian biting dissonances of the ensuing decade, a prominent weapon in his modernist arsenal. He would reuse the "bite" in high relief to represent the fatal stabbing of *Don Juan* (over A, measures 586–89; compare the love pang in the *molto tranquillo* codetta to the G-major idyll, over G, measures 302–4); to suggest fever onslaughts in *Tod und Verklärung* (for instance, in the principal theme, measure 96, over C, and in the two most notorious of the four strident, brass-led dissonances in the developmental space, over C and D, measures 278 and 287); and to illustrate the anarchic horse ride–romp of *Till Eulenspiegel* through the "wives in the marketplace" (over D, measures 135–39; cf. the parallel passage, Till "hidden in a mousehole," over G, measures 157–65), and so on. The locus classicus of the dissonance in the earlier canonic repertory occurs at the climactic point of the development of the Eroica Symphony's first movement.

18. See, e.g., the discussion in Edward Aldwell and Carl Schachter, *Harmony and Voice Leading*, 2d ed. (New York: Harcourt Brace Jovanovich, 1989), pp. 53–56, 278–81.

19. The settling onto the tonic F here is the result of neither implicit nor explicit parallel motion. Rather, the F♯-triad predecessor of the F chord is probably best considered as falling into the conceptual family of augmented

sixths that resolve to the tonic. Thus the F♯ is revealed here to function enharmonically as a G♭, or ♭2̂ of the true tonic, F. (See Aldwell and Schachter, p. 496, for a discussion and a strikingly similar example from Schubert; the principal difference—and a significant one, to be sure—is that in *Macbeth* the actual "augmented-sixth" pitch itself, E♮, is not present, whereas the corresponding pitch does appear, almost as an afterthought, in the Schubert. In terms of function the E♮ may perhaps be considered to be implied. Strauss's curious spelling of the chord at this point, F♯–B♭–C♯, serves to unsettle the prior F♯-major spelling [measures 106–8], with A♯, but it is still not a correct functional spelling.)

20. Cf. also Brahms's more recent (for Strauss) *Tragic Overture*, with a single, marchlike developmental episode in slower tempo. Unlike the Liszt and Wagner examples, however, this episode is more emphatically marked with the "developmental" principle.

21. On the tradition of the use of the tam-tam and (secondarily) the cymbal as a death image, see Constantin Floros, *Gustav Mahler: II: Mahler und die Symphonik des 19. Jahrhunderts in neuer Deutung* (Wiesbaden: Breitkopf and Härtel, 1977), pp. 311–16, 367–68. Floros's claims are buttressed at least by the reception tradition represented by Nodnagel, who in 1902 also singled out this cymbal crash (Beckenschlag) as the moment of the death; see n. 12.

22. As is demonstrated by Warfield (see n. 1), the existing evidence suggests that in the little-known preliminary version of the work (9 January 1888) what I propose to be the recapitulatory space was considerably longer and more diffuse than that of the final version, particularly in the measures following the final version's measure 482. These additional measures, which are not totally recoverable, seem to have included a "premature" statement of the so-called Macduff fanfare in D major that almost immediately rejoined the music of the exposition at the equivalent of measure 10 or 11 and seems to have proceeded with a near-literal recapitulation of the "first Macbeth theme" (at least measures 11–17, and possibly some earlier bars as well), perhaps eliding near its end into the D-minor "Macbeth" cadential material (and death of Macbeth?) that we also find in the final version before the coda. (For another transcription of the "premature" Macduff fanfare, see Williamson, p. 7.)

In this preliminary version it would seem that Strauss was suggesting that Macbeth attempts to initiate at least two redemptive "recapitulations" (the first begins with the D-minor Macbeth-strides [final version, measure 324]; the second with the later-omitted D-major fanfare that soon decayed into the exposition's measure 10 or 11), both of which are doomed to failure. This layout of events may also be adapted to the poetic idea proposed above: despite the inordinate length and diffusion of the whole, the argument may still be maintained that both events were to be heard under the category of "recapitulatory space" following a doubly divided, episodic development. Or, restated from a slightly differing point of view: the first attempted (or false) "recapitulation" could be considered to decay into a development—producing, in effect, a third developmental episode—which itself is constituted from the ruins of a failed recapitulation. In any event, further nuancing the formal status of a discarded and not completely recoverable "Entwurf" need not detain us any longer. Our principal aim here is to confront the revised, authorized version.

23. The generally cautious Specht, p. 179, suggested that this passage might have been intended to be Lady Macbeth's sleepwalking scene, an interpretation that seems difficult to defend.

24. For a somewhat broader view of this dominant-tonic cadence, as well as the one in measures 479–81, see n. 16.

25. Richard Strauss, "Recollections of My Youth and Years of Apprenticeship," *Recollections and Reflections,* ed. Willi Schuh, trans. L. J. Lawrence (London: Boosey and Hawkes, 1953), p. 139. This essay, undated in the edition cited here, is given the date "ca. 1940" by Robert Bailey in *The New Grove* (see n. 8).

26. Indeed, since Reimann stands alone on the one point of his interpretation that Strauss did inadvertently verify, it may be argued that the case to consider his program more carefully is strengthened (p. 15: "Ganz aus der Ferne ertönen Macduff's Fanfaren und sein Siegesmarsch").

27. Curiously, this Macbeth-heroic connotation may have been the one originally implied in the theme's first ("recapitulatory") appearance in the preliminary version, which was deleted in the second and final versions. See n. 21.

Ruhe, meine Seele!

and the *Letzte Orchesterlieder*

TIMOTHY L. JACKSON

For Tova and Marshall Train

This essay explores subtle, yet vital, musico-poetic relationships between Richard Strauss's early song *Ruhe, meine Seele!* (1894) and his
last orchestral songs (1946–48), a connection created through a musical motive that sets the word *Not* at the climax of *Ruhe, meine Seele!*[1]
Strauss recomposed this *Notmotiv* in *Im Abendrot, Frühling, Beim
Schlafengehen,* and *September.* The especially close connection between
Ruhe, meine Seele! and *Im Abendrot* through the *Notmotiv* sheds new light
on why Strauss orchestrated *Ruhe, meine Seele!* just after completing *Im
Abendrot* but before finishing the remaining orchestral songs. Strauss
returned to *Ruhe, meine Seele!* in 1946–48 not merely because it had
relevance to his postwar experience but for compositional reasons. He
may well have been haunted by the irresolution of the *Notmotiv* in
Ruhe, meine Seele! as compositional unfinished business that required
resolution before his death. That sense of reconciliation would be
found in the orchestral postlude to *Im Abendrot.* Performing the 1948
orchestral version of *Ruhe, meine Seele!* immediately before *Im Abendrot*
allows the listener to perceive the suspension of the *Notmotiv* prepared
in *Ruhe, meine Seele!* and resolved at the end of *Im Abendrot.* By integrating *Ruhe, meine Seele!* into the so-called *Four Last Songs,* we hear
them in a new way truer to Strauss's intentions. That these five songs
form a unified cycle is supported by biographical, musicological, and
analytical evidence.

The orchestrations, arrangements, and reworkings of earlier material in Strauss's last creative period accords with his generally retrospective outlook. They also confirm accounts of Strauss's atemporal
capacity to recall and reactivate compositional ideas. Ernst Roth
(Strauss's friend, the senior editor at the music publisher Boosey and
Hawkes) reports: "He always carried a sketchbook with him. But he

could first use sketches from the year 1900 twelve years later. To this belong both order and reflection."[2] The larger context of Strauss's compositional activity in the 1940s shows that musical ideas exist in an eternal present to be reactivated, reworked, and renewed.

Strauss scholars have long debated whether the composer actually considered the four last orchestral songs a complete unit. The songs were published posthumously by Boosey and Hawkes under the title *Vier letzte Lieder,* which originated with Roth. His impulse to give the songs a collective title correctly suggests that these works form a cycle, but his modifiers fall short of the mark. If one accepts the notion of including *Ruhe, meine Seele!* one must acknowledge five rather than four last songs. Roth's use of the term "last" is equally inappropriate, for scholars have known about Strauss's true last song, *Malven,* for many years. Of course this work, for voice and piano, has nothing to do with the late orchestral songs; it is little more than an *Albumblatt,* an homage-type piece dedicated and given (unpublished) to Maria Jeritza, who helped Strauss through difficult times. Thus, *Letzte Orchesterlieder* is more accurate and leaves open the possibility of including the 1948 orchestration of *Ruhe, meine Seele!* within the canon.

Alan Jefferson downplays the cyclic aspect of the *Letzte Orchesterlieder* and suggests that Strauss intended to write more orchestral songs, observing that "1948 was spent partly in Montreux and partly in Pontresina. Strauss was composing in leisurely fashion a number of orchestral songs for soprano, to poems which had caught his fancy. Three of them are by Hesse and the fourth by Eichendorff. *He did not necessarily consider these, which have different instrumentation, as a group, and there was a fifth which was never written—but they have come to be known as the Four Last Songs*" [my emphasis].[3] In fact, Strauss considered setting two more poems by Hesse, *Nacht* and *Höhe des Sommers* but chose not to for reasons to be explained presently.

Willi Schuh, Strauss's friend from the 1930s onward, contradicts Jefferson.[4] Alan Frank simply assumes that Strauss intended the songs to be performed as a set, observing that "the setting of Eichendorff's *Im Abendrot,* though written a few months [May 1948] before the others, is clearly intended as the last of the group, in whatever order the previous ones are sung."[5] Other commentators have accepted the songs as an incomplete set, believing that Strauss intended to compose more orchestral songs, but his death prevented it. Historical background, analysis of the works themselves, and examination of the autograph sources, however, negate this romantic view of death seizing the pen from the composer's hand. Strauss, of course, left a related major project unfinished—the choral setting of Hesse's

Besinnung—but even here death was not responsible for interrupting his work. Strauss had deliberately set the work aside, remarking that the projected fugue had become "too complicated."

Strauss selected performers for the premieres of almost all his late works: the *Metamorphosen*, the *Sinfonie für Bläser*, the *Konzert für Oboe*, and the *Duett-Concertino*. Unfortunately, no documents in which Strauss discusses the premiere of his newly completed orchestral songs have come to light. However, Edwin McArthur, Kirsten Flagstad's accompanist and close friend, reports that Strauss had, in fact, begun to organize such a premiere:

> Richard Strauss had chosen her [Flagstad] to give the world premiere of his now famous *Four Last Songs*, the only condition being that there be a first-class conductor. The "first class conductor" was none other than Wilhelm Furtwängler, her favorite of all. . . . She had always not only had the greatest admiration for Strauss, but a pleasant professional memory of him as well. In 1933, when singing her first season at Bayreuth, she had been chosen as the soprano soloist for a performance of Beethoven's Ninth Symphony and Richard Strauss had conducted the performance.[6]

McArthur's testimony is vital, for if Strauss had already selected Flagstad for the premiere, he must have regarded the cycle of orchestral songs as complete.

Strauss's alleged choice of Flagstad is revealing. She was no longer in her prime, and other considerations likely played a part in Strauss's selection. Flagstad, like Strauss, found herself under siege after the war on account of her connections with National Socialists. She had returned to Norway during the Nazi occupation to be with her husband, who was later convicted of collaborating with the Third Reich and died in prison. Flagstad could well empathize with Strauss's postwar predicament and with the expression of weariness articulated in these songs. At the premiere, which took place on 22 May 1950, the four songs were presented in the following order: *Beim Schlafengehen, September, Frühling*, and *Im Abendrot*. Roth later revised this order to the now well known *Frühling, September, Beim Schlafengehen*, and *Im Abendrot*.

That Strauss himself neither gave the orchestral songs a collective title nor specified an order in which they should be performed would appear to strengthen either of the following arguments: first, that the songs are simply occasional pieces composed in an additive manner and do not constitute a cycle; or second, that the songs do represent a cycle, but one that is unfinished. But the absence of an authentic title neither invalidates the cyclic interpretation nor proves that the cycle is incomplete. Indeed, it is instructive to compare the genesis of the *Letzte Orchesterlieder* with the *Sinfonie für Bläser*, for an additive manner of composing can be seen in the genesis of both works. In the *Sinfonie für Bläser*, the eventual last movement (*Einleitung und Allegro*) was conceived first as a potentially independent work and the preceding movements were added later. If *Im Abendrot* is understood—as I think it must be—as the last song of the cycle, the same process of beginning with a potentially independent song, which then becomes the last movement of a larger composition, may be observed. Although the movements of the *Sinfonie* were composed additively within the time span of more than a year, by recomposing motivic ideas from the *Einleitung und Allegro* in the *Allegro con brio*, Strauss clearly intended the four movements to comprise a unified whole. Since the composer was unable to invent a collective title for all four movements, Roth proposed the title *Sinfonie für Bläser*, which he accepted. Although Strauss neither decided on a collective title for his last orchestral songs nor lived to sanction their publication under the title *Vier letzte Lieder*, there is no evidence to contradict the notion of these songs as a complete cycle.

The literature suggests that most commentators, listeners, and performers feel intuitively that the four orchestral songs constitute a cycle with *Im Abendrot* as its endpoint. However, if one accepts the cyclic interpretation, and even agrees with the assertion of a musical-poetic connection between the orchestral version of *Ruhe, meine Seele!* and these songs, the question remains: did Strauss want *Ruhe, meine Seele!* to be performed within the cycle, or was the motivic connection intended to remain secret? Admittedly, we cannot definitively answer the question based on surviving evidence, but the fact that the orchestration of *Ruhe, meine Seele!* immediately followed completion of *Im Abendrot* strongly suggests that Strauss wanted to make the connection overt and that he wanted it to be heard in performance.

The Autobiographical Significance of Strauss's Last Two Song Orchestrations and the *Letzte Orchesterlieder*

Roth's memoirs and the published correspondence between Strauss and Schuh, as well as a series of articles by the latter, offer important information about Strauss's state of mind in his last years. Roth describes Strauss's mood immediately after the war: "I always returned deeply depressed from my frequent visits to Strauss. Something must be done to rescue Strauss from his end-of-the-world mood, which even his avid Goethe reading could not dispel."[7] At the urging of Schuh, Roth, and family members (especially his son Franz), Strauss turned to composition in an effort to cope with depression. The result was the works without opus number, which he referred to with a certain bitter irony as *Handgelenksübungen,* or "wrist exercises."

Strauss's therapy through composition resulted in two very different types of works. In the *Sinfonie für Bläser (Fröhliche Werkstatt),* the *Konzert für Oboe,* and the *Duett-Concertino,* Strauss escaped unpleasant reality by returning to the "happy workshop" of baroque and classical masters. These intriguing compositions are written in a uniquely Straussian neo-classical language. In the *Metamorphosen,* the orchestrations of *Ruhe, meine Seele!* and *Ich liebe dich,* and the *Letzte Orchesterlieder,* Strauss expressed his feelings of despair in a decidedly late-romantic idiom.

The contrast of style and content between the light and serious works could not be more striking. However, the overlapping and interpenetration of both serious and lighter works in compositional chronology and in the sketchbooks reflects a deeper spiritual unity. The lighter works and arrangements are the flip side, the alter ego, of the serious compositions. And both types of "wrist exercises," the light and the serious, represent two sides of the great German music tradition—classic and romantic—of which Strauss believed himself to be the sole remaining proponent.

With the works in a lighter vein, Strauss reaffirmed the values of the great French-Italian baroque and Viennese classical masters, exalting craftmanship and therein finding consolation. The lighter works of the last period, the *Sinfonie für Bläser,* the *Konzert für Oboe,* and the *Duett-Concertino,* exhibit a serene delight in craftmanship and in playful intellectual sophistication; these works are spiritually related meditations on the music of Mozart. On the last page of the *Partitur* for the fourth movement of the *Sinfonie,* Strauss writes: "Fröhliche Werkstatt / Den Manen des göttlichen Mozart am Ende / eines dankerfüllten Lebens / Richard Strauss. Garmisch, 9 Januar 1944." A similar affection for the classical masters is reflected in a sketch bearing the inscription "Dem Andenken Franz Schuberts" in one of the *Metamorphosen* sketchbooks (probably from January–February 1944) and in a "free harmonization" from Beethoven's A-minor String Quartet in a sketchbook that also contains sketches for the *Duett-Concertino* (probably from mid-1947).[8]

But it was in late-romantic orchestral songs that Strauss sought to express the *Not* of the postwar period—both his own personal *Not* and the larger *Not* of Europe. Since *Not* is the subject of the newly composed songs, it is not surprising that all four carry dedications to friends who tried to ameliorate Strauss's personal anxiety. *Im Abendrot* and *Frühling* are respectively dedicated to Roth and Schuh (and their wives), for their efforts to rehabilitate Strauss. *Beim Schlafengehen* and *September* are respectively dedicated to Adolf Jöhr (Strauss's Swiss banker) and his wife, and to the Seerys (Maria Jeritza and her husband), for their financial and moral support when Strauss found himself cut off from his sources of income.

Although the German word *Not* is cognate to the English word "need," *Not* is stronger and has untranslatable religious and philosophical connotations. The English words "anxiety," "fear," "vulnerability," and even "dire need" do not adequately circumscribe all German connotations. I am convinced that it was the relevance to his present circumstances of the last, climactic verse of *Ruhe, meine Seele!* ("Diese Zeiten sind gewaltig, / Bringen Herz und Hirn in Not— / Ruhe, ruhe, meine Seele, / Und vergiss, was dich bedroht") that brought Strauss back to the early 1894 song in the immediate postwar period. And although it is impossible to prove that Strauss contemplated orchestrating *Ruhe, meine Seele!* as early as April 1946, when he began thinking about an orchestral setting of *Im Abendrot,* the motivic connection between *Ruhe, meine Seele!* and an early *Im Abendrot* sketch suggests that these two songs formed the very nucleus of the eventual *Letzte Orchesterlieder.* According to my reconstruction of chronology, it was only eight months later, in January 1947, that Strauss decided to add Hesse's *Frühling* to the two nuclear songs; the decision to set yet two more Hesse poems, *Beim Schlafengehen* and *September,* was taken in July–August 1948, immediately after the preceding three songs had already been orchestrated.

Eichendorff's *Im Abendrot,* Hesse's *Frühling, Beim Schlafengehen,* and *September,* and Henckell's *Ruhe, meine Seele!* are all related through the concept of *Not.* Hesse's poetry was an attractive source not only for its intrinsic value but because Strauss no doubt felt kinship with Hesse: like Strauss, Hesse had left his native Germany for exile in Switzerland.[9] To facilitate comparison, the five poems are presented here in both German and English (my translation):

RUHE, MEINE SEELE! (Henckell)

REST, MY SOUL!

Nicht ein Lüftchen regt sich leise;
Not even a breeze stirs gently;

Sanft entschlummert ruht der Hain.
The grove rests sleeping softly.

Durch der Blätter dunkle Hülle
Through the dark cover of leaves

Stiehlt sich lichter Sonnenschein.
Steals beaming sunshine.

Ruhe, ruhe, meine Seele,
Deine Stürme gingen wild,
Hast getobt und hast gezittert,

Wie die Brandung, wenn sie
    schwillt.

Diese Zeiten sind gewaltig,
Bringen Herz und Hirn in Not—

Ruhe, ruhe, meine Seele,
Und vergiss, was dich bedroht.

Rest, rest my soul,
Your storms were wild,
You have raged and you have
    trembled

Like the breakers when they
    swell.

These times are momentous,
They place heart and mind
    in need—

Rest, rest my soul,
And forget what threatens you.

IM ABENDROT (Eichendorff)

Wir sind durch Not und Freude
Gegangen Hand in Hand;
Vom Wandern ruhn wir beide[10]
Nun überm stillen Land.

Rings sich die Täler neigen.
Es dunkelt schon die Luft,
Zwei Lerchen nur noch steigen
Nachtträumend in den Duft.

Tritt her, und lass sie
    schwirren,
Bald ist es Schlafenszeit,
Dass wir uns nicht verirren

In dieser Einsamkeit.

O weiter, stiller Friede
So tief im Abendrot
Wie sind wir wandermüde—

Ist dies[11] etwa der Tod?

IN THE SUNSET

We have, in need and joy,
Gone hand in hand;
From wandering let us rest
Now in this silent land.

The valleys press around us,
Soon the air will darken,
Two larks rise,
Dreaming in the fragrance.

Come here, and let them
    whirr—
Soon it will be time to sleep—
So that we do not lose
    ourselves
In this loneliness.

O wide, still peace
So deep in the sunset
How tired we are of
    wandering—
Is this perhaps death?

FRÜHLING (Hesse)

In dämmrigen Grüften
Träumte ich lang
Von deinen Bäumen und blauen
    Lüften
Von deinem Duft und Vogelsang.

SPRING

In shadowy grottoes,
I dreamt long
Of your trees and blue skies,

Of your fragrance and
    birdsong.

Nun liegst du erschlossen In Gleiss und Zier, Von Licht übergossen Wie ein Wunder vor mir.	Now you lie opened up In glitter and ornament, Bathed in light Like a wonder before me.
Du kennst mich wieder, Du lockest mich zart, Es zittert durch all meine Glieder Deine selige Gegenwart.	You also recognize me You sweetly tempt me, Your blessed presence Trembles through all my limbs.

Beim Schlafengehen (Hesse)	Going to Sleep
Nun der Tag mich müd gemacht,	Now the day has made me tired,
Soll mein sehnliches Verlangen Freundlich die gestirnte Nacht Wie ein müdes Kind empfangen.	Let the starry night Receive my ardent demand, As if [I were] a tired child.
Hände lasst von allem Tun,	Hands, leave off from every action,
Stirn vergiss du alles Denken. Alle meine Sinne nun Wollen sich in Schlummer senken.	Brow, forget all thinking. All my senses now Wish to sink into slumber.
Und die Seele unbewacht Will in freien Flügen schweben, Um im Zauberkreis der Nacht Tief und tausendfach zu leben.	And the soul, unfettered, Wants to soar in free flight In the magic circle of night, Deeply and a thousandfold to live.

September (Hesse)	September

Der Garten trauert,
Kühl sinkt in die Blumen der
    Regen.
Der Sommer schauert
Still seinem Ende entgegen.
	The garden mourns,
	Rain sinks cool into the
	    flowers.
	Summer trembles quietly,
	Faced with its end.

Golden tropft Blatt um Blatt Nieder vom hohen Akazienbaum. Sommer lächelt erstaunt und matt	Leaf after leaf drops, golden Down from the high acacia. Summer smiles astonished and faintly
In den sterbenden Gartentraum.	Into the dying garden-dream.

Lange noch bei den Rosen	Long yet by the roses
Bleibt er stehen, sehnt sich nach	It remains standing, longing
Ruh.	for rest.
Langsam tut er die grossen	Slowly the big
Müdgewordenen Augen zu.	Tired eyes are closed.

The similarity of diction and imagery in Henckell's *Ruhe, meine Seele!* and Eichendorff's *Im Abendrot* is particularly striking. Strauss, who had a keen ear for puns and word games, surely noticed the signal importance of the word *Not* in both *Ruhe, meine Seele!* and *Im Abendrot*. In *Ruhe, meine Seele!* it occurs in the climactic line "Bringen Herz und Hirn in *Not,*" while in *Im Abendrot* it appears in the first line, "Wir sind durch *Not* und Freude / Gegangen . . ." Other key words in both poems rhyme with *Not*—*bedroht, Abendrot, Tod*—and with *Roth*, the dedicatee of *Im Abendrot*.

Ruhe, meine Seele! opens by contrasting a peaceful, sunlit grove of trees with the disquiet of the speaker's soul. The grove enjoys the "rest" that the man himself seeks, underscored by repetition of the verb *ruhen:* "Sanft entschlummert *ruht* der Hain. . . . *Ruhe,* meine Seele!" The cause of the narrator's angst is made clear by the beginning of the last strophe: "These times are momentous / They place heart and mind in need." The soul's quietude is threatened by social cataclysm, which finds its counterpart in "inner storms." Only by forgetting outward circumstances can the speaker attain peace ("Rest, rest my soul / And forget what threatens you"). Surely this last strophe brought Strauss back to his 1894 song in the bleak April of 1946. Strauss may well have had this phrase in mind when he clipped a newspaper article on the plunder of Dresden, which he pasted immediately above his *Abschrift* of *Im Abendrot* in his *Schweizer Tagebuch*, probably in January 1947 (see Figure 1). Understood in light of contemporaneous events, the *Not* of the first line of *Im Abendrot*, "Wir sind durch *Not* und Freude gegangen," refers to the experience of both the war and its aftermath.

Eichendorff's *Im Abendrot* describes two elderly people, presumably man and wife, wandering through a darkening valley at sunset. They have reached the end of a long life together. Eichendorff's tired wanderers become Strauss and his wife Pauline in exile from their Garmisch home, whose only relief from *Not* will be in death. They wonder whether their "tiredness of wandering" is symptomatic of their own imminent deaths. The entire poem gravitates toward the final question—"Ist das etwa der Tod?"—which Strauss further intensifies and personalizes by changing Eichendorff's *das* [that] to *dies* [this].

The first "Ouchy" *Abschrift* from April 1946 suggests that Strauss copied the last line exactly as Eichendorff wrote it. Given the difficulty of deciphering Strauss's handwriting on the *Schweizer Tagebuch* page, it is impossible to determine with certainty whether the change is now present. Nevertheless, from close scrutiny it seems that the change of *das* to *dies* is present in the *Tagebuch* copy. Thus, Strauss appears to have made the textual change in the process of recopying the poem in January 1947.

While the change of *das* to *dies* may well have been unconscious, the intensification is symptomatic of Strauss's deeply felt, auto-biographical readings of *Ruhe, meine Seele!* and *Im Abendrot* in 1946–48. Within the context of *Im Abendrot, Not* also refers to the "need" of the old couple to know whether the peace of the sunset corresponds to the peace of death. In Strauss's setting, the question "Ist dies etwa der Tod?" is perceived as rhetorical only after it has been answered by the orchestra in the postlude, which, representing nature, responds with an ineffable affirmation.

Although the word *Not* does not appear in the three Hesse poems set by Strauss, in each of them the speaker wishes to be set free from his worldly cares—his *Not*—by death. The "shadowy grottoes" at the beginning of *Frühling* can be interpreted as the *Not* of mundane existence; the soul, hibernating in the phenomenal world filled with *Not*, dreams of spring or paradise, death being the "wonder" through which it can be reborn. In both *Beim Schlafengehen* and *September,* the soul also longs for death as a release from *Not.* In the first two stanzas of *Beim Schlafengehen,* the narrator expresses a wish to die; the third stanza describes the flight of the soul into the realm of death, represented by the night sky. Day, or life, has made the speaker tired. He wants to be received into the "magic circle of night" to die because, paradoxically, only then can he live. In *September,* as in *Frühling,* the wish to die is once again experienced in a "dream." In *September,* the garden—metaphorically the soul—dreams of summer's death, which is the death of the garden itself. In the garden's dream, summer appears as a being with a mouth that smiles and eyes that close. Summer is astonished by its impending death; it remains standing by the flowers until the last possible moment until, "longing for rest," it accepts the inevitable.

Beim Schlafengehen and *September* are linked to *Ruhe, meine Seele!* and *Im Abendrot* through the word-concepts *müde* and *ruhe.* In *Im Abendrot,* the old couple is "wander*müde*" [tired of wandering]. The opening line of *Beim Schlafengehen* also stresses fatigue: "Nun der Tag [hat] mich *müd* gemacht" [Now the day has made me tired]. The speaker describes himself as a "*müdes* Kind" [tired child]. Finally, in the last line of *September*, the word "tired" recurs in the climactic image of the "*müd*gewordenen Augen" [tired eyes].

Unlike most of the earlier orchestrations of the teens and thirties, the orchestration of *Ruhe, meine Seele!* is a special compositional moment intimately connected with contemporary events in Strauss's life, the very events that bear upon the genesis of the *Letzte Orchesterlieder.* Some scholars have argued that Strauss simply orchestrated old songs when he found himself at compositional loose ends. Del Mar, for example, would contend that the orchestration of *Ruhe, meine Seele!* is not distinguished from Strauss's other song orchestrations: "He was, in those last years, in any case rather prone to filling in his time in orchestrating the odd song when he had no other composition in hand."[12]

Del Mar's comment, which implies that Strauss adopts an almost casual approach to the orchestration of the "odd song" whenever time permits, simply does not square with the facts. A survey of the dates of song orchestrations shows that the composer orchestrates systematically; he either orchestrates songs in groups for singers for anticipated performances or as homages to individuals. *Waldseligkeit* (Op. 49, no. 1), *Winterweihe* (Op. 48, no. 4), *Winterliebe* (Op. 49, no. 5), *Freundliche Vision* (Op. 48, no. 1), and *Der Arbeitsman* (Op. 39, no. 3) were all orchestrated for Elisabeth Schumann between 15 June and 12 December 1918. The orchestrations then cease for fifteen years. The next group of orchestrations, intended for Viorica Ursuleac (wife of Clemens Krauss), dates from 1933. Between 3 and 22 September, Strauss orchestrates *Frühlingsfeier* (Op. 56, no. 5), *Meine Auge* (Op. 37, no. 4), *Befreit* (Op. 39, no. 4), and *Lied der Frauen* (Op. 68, no. 6). The orchestration of the homage song to Joseph Goebbels, *Das Bächlein* (AV 118), follows on 6 April 1935. The orchestration of *Zueignung* (Op. 10, no. 1) on 19 June 1940 is an homage to Ursuleac. Strauss is then inspired to orchestrate the remaining *Brentano-Lieder* (Op. 68, nos. 1–5) for Ursuleac between 3 July and 2 August 1940; he also thins the orchestration of the 1933 version of *Lied der Frauen* (Op. 68, no. 6).

Prior to 1943, there are only two exceptions to the principle of orchestrating lieder in groups; these are the orchestrations of *Das Bächlein* and *Zueignung.* Furthermore, between 1918 and 1940, the groups of orchestrations are directly attributable to the possibility of performance by the singers mentioned here; the 1918 orchestrations are inspired by and intended for the voice of Elisabeth Schumann, while the 1933 and 1940 orchestrations may be credited to Ursuleac. After 1918, only two orchestrations stand out as isolated, entirely spontaneous compositional acts: *Ich liebe dich* (orchestrated on 30 August 1943) and *Ruhe, meine Seele!* (orchestrated on 9 June 1948); these two orchestrations are related to Strauss's personal circumstances during and after the war.

It is important to note the continuing personal significance of songs for Strauss. The main body of his songs dates from before 1906; they were intended to be sung by his wife, Pauline. When she stopped giving *Liederabende* in 1906, Strauss largely turned away from lieder to concentrate on other genres. After 1906, Strauss continued to associate lieder with memories of his wife's voice and with the period in their lives when they performed together. Barbara Petersen points out, in a footnote to a table of orchestrations in her dissertation, the "large number of compositions and orchestrations created on and near" 10 September, the Strausses' wedding anniversary.[13] Roth recounts that

> Strauss himself insisted that no one had so incomparably sung his lieder as [Pauline]. . . . But when Strauss lay in the clinic in Lausanne in 1948, he and I could not remember the title of the song that begins with the line "Du solltest nicht weinen." I recalled this to Frau Pauline later in the evening and without the slightest hesitation, she said, "the song is *Befreit.*" And with great earnestness she added: "It is a very beautiful song," and in a well-sounding half-voice she sang it through to me. Now, half a century is a long time to remember something that one does not treasure.[14]

In striking contrast to the orchestrations for Schumann and Ursuleac, the late orchestrations of *Ich liebe dich* and *Ruhe, meine Seele!* and the *Letzte Orchesterlieder* are not created for a particular voice in an anticipated performance but rather for idealized voices in posthumous performance. In these last orchestrations and orchestral songs, the voices now assume autobiographical significance. The soprano of the piano-vocal version of *Ich liebe dich* is changed to a heroic tenor, perhaps Strauss's idealized voice, while the soprano voice of *Ruhe, meine Seele!* and the *Letzte Orchesterlieder* may be a reincarnation of Pauline's voice. This autobiographical interpretation of the voices in the orchestrations of *Ich liebe dich* and *Ruhe, meine Seele!* suggests a connection between the texts of these songs and the Strauss family's circumstances when the orchestrations were made.

The orchestration of *Ich liebe dich,* dated 30 August 1943, was undertaken at a time when Strauss was acutely aware that the lives of his daughter-in-law, Alice Grab Strauss, and his grandchildren were endangered by the Nazi environment because of their Jewish background. Strauss's letter to Hans Frank, dated 3 November 1943, was clearly intended to protect his family.[15] In this context, the last two stanzas of *Ich liebe dich* assume a new and terrible relevance to the fate of Jews in Nazi Germany:

Und irrst du verlassen,	And if you roam, rejected,
Verbannt durch die Lande;	Outcast, through the countryside,
Mit dir durch die Gassen	With you through the streets
In Armut und Schande!	In poverty and disgrace I will go.
Es bluten die Hände,	Our hands may bleed,
Die Füsse sind wund,	Our feet be sore,
Vier trostlose Wände,	Four pitiless walls,
Es kennt uns kein Hund.	No dog recognizes us.
Steht silberbeschlagen,	When silver-edged stands
Dein Sarg am Altar,	Your coffin at the altar,
Sie sollen mich tragen	They will have to carry me
Zu dir auf die Bahr;	To you on your bier;
Und fern auf der Heide	Whether far away on the heath,
Und stirbst du in Not,	Whether you die in need,
Den Dolch aus der Scheide,	My dagger drawn from its sheath,
Dir nach in den Tod.	I will follow you in death.

The relevance of the text to the Strausses' family circumstances at the time hardly requires further explanation. Most interesting is the wording of the climactic final three lines: "Und stirbst du in Not, / Den Dolch aus der Scheide, / Dir nach in den Tod." The association of *Not* with *Tod*, which later forges the connection between *Ruhe, meine Seele!* and *Im Abendrot*, brings Strauss back to *Ich liebe dich* in 1943.

In the orchestrations of *Ich liebe dich, Im Abendrot,* and *Ruhe, meine Seele!* the timpani point to the sinister and dark forces threatening the speaker. The short, jabbing *Paukenmotiv* of *Ich liebe dich* recurs in *Ruhe, meine Seele!* and *Im Abendrot,* only to be dispelled in the postlude to *Im Abendrot.* Thick brass chords, composed of four interlocking horns supported by trombones, suggest death and appear in the orchestral postludes to all three songs. In sum, the orchestrations of *Ich liebe dich* and *Ruhe, meine Seele!* carry a deep personal significance for Strauss that extends well beyond the exigencies of performance possibilities or the simple filling-in of time between other projects. The orchestration of each of these songs is not merely an enlargement of the original piano accompaniment for larger forces. The *process* of orchestration is a poetic act whereby the old song becomes a new composition relevant to present circumstances.

Chronology of the Sources and the Cyclic Aspect

Reconstruction of compositional chronology combined with examination of the song texts supports the contention that the five last orchestral songs (including the orchestrated *Ruhe, meine Seele!*) constitute a closed cycle.[16] Although Schuh mentions that Strauss considered setting a series of Hesse poems, in addition to those actually set, only *Nacht* and *Höhe des Sommers* were ever serious candidates for orchestral songs. Subsequent investigators have neglected to compare the texts of these rejected Hesse poems with the chosen poems to seek reasons why the poems were set or rejected in a particular sequence. But by systematically reconstructing compositional chronology and by comparing the accepted and rejected poems in order of composition, it is possible to show that Strauss was especially careful to maintain consistency of imagery, temporal symbolism, and diction, and to avoid redundance. Since redundance would only be problematic if performance of the songs as a cycle were contemplated, Strauss's care in this respect may taken as evidence that he understood the newly composed orchestral songs as a cycle and not as isolated, occasional settings. Thus, source evidence leading to new chronology, along with literary analysis of the poetry, combine to support the corollary hypotheses that, first, the chosen poems form a complete and self-contained poetic statement; and second, Strauss contemplated no further settings beyond those orchestrated.

Before setting a poem, whether for solo voice or chorus, Strauss sometimes copied the poem into his pocket sketchbooks. In the act of copying, he may have already heard the outlines of the setting, making annotations of keys, pitches, and formal sections in his copy. Two *Abschriften* of Eichendorff's *Im Abendrot* have survived, showing that Strauss was preoccupied with setting this poem for at least two years, 1946–48. Unfortunately, neither *Abschrift* contains musical or other annotations. In November 1987, a sketchbook resurfaced at Sotheby's; it contains what is presumably the first *Abschrift* of Eichendorff's *Im Abendrot*, dated "Ouchy 3. April 46." During his Swiss exile, Strauss kept a diary, the so-called *Schweizer Tagebuch,* in which he pasted and commented on newspaper articles that captured his interest. Although the *Tagebuch* has not been made available to the public, the late Frau Alice Strauss kindly provided a copy of the page on which Strauss recopied *Im Abendrot* (see Figure 1).

Immediately above his *Abschrift*, Strauss pasted in a newspaper article, "The Fate of the Dresden Collections." Dresden was Strauss's "glückliche Stadt"; it had seen nine of his opera premieres, and the

Vom Schicksal der Dresdner Sammlungen

K. A. Nach dem Einmarsch der Russen wurden verlagerten Bestände der *Gemäldegalerie* und s *Kupferstich-* und *Handzeichnungskabinetts* von m Sowjets nach dem Schloß Pillnitz bei Dresden erbracht. Diese Maßnahme erfolgte durch die sogenannte „Trophäenkommission", die aus vier Offizieren bestand. Schloß Pillnitz wurde sodann hermetisch abgeschlossen und war nur Russen oder in Begleitung von Russen befindlichen Personen zugänglich. Was sich in dieser Zeit im Schloß abgespielt hat, läßt sich nicht mit Genauigkeit feststellen. Es ist sicher, daß die Spitzenwerke der Galerie nach Rußland abtransportiert wurden. Ebenso wahrscheinlich ist es aber auch, daß ein großer Teil der Galerie illegal in alle möglichen Hände gelangte. Die Russen hatten das Prinzip aufgestellt, daß alle *deutschen* Bilder als Restbestand in Dresden bleiben sollten. Aber auch diese Linie wurde nicht eingehalten und es sind zahlreiche Bilder des 19. Jahrhunderts aus verschwunden. Am krassesten drückte sich dies bei der Kupferstichsammlung aus. Hier blieb von dem herrlichen Bestand an Graphik des 15. Jahrhunderts, wohl durch Zufall, nur noch eine Mappe erhalten. Der erhaltene Bestand ist ganz kümmerlich. Erwähnenswert ist, daß selbst ein Werk von nationaler Bedeutung, wie das von Caspar David Fried-

rich lückenlos verschwand. Im Jahre 1946 wurde kurfristig der Befehl erteilt, Schloß Pillnitz in ein Zentralmuseum des Landes Sachsen zu verwandeln. Bei dieser Gelegenheit konnten die deutschen Septstellen die traurige „Sichtung" der Bestände vornehmen. Von den beiden Sammlungen von Weltruf ist nur noch ein ganz kümmerlicher Bestand vorhanden, der von manchem Provinzialmuseum weit übertroffen wird.

Besonders tragisch gestaltete sich das Schicksal der *Porzellansammlung*. Der gesamte ostasiatische Bestand (China und Japan), der Weltruf hatte, und von August dem Starken mit einem Sonderschiff aus Ostasien nach Europa gebracht worden war — ging bis auf wenige Einzelstücke verloren. Er verfiel wie die unersetzlichen Meißner Vögel und Augustus-Rexvasen aus dem Residenzschloß der Zerstörung. Die Abteilung Meissen der Porzellansammlung fiel den merkenswertes Unternehmen. Die geschlossen in die Hände der sowjetischen Behörden und es ist zu hoffen, daß wenigstens dieser Bestand unbeschädigt erhalten geblieben ist.

Das gesamte *Grüne Gewölbe* und die Hauptobjekte des *Historischen Museums* fielen in der Festung Königstein in die Hände der Sowjets und wurden nach Rußland verbracht. Es ist zu hoffen, daß die für die Sowjetunion bestimmten Sammlungsteile der Galerie, des Kupferstichkabinetts und des Grünen Gewölbes wenigstens dort angekommen und so der Kulturwelt erhalten geblieben sind. — Die in unmittelbarer Nähe Dresdens liegenden *Schlösser* Augusts des Starken, Pillnitz und Moritzburg, wurden von russischen Truppen und freigelassenen Polen geplündert, wobei unersetzliche Kulturwerte zugrunde gingen.

porte, die beraubt wurden oder in die Hände polnischer Parisiner. leider; ließen, eine gewisse Befürchtung nicht verstummen. Von norwegischer Seite wurde bisher verlautbar, daß die „Sixtinische Madonna" in Moskau ausgestellt worden sei. Die allgemeineren Bestände des Historischen Museums, die aufs Land verlagert worden waren, wurden gestendsten der Welt, wurde vor den Sowjets in der Form liquidiert, daß die Münzen aus den Kästen nach ihrer Materialbeschaffenheit in Säcke geschüttet und zum Einschmelzen fortgefahren wurden. Die *Landesbibliothek*, die wegen ihrer riesigen Umfangs nicht verlagert werden konnte, fiel dem britischen Bombardement vom 13. Februar 1945 zum Opfer. Die verlagerten wertvollsten Werke, unter denen sich unersetzliche Handschriften befanden, wie die mathematischen Bücher von Dürer, die Partitur der h-Moll-Messe von Bach u. s. f. wurden nach einem Wasserrohrbruch im Bergunsert zerstört.

Beim Bombenangriff auf Dresden ging ein Verlagerungstransport mit Bildern des 19. Jahrhunderts durch Brand verloren. Dabei gingen alle Bilder der Rayskis zugrunde. Die Bestände des Mathematisch-Physikalischen Salons, einer einzigartigen Sammlung, teilten das Schicksal des Historischen Museums.

Figure 1. Facsimile of a page from Strauss's *Schweizer Tagebuch*, circa January 1947, containing his *Abschrift* of Eichendorff's *Im Abendrot*. Courtesy of the late Frau Alice Strauss

city's art treasures were no less dear to the composer than the Staatskapelle itself. The newspaper report of the destruction of important works of art, as well as the plunder of surviving treasures by the occupying Russians, caused Strauss great pain and anxiety. Although the date of the article cannot be ascertained from the pasted clipping (Strauss cut off the header from the newspaper), one may assume from the retrospective perspective of the observation in the first line of the second column ("Im Jahre 1946 wurde . . .") that the article dates from January 1947.[17] Above his *Abschrift*, Strauss wrote, "1945 The Mongols in Europe!"—clearly referring to the beginning of the Russian occupation as described in the article. Perhaps Strauss entered both the article and the poem into his scrapbook at the same time, in January 1947.

In the introduction to the published score, Roth states that the first sketches ("die ersten *Skizzen*") for *Im Abendrot* date back to late 1946 or early 1947. It is significant that he speaks unequivocally of "sketches," for only one brief sketch survives in the Garmisch collection. However, everything known of Strauss's compositional method— he usually wrote out his compositions in full in the sketchbooks prior to embarking on the *Particell*—combined with internal evidence of the Garmisch sketch, supports Roth's observation.[18] Roth died in 1971 and his widow retains ownership of the *Particell* (published in facsimile). The whereabouts of these sketches remain a mystery. Since further sketches are also mentioned but never actually quoted by other writers after Strauss's death, these references may well be based solely upon Roth's testimony. Perhaps the *Im Abendrot* sketches were given away by Strauss himself and were not in the Garmisch collection at the time of his death. Since these sketches would have been needed until the *Particell* was finished, on 27 April 1948, this is the earliest date that sketches for *Im Abendrot* could have passed out of Strauss's hands. *Im Abendrot* sketches were possibly given away in connection with the premiere; Strauss and later his family often presented sketches to the performers of premieres. Perhaps Flagstad received them; Furtwängler's wife has confirmed that Furtwängler did not receive any. The fact that a potentially substantial body of sketches for *Im Abendrot* has disappeared en masse suggests that yet another sketchbook from the years 1947–48 may eventually surface.

．

The single preliminary sketch for this song is in a sketchbook (Tr. 136) at the Richard Strauss–Archiv, and it is highly informative. Along with the sketch for *Im Abendrot*, Tr. 136 contains drafts for *Die Rache der Aphrodite*, a ballet-pantomime. The idea for this work occurred to Strauss as early as January 1945. Schuh reports that the project languished in May 1946 when Strauss turned his attention to orchestral fantasies on themes from *Die Frau ohne Schatten* and the *Josephslegende*.[19] If, as Schuh reports, *Die Rache der Aphrodite* was abandoned in May 1946, the sketches for this work preserved in Tr. 136 must have been entered prior to that date. Page analysis of the sketchbook suggests that the single sketch for *Im Abendrot* predates surrounding sketches for *Die Rache der Aphrodite*. Thus, the *Im Abendrot* sketch may date from April 1946, shortly after the first "Ouchy" *Abschrift* of 3 April 1946 and before *Die Rache der Aphrodite* was dropped in May 1946. According to my reconstruction of chronology, the *Im Abendrot* sketch in Tr. 136 falls between the "Ouchy" *Abschrift* of April 1946 and the *Tagebuch Abschrift* of January 1947, which it antedates by as much as six months.

Page analysis combines internal evidence of the sequence of sketches with the relationship between blank and filled pages at given stages in the compositional process to yield chronology. Its basic principle is space availability: sketches that block other sketches must be entered earlier. Page analysis of Tr. 136 is complicated by the fact that *Die Rache der Aphrodite* is unfinished; one cannot reconstruct the sequence of sketches using the finished work as a guide. It is, however, revealing that an F-minor "Klage" sketch beginning on p. 50 links up with its continuation on p. 43. Figure 2 shows that the continuation of the "Klage" sketch is blocked by the "Marschartig" sketch on p. 51, which must already have been in place. Strauss therefore looked back in the sketchbook for free pages and found four blank pages, pp. 43–46. The fact that he did not continue the "Klage" sketch earlier on p. 40 suggests that pp. 40–42 were already occupied by the sketch for *Im Abendrot*. Pp. 43–46 had probably been left blank for further sketching of *Im Abendrot*, but as Tr. 136 filled up with sketches for *Die Rache der Aphrodite*, Strauss may have turned to another, now missing, sketchbook to develop his ideas for *Im Abendrot*. This external evidence for the sketch's earliness is confirmed by the study of its content.

The existence of two *Abschriften* of the poem *Im Abendrot* from different periods indicates long and intense preoccupation with its setting. My April 1946 dating of both the "Ouchy" *Abschrift* and the Garmisch *Im Abendrot* sketch and January 1947 dating of the *Tagebuch Abschrift* suggest that although Strauss put the *Im Abendrot* setting aside at least twice, he continued to think about it. The time span between 3 April 1946, the date of the "Ouchy" *Abschrift*, and 27 April 1948,

PAGE NO.	TITLE	KEY	TIME SIGNATURE
38	*Nymphe*	D♭ major	$\frac{2}{4}$
39	*Allegretto*	E♭ major	$\frac{2}{4}$
40	*Im Abendrot* (Eichendorff)	E♭ major	$\frac{4}{4}$
41			
42			
43	"Klage" (continued)	F minor	$\frac{4}{8}$
44			
45			
46			
47		G major	$\frac{3}{4}$
48	*Schnell*	G major	$\frac{3}{4}$
49	*Moderato*	D♭ major	$\frac{6}{4}$
50	"Klage," *Andante*	F minor	$\frac{4}{8}$
51	"Marschartig"	C major	$\frac{6}{4}$
52			
53	*Allegretto*	C major	$\frac{6}{4}$
54	Blank		
55			
56		D major	$\frac{4}{4}$
57	*Sinfonische Melodie*	E♭ major	$\frac{4}{4}$

Figure 2. Diagram of pp. 38–57 in sketchbook Tr. 136

the day on which Strauss completed the *Particell*, is just over two years. During this period, Strauss worked on other compositions and also traveled to England (4 October to 1 November 1947).

Precisely when Strauss began considering a cycle of orchestral songs that would include Eichendorff's *Im Abendrot*, Hesse poems, and also the orchestration of the 1894 setting of Henckell's *Ruhe, meine Seele!* cannot be determined. Strauss initially copied *Frühling* onto the first page of Tr. 137. This *Abschrift* is undated. The cover of the sketchbook bears the date and place "1947, Verenahof" in Strauss's own hand. The first page of the sketchbook is dated 15 December 1946, but this date would appear to refer to earlier sketches on the same page—namely, early drafts for the *Duett-Concertino*.

Based on Strauss's own dating of Tr. 137, it is likely that he copied out *Frühling* in 1947, possibly in January, at the same time he copied *Im Abendrot* into the *Schweizer Tagebuch*. This dating is confirmed by Schuh, who states that it was in 1947 (not in 1946), that an "admirer" of Hesse introduced Strauss to Hesse's poetry.[20] This dating would document Strauss's interest in setting Hesse's poetry at least a year before he completed the *Particells* for *Im Abendrot* (dated 27 April 1948) and *Ruhe, meine Seele!* (dated 9 June 1948) and would, in turn, lend credence to the idea that Strauss began to conceive of the Henckell, Eichendorff, and Hesse settings as a cycle of poetically and musically interrelated orchestral songs at a very early stage in the compositional process.

Undated musical sketch drafts of *Frühling* are found in Tr. 143. Although the later part of this sketchbook also contains sketches for Strauss's very last vocal works, *Malven* and *Besinnung*, the sketches for *Frühling* still probably predate the sketches for *Beim Schlafengehen* and *September* in Tr. 142. These two sketchbooks were thus not filled in strict chronological order; rather, Strauss entered ideas in the two sketchbooks in a complex sequence. Tr. 143 contains two drafts for *Frühling* plus a page of studies. Drafts 1 and 2 are set down in a combination of two different colors of ink: that of a black fountain pen and that of a blue ballpoint pen. In Draft 1, the earlier layer is in black ink, which has been revised with a blue ballpoint pen. In Draft 2, the earlier layer is in blue ballpoint pen, with some additions in black fountain pen.

The unpublished memoirs of Adolf Jöhr, Strauss's Swiss banker, provide important new information concerning the genesis of *Beim Schlafengehen* and thus of the *Letzte Orchesterlieder* as a whole. The *Particell* for *Beim Schlafengehen* was begun while Strauss was staying with the Jöhr family in Zurich. Jöhr reports:

If my memory is correct, it was after our meeting in Rosenberg (28 July 1948), that Richard Strauss, as he came out of his room for lunch, held in his hand a folio [*Quartblatt*] written on two sides, and overwhelmed me with the remark "Here I have a new song on a text by Hermann Hesse, which I have dedicated to you and your wife." Apparently, he had unearthed the volume of Hesse's *Collected Works* from my library and studied it in the evening before retiring. I thanked him immediately for the dedication, but did not have the courage to ask him to give me the original as a gift; perhaps I was also put off by the difficulty of deciphering the manuscript more scribbled than written in the fine handwriting of the master. Apparently, it was the original *Particell* with worked-out vocal line, but only an indicated accompaniment, which he worked up and completed afterward in Pontresina. I received a photocopy of the manuscript *Partitur* through the good offices of Dr. Schuh after Richard Strauss's death and later the original from the legacy through the generosity of the heirs.[21]

Jöhr's description is precise; he observed a single sheet of folio paper written on both sides. He could not, then, be referring to the nine pages of sketches found in Tr. 142. Further evidence suggests that Jöhr did, in fact, see the *Particell*. However, Jöhr's statement that Strauss "unearthed" the Hesse volume in his library might imply that, while staying with Jöhr, Strauss first discovered and set the Hesse poem in a single night. This contention is not borne out by the sources.

The precise date of the visit, shortly after the meeting in Rosenberg on 28 July 1948, postdates by ten days Strauss's completion of *Frühling* (*Particell* and *Partitur* for *Frühling* are dated 20 June and 18 July 1948, respectively). As already noted, the *Abschrift* of *Frühling* suggests that Strauss had been interested in setting Hesse as early as January 1947. It is, therefore, doubtful that Strauss discovered Hesse's poetry while staying with the Jöhrs in 1948; rather, he had been thinking of setting a number of Hesse poems for some time, probably for more than a year prior to the Jöhr visit.

Although Strauss could work very quickly once he had formulated a compositional idea, it is highly unlikely that he produced both sketches and *Particell* for *Beim Schlafengehen* in a single night. Assuming from his precise description that Jöhr did see the *Particell* for *Beim Schlafengehen*, Strauss had probably already completed the sketches for this song in Tr. 142 in the ten days after finishing *Frühling* and prior to visiting Jöhr—that is, between 18 July and the first days of August

1948. If this interpretation is correct, it was during his stay with Jöhr—shortly after 28 July 1948—that Strauss completed the *Particell* for *Beim Schlafengehen*. Strauss borrowed Jöhr's Hesse volume while completing the *Particell* and decided to dedicate *Beim Schlafengehen* to the Jöhrs in appreciation of their hospitality.[22] The *Partitur* was completed a few days later on 4 August 1948.

The sketch for *September* is found in Tr. 142, three pages after the sketch for *Beim Schlafengehen*. In this sketchbook, immediately after completing the sketch of *Beim Schlafengehen*, Strauss continued sketching an eventually abandoned *Violinkonzert* and began to sketch another Hesse poem, *Nacht*, which also remained unfinished. Strauss's memorandum accompanying the sketch for *Nacht* shows that it was also intended to be an orchestral song. This sketch is remarkably tentative, and, unlike in other song sketches of this late period, the vocal line is omitted. Strauss did not progress very far before abandoning both poem and sketch. After rejecting *Nacht*, Strauss considered setting two more Hesse poems, which he copied out at the bottom of two facing sketchbook pages: *September* and *Höhe des Sommers*. Strauss chose *September* and began the sketch immediately above it. The sketch for *September* is dated 10 August 1948.

The central theme that manages to weave itself through all these late songs is the approach and ultimate acceptance of death. Strauss's initial exploration (April 1946 to January 1947) of this theme involved only two songs: *Ruhe, meine Seele!* and *Im Abendrot*. These two songs are the most closely related (poetically and motivically) of the *Letzte Orchesterlieder*, and they form a kind of paired unit: *Ruhe, meine Seele!* serving as a prelude before death and *Im Abendrot* as a meditation on the subject of death itself. Hesse's *Frühling* was added to the pair in January 1947. With the composition of that song, a time-of-year cycle was juxtaposed with the time-of-day cycle already inherent in the first two songs. Thus, death is also reflected in the changing of the seasons: from spring's birth to winter's death. This dual metaphor is especially clear in *Im Abendrot*, which functions both as dusk in the day cycle and as winter in the seasonal cycle. Strauss's decision to add more Hesse settings seems to have been made relatively late in the compositional process—after the composition of *Frühling* in mid-July 1948. *Beim Schlafengehen*, with its day-versus-night imagery, would be an addition to the day cycle and *September* would fill out the seasonal cycle with the passing of summer into autumn.

Consideration of the proper sequence of events within the seasonal and day cycles supports Roth's sequence of songs, along with the interpolation of *Ruhe, meine Seele!*

1. *Frühling* (spring viewed through winter)
2. *September* (summer viewed through autumn)
3. *Beim Schlafengehen* (day viewed through night)
4. *Ruhe, meine Seele!* (recitative: meditation before death)
5. *Im Abendrot* (aria: winter, dusk, death)

Performed in this order, death (winter and dusk) is the endpoint of the two interlocking time cycles of seasons and times of day. In the first two songs, *Frühling* and *September*, spring passes into autumn, while in *Beim Schlafengehen* day passes into night. *Im Abendrot* closes both cycles as winter and dusk. The persona's perspective is oriented from the end of both time cycles. The entire set of songs is weighted toward the darkness of night and winter: in *Frühling*, spring is viewed from wintry hibernation; in *September*, summer is viewed retrospectively from autumn; while in *Beim Schlafengehen*, day is viewed retrospectively from night.

This analysis of the thematic subtext helps explain Strauss's choice of *Beim Schlafengehen* and *September* in mid-July–early August 1948. In the last two weeks of July 1948, after creating a winter and a spring song (*Im Abendrot* and *Frühling*) and orchestrating a meditation (*Ruhe, meine Seele!*), Strauss turns to a day-night setting, *Beim Schlafengehen*. Once the seasonal and day cycles have been established with the completion of *Beim Schlafengehen* it becomes difficult to find poems that fit comfortably into one of these cycles and yet are not redundant. While remaining true to his underlying concept, Strauss must be careful to observe the principles of contrast and variety. By restricting his final choice of Hesse poems to three-stanza poems, Strauss seems to have decided that the weightier four-stanza *Im Abendrot* should be the culmination of the group.

After completing *Beim Schlafengehen* on 4 August 1948, Strauss briefly considers setting *Nacht:*

NACHT

Mit Dämmerung und Amsel-
    schlag
Kommt aus den Tälern her die
    Nacht.
Die Schwalben ruhn, der lange
    Tag
Hat auch die Schwalben müde
    gemacht.

NIGHT

With dusk and the cry of
    blackbird
Night approaches out of the
    valleys.
The swallows rest, the long
    day
Has also made the swallows
    tired.

Durch Fenster mit verhaltenem Klang	The restrained tone of my violin
Geht meiner Geige milder Streich.	Passes through the window.
Verstehst du, schöne Nacht, den Sang—	Do you understand, beautiful night, the song—
Mein altes Lied, mein Lied an dich?	My ancient song, my song to you?
Ein kühles Rauschen kommt vom Wald,	A cool breeze comes from the wood,
Dass mir das Herz erschauernd lacht,	So that my heart, feeling it, laughs,
Und leis mit freundlicher Gewalt	And gently with a friendly force,
Besiegt mich Schlummer, Traum und Nacht.	Slumber, dream, and night overwhelm me.

Beautiful as this poem is, Strauss quickly rejects it. *Nacht* is too closely related to the already-composed *Beim Schlafengehen*, also a night poem. The redundancy is one not only of subject matter but also of wording, as is revealed by a comparison of the opening of *Beim Schlafengehen*—"Nun der Tag [hat] mich müd gemacht"—and the third and fourth lines of *Nacht*—"der lange Tag / Hat die Schwalben müde gemacht." Furthermore, in *Beim Schlafengehen*, Strauss had already composed a long melisma for solo violin, which alludes to the second stanza of *Nacht* and to Strauss's own remark "später als Geigenmotiv."

Strauss realizes that night is encompassed by *Beim Schlafengehen* and returns to the cycle of the seasons. The remaining seasons are summer and autumn. In the week between 4 August (completion of the *Partitur* for *Beim Schlafengehen*) and 10 August (completion of the sketch for *September*), Strauss considered both *Höhe des Sommers* and *September* and copied these poems on facing pages of Tr. 142.

HÖHE DES SOMMERS	HIGH SUMMER
Das Blau der Ferne klärt sich schon	The blue of the distance already clarifies itself,
Vergeistigt und gelichtet	Spiritualized and lightened
Zu jenem süssen Zauberton,	To that sweet magic tone,
Den nur September dichtet.	Which only September poetizes.

Der reife Sommer über Nacht	Ripe summer, through the night,
Will sich zum Feste färben,	Wants to color itself festively
Da alles in Vollendung lacht	So that everything in fulfillment laughs
Und willig ist zu sterben.	And is willing to die.
Entreiss dich, Seele, nun der Zeit,	Tear yourself away, soul, now is the time,
Entreiss dich deinen Sorgen	Tear yourself away from your cares
Und mache dich zum Flug bereit	And make yourself ready for flight
In den ersehnten Morgen.	Into that longed-for morning.

A comparison of *September* and *Höhe des Sommers* reveals once again that Strauss had to choose between the two poems. Both are autumnal poems that refer to summer retrospectively—*Höhe des Sommers* explicitly mentions "September," while *September* mentions "summer." But, in the case of *Höhe des Sommers*, there is a problem: redundancy of wording and metaphor with the previously set *Beim Schlafengehen*, whose climactic last stanza begins, "Und die Seele unbewacht / Will sich in freien Flügen schweben," while in *Höhe des Sommers*, the climactic last stanza reads, "Entreiss dich, Seele, nun der Zeit, / Entreiss dich deinen Sorgen / Und mache dich zum Flug bereit." A further problem is the explicit mention in *Höhe des Sommers* of both *Nacht* and *Zauber*, concepts that have already figured prominently in *Beim Schlafengehen*. *September*, on the other hand, has its own autonomous garden imagery, which, while filling the remaining seasons within the season cycle, does not overlap with the imagery and diction of the poems already set. Strauss therefore rejected *Höhe des Sommers* without even attempting a setting, and chose *September*—thus completing the cycle of the *Letzte Orchesterlieder* texts.

Resolution of the *Notmotiv* in *Im Abendrot*

The *Notmotiv* is shown in Example 1. *Not* is represented by uncertainty of tonal identity (G♭ or F♯?) and by disconcerting semitonal displacement in the bass, D displacing E♭.[23] The *Notmotiv* is untransposed; it involves only this particular constellation of pitches: G♭ becoming F♯ in the upper voice, supported by E♭ and D♮ in the bass. The importance of absolute pitch in Strauss's compositional thinking cannot be underestimated.[24] As he read through texts for vocal compositions, Strauss often already heard absolute pitches, chords, and tonalities; he made marginal notes of these, and later incorporated them into musical sketches. The present study of the genesis of *Im Abendrot* further underscores the importance of absolute pitch relationships; Strauss transposes the end of the *Im Abendrot* sketch in order to restate the *Notmotiv* at its original pitch. Transpositional invariance of the *Notmotiv* facilitates perception; if the *Notmotiv* were transposed from song to song, in combination with all the other variant features, it would be difficult if not impossible to hear. Although each of the five orchestral songs possesses its own unique motivic, tonal, rhythmic, and formal aspects, the *Notmotiv* is worked into the structure in each of the five songs—at different structural levels ranging from foreground to background.

Example 1. The *Notmotiv*

For our purposes here, however, the focus will be limited mainly to the motivic relationship between *Ruhe, meine Seele!* and *Im Abendrot.*[25] Example 2a shows the *Notmotiv* at the climax of *Ruhe, meine Seele!* at the exclamation, "Diese Zeiten sind gewaltig, / Bringen Herz und Hirn in Not" (measures 29–33);[26] Example 2b shows the *Notmotiv* at the end of *Im Abendrot* coinciding with the climactic question "Wie sind wir wandermüde—/ Ist dies etwa der Tod?" (measures 67–76). Thus, *two* reminiscences of early works are superimposed at the end of *Im Abendrot:* the "theme of the artist's ideology" (Del Mar's designation) from *Tod und Verklärung* (1889) and the *Notmotiv* from the climax of *Ruhe, meine Seele!* (1894).[27]

At the climax of *Ruhe, meine Seele!* Strauss represents *Not* through the unfulfilled "need" of the high $g\flat^2 = f\sharp^2$ to resolve upward as a leading tone to g^2. But the irresolution of the high $f\sharp^2$ is never addressed. The vocal line immediately plunges into the lower octave without returning to the upper register. The narrator wants to ignore *Not,* to put it out of mind. Notice the emphasis placed on "und vergiss" [and forget] through repetition (the only word repetition in

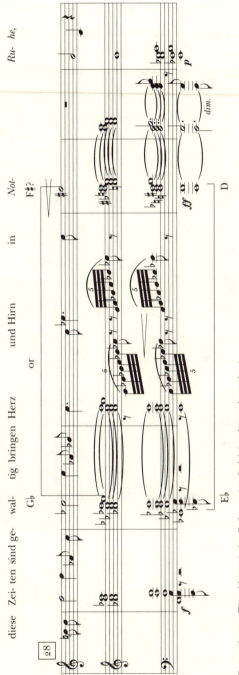

Example 2a. The *Notmotiv* in *Ruhe, meine Seele!* (orchestral version)

Example 2b. The *Notmotiv* in *Im Abendrot (Particell)*

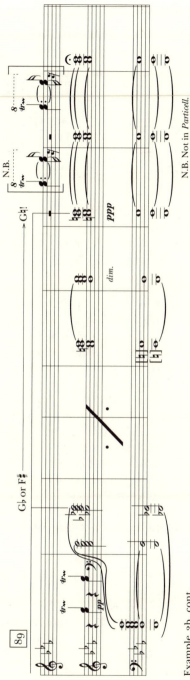

Example 2b, cont.

the setting). At these words, Strauss represents forgetting by "forgetting" F♯ (associated with *Not* throughout the song) and replacing F♯ with F♮ within the descending line G–F–E♭–D–C (measures 35–42).[28]

Example 2c. The *Notmotiv* in *Im Abendrot* (sketch, measures 4–6)

In 1946–48, to articulate the *Not* of "the times," Strauss returns to the *Notmotiv* in *Ruhe, meine Seele!* But this song does not provide a satisfactory resolution to the *Notmotiv*—a real sense of comfort in times of great distress. And when the *Notmotiv* is taken up again at the end of *Im Abendrot*, semitonal *root* displacement (as the E♭-minor triad is twice displaced down a semitone to the D-major triad within the *Notmotiv* in measures 68–72 and 80–84) forcefully depicts the *Not* of the wanderers, the *rootlessness* and humiliation of their exile.

One commentator has claimed that the vocal line in *Im Abendrot* breaks off "pathetically" at the question "Ist dies etwa der Tod?"[29] I interpret the *Ruhe, meine Seele!–Im Abendrot* pairing—indeed the entire proposed sequence of songs—as analogous to a Delphic ritual, whereby the soul approaches the oracle to pose a question. But there is nothing pathetic, self-pitying, or maudlin in the asking of the question; on the contrary, the actual positing of the question represents a great triumph over adversity. In spite of having been forced to wander in exile, in spite of its *Not*, the soul has found its way to the sacred place and is there able to articulate its fateful question.

Strauss—and much of Europe, for that matter—stood in need of a comforting reply. But the agnostic composer could not find solace in a traditional religious response. Thus, the reply cannot come from a deity or oracle but rather must come from the inarticulate voice of the orchestra representing nature. Nevertheless, nature's response, when it comes, is that the miracle of death is simultaneously the

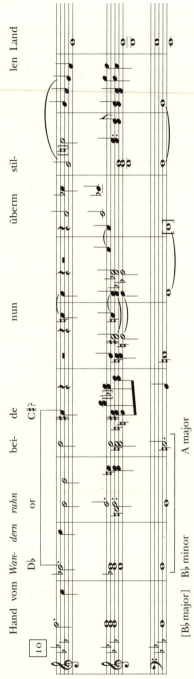

Example 2d. The *Notmotiv* in *Im Abendrot* (sketch, measures 10–16)

miracle of birth. The subtle way in which nature (the orchestra) answers the soul (the voice) is central to Strauss's expressive goal. At the point where the *Notmotiv* and the theme of the "artist's ideology" are superimposed (measures 71–72), the theme enters tentatively, emerging from the most profound depths (the low A of the horn) to create the effect of a miraculous resurrection from the realm of death. This theme from *Tod und Verklärung*, the personification of the composer's creative ego, emerges like an apparition from the under-world, called into being by the speaker's great *Not*. As this theme, which is repeated more emphatically in a higher register (after the voice breaks off, measures 76–77), melds with the orchestra to become part of the repetition of the question (measures 77–78), the apparition dissolves into nature. This moment of dissolution in death is simultaneously an act of creation; the theme (the spirit of the dying soul) impregnates the orchestra (inanimate nature), bestowing consciousness upon it.

In transmuting nature's miracle of regeneration—its miraculous creation of new being—into a visual metaphor, it is as if the reflection in the mirror were to assume its own independent existence. In Strauss's musical metaphor, the echo begins to assume a life of its own. Under normal circumstances, nature should be dumb; without its own voice, it should only be capable of reflecting the soul's living voice. Thus, if nature is to echo the soul, measures 77ff. should literally repeat measures 65ff. But the repetition in measures 77ff. is nonliteral; it comes alive. Nature's response is an echo of the soul, but an echo that, through the labor of transformation, brings forth new, independent life.

In measures 77–92, the orchestra echoes the enharmonic question embedded in the *Notmotiv:* is G♭ really F♯? The answer is deferred until the last chord in measure 95: yes, G♭ *is* F♯ because it resolves as a leading tone to G♮. Thus, one can legitimately speak of the resolution to G♮ in the *Im Abendrot* postlude of the suspended G♭/F♯ prepared in *Ruhe, meine Seele!* For Strauss, this resolution of the *Notmotiv* is part of a healing process whereby both personal and collective *Not* is resolved in nature.

Example 3 shows the colossal enlargement of the *Notmotiv* in the background of *Im Abendrot*, welding the first three stanzas into a single tonal progression: I–V/V–V.[30] This background enlargement (E♭ major in measure 1 to E♭ minor in measure 50, which is then tonally displaced down a semitone to D major in measure 52) wondrously foreshadows the previously discussed foreground statements in the postlude (the motions from E♭ minor to D major in measures 68–72

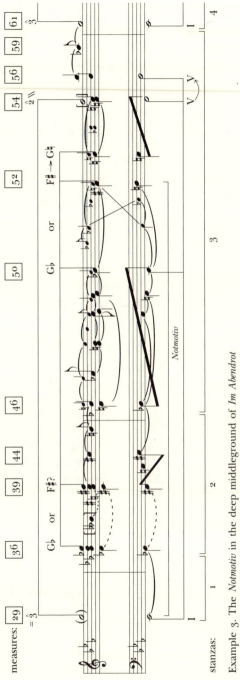

Example 3. The *Notmotiv* in the deep middleground of *Im Abendrot*

and 80–84). The *Notmotiv* emerges close to the foreground in the shift from the Eb-minor chord to the D-major triad in measures 50–52. Although Gb/F♯ resolves to G♮ within the C-minor chord in measure 53 in the middleground (foreshadowing the definitive resolution to G♮ at the end of the song), F♯ is prevented from resolving to G♮ in the foreground by the descending chromatic passing tones in measure 52. By suggesting a resolution to the goal G♮ in the middleground and at the same time obscuring it in the foreground, Strauss subtly illustrates "losing the way" ("Dass wir uns nicht verirren").

Example 4 presents a transcription of the sketch for *Im Abendrot* in Tr. 136. The sketch begins with an abbreviated orchestral introduction and fuses introduction and first stanza into a single entity. Internal evidence, such as the absence of important surface motives like the rising and falling third motive, confirms the sketch's earliness in the compositional process, as has already been suggested by other, external factors. Observe, however, that Strauss already realizes a variant of the opening accompaniment horn motive. Perhaps working quickly and from memory, Strauss changes Eichendorff's "Vom Wandern ruhn wir beide," omitting the word "wir."[31]

.

It is of considerable interest to us that the sketch's measures 4–6 (Example 2c) adumbrate the foreground presentation of the *Notmotiv* in the final version of the postlude, measures 68–72 (Example 2b) and 80–84. The two downward semitonal displacements of Eb major to D major in measures 4–6 of the sketch foreshadow the two downward semitonal displacements of Eb minor to D major in measures 68–72 and 80–84 of the final version. Notice that, while measures 4–6 of the sketch contain the parallel tenths of the *Notmotiv* and three of its four tones (Eb, D♮, and F♯), the enharmonic transformation of Gb into F♯ is missing because Eb *major,* rather than minor, moves down to D major.[32]

How does Strauss achieve the final version's statement of the *Notmotiv* in measures 68–72, with its emphatic enharmonic transformation of Gb into F♯ (marked by the sforzando on Gb in measure 68)? Although many intervening sketches may be missing, measures 10–16 of this early sketch (Example 2d) provide the vital clue. Like measures 4–6, these measures foreshadow measures 68–72 of the final version, but *transposed up a fifth.* Thus the displacement of Eb minor by D major in the final version is represented in the sketch by the displacement of Bb minor by A major. Where the final version hinges on the enharmonic transformation of Gb into F♯, the sketch features

Example 4. Transcription of the *Im Abendrot* sketch in sketchbook Tr. 136, pp. 40–42

the enharmonic transformation of D♭ into C♯. The expressive 4–3 suspension in the vocal line in measure 13 of the sketch is transferred to measure 68 of the final version. The halting declamation created by rests in the vocal line at "Beide . . . nun . . . überm," reappears in the final version of the last stanza at "wandermüde . . . ist dies . . . etwa . . . der Tod?" At some point in the compositional process—it is impossible to say when because of the lacuna in the sources—Strauss realized that transposing the sketch reading of measures 10–16 down a fifth would reproduce the *Notmotiv* at its original pitch at the climax of *Ruhe, meine Seele!*—the pitch already suggested by the nonliteral statement of the *Notmotiv* in measures 4–6 of the sketch.[33] Surely this transposition was suggested by textual association between "von *Wandern ruhn* Beide" in the first stanza, "*wander*müde" in the last stanza, and "*Ruhe, ruhe*, meine Seele!" Thus, motivically and in terms of compositional genesis, *wandern*, *Not* and *Müde* in *Ruhe, meine Seele!* and *Im Abendrot* are linked as cause and effect, whose resolution will be the absolute *Ruhe* of death.

Transposing measures 10–16 of the sketch down a fifth restates the *Notmotiv* at its original pitch. The enharmonic transformation of D♭ into C♯ in the sketch becomes, through transposition, the enharmonic transformation of G♭ into F♯. If the G♭-equals-F♯ transformation is to be *the* central issue in *Im Abendrot*—as it is in *Ruhe, meine Seele!*—then any residue of the sketch's D♭-equals-C♯ transformation must be eliminated. If, during composition of *Im Abendrot*, Strauss takes steps to concentrate enharmonic transformation in the G♭/F♯ enharmonic pair, this constitutes further evidence that transposition of the *Notmotiv* to its original pitch is not fortuitous but a deliberately calculated compositional effect. Such evidence exists in the *Particell*.

Example 5 compares the sketch, *Particell*, and final versions of "gegangen Hand in Hand." In measures 8–10 of the sketch and in the corresponding place in the *Particell* (measures 27–28), D♭ rises as if it were C♯ to D♮ while the bass arpeggiates D♭-F♯-B♭ (Examples 5a–5b). To avoid any suggestion of the enharmonic transformation of D♭ into C♯, Strauss revises measures 27–28 in an "Einlage" at the end of the *Particell*. The revision, which yields the final version of these measures, transposes D♭ rising as if it were C♯ to D♮ down a fifth to become G♭ rising as if it were F♯ to G♮ in the bass (Example 5c).

Practical Results of the Discovery

If the alleged motivic connection between the *Letzte Orchesterlieder* and *Ruhe, meine Seele!* exists, two related questions spring to mind: first,

Example 5a. *Im Abendrot* (sketch, measures 8–10)

Example 5b. *Im Abendrot* (*Particell,* measures 25–28)

was Strauss conscious of it? And second, if he was conscious of it, why did he fail to alert posterity in a memorandum or note? The second question may be quickly dispensed with. It is doubtful that Strauss would have offered an explanation of this kind; he rarely discussed substantive compositional issues, and then only in the most general terms. To answer the first question, it is necessary to differentiate between verbal and analytical consciousness on the one hand and intuitive tonal and compositional consciousness on the other as two distinct modes of thought. It is thus reasonable to assert that Strauss was indeed conscious of the connection at the level of tonal consciousness, even though he may have been unable to explain it verbally or in a series of Schenkerian graphs, a method of analysis with which

Example 5c. *Im Abendrot* ("Einlage" at the end of the *Particell,* containing the final version of measures 27–28)

he was entirely unfamiliar.[34] Oswald Jonas—who of Schenker's pupils was the most concerned with autograph study—applied himself to the question of the relationship of analytical Schenkerian thinking to the creative process in a series of paragraphs entitled "Conscious or Unconscious Creation":

> The question that is continually being asked by readers, both lay people and also trained musicians, arises out of the doubt whether the genius was conscious of all of the aspects pointed out by analysis and whether the creator actually worked according to plan and not rather with "bare feeling." Implicitly, this view places unconscious creativity above the other. . . . The posing of the question in itself rests on a logical error and a false conception of "consciousness." Just as there is conceptual thought, so there is strictly visual [*anschauliches*], namely artistic thought. This, however, is not to be called less conscious than the other. The visualization [*Anschauung*] of the sonority—if one can transfer the sense of this word to the ear—is inborn in the ear of the genius and is, therefore, in the act of creation absolutely conscious. If, in the interpretation of the process, we were compelled to translate it into our conceptual thought, this is merely a translation

of visualization [*Anschauung*] into concept [*Begriff*], but in no way
do we draw the unconscious into the conscious.[35]

Jonas then cites an example of motivic enlargement from J. S. Bach's
Prelude in F major (BWV 927) whereby Bach expands a neighbor-
note motive from measure 4 to bind the composition into a "unity."
Jonas continues: "This may be called conscious creation, not in the
sense of concept-thinking [*begrifflich*] but anchored in the ear, inborn
consciousness of the sonority [*Klangbewusstsein*]. So also it may be understood that the reverse course—out of concept-thinking alone—
which would want to sketch or compose such a piece, is impossible
and that such a piece will be stillborn, while it does not arise out of
the conscious living visualization [*Bewusstsein lebendiger Anschauung*]."[36]
Here, in my view, is where the study and analysis of the *Im Abendrot*
sketch assumes great significance; for careful analysis of this sketch
in its proper historical-biographical context reveals the composer's
strictly compositional consciousness—his *Bewusstsein lebendiger
Anschauung*—of the *Notmotiv,* which can plausibly be shown to guide
the evolution of the work.

The belief that musicology is a science in search of incontrovert-
ible facts has prompted a massive effort to catalog and transcribe
sketches and autographs. In a still-controversial essay on Beethoven
scholarship, Douglas Johnson states:

> At issue here is the purely musical significance of the sketches.
> . . . The great growth of analytical technique in our own cen-
> tury (so the argument continues) has led to a far more sophisti-
> cated discussion of internal relationships than was hitherto pos-
> sible, and as our questions have become more sophisticated, so
> too must our resources. Analysis has admittedly become difficult.
> It would be foolish to reject help from any quarter. So, then, we
> take another look at the sketches. *The results thus far are disap-
> pointing. Is there a single important analytical insight derived from the
> sketches which has become common knowledge among musicians?* [my
> emphasis][37]

The facts that emerge from studies of paper, revisions, concordances,
and so on may well have some intrinsic value of their own, but I share
Johnson's concern that these facts can become irrelevant to our general musical culture. I hope that the connection I have drawn between
Ruhe, meine Seele! and *Im Abendrot,* based in part upon sketch study,
will indeed "become common knowledge among musicians," enrich-
ing our experience of these works, as performers and contemplators.

Indeed, the ultimate aim of the foregoing discussion is to put these findings into practice, to find practical ramifications for a broader musical audience.

The strong musico-poetic link between *Ruhe, meine Seele!* and the *Letzte Orchesterlieder* requires us to rethink the way in which we program the so-called *Four Last Songs*. Omitting the orchestral *Ruhe, meine Seele!*—which must be interpolated before *Im Abendrot*—presents Strauss's *Letzte Orchesterlieder* in a fragmention. Performing *Ruhe, meine Seele!* before *Im Abendrot*, however, makes the strong musical connection audible. Future performances and recordings of the *Letzte Orchesterlieder* may now restore this late song cycle to its original concept.

Im Abendrot should be performed last because it is a portrayal of winter's death, because it is the longest song (four stanzas as opposed to the Hesse and Henckell poems' three) and because, orchestrally, it is the heaviest. *Frühling*, the antipode to winter, works best at the beginning. *September* is most effective after *Frühling* because in the poem summer is put to sleep; spring has turned into summer, which must die in autumn. Thus three of the four seasons have been accounted for in the first two songs. *September* also follows *Frühling* smoothly because, like *Frühling*, it is lightly orchestrated. *Beim Schlafengehen* and *Ruhe, meine Seele!* share a meditative quality. *Beim Schlafengehen* presents the soul's desire to "sleep," while in *Ruhe, meine Seele!* the narrator enjoins his soul to rest. *Ruhe, meine Seele!* articulates the soul's fear, its great need brought on by the "momentous times." The soul's *Not*-cry is finally answered by the voice of nature, represented by the orchestra in the postlude to *Im Abendrot*.

One of Jefferson's arguments that Strauss did not necessarily consider the *Letzte Orchesterlieder* a group is their variety of instrumentation. The orchestration, however, shows a remarkable consistency of instrumental symbolism that contributes to the overall impression of unity. Orchestration is not simply a technique of coloration but also a kind of instrumental symbolism in which particular instruments used in certain ways have certain connotations. Trombones, for example, are traditionally extra brass, borrowed from ceremony. Their association with death and the underworld dates back centuries. The connotation of the "last trump" has never been entirely lost; in both *Ruhe, meine Seele!* and *Im Abendrot* the choir of three trombones is associated with death.[38]

The proposed order of performance represents a smooth progression from lighter to heavier orchestration. The final *Im Abendrot* is the only song to employ the contrabassoon, which is needed to support the low sound-mass in the postlude properly. The contrabassoon, like the low brass, also has funereal connotations.[39] As the persona draws closer to death, the brass and timpani increase in weight and prominence. The trombones enter discreetly in *Beim Schlafengehen* and are intensified through *Ruhe, meine Seele!* and *Im Abendrot.*

Performed immediately before *Im Abendrot,* the somewhat declamatory *Ruhe, meine Seele!* has the effect of a meditative recitative before an aria. At the words "Not und Freude" in the first phrase of *Im Abendrot,* the voice picks up the unresolved G♭/F♯ that set *Not* at the climax of *Ruhe, meine Seele!* The G♭/F♯ ambiguity of the *Notmotiv* is then extended through *Im Abendrot* and resolved. The threatening timpani strokes of *Ruhe, meine Seele!* return in the orchestral introduction to *Im Abendrot* only to disappear with the final attainment of peace in the postlude.

The solo violin features in the orchestrations of *Im Abendrot, Beim Schlafengehen,* and *Ruhe, meine Seele!* Solo violin, perhaps since Beethoven, has had the connotation of the individual human soul separated from the mass of humanity, represented by the main body of strings.[40] In Strauss's song orchestrations, solo violin again represents the individual human soul. A noteworthy feature of the orchestration of *Ruhe, meine Seele!* is the division of the rising arpeggio figures between the solo violin and the harp and celesta. Examination of the Keilberth manuscript (the *Partitur*) reveals that celesta and harp were added as an afterthought ("nachgetragen zu Seite 2, II bis V Takt"). Strauss realized that there are, in fact, two entities combined in the arpeggio figure: the sunlight—represented by the "shimmering" harp and celesta—and the human soul—portrayed by solo violin—yearning upward to meet it. Harp and celesta timbrally preserve a certain objectivity and separation from the violin, as the soul ascends along the ray of light (harp and celesta) into the realm of death. The same upward yearning of the soul in death is represented by the solo violin in *Beim Schlafengehen* and *Im Abendrot.* The ever-higher melismatic rhapsodizing of the violin solo in the third stanza of *Beim Schlafengehen* depicts "die Seele unbewacht" ascending in "freien Flügen" into the "Zauberkreis der Nacht"; while the solo violin rhapsodizing at the end of the second stanza and in the third stanza of *Im Abendrot* responds to the verb "steigen." In *Im Abendrot,* the upward yearning of the solo violin represents the longing of the old couple's souls to join the two larks, represented by the high flute trills in thirds.

A study of the change in the persona through the songs in the new recommended sequence reveals a subtle increase in the number of narrative voices. In *Frühling, September, Beim Schlafengehen,* and *Ruhe, meine Seele!* the vocal line represents only one speaker, the solitude of the individual human soul; but in *Im Abendrot,* the singing voice represents a fusion of two voices, speaking of "wir." This increase from one to two voices, from the singular to the plural in *Im Abendrot,* further supports the placement of this song at the end.

If the persona of the first four songs is understood as the composer's own spiritual voice, it is only after the catharsis of *Ruhe, meine Seele!* that he is able to join his wife in death, the two voices meeting in "wir," the first word of Eichendorff's poem. The concept of "two voices in one" in *Im Abendrot* is supported by the accompaniment not only by the larks trilling in thirds but more profoundly by the parallel octaves between the outer voices in the orchestral postlude. At the beginning of the song, the lovers are united in the rich parallel thirds and sixths of life, love, and nature; but, by the postlude, they are completely fused in the one ultimate unity, the barren octaves of death.[41]

Placed before it, the anxious tone of *Ruhe, meine Seele!* sets the triumphant character of *Im Abendrot* in higher profile. Many sopranos and conductors overlook this aspect of *Im Abendrot* and perform the orchestral introduction as a depressed, Adagio funeral march. But this interpretation misreads both the mood of the song and Strauss's initial tempo indication. Strauss writes *Andante,* not *Adagio;* there must be a gradual and progressive slowing down from the opening *Andante* through the *immer langsamer* at letter G to the *rit. sehr langsam* at letter I. Furthermore, the orchestral introduction represents a fusion, a superimposition of elements of both the Andante introduction and the Adagio postlude. The polyphony of rhythmic values, faster in the strings and upper winds ("life"), and long and sustained in the brass ("death"), is only made clear at a faster tempo. As the lovers journey into the valley of death, the introduction's "life" (Andante) can then be progressively stripped away to reveal the postlude's "death" (Adagio). The orchestral version of *Ruhe, meine Seele!* can, on the other hand, be taken as slowly as Strauss's *Langsam* and his broadening of the durational values of the piano version suggest.

This examination of the connection between *Ruhe, meine Seele!* and the *Letzte Orchesterlieder* through the *Notmotiv* reveals a hitherto unknown dimension of the creative world of the late Strauss that deserves attention. In spite of serious political mistakes, the picture emerges of a man who did not lose either his self-dignity or his artistic sensitivity. Moved by suffering, not just his own, but the *Not* of Europe, which he represented through recomposition of the *Notmotiv* in the *Letzte Orchesterlieder*—Strauss the composer reacted to the times and circumstances with great compassion and sincerity. Early on,

Strauss expressed his dislike of Bruckner's music because of its religiosity, and, despite the approach of his own death, Strauss did not change his mind.[42] In these late songs, however, he does find faith: not the Christian faith of the devoutly Catholic Bruckner, but the human faith of a man who has lived, worked, and now must die. Devoid of any ulterior motives, devoid of any reference to reward or punishment, perhaps this is the purest and noblest faith a human being can attain.

APPENDIX: SECONDARY LITERATURE ON THE
Letzte Orchesterlieder

Carner, Mosco. "Strauss's Vier letzte Lieder." In *Monthly Musical Record* 80 (1950): 172–77.

Colson, William Wilder. "Four Last Songs by Richard Strauss" and "Concerto for Violoncello and Orchestra (Original Composition)." D.M.A. dissertation (vols. 1 and 2), University of Illinois at Urbana-Champaign, 1975.

Del Mar, Norman. *Richard Strauss: A Critical Commentary on His Life and Works.* 3 vols. London: Barrie and Rockliff, 1965–72.

Frank, Alan. "Strauss's Last Songs." In *Music and Letters* 31 (1950): 172–77.

Garlington, Aubrey S. "Richard Strauss's Vier letzte Lieder: The Ultimate *Opus Ultimum.*" In *Musical Quarterly* 73, no. 1 (1990): 79–93.

Hutchings, Arthur. "Strauss's Four Last Songs." In the *London Times* 91, no. 1294 (1950): 465.

Jefferson, Alan. *The Lieder of Richard Strauss.* London: Cassell, 1971.

Kohler, Stephan. "Besinnung und Abschied," program notes for a performance of the *Vier letzte Orchesterlieder* under the direction of Herbert von Karajan, 30 December 1980.

Krebs, Harald. "Alternatives to Monotonality in Early Nineteenth-Century Music." In *Journal of Music Theory* 25 (1981): 1–15.

Petersen, Barbara. "Richard Strauss in 1948–49: *Malven, September, und letzte Briefe an Maria Jeritza.*" In *Richard Strauss–Blätter* 13 (1985): 1–18.

Redlich, Hans. "Aus dem Nachlass von Richard Strauss." In *Das Musikleben* 3 (1950): 226.

Rockwell, John. "A Song by Richard Strauss Discovered." In the *New York Times* (Saturday, 15 September 1984): 1 and 11.

Rolf, Marie, and Elizabeth West Marvin. "Analytical Issues and Interpretive Decisions in Two Songs by Richard Strauss." In *Intégral* 4 (1990): 67–103.

Roth, Ernst. Introduction to the Hawkes Pocket Score of the *Vier letzte Lieder.* Hawkes Pocket Score no. 667, pp. 2–4. London, 1950.

Schuh, Willi. "Die Vier letzte Lieder von Richard Strauss." In *Schweizerische Musikzeitung* 90 (1950): 301–4.

Strickert, Elizabeth. "Richard Strauss's 'Vier letzte Lieder': An Analytical Study." Ph.D. dissertation, Washington University, 1975.

Tenschert, Roland. "Richard Strauss's Schwanengesang." In *Österreichische Musikzeitschrift* 5, nos. 10/11 (1950): 225–29.

Wanless, Susan. *Richard Strauss. Vier letzte Lieder.* Leeds: Mayflower Enterprises, 1984.

NOTES

1. This essay grew out of remarks made by Carl Schachter in a seminar on composers' autographs given at Queens College (CUNY) in the spring of 1983. Schachter presented a page of Chopin's sketches for the Mazurka in E minor, Op. 41, no. 1, and the Prelude in E minor, Op. 28, no. 4, both pieces in an early stage of the compositional process. The pieces are sketched on the same piece of manuscript paper; the Mazurka is sketched on the top four systems, the Prelude on the lower two systems. Schachter pointed out that not only were both pieces in the same key but there appeared to be a hidden motivic connection between the structure of the melodic lines. The sketches further reveal that these two melancholy pieces spring from the same compositional matrix and have a spiritual kinship with each other. It was this idea of kinship that, when I went back to some notes I had made on the two Strauss songs, alerted me to the possibility of an analogous connection between them. This project could not have been undertaken without the assistance of many people in North America and Europe. I am grateful to the late Frau Alice Strauss for permission to examine the original manuscripts in the Richard Strauss–Archiv in Garmisch. Dr. Franz Trenner (Munich) kindly arranged for me to consult Strauss documents in Garmisch and various private collections. The late Dr. Willi Schuh made a special effort to show me the *Frühling Particell* in spite of chronic illness. Special thanks must be given to the staffs of the Bayerische Staatsbibliothek, Musikabteilung, the Österreichischer National Bibliothek, Musiksammlung, the Archiv der Wiener Philharmoniker, and the Pierpont Morgan Library, who patiently brought me the many autographs, microfilms, and volumes I required. I wish to thank Frau Elisabeth Fürtwängler, Mrs. Kate Roth, Mrs. Edwin McArthur, Dr. Paul Sacher, and Dr. Norman Del Mar for replying to my inquiries. My thanks also to Frau Krüger (Zurich) and Frau Ingeborg Keilberth (Grünwald), who allowed me to consult autographs and memoirs in their possession. I gratefully acknowledge support from the following scholarly institutions: the Social Sciences and Humanities Research Council of Canada (SSHRCC), the Deutscher Akademischer Austauschdienst (DAAD), and the Österreichischer Akademischer Austauschdienst (ÖAD). Finally, I would like to thank a number of scholars who have advised me with this project: Carl Schachter, Saul Novack, Charles Burkhart, Rufus Hallmark, and Joel Lester (CUNY Graduate Center), Thomas Stoner (Connecticut College), and Bryan Gilliam (Duke University).

2. Ernst Roth, *Musik als Kunst und Ware. Betrachtungen und Begegnungen eines Musikverlegers* (Zurich: Atlantis, 1966), hereafter referred to as "German version"; translated as *The Business of Music. Reflections of a Music Publisher* (London: Faber, 1969), hereafter referred to as "English version." My translation of Roth, German version, p. 189.

3. Alan Jefferson, *The Life of Richard Strauss* (Newton Abbot: David and Charles, 1973), p. 224.

4. Willi Schuh, "Die Vier letzte Lieder von Richard Strauss," *Schweizerische Musikzeitung* 90 (1950): 301–4.

5. Alan Frank, "Strauss's Last Songs," *Music and Letters* 31 (1950): 172–77.

6. Edwin McArthur, *Kirsten Flagstad* (New York: Knopf, 1965), pp. 289–90. Unfortunately, McArthur does not provide details and his surviving wife could not add anything to his testimony. Nevertheless, McArthur documents Flagstad's presence in Zurich in January and May of 1947 and April of 1948, observing that she always stayed at her favorite hotel, the Dolder Grand, and that she sang in her "beloved" Stadttheater. It may have been during one of her Swiss sojourns that Strauss and Flagstad discussed the performance of the *Letzte Orchesterlieder.*

7. Roth, German version, p. 198.

8. The sketch "Dem Andenken Franz Schuberts" is in a sketchbook in the Bayerische Staatsbibliothek, Mus. Mss. 9986 (see Günter Brosche and Karl Dachs, eds., *Richard Strauss Autographen in München und Wien* [Tutzing: Schneider, 1979]), while the sketch "frei harmonisiert nach Beethovens Amollquartet" is in Tr. 137. Dr. Trenner's numbering of the 144 sketchbooks in the Garmisch Richard Strauss–Archiv is adopted throughout this study (see Franz Trenner, *Die Skizzenbücher von Richard Strauss aus dem Richard Strauss–Archiv in Garmisch* [Tutzing: Schneider, 1977]).

9. Hesse and Strauss met in Switzerland, as the former reports in a letter (23 June 1957) to Herbert Schulze. Strauss's admiration for Hesse's poetry did not match the poet's opinion of Strauss's music; indeed, one cannot help being reminded of Goethe's negative reaction to Schubert's settings of his poetry or of Schopenhauer's lack of enthusiam for Wagner's operas:

> I never had a strong affinity for Richard Strauss. I never heard most of his operas. For a while, in midlife, his orchestral pieces like *Don Juan* and *Eulenspiegel* amused me. Then he began to disappear from view; the celebrations for him under Hitler and his homage to him [Hitler] made him an anathema to me. I was really surprised to meet him, already very old, one day in a Swiss hotel, and he said to me that someone had given him my poems to read and he was in the process of setting some of them. The songs themselves strike me like all of Strauss's music: virtuoso, refined, full of beautiful craftsmanship, but without a deeper purpose other than themselves [*nur Selbstzweck*]. I have heard them only a few times on the radio. (Hermann Hesse, *Music: Betrachtungen, Gedichte, Rezensionen, und Briefe,* ed. Volker Michels [Frankfurt: Suhrkamp, 1986], p. 208)

10. Strauss omits the word *beide* in the *Particell* but not in the early sketch. Perhaps Strauss felt that *beide* is redundant after the very strong *wir* with which the poem opens.

11. Changed from Eichendorff's *das*; see pp. 98–99.

12. Letter to me (7 October 1984) in reply to a preliminary report of this project.

13. Barbara Petersen, *Ton und Wort: The Lieder of Richard Strauss* (Ann Arbor: UMI Research Press, 1977), p. 108

14. Not in Roth, English version; my translation of the German version, p. 192.

15. For information on the letter to Frank, see the *Werkverzeichnis*, vol. 3, pp. 1305–6.

16. The present discussion is based on personal examination of the known sources, in both public and private collections. 1. The sketch for *Ruhe, meine Seele!* is in Tr. 2. The *Stichvorlage* is in the Pierpont Morgan Library, New York, Lehman Deposit, Albrecht 1802A. The *Partitur* is in the possession of Ingeborg Keilberth, Grünwald. 2. An early sketch for the opening stanza of *Im Abendrot* is in Tr. 136, pp. 40–42. The *Particell* (four pages), now in the possession of Kate Roth (the widow of Ernst Roth), has been reproduced in facsimile (Peter Presse, Darmstadt, 1967). The *Partitur* (ten pages) is in the Richard Strauss–Archiv in Garmisch (a microfilm may be consulted in the Bayerische Staatsbibliothek). 3. The first draft of *Frühling* is in Tr. 143, pp. 2–7; the second draft is in Tr. 143, pp. 8–15. Until his death, the *Particell* (four pages) was in the possession of Willi Schuh, Zurich. Schuh kindly made a photocopy of this autograph available to me when I visited him in March 1986. The *Partitur* (eleven pages) is in the Strauss-Archiv in Garmisch (a microfilm may be consulted in the Bayerische Staatsbibliothek). 4. The first draft of *Beim Schlafengehen* is in Tr. 142, pp. 6–7, 9, 12–16. Franz Trenner in *Richard Strauss—Werkverzeichnis*, vol. 3, relying on information from Schuh, incorrectly reports the *Particell* in the possession of the heirs of Jöhr in St. Gall; an inquiry has confirmed that Jöhr never received the *Particell*, although according to Jöhr's unpublished memoirs concerning his friendship with Richard Strauss, Strauss showed Jöhr the *Particell*. It is therefore definitely known to have existed but has since vanished. Further inquiries concerning its present whereabouts were unsuccessful. The *Partitur*, however, is in the possession of Jöhr's daughter, having been given to that family by the composer's son, Franz. 5. The first draft of *September* is in Tr. 142, pp. 20–26. The autograph *Particell* for *September* along with the manuscript of *Malven* belonged to the estate of the singer Maria Jeritza. The estate was sold on 12 December 1984 at Sotheby's in New York and is now in the Pierpont Morgan Library, Lehman deposit. The *Partitur* (ten pages) is in the Strauss-Archiv in Garmisch (a microfilm may be consulted in the Bayerische Staatsbibliothek).

17. This is the kind of retrospective article that appears around the turn of the year and discusses major events of the preceding year.

18. See pp. 122–24 for my analysis of the *Im Abendrot* sketch.

19. See Willi Schuh, "Unvollendete Spätwerke von Richard Strauss, Ein kurzer Rechenschaftsbericht," *Schweizerische Musikzeitung* 90 (1950): 395.

20. Schuh, "Die Vier letzte lieder von Richard Strauss," in ibid., p. 302.

21. I came across the Jöhr memoir in the course of trying to locate the *Particell* for *Beim Schlafengehen*. The Jöhr family does not own the *Particell* (as listed in the *Werkverzeichnis* and reported by all subsequent authors); however, the family did receive the *Partitur*. Before he died, Jöhr, a prominent and highly cultured banker, wrote his memoirs and presented them to his children as a gift.

22. Strauss was also deeply grateful to Jöhr for looking after his financial affairs.

23. The bass displacement represents "rootlessness"; see p. 118.

24. See Charlotte E. Erwin, "Richard Strauss's Presketch Planning for *Ariadne auf Naxos*," *Musical Quarterly* 67, no. 3 (1981): 348–65; Bryan Gilliam, "Strauss's Preliminary Opera Sketches: Thematic Fragments and Symphonic Continuity," *19th-Century Music* 9, no. 3 (1986): 176–88; and his *Richard Strauss: "Elektra"* (Oxford: Oxford University Press, 1991), especially chap. 4, "*Elektra*: Summary of the Tonal Structure," pp. 67–74. See also Derrick Puffett, "'Lass Er die Musi, wo sie ist': Pitch Specificity in Strauss," pp. 138–63, here.

25. For a detailed discussion of the *Notmotiv* in all five songs, see Timothy L. Jackson, "The Last Strauss: Studies of the *Letzte Lieder*" (Ph.D. dissertation, the Graduate Center of the City University of New York, 1988). The *Notmotiv* also has a durational aspect: in all five songs, it is associated with durational expansion.

26. The measure-number references in this article are to the orchestral, not the piano-vocal, version of *Ruhe, meine Seele!* Notice that Strauss expands the setting of *Not* from one measure (piano-vocal version, measure 30) to two measures (orchestral version, measures 32–33).

27. Norman Del Mar, *Richard Strauss: A Critical Commentary on His Life and Works*, 3 vols. (London: Barrie and Rockliff, 1965–72), vol. 1, p. 81.

28. In Schenkerian terms, the descending *Urlinie* from $\hat{5}$.

29. Mosco Carner, "Strauss's Vier letzte Lieder," *Monthly Musical Record* 80 (1950): 177.

30. A pedestrian "common sense" interpretation reads a large-scale arpeggiation: I (first stanza, measures 20–35)–♭III (second stanza, measures 36–45)–V (third stanza, measures 46–60). According to this interpretation, the beginning of each stanza coincides with the beginning of a new prolongation. In my view, however, this reading obscures Strauss's subtle overlap between harmony and poetic design in the third stanza. In my analysis, the beginning of the third stanza is harmonically bridged over: the dominant in measure 46 (at the beginning of the third stanza) is not a fundamental harmony, but rather leads to the minor tonic in measure 50 (in the middle of the stanza), which *is* a fundamental harmony (since it connects with the initial tonic, measure 20). According to the "common sense" reading, the renotation of G♭ minor as F♯ minor in measure 39 is simply a matter of no-

tational convenience. I suggest that this turn to F♯ minor has motivic significance beyond notational convenience: by hearing the enharmonic transformation of G♭ into F♯ in measures 36–39 caught within tonic prolongation, this transformation is heard within an enlargement of the *Notmotiv.*

31. Later, in the *Particell,* Strauss restores *wir* but omits *beide* (see the discussion of the poem).

32. Notice, however, that a motion from E♭ major to D major controls the setting of the first three stanzas (measures 20–52, Example 3) and the last stanza (measures 61–72).

33. The D-major triads containing F♯ at the words *sind* and especially *Not* in measures 5–6 of the sketch are marked by sforzandi. These sforzandi in the sketch become the sforzando on G♭ in the final version of the postlude (measure 68). This sforzando emphasizing the G♭ equals F♯ enharmonic transformation within the *Notmotiv* is, in turn, associated with the great crescendo on the climactic f♯^{2} at *Not* in *Ruhe, meine Seele!* (measures 32–33).

34. An important statement by Strauss on his creative process can be found in Richard Strauss, *Betrachtungen und Erinnerungen,* ed. Willi Schuh (Zurich: Atlantis, 1981), p. 165: "A motive or a two- to four-measure melodic phrase occurs to me directly. I set it down on paper and immediately expand it to an eight-, sixteen-, or thirty-two-measure phrase, which naturally does not remain unmodified but, after a shorter or longer setting-aside, is gradually worked into the final form, which then must withstand the most strenuous self-criticism. This work progresses in such a way, that it comes to the innermost stage [*Linie*] to wait for the time when imagination is capable and ready to help me further. But the readiness is mostly evoked and facilitated by a great compulsion, after long reflection, also . . . deep excitement (even rage and anger). This spiritual process belongs not only to the realm of inborn talent but to self-criticism and self-development. 'Genius is hard work,' Goethe is supposed to have said. But industriousness and the desire to work is inborn and not only instilled." The kind of rhythmic expansion Strauss mentions can be observed in the drafts for *Frühling* (see Timothy L. Jackson, "The Last Strauss," pp. 126–32). Strauss speaks of developing a composition to that stage [*Linie*] at which "imagination" or, perhaps better, inspiration is able to carry him further. Evidence of this process of halting and waiting for inspiration can be seen in the genesis of large works such as the *Metamorphosen* (see Timothy L. Jackson, "The Metamorphosis of the *Metamorphosen,*" in *Richard Strauss: New Perspectives on His Life and Work,* ed. Bryan Gilliam (Durham, N.C.: Duke University Press, 1992). The great emotions, including "rage and anger," are borne out by some of Strauss's verbal exclamations entered in the manuscripts. In *Begegnung mit Richard Strauss* (Vienna and Munich: Doblinger, 1964), p. 33, the conductor Karl Böhm prefaces his own quotation of Strauss's statement with several provocative remarks: "Strauss seldom expressed himself concerning his own creative process. This is natural, while the process takes place in the realm of the unconscious, uncontrolled by reason. Nevertheless, the master often spoke with me about this impor-

tant question and later also put his ideas into writing." Böhm's prefacing statement that "the creative process takes place in the realm of the unconscious, uncontrolled by reason" is not in accord with Strauss's statement. Strauss never relegates the creative process entirely to the unconscious; on the contrary, his description contains words that suggest conscious effort: "self-criticism," "long reflection," and "hard work."

35. Oswald Jonas, "Bewusstes oder unbewusstes Schaffen," *Der Dreiklang* 2 (1937): 54.

36. Ibid., p. 55.

37. Douglas Johnson, "Beethoven Scholars and Beethoven's Sketches," *19th-Century Music* 2 (1978): 13.

38. The trombone and trumpet fanfares, which Strauss adds to the beginning of *Ich liebe dich*, are not simply "lusty," as one writer describes them (Alan Jefferson, *The Lieder of Richard Strauss* [London: Cassell, 1971]); they also have eschatological connotations. The melodic use of trombones at the phrase "mit dir durch die Gassen in Armut und Schande!" carries special significance under the circumstances.

39. See, for example, the instrumentation of Mozart's *Mauerische Trauermusik*, KV 477 (479a).

40. Strauss's *Morgen* (Op. 27, no. 4), orchestrated in 1897 for Pauline, provides an eloquent example of his earlier use of solo violin to evoke the human soul. (The Op. 27 songs—including *Ruhe, meine Seele!*—were Richard's wedding gift to Pauline; as such, they continued to have a special significance for the Strausses long after Pauline retired.) In *Morgen*, the solo violin represents the lovers' souls in blissful communion; at the point where the souls are struck "dumb," the solo violin ceases to speak. A further interesting use of the solo violin may be seen in the 1906 orchestration of Strauss's only overtly religious song, the setting of Heine's *Die heiligen drei Könige aus Morgenland*, dedicated to the composer's mother. The song opens with divided lower strings, muted, which depict the darkness of the night in which the three kings journey toward Bethlehem. Solo C-major trumpet, already indicated in the sketches, represents the triumphant Saviour. In the orchestral postlude, just at the point where the voice melismatically fades out, solo violin enters, transforming verbal into nonverbal "singing" of the individual soul.

41. See Timothy L. Jackson, "Richard Strauss's *Winterweihe*—An Analysis and Study of the Sketches," *Richard Strauss–Blätter* 17 (1987): 28–69, for a discussion of Strauss's use of parallel sixths to represent two people in love.

42. Strauss's antipathy toward Bruckner never softened, as is revealed by an ironic reference to "Brucknerscher Orgelruhe" in the letter to Böhm concerning the *Metamorphosen* (see Jackson, "The Metamorphosis of the *Metamorphosen*").

"Lass Er die Musi, wo sie ist":

Pitch Specificity in Strauss

DERRICK PUFFETT

BARON:	Was will die Musi? Hab' sie nicht bestellt.
WIRT:	Schaffen vielleicht, dass man sie näher hört.
	Im Vorsaal da is Tafelmusi!
BARON:	Lass Er die Musi, wo sie ist.
BARON:	What's the music for? I didn't order it.
LANDLORD:	Perhaps you'd like to hear it closer?
	In the foyer there . . . it's table-music!
BARON:	Leave the music where it is.[1]

This essay is concerned with a topic that may seem narrow but actually has the most wide-ranging implications. In works employing a leitmotivic technique—usually dramatic works—under what conditions does Strauss decide to restate his musical material at the original pitch rather than in a transposed form?[2] How is the material adapted, if it is adapted, to suit its new context, and what effect does it have on its new environment? How is Strauss's practice in this regard related to his conception of the leitmotif in general, and to his ideas about key association and musical characterization? What is the relationship between such fixed-pitch references and the large-scale tonal plan? And to what extent does Strauss's practice vary over the years?

Most of these questions can only be posed, not answered, here. For a study of this sort to be authoritative it would need to be comprehensive: that is, it should consider *all* the leitmotifs in *all* the dramatic works (this naturally begs the question "what is a leitmotif?"), answering *all* the questions as fully and rigorously as possible. Since comprehensiveness is not possible in this essay, rather than aim at a pseudocomprehensiveness I prefer to err on the speculative side and broaden the discussion to include nondramatic works in those cases where Strauss's thematic and motivic usage seems to be influenced by leitmotivic technique.

· 138 ·

In a chapter entitled *"Salome* as Music Drama" in the Cambridge Opera Handbook devoted to that work,[3] I attempted to define as accurately as possible Strauss's leitmotivic technique in *Salome*—which admittedly turns out to be something of an extreme point, in at least two respects (the number of pitch-specific motives used and the subtlety with which the pitch-specific property of the motive is integrated into the drama) where Strauss's leitmotivic practice is concerned. Strauss's *conception* of the leitmotif I described as "simplistic," inasmuch as it seems to derive from the kind of Wagner analysis (fashionable at the turn of the century and still prevalent in some quarters) that assigns a specific extramusical meaning to each motive. That Strauss himself saw the leitmotif in this way is suggested by his sketches, which in the case of *Salome* list motives under such designations as "Salome," "Herod's covetousness," "the death sentence," and so on.[4] When we turn to the works themselves we find that Strauss's *practice* is more complex than his attitude leads us to expect. His practice may be characterized as "progressive" in the sense that each recurrence of a motive tends to take us farther and farther away from the definitive statement; that there is usually a definitive statement is consistent with his simplistic idea of the motive and is one of the qualities that distinguish his use of the motive from Wagner's.[5] In the process of varying a motive, pitch is naturally a crucial factor: as in Wagner, a motive may be varied by being transposed. It follows that pitch is also a crucial factor in defining the identity of a motive in those cases where it is *not* transposed (or, to be more precise—since transposition is rarely excluded altogether—where the motive is varied rhythmically or in some other way). Motives that adhere to a particular pitch level may be termed "pitch-specific."

Two significant examples are discussed in my *Salome* chapter. The first is Narraboth's motive, which clings to its original pitches at almost every one of its appearances except toward the end of scene 3, when (to suggest his anguish at the sight of Salome trying to seduce Jochanaan) it is heard in several different transpositions, reverting to its original pitch, however, at the moment when Narraboth kills himself—a rhetorical device of supreme dramatic power. The second is the Salome motive from the beginning of the opera, which, though not always confined to its original pitches, continually subjects those pitches to diatonic and enharmonic reinterpretation, most notably when Salome is given the Baptist's head.[6] In both cases the pitch-specific quality of the motive is made the means of achieving a powerful dramatic effect—Narraboth's obsessive love for Salome and Salome's intransigence are dramatic forces that can be effectively expressed through the ostinato-like reiteration of particular pitches—and in both cases the return of the motive to its original form after all the intervening transpositions and reharmonizations has *formal* ramifications that bear on the organization of the work as a whole.

I

One way of approaching this topic is through Strauss's use of quotation.[7] As an inveterate quoter of his own and other people's music Strauss can be counted on to preserve the original pitch of his quoted material wherever possible—and for an obvious reason: the pitch is an essential part of its identity (or at least it was considered so by Strauss). Thus in the song "Hochzeitlich Lied," Op. 37, no. 6 (1898), for instance, where he quotes the Venus motive from Wagner's *Tannhäuser,* he does so at the original pitch, that is, in F♯ major.[8] Since the key of the song is D♭ this presents no problem, F♯ (= G♭) being in a simple subdominant relation to it, though it is significant that Strauss writes out the quotation in sharps, not flats. The chord supporting the first note of the quotation, C♯, is a characteristic Straussian $^6_4$, and Strauss approaches it via an augmented sixth. The second (and last) chord of the quotation is a diminished seventh, which enables the composer to leave F♯ as smoothly as he entered it. These hackneyed chords, for which Strauss has often been criticized, are in fact an essential part of his vocabulary: they allow him to move in and out of his "quoted" keys (or the keys implied by his leitmotifs) with minimum fuss.[9] More interesting is the tonal-harmonic function of the quotation (its "meaning" is clear enough), which seems to be to highlight the note A. This note has acted as a harmonic irritant since the opening bar, causing the unusual juxtaposition of D♭ major and a dominant seventh of B♭ minor, and it is into the latter chord that the diminished seventh is transformed (one can hardly speak of a resolution) as we reach the end of the quotation (Example 1). From this chord Strauss can easily return to D♭.

The many quotations from Strauss's and other composers' works in the song cycle *Krämerspiegel* (1918) are nearly all at the original pitch, though not the quotation from *Tod und Verklärung* (no. 8, bars 76–77), which, however, uses the same D major as it does thirty years later when it reappears in the *Four Last Songs*. In most cases the tonal relationship between quotation and surrounding material is simple and not interesting enough for comment. The same applies to the later song "Zugemessne Rhythmen" (1935), in which the humorous

Example 1. Quotation of the Venus motive from Wagner's *Tannhäuser* in "Hochzeitlich Lied," Op. 37, no. 6

quotations from Brahms's First Symphony, *Tod und Verklärung* (this time in the "right" key),[10] and Wagner's *Die Meistersinger* are easily absorbed into the prevailing C major.

Things are not quite so simple when Strauss quotes two or more passages in different keys, both of which he wishes to preserve in the new context. The locus classicus for this is of course the "Hero's Works of Peace" section in *Ein Heldenleben*. Here Strauss quotes from nine of his previous works; it is hard to be sure of the exact number of quotations,[11] since in addition to the obvious references there are a few subliminal ones,[12] but there are at least thirty-three, of which about two thirds retain the original pitch.[13] Now, so long as successive quotations are in the same key, as is the case with the first three references to *Don Quixote,* there is no problem. However, when Strauss juxtaposes passages that were formerly in different keys, his desire to maintain the original pitch levels can lead to awkward results. The first reference to *Don Juan,* for instance (see n. 13), invokes a theme that was originally accompanied by $^6_4$ harmony: hence, E major over a B pedal for what is now fig. 83/5, B major for fig. 83/6, and E major for fig. 83/7. But Strauss's desire to have a B-major chord at fig. 83/7 (so that the second reference to *Don Juan* and the quotation from *Also sprach Zarathustra* can be in their original keys), coupled with the fact that he has approached the first reference to *Don Juan* via the dominant of G major, leads him to change the order of the chords in the progression: hence, B major for fig. 83/5, E major for fig. 83/6, and B major (prepared by an applied dominant on the second half of fig. 83/6) for fig. 83/7. This works well enough for fig. 83/5 but leaves the F♯ on the second beat of fig. 83/6 high and dry: formerly a chord note, with the previous G♯ acting as appoggiatura, it is now reduced to the role of a dissonant passing note without resolution (Example 2).

Example 2. Successive references to *Don Juan* and *Also sprach Zarathustra* in the "Hero's Works of Peace" section of *Ein Heldenleben*

A second example of unsuccessful juxtaposition occurs at fig. 87. Here Strauss combines two themes from *Tod und Verklärung,* one originally in C major (the "ideology" theme in the bass) and the other originally in G. Strauss has to settle for one or the other and opts for G major, with a cadence onto a triad of G at fig. 87 itself. This leaves the note C in the bass unaccounted for. In the original (C-major) context, C is naturally understood as the first note of a third-progression, C–D–E, which reduces to the consonant interval of a third at the middleground. Here, however, it is the interval G–D that is consonant, leaving the C to be explained as—what? Another passing note? But then it would have to come from a B (Example 3).

[reduction]
fig. 86/6   fig. 87

Example 3. Juxtaposition of two themes from *Tod und Verklärung* in the "Hero's Works of Peace" section of *Ein Heldenleben*

The F♮s in the two quotations from *Till Eulenspiegel* (fig. 88/3–4) prompt no more than a momentary shudder, though one can imagine what Schenker would have said.[14] But it is hard to understand the clash of A♮ (clarinet 1) and A♭ (trombone 3) at fig. 89/4; again, this seems to be caused by Strauss's desire to retain the original pitch levels of the two themes in question (the clarinet is referring to an earlier passage in *Heldenleben,* probably the music of the second violins at fig. 3/5, though if Strauss had gone back a bit farther, to fig. 3 itself, he would have found the same music in D♭). The clash of I and V in G♭ major (figs. 91/4, cellos and violins; and 91/7, horns 3–4 and violins) is also a little hard to take, though here all the themes concerned are actually in the same key.

It may seem pedantic, even ridiculous, to chastise Strauss for "mistakes" of harmony or voice leading that he could obviously have corrected if he had wanted to, especially since they occur in a work written at the very end of the nineteenth century. Tethys Carpenter, discussing *Elektra,* claims that "it makes no difference if there are, briefly, a few 'wrong' notes in his voice leading."[15] But if one believes in critical evaluation one has to respond that, on the contrary, it is just this sort of thing that makes *all* the difference—between a first-rate composer such as Wagner, say, and the kind of "first-class second-rate composer" that Strauss knew himself to be.[16] Theodor Adorno once took Strauss to task for his cavalier regard for detail, citing as an example two notes in the opening theme of *Heldenleben.*[17] Though I would not necessarily choose this particular example, I would agree that one does not find in Strauss the same "inevitable" relationship between detail and whole, the small and the large, that one finds in the very greatest composers. The kind of scrape he gets himself into, again and again, in the "Hero's Works of Peace" section is a good example of what I mean. Such problems are in many cases, as I have shown, a direct result of his insistence upon quoting material at the original pitch level.

The same insistence is evident in the Wagner quotations in *Feuersnot*. Here the Valhalla motive from *The Ring* and the opening horn call of *The Flying Dutchman* are given in their original keys (Db major and D minor respectively), as is the quotation from Strauss's own *Guntram* (the "war" motive in C minor) a little later.[18] These quotations are skillfully absorbed into their new environment, as a result of a circle-of-fifths progression (Eb–Ab–Db, the last being treated as bII of C minor, the new context) in the first case, the use of blunt unisons in the second and an enharmonically reinterpreted diminished-seventh chord in the third. The quotations from Wagner and (once again) Strauss in the *Bourgeois Gentilhomme* music are, if anything, even more ingenious. References (in no. 9, "Das Diner") to "Rhine salmon" and "saddle of lamb" evoke quotations of the Rhine motive from *The Ring* (first in A minor and then in its native Eb major, the latter followed by an abrupt shift to V of the prevailing A minor) and of Don Quixote's sheep (the C–C#–D clusters, within an extended F# minor, resolving neatly onto a dominant seventh of G—see Example 4).

But perhaps the most marvelous of these passages involving quotation, in subtlety almost rivaling Wagner himself, is the quotation from *Tristan* in *Ariadne auf Naxos*. The Tristan chord (suggested by the reference to Circe's "magic drink") is quoted once at its original pitch, but it is prepared by two previous statements, each a major third higher than the next. This interval of transposition is obscured by the semitonal voice leading, with each chord blending perfectly into the next; and the whole passage is unified by a B pedal in the bass (part of a middleground I–V arpeggiation in E major), which is reinterpreted as Cb at the moment when the Tristan chord sounds at its original pitch (fig. 202) before being reinterpreted once again as B, V of E (Example 5). There is no cadence; the arrival at V is followed by a liquidation of the melody (fig. 203/5ff.), which ensures that the quotation is left behind as gradually as it is reached.

The numerous opera quotations in *Intermezzo, Die schweigsame Frau,* and *Capriccio* adhere to the original pitches so far as the constraints of the individual passage allow. Thus in the second little cluster of quotations in *Die schweigsame Frau* (act 1, fig. 86) the *Rigoletto* quartet is cited at its original pitch (Db major), as is Barak's "Mir anvertraut" from *Die Frau ohne Schatten* (also in Db); but "La donna è mobile" is

Example 4. Quotation of Don Quixote's sheep in the *Bourgeois Gentilhomme* music

transposed (to D♭ from B). No doubt the interval of a tone between the two original keys would have presented problems. For a similar reason, although the interval is different, the quotation from *Tod und Verklärung* in the *Four Last Songs* is transposed from C to D, as has already been mentioned. But the reference to the slow movement of the *Eroica* Symphony in *Metamorphosen* is of course at the original pitch (C minor). Norman Del Mar quotes a sketch for *München: Ein Gedächtniswalzer* showing an early G-minor version of the theme later used in *Metamorphosen*.[19] One is bound to ask which came first, the decision to transpose it to C minor or the idea of quoting from the *Eroica*? But this is a chicken-and-egg problem that probably cannot be solved. A more interesting question concerns the point at which Strauss decided to end *Metamorphosen* in C minor. If the quotation

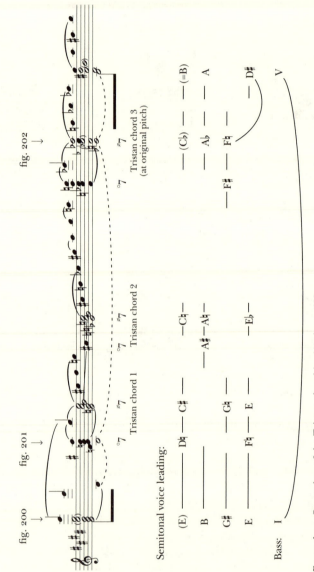

Example 5. Quotation of the Tristan chord in *Ariadne auf Naxos*

only suggested itself during the process of composition, as Strauss himself maintained, it is a remarkable coincidence that C minor is prepared as early as bars 7–10. Or did Strauss rewrite the opening of the piece after deciding on a C-minor ending?[20]

II

Before launching into a consideration of Strauss's leitmotivic practice, it is worth spending a moment on the tone poems. It is obvious that his thematic usage in *Also sprach Zarathustra,* for example, is heavily dependent on the leitmotif: the way that individual themes stick to specific keys (nature = C major; the mind of man = B major/minor), the strongly characterized nature of the themes themselves, and the symbolic way in which keys are played off against each other[21] are all closely related to Wagnerian practice. It would be idle to suggest that Strauss is either more or less consistent than Wagner in these respects; both composers' works show a great variety of treatment. However, there is an element of the systematic in the younger Richard's work—an effect of his "simplistic" view of the leitmotif, no doubt—which is foreign to Wagner, the great pragmatist, and which places Strauss firmly in the company of Schoenberg, Scriabin, and others of their generation.

A simple example of this is the organization of keys in the *Symphonia Domestica:* F major for father, B major for mother, and D major (symmetrically dividing the tritone) for baby.[22] A more interesting one is the tendency of themes—the opening melodic gestures of *Till Eulenspiegel* and *Don Quixote,* for example—to be conceived as merely a succession of pitches, without harmony or rhythm (certain harmonizations may be *implied*), a tendency that has more than a little in common with twelve-tone technique.[23] Even Wagner never thought of themes as abstract, de-rhythmized note successions. Strauss seems to be thinking in terms of transformation from the outset: as the "bare bones" of his themes are fleshed out with one harmonization, one rhythmic structure, after another, so his themes can take on any expressive character he wishes. The importance of fixed pitch in all this (and here the difference between Strauss, a committed tonal composer, and the dodecaphonists is most obvious) is that certain effects become possible only when conceived against a background of what might be called tonal invariance. One reason why *Don Quixote* is cast as a set of variations is that the regular recurrence of the same pitch material gives Strauss the opportunity to reexamine and reinterpret it constantly in the light of his changing expressive needs (the Don's different adventures).

In the introduction, for example,[24] he sets the opening theme against itself in two different keys—D minor and D♭ major—simultaneously, the idea presumably being to offer two opposing interpretations of the note F, as minor and major third respectively. A few bars later the same move is repeated but with the final F (formerly associated with the D-minor version of the theme) altered to F♯. This in turn sets up an opposition between F♯ and F, the goal notes of the two statements and the pitches associated throughout the work with the characters Don Quixote and Sancho Panza. The two pitches are successively tonicized in Variation 3—which gives a new twist to the opposition already established between D major and D minor. Strauss's practice here is very close to opera. And if his operas have sometimes been described as symphonic poems with voice parts added, it can also be said that the symphonic poems cry out for the extra dramatic dimension provided by living and breathing characters on a stage.

III

To the operas, finally. *Feuersnot* has two themes that cling to their original pitches: the children's "Maja maja maja mö!"—which is always heard in D major[25] and usually approached from it, except on one occasion when it is approached from A♭ (fig. 126/4: the augmented-sixth chord is brought once more into service here)—and, more interestingly, the five-note motive associated with Kunrad. Actually this should perhaps be described as a *six*-note motive, since, on its earliest appearances at least, it is stated against the background of a pedal F♯. In this form, which implies the dominant of B minor, it is restated at fig. 21. After an expressive transposition (and rhythmic transformation) at fig. 22, it reverts to its original pitch level, though transferred up two octaves, at fig. 23/3. The point about this last version is that it is harmonized with a dominant seventh of A minor (A minor rather than major because of the F♮s), though the continuation (B♯–C♯ on the word "stinkts") enforces an A-major resolution. So the F♯ has to go, leaving the motive in its familiar five-note state. This version is reharmonized again (F minor leading to A major) at fig. 24, before its liquidation on the next page of vocal score. At fig. 26/9 it is reharmonized yet again with a diminished seventh that implies D minor, though this is reinterpreted enharmonically so as to resolve in B minor; at fig. 29/2 it is supported by V of E; at fig. 31 it is absorbed into a new diminished seventh, one on D♯ (the F♯ is temporarily reinstated here, giving F the status of a passing note); and from fig. 32 onward it is subjected to a whole host of fresh interpretations—alternating diminished sevenths on G♯ and A♯ (fig. 32/5–6), diminished sevenths on G♯ alternating with dominant sevenths on C♯ (fig. 33), V of C going to V of F minor (fig. 34), B minor with a flatted fifth (fig. 36/8), F♯ minor (fig. 38/4), V of B major (fig. 39/ 11), and so on—while generally adhering to the original pitch level. Of course there are exceptions: the motive is occasionally transposed. But what most impresses about Strauss's development of the motive is the obstinate, well-nigh obsessive way in which he works out the implications of his chosen pitches, turning the motive over and over at its original pitch level like a dog chewing a bone. The statements at fig. 54/2 (B major, the F♯ once again reinstated) and fig. 57/11 (B♭ minor!) are especially remarkable.[26] One could go through the whole opera like this. Admiration for virtuoso technique is tempered only by the thought that Strauss seems to have found no wider resonance for his material, such as he does in some of his later operas. F♯ is rarely tonicized, for example (though the emergence of F♯ minor at the beginning of the climactic interlude—fig. 220—is both apposite and striking), so that the possibility of interaction between motive and large-scale tonal structure, or between motive and characterization, is hardly explored. Instead the various statements of the motive, transposed and untransposed, are strung out like pearls on a string.[27]

Passages from *Salome*, perhaps Strauss's greatest achievement in this field, have already been discussed. The essential point is that the keys associated with particular motives (which in turn tend to be associated with characters in the opera) are also fundamental to the large-scale organization of the work, thus bringing about precisely the sort of integration that *Feuersnot* lacked. The fact that the opera ends in C minor cannot be separated from the fact that C minor is the key associated with the "death sentence" motive (which rings out as Herod orders his guards to "kill that woman!"); the pitch C is also associated with Herod himself, whose ambiguous C-minor/major/whole-tone harmony has been set up in opposition to Salome's C♯ ever since his first entrance.[28] Salome's C♯, present since the very beginning of the opera (where it is introduced by her largely pitch-specific motive), is tonicized with overwhelming force in the interlude following her encounter with Jochanaan, recalled briefly during the Dance of the Seven Veils and made the starting point and conclusion of her final monologue, which effects the same progression from C♯ minor to C♯ major as does the work as a whole up to this point. (The C-minor ending is as startling as it is abrupt.) Operating alongside or within these large-scale tonal processes are tonal associations or references of a more local kind, such as the E♭ minor associated with the cistern and the D minor of the Jews. These provide the basis for self-contained sections, or "set pieces," such as the Jews' squabble, which play the role of scherzo in Strauss's one-movement dramatic symphony. The motives of the cistern and the Jews, in fact, together with the C-minor "death sentence" motive, are the only motives that are pitch-specific in a strict sense. Motives confined *exclusively* to one pitch level are rare, in *Salome* as in the later operas; even Narraboth's motive wanders to other levels, though it is later restored to its original pitch, as we have seen, with supreme dramatic force.

The association of motives with particular pitch levels (one cannot always say they are associated with particular *keys,* such is the nature of the musical language of the work[29]) leads to passages of great instability, and even to momentary bitonality, as motives are rapidly juxtaposed with, and sometimes superimposed upon, one another (Example 6).[30] Obviously this is a major contributory factor where the "neurotic," highly fragmented style of the work is concerned. Yet it can also be said that such motives, in clinging to their original pitch levels, have a *stabilizing* effect, providing so many reference points or islands of safety within the sea of chromatic flux. Perhaps this is how Strauss thought of them. After all, so many occurrences of C♯ minor (or D minor, or whatever) *almost* add up to an all-embracing tonic. And Strauss was never one to abandon the security of tonality altogether.

This being the case, it is perhaps surprising that *Elektra* does not make more use of pitch-specific motives. There *are* such motives, as I have written elsewhere,[31] but their effect on the large scale is curiously perfunctory. As in *Salome,* there are clearly defined associations between keys and characters (Chrysothemis and E♭ major, for example), but these associations are rarely articulated by motivic means. Rather, each character has a pool of more or less sharply defined material (more in the case of Elektra, with her famous chord; less in the case of Orestes), which may be drawn upon to provide long melodies as well as terse motives. That these melodies are sometimes depressingly undistinguished, by comparison with those in *Salome* on the one hand and *Der Rosenkavalier* on the other, is one reason why characters like Orestes and Chrysothemis hardly seem to come to life. More vital by far is the dissipated Klytämnestra with her stock of short,

Example 6. Interplay of pitch levels in *Salome*

memorable motives. As in *Salome,* again, there are passages in which
the rapid juxtaposition of motives (pitch-specific or not) produces a
highly fragmented effect. The passages beginning at figs. 136/2 and

181 (the latter extending through to fig. 186) are good examples. When the material is impressive, as it is here—really unpleasant characters always bring out the best in Strauss—the density of the musical argument, with almost every note throbbing with extramusical meaning, recalls Wagner. Elsewhere it is Stravinsky who is recalled, or rather anticipated, in the blocklike construction, the unexpected juxtapositions and oppositions, the importance of rhythm and register in defining the musical material.

Strangely enough it is Stravinsky, too, who is recalled (though the comparison would not have been to his pleasure) in *Rosenkavalier*. The string of waltzes near the beginning of act 3 (fig. 27ff.), often offset and accompanied by contrasting material—trilling woodwind for the lighted candles, a stolid $\frac{4}{4}$ for Ochs—seems in its disconnected (Adorno would have said "alienated") way to anticipate *The Rite of Spring*. The point should not be labored, however. In other respects, most notably in its handling of pitch-specific material, the work recalls *Salome*. Of many wonderful examples only a few can be mentioned. The first four-bar phrase of the prelude—horns answered by strings—sets up an opposition between sharps and flats (mediated by the enharmonic change of G♯ to A♭) that is worked out in more specific terms (E major versus E♭) in the opening scene, the dialogue between Octavian and the Marschallin, and then in the later exchange between them. It would be too schematic to say that each of these characters is associated with a particular key, though there is a certain amount of truth in this (why else should there be a sudden surge of E♭ major when the Marschallin enters in act 3?).[32] Rather, the music moves with the ebb and flow of emotion, touching on one key and then another in such a way that it is sometimes Octavian who sings in E, sometimes the Marschallin (and similarly with E♭). At times a third key is introduced, F major, associated with the Feldmarschall. The dialectic between these keys, and between the themes associated with them, reflects the interplay between the characters (and acts as a metaphor for it) without having to resort to a rigid system of correspondences: often it is the theme, rather than the character, that seems to recall the key, or the key that recalls the theme. A passage like that beginning at fig. 72, or (a little later) stretching from fig. 108/3 to Fig. 109/3 (Example 7), is wonderfully subtle and allusive.

The richness of harmonic relations that distinguishes this work is possible only because theme, key association, and musical characterization are in perfect balance. When the prelude to act 2 moves vertiginously from D minor (as minor dominant of G major) to D♭, with

Example 7. Interplay of key areas in *Der Rosenkavalier*

(Baron setzt sich zögernd und bemüht sich, der hübschen Zofe nicht völlig den Rücken zu kehren)

Example 7, cont.

one of Strauss's ubiquitous diminished sevenths serving as the only link between them, the modulation is not only thrilling in itself because it is "dangerous"—only Strauss could get away with it—but also meaningful in ways that have become familiar to us. The theme with the falling seventh sets up resonances with similar themes earlier in the opera—the Marschallin's E-major theme from act 1, fig. 8 (and especially fig. 327ff.), where the seventh falls from $\hat{3}$ to lower $\hat{4}$, her G-minor theme from fig. 307 ($\hat{3}$ to lower $\hat{4}$ again but in the minor; the effect is quite different), and Octavian's E♭-major melody from fig. 314 ($\hat{5}$ to lower $\hat{6}$)—but what is even more striking is the D♭-major sonority, which has long been associated with Ochs. We have even had him associated with this theme before, in the middle of the levée scene (fig. 243/3), where it symbolizes his marital aspirations and what he hopes to get from the house of Faninal. So theme, key, and character combine to create a nexus of meanings that exists quite separately from the immediate, short-term effect of the modulation itself, which, rather, suggests the excitement and bustle *chez* Faninal just before the arrival of the Rose Cavalier.

One other pitch-specific theme in this opera must not go unmentioned: that of the Silver Rose. This theme spreads its aura of G♭ major around everything it touches, starting with brief references (act 1, fig. 113) and gradually becoming more explicit (figs. 129 and 264/4).[33] When we come to the Presentation of the Silver Rose itself (act 2, fig. 24/3), G♭ major is rewritten as F♯! Thereafter the theme can take either form, sharp or flat (and be transposed to other pitch levels, as at fig. 56).

Nothing in the later operas can match this. The Prologue to *Ariadne*—written after the rest of the work, of course—delights with its rapid juxtaposition of characterizing themes and keys. Even within the little overture, pitch-specific material—the F-major music of the clowns at fig. 3, the D-minor music at fig. 4, and the D♭ $^6_4$ at fig. 4/ 4, not to mention the C major of the Composer at the very beginning—is being established. These themes and motives often succeed one another by means of an interrupted cadence, which becomes almost a motive (or an in-joke) in itself. After the overture the characters introduce themselves (as Tenor, Prima Donna, and so on) with the themes they are associated with in the opera. Sometimes the succession of ideas and keys is kaleidoscopic: the juxtaposition of B♭ major (Ariadne's *Bote*) and E major (Zerbinetta) via an augmented sixth of A at fig. 65/3–5, the passage from D♭ (death) through A (= B♭♭, the "interrupted cadence" progression again) and V of F♯ minor (these last two keys being associated with Bacchus) to D as V of G minor (Ariadne) between figs. 79 and 81, or the progression from C♯ minor (= D♭ again) through A (another interrupted cadence) and D♭ proper to B (the nearest we can get to E, for Zerbinetta), C, and D♭ between figs. 85 and 88. The only thing that disappoints is the quality of the thematic material, which is not always very good.

This is also a problem (and by no means the only one) in *Die Frau ohne Schatten*. The few pitch-specific motives—those associated with Keikobad, the falcon, and the talisman—tend to get lost in the welter of busy, rather anonymous invention; some of the best ideas (such as Barak's "Mir anvertraut") are not strictly motivic. The key symbolism is as confused and confusing as Hofmannthal's psychologizing. On the other hand, there are some ideas, such as the shadow motive, that are really distinctive, but this is largely because of their unusual sonority (in this case, a mixture of seconds and fourths, emphasized by the deliberately weird orchestration). The parts are decidedly more attractive than the whole.

Curiously enough, this is the direction in which the later operas seem to go, though mercifully there is nothing quite like *Die Frau ohne Schatten*. From *Intermezzo* onward Strauss appears to be losing interest in pitch-specific motives.[34] Perhaps he felt that with the simpler, more diatonic harmony of these works (Strauss's harmonic evolution is of considerable interest in itself) there was no need for the stabilizing effect the technique offered. Instead we find him experimenting with new types of harmony, especially sonorities involving the interval of a fourth. This can be combined with seconds (as in the shadow motive of *Die Frau ohne Schatten*), thirds (as in the music associated with Baron Lummer in *Intermezzo;* music of this kind had already been anticipated in *Ariadne*), or more fourths (as in the Apollo motive from *Daphne*); there is also the dreaded cacophony of the parrot—cluster harmony as well as fourths—in *Die schweigsame Frau*.[35] It is idle to look for connections with Hindemith or other fourth-obsessed composers of the 1920s; even when Strauss is at his most "modern," as in the skat party from *Intermezzo,* he never sounds like anyone but himself. Some of the sonorities in the later operas (*Daphne* in particular comes to mind) are marvelously distinctive—really quite original—and could perhaps have become the basis of an expanded tonal language, similar to those suggested by Busoni in the more adventurous parts of *Doktor Faustus,* by Schreker in *Christophorus,* and by Weill in some of his works of the 1930s. But Strauss by this time had no interest in "expanding the language." His concern was increasingly with refinement, with a purification of his harmonic style, which makes parts of *Capriccio* sound like late Fauré.

Two of the rare examples of pitch-specific motives from the late (or latish) works will be discussed by way of conclusion.[36] The first is the offstage Arab music, which Del Mar amusingly describes as "wailing,"[37] in the second act of *Die ägyptische Helena.* It outlines part of a scale of D minor with sharped fourth—surely the tritest form of "orientalism"—but is nevertheless more exotic than it looks. For the scale is supported in the orchestra not only by triads of D minor/major (figs. 120/7, 137/6, and 150/3) but also by seventh chords on E (fig. 123/3), G (fig. 150/9), C♯ (fig. 151/5), and B♭ (fig. 151/9)—in other words, by all the possible triads on the notes of the diminished-seventh chord C♯–E–G–B♭. If one put all these notes together one would have an octatonic scale. For the rest, the constant reinterpretation of the individual pitches as the various permutations are worked out (the note F, for example, acts as a minor third in D minor but as a major third in C♯ major) is fully in line with the principles already observed in *Don Quixote.* There is not much more to say about the Arab music than this—it has no "wider resonances"—but the motive deserves its place in the harmony books of the twenty-first century as an example of one of the crankier (though rather endearing) experiments of the twentieth.

Finally, *Die schweigsame Frau:* the Silent Woman finds expression in a four-note motive (on its first appearance, at fig. 45/6, set to the very words "schweigsame Frau"), which clings tenaciously to its original pitches[38]—C, B, D♯, E—while being constantly reharmonized. This is the technique of *Feuersnot* and *Salome* all over again, but with a new, zany quality lacking in the earlier works. It would be tedious to describe every statement (or even to list them, except in a note[39]); suffice it to call attention to just a few of the most ingenious reharmonizations, those at act 1, figs. 49/2–3, 56/3–4, and 134/9;

and act 2, figs. 17/10–11, 21/10–11, and 129/4 (Examples 8a–g). Strauss's invention was rarely more fertile.

a. Act 1, fig. 45/6

b. Act 1, fig. 49/2–3

c. Act 1, fig. 56/3–4

Example 8. Reharmonizations of the Silent Woman's motive in *Die schweigsame Frau*

d. Act 1, fig. 134/9

Der Barbier

Jetzt soll ich noch bis morgen für den Herrn sein schweigsames Fräulein finden!

e. Act 2, fig. 17/10–11

Der Barbier

Gna - den gil - ti - ges Sig - num.

f. Act 2, fig. 21/10–11

Der Barbier

[Mad-]chen - herz___ ist scheu,___ nur Ver -

Example 8, cont.

g. Act 2, fig. 129/4

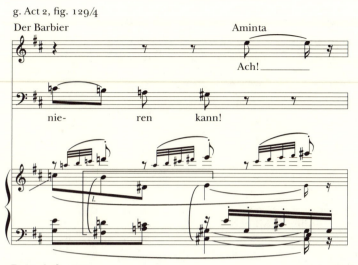

Example 8, cont.

IV

Despite his modernisms, which are never so obvious as when one studies a particular technique in detail—this essay might almost have been
called "Strauss the Progressive"—Strauss's aesthetics remained firmly
rooted in the nineteenth century. Perhaps his penchant for pitch-
specific themes, more pronounced at some times of his life than at
others, reflects a simple belief in inspiration: "Melody . . . is one of
the most noble gifts which an invisible deity has bestowed on mankind. . . . The melodic idea which suddenly falls upon me out of the
blue, which emerges without the prompting of an external sensual
stimulant or of some spiritual emotion . . . appears in the imagination immediately, unconsciously, uninfluenced by reason. It is the
greatest gift of the divinity and cannot be compared with anything
else."[40] In other words, if melody is a gift from God, why change it?
Although Strauss is well aware of the sheer hard work that goes into
composition (he writes about it at length), his attitude is basically that
of Elgar, who thought there was music in the air around him; it only
had to be written down. The composer is a transcriber, not a creator. In the same way Strauss was surprisingly ready to accept, merely
because they seemed to come to him "out of the blue," melodic ideas
that a more self-critical artist might have rejected.

Of course the decision to restate a piece of musical material at one pitch rather than another is an intellectual one, and its effects can be described in any amount of detail. But in the end one returns to an image of the composer working at a desk: his reasons for doing things are, finally, as unknowable as the nature of inspiration itself. Strauss might have been glad that someone was taking a technical interest in his music. But sooner or later he would have shrugged his shoulders, acknowledged the ultimate futility of all human inquiry— and got back to work.

NOTES

1. *Der Rosenkavalier,* act 3. Translation from the booklet accompanying the Karajan recording (EMI SLS 810).

2. Throughout this essay octave transpositions are regarded as equivalent to the original pitch.

3. *Richard Strauss: "Salome,"* ed. Derrick Puffett (Cambridge: Cambridge University Press, 1989), pp. 58–87.

4. Ibid., p. 65.

5. Ibid., pp. 69–74. The word "simplistic" is actually Carl Dahlhaus's (see the quotation on p. 61).

6. Ibid., pp. 71–72, 76–82.

7. For a survey of Straussian quotations see the chapter "Zitate und Selbstzitate" in Roland Tenschert, *Dreimal sieben Variationen über das Thema Richard Strauss* (Vienna: Frick, 1944), pp. 156–61.

8. Since F♯ is not tonicized (i.e., there is no V–I cadence) it is not quite correct to say that the quotation is "in" F♯, though the aria from which it is taken certainly is.

9. Exactly the same techniques are used in the song "Die Ulme zu Hirsau," Op. 43, no. 3 (1899), which quotes the chorale "Ein' feste Burg" (E major in an F-major context): augmented sixth for entering the new key, diminished seventh for leaving it.

10. How to decide which key is the "right" one when the passage quoted may occur many times, and in as many different keys, in the original source? In this case the answer is easy: the "definitive" statement of the theme is clearly that which appears at the beginning of the final, "Transfiguration" section (in C major), in relation to which all the previous statements are to be understood as anticipations. As it happens, we have a note by Strauss himself on this point: "*Tod und Verklärung* makes the main theme its point of culmination, and does not state it until the middle." Quoted in Willi Schuh, *Richard Strauss: A Chronicle of the Early Years 1864–1898,* trans. Mary Whittall (Cambridge: Cambridge University Press, 1982), p. 179.

11. Norman Del Mar gives a reasonably complete list in *Richard Strauss: A Critical Commentary on His Life and Works* (London: Barrie and Rockliff, 1978), vol. 1, p. 177.

12. For example, the possible reference to the cross motive from *Guntram* in tuba and double basses at the three bars beginning fig. 91.

13. Again, it is not possible to give an exact number, since when quoting from *Guntram,* for instance, Strauss could be referring to any one of several statements of a particular theme (though in most cases he was obviously not concerned about referring to a specific passage). It is fairly clear, however, that the most substantial quotation from *Guntram* (violins at fig. 91) refers to the end of the opera.

The quotations that retain their original pitch are as follows:

Heldenleben Passage	Original Source
Fig. 83/5,* horns 1–4	*Don Juan,* letter Y
Fig. 83/7, violins 1	*Don Juan,* letter D/20
Fig. 83/7, violins 2	*Zarathustra,* bars 3off., but in the major version from p. 108**
Fig. 87, double basses	*Tod und Verklärung,* letter Y/13
Fig. 87, violins 1	*Tod und Verklärung,* letter L/19
Fig. 87/3, flute 1	*Don Quixote,* opening
Fig. 87/4, English horn	*Don Quixote,* p. 169**
Fig. 87/5, violins	*Don Quixote,* bars 4–5
Fig. 88, oboe 1	*Don Juan,* letter L/4 (N.B.: modification in second half of first bar)
Fig. 88, violas and cellos	*Don Juan,* letter L/1
Fig. 88/3, E♭ clarinet	*Till Eulenspiegel,* p. 8**
Fig. 88/4, bass clarinet	*Till Eulenspiegel,* p. 8**
Fig. 89/3, trombone 3	*Guntram,* "redemption" motive
Fig. 89/7, cellos and basses	*Tod und Verklärung,* letter Y/13
Fig. 89/7, trumpet 1	*Zarathustra,* p. 128**
Fig. 90, cellos and basses	*Macbeth,* p. 15**
Fig. 90/3, violas	*Macbeth,* pp. 6–7**
Fig. 90/4, horn 2	*Macbeth,* p. 13**
Fig. 90/6, violas	"Traum durch die Dämmerung," bars 18–22 (N.B.: notated in G♭, not F♯)
Fig. 91, violins	*Guntram,* end of act 3
Fig. 91, cellos	*Don Quixote,* p. 75** (N.B.: notated in G♭, not F♯)
Fig. 92, cellos	*Tod und Verklärung,* letter O/11
Fig. 92/3, violas	*Zarathustra,* bars 3off. (minor version this time)

*i.e., five bars after fig. 83, including the bar headed by the rehearsal number; this referencing system will be used throughout the essay
**references are to the Eulenburg miniature score

14. For his reaction to an "unmotivated" modulation in *Don Quixote* see the *Harmonielehre* (Vienna: Universal, 1906), pp. 299–300. This passage was cut in the English edition.

15. "The Musical Language of *Elektra,*" in *Richard Strauss: "Elektra,"* ed. Derrick Puffett (Cambridge: Cambridge University Press, 1989), p. 85. Later in the same chapter (p. 91) Carpenter quotes Strauss's condensation of the beginning and end of Wagner's *Tristan,* a jeu d'esprit that unfortunately contains a flagrantly bad example of voice leading (the unresolved D in the penultimate bar).

16. See Del Mar, *Richard Strauss*, vol. 1, p. xii.

17. "Richard Strauss," trans. Samuel and Shierry Weber, *Perspectives of New Music* 4, no. 1 (Fall–Winter 1965): 19.

18. Fig. 186.

19. *Richard Strauss*, vol. 3, p. 421.

20. I am informed by the editor of this volume that Strauss *always* thought of *Metamorphosen* in C minor. See Timothy L. Jackson, "The Metamorphosis of the *Metamorphosen*," in *Richard Strauss: New Perspectives on the Composer and His Work*, ed. Bryan Gilliam (Durham, N.C.: Duke University Press, 1992), a source that of course was not available to me at the time of writing.

21. Cf. Strauss's humorous gloss on the ending, which interprets the B major/C major opposition in the light of a weather report. Kurt Wilhelm, *Richard Strauss: An Intimate Portrait*, trans. Mary Whittall (London: Thames and Hudson, 1989), p. 75.

22. See the note in sketchbook 10 quoted in Franz Trenner, *Die Skizzenbücher von Richard Strauss aus dem Richard Strauss–Archiv in Garmisch* (Tutzing: Schneider, 1977), p. 21.

23. See my discussion of these issues in *The Song Cycles of Othmar Schoeck* (Bern: Haupt, 1982), pp. 193–95.

24. Pp. 26–27 of the Eulenburg miniature score. Graham H. Phipps has discussed this passage in detail: see "The Logic of Tonality in Strauss's *Don Quixote*: A Schoenbergian Evaluation," *19th-Century Music* 9, no. 3 (Spring 1986): 200–202. Though I find Phipps's article more than a little confused, I am grateful for its having brought the passage to my attention.

25. It appears at figs. 6, 45, 81/10, 96/7, 126/4, and 151.

26. Cf. also those at figs. 58, 85/15, 147/11, and 172/13.

27. Cf. Adorno: "Everything becomes brittle; even the Wagnerian mirror breaks. Among the arts of his predecessor, Strauss spurns the most important, that of transition. Instead, motifs—often of minimal importance—line up like pictures on an unending filmstrip, at times virtually unrecognizable in the background of the sound events . . . It is idle to argue whether this picture-like quality, the tumult of juxtaposed elements, causes the short-windedness of the individual melodic formations, or whether it is produced by them as a peculiar feature of Strauss's musicality. The hand behind the magic lantern can change pictures so swiftly that their monadlike aspect is no longer recognizable. Strauss was a composer in the most literal sense, one who 'puts together.'" "Richard Strauss, Part II," trans. Samuel and Shierry Weber, *Perspectives of New Music* 4, no. 2 (Spring–Summer 1966): 116. This is a negative way of describing another of Strauss's "modern" aspects, the blocklike, almost Stravinskian effect of some of his thematic and tonal juxtapositions.

28. For more on the C♯/C opposition see Tethys Carpenter, "Tonal and Dramatic Structure," in *Richard Strauss: "Salome,"* pp. 94–97.

29. The intensely chromatic material associated with Herod (see the whole stretch from fig. 155 to fig. 172) is a good example.

30. From fig. 79. Other notable examples are at figs. 26, 48, 51/4ff., 83, 187/4, and 298ff.

31. See my comments on the Aegisthus motive in *Richard Strauss: "Elektra,"* pp. 39–40. Certain of Klytämnestra's motives also adhere to fixed pitch levels.

32. Fig. 210. On Strauss's annotations in the *Rosenkavalier* libretto see Willi Schuh, "Hugo von Hofmannsthal und Richard Strauss: Legende und Wirklichkeit," in *Umgang mit Musik* (Zurich: Atlantis, 1972), pp. 173–202.

33. There are further allusions to G♭ at figs. 180, 198, and 225.

34. Two exceptions in *Intermezzo* are the Frau's cries of "Anna! Anna!" which appear at the opening in a context of C and at figs. 109/8 and 116ff. in a context of D, and the opening motive itself, which, however, returns as many times in transposed forms as it does at the original pitch. (One interesting reharmonization of the latter occurs at fig. 195/4ff., where it incorporates an A♭-minor triad with the second note, not the first, being taken as the chord note.)

35. Act 3, figs. 14/5–16, 16/9–12, and 28/1–8. (It is doubtful that Strauss knew any Cowell.)

36. There are many examples of key association in a more general sense, but these cannot be discussed here.

37. *Richard Strauss,* vol. 2, p. 338.

38. There are in fact some transposed versions, but these are far outweighed by the number of pitch-specific ones.

39. See act 1, figs. 45/6–7, 46/1–3, 47/4, 47/6, 49/2–3, 56/3–4, 73/3, 93/14–15, 101/8–10, 106/3–4, 134/9–10, 149/4, 152/6–7, and 153/1–2; act 2, figs. 14/3, 15/1–3, 15/5–7, 17/3–4, 17/10–11, 21/10–11, 37/3, 48/6, 50/6, 52/5–6, 53/2, 53/4–5, 55/1–2, 60/7, 64/5, 77/7–9, 77/12, 80/7–8, 118/1–8, 119/2–8, 125/15, 127/7–8, 129/4, 142/2, 142/5–6, 145/1–2, 145/5–6, 146/5–6, 159/6–7, 160/6, 161/2, 165/2–4, 165/9–11, 166/6–8, and 168/2; act 3, figs. 31/19–20, 34/3–4, 34/8–9, 51/4, 51/11, 52/10, 62/2–16, 78/1–3, 92/13, and 93/1. This is probably not a complete list; it is impossible to be sure that one has found every statement.

40. "On Inspiration in Music," in *Richard Strauss: Recollections and Reflections,* ed. Willi Schuh, trans. L. J. Lawrence (London: Boosey and Hawkes, 1953), p. 112.

Richard Strauss

and the Question

MICHAEL P. STEINBERG

This essay will attempt to examine the politics of Richard Strauss in the 1930s. It will not rehearse or focus on the well-known chronology of Strauss's affiliation with the Nazis. We know well that Strauss served as president of the newly created *Reichsmusikkammer* [Reich music chamber] from 1933 to 1935, when he was removed following the Gestapo interception of a letter to Stefan Zweig. Which of these milestones is the more significant—the service or the removal and its circumstances—has continued to generate judgments of the composer's politics, unproductively. Recently, a German monograph on Strauss in the years from 1933 to 1935 has revealed a deeper reserve of enthusiasm for Nazi policy than had previously been known.[1] But almost any level of political participation or implication remains secondary, even incidental, when the personality in question remains significant for a realm of mind and sensibility where autonomy and apoliticality can be cited. For Strauss, this realm is music.

For Martin Heidegger, the realm is philosophy. Richard Strauss and Heidegger in the early years of Nazi rule can be compared fruitfully. Both served the state briefly in highly visible positions: Strauss in the *Reichsmusikkammer*, Heidegger as rector of the University of Freiburg. Until the late 1980s, the brevity of these affiliations was cited as evidence of their insignificance. In the case of Heidegger, this argument has been decisively undermined. But the question of the relationship of politics to philosophy continues to command attention. The extent to which Heidegger's philosophy is ideologically compatible with Nazi cultural politics haunts his readers—or should. And the formulation of this last sentence is a mild one: I speak of compatibility rather than service.

How the case of Heidegger can inform the case of Strauss is the question I want to pursue in this essay. At stake is the political sensibility of music. I want to try to define this sensibility from within Strauss's creative process: his synchronic and diachronic variety of musical styles; his choice and treatment of texts for songs and opera; and what might be called his politics of musical self-quotation. From these sources, I will try to examine the "politics of the spirit" of Richard Strauss.

.

The phrases "politics of the spirit" and "Richard Strauss and the Question" echo Jacques Derrida's 1987 book *De l'esprit: Heidegger et la question,* translated as *Of Spirit: Heidegger and the Question.*[2] I begin by positing Derrida's monograph on Heidegger as a model for my essay on Strauss and by suggesting that Heidegger's philosophy of the spirit, his interest in myth in general and in Hölderlin in particular, and the problem of drawing a line between his philosophy and his professional and political career all establish a significant parallel to the case of Richard Strauss.

The Politics of the Spirit: Heidegger

When Jacques Derrida published *De l'esprit* in 1987, the revised political biography of Martin Heidegger had become well known. The separate peace that contemporary phenomenologists had made with Heidegger and his politics had been shattered, although the new political biography, and the subsequent new reading of the philosophy, remained—and remain still—contested issues. It had always been a simple matter of record that Heidegger had been appointed rector of the University of Freiburg in 1933. He joined the party on 1 May. His inaugural address, the *Rektoratsrede,* delivered on 27 May, was a clear document of collaboration with the National Socialist government. The address's title was "The Self-Determination of the German University." By the term Heidegger meant the symbiosis of university, nation, and people: a philosophical argument for the politics of *Gleichschaltung.* But Heidegger resigned this position after a year, and posterity had been comfortable with two assumptions. First, the resignation was interpretable as a prescient dissatisfaction with Nazi politics and university policy—an early moral position consistently reinforced in post-1945 utterances by Heidegger himself. Second, politics did not carry over into philosophy. This second position resulted partly from the tendency to focus on the early Heidegger, specifically on *Being and Time,* published in 1927. Heidegger himself referred portentously to the "turn" [*Kehre*] in his work of the subsequent period, and here many of his readers had chosen to remain myopic, as the political grounds of much of the work in the 1930s are clearly compatible with the nationalist neoromanticism of Nazi cultural politics. It argues in and for what Theodor Adorno called "the jargon of authenticity."

Adorno's short book of that name, published in 1964, had been digested and too hastily rejected by scholars for whom Heidegger was philosophically important.[3] Its political critique seemed to gain momentum through disregard for Heidegger's philosophical subtlety. Adorno had chosen to identify Heidegger's ideology from within his language and neologisms, and these aspects of his writing had come for many of his readers to signify and bear his greatest philosophical validity and innovation. The new attack on Heidegger was thus initiated in the realm of political biography, with a revised philosophical reception following suit. Both occurred in France, where his presence continued to be greatest.[4] In his *Heidegger et le nazisme,* Victor Farias argued that Heidegger had been a convinced adherent of National Socialism from before 1933 through 1945. A German biography by Hugo Ott corrects many errors of Farias but does not substantially alter his contextual picture.[5]

The extent to which French intellectual life still felt itself linked to Heidegger became evident in the rash of books that greeted and augmented the "Heidegger scandal."[6] Whereas the typical reaction among American continental philosophers was to agree to the jettisoning of the person so long as the philosophy could be salvaged, the French reaction was to work through the conundrum of person, politics, and philosophy in a more analytical and self-analytical manner.[7] Derrida's short book is perhaps the most remarkable for its penetration and judiciousness. In identifying "the politics of the spirit" as the defining ideological strand in Heidegger's work from 1933 at least to 1953, he redefines Heidegger's *Kehre* in a way that shows its philosophical elegance to be wedded to neoromantic nationalism.[8] The argument's only weakness is its failure to acknowledge Adorno.

"Heidegger and the Question," Derrida's subtitle, refers to two planes of discourse. First, there is the question of philosophy itself, the possibility of philosophy—the question of the question. Second, there is the *specific* question—*the* question that haunts—and that is the question of Heidegger's politics and its relation to his philosophy. More specifically, it is the question of the politics of Heidegger's philosophical imagination.

Derrida begins by tracing the appearance of the word "spirit" [*Geist*] and its variations in Heidegger's writings. In *Being and Time,* the word appears several times in quotation marks. It appears therefore as someone else's concept, a vestige from another era that resists present-day legitimacy on its own terms. The word appears for the first time without the dismissive quotation marks in the Rectorship Address of May 1933. The word presents itself, on this theatrical occasion, as a phenomemon, as a philosophical and historical agent.

Derrida is right to emphasize the theatricality of the occasion and of the appearance of the word. The occasion is a ceremony, but a self-conscious one. Heidegger makes it celebrate the union of north German intellectuality and south German performance itself. The University of Freiburg sits at the crossroads of the German intellectual world. Heidegger, a Swabian, Catholic philosopher, takes over its rectorship and in his inaugural address celebrates the literal Catholicization of German philosophy. Spirit becomes theatrical; it becomes its own representation. Philosophy and the university become the intellectual and institutional loci for the realization of spirit as matter and agency—in another word, as politics. Derrida puts it as follows: "In the wings, spirit was waiting for its moment. And here it makes its appearance. It presents itself. Spirit *itself,* spirit in its spirit and in its letter, *Geist* affirms itself through the self-affirmation of the German university. Spirit's affirmation, inflamed."[9]

The purpose of the German university, as affirmed in 1933, is to define philosophical and political leadership as identical. The university must lead, and the apposite nouns are of course *Führung* [leadership] and the *Führer*—the leader, in this case Heidegger, as rector. In Derrida's words, "the self-affirmation of the German university will be possible only through those who lead, while themselves being led, directors directed by the affirmation of this spiritual mission."[10] Spirit is thus an attribute of mind that becomes real as an attribute of action, of politics. Heidegger's final imperative is to define this phenomenon as *essentially German.* He does this, as Derrida points out, through a philological conceit. The articulation of the conceit appears only twenty years later, however, in the 1953 essay on the poet Georg Trakl. Here, Heidegger defines *Geist* as flame, thus setting it apart from the words that in other languages connote "spirit":

> Spirit's affirmation, inflamed. Yes, *inflamed:* I say this not only to evoke the pathos of the *Rectorship Address* when it celebrates spirit, not only because of what a reference to flame can illuminate of the terrifying moment which is deploying its specters around this

theater [i.e., the lecture hall where Derrida first gives this text], but because twenty years later, Heidegger will say of *Geist,* without which it is impossible to think Evil, that *in the first place* it is neither *pneuma* nor *spiritus,* thus allowing us to conclude that *Geist* is no more heard in the Greece of the philosophers than in the Greece of the Gospels, to say nothing of Roman deafness: *Geist* is flame. And this could, apparently, be said, and thus thought, only in German.[11]

With understatement and perhaps even, unfortunately, some awkwardly placed preciousness, Derrida does record, later in the book, his horror at the fact that Heidegger articulated the identification of spirit with flame in 1953, after the Holocaust: "What is spirit? Final reply, in 1953: fire, flame, burning, conflagration. *Twenty years later,* then, and what years!"[12] But even without this later, and most horrifying, move, Heidegger's 1933 politics of the spirit is fully formed and coherent. The equation of philosophy and politics equals in turn the equation of Germanness with cultural authenticity. The affirmation of spirit is the affirmation of Germanness and Germany. Heidegger speaks of the renewal of "our historico-spiritual existence" [*unseres geschichtlich-geistigen Daseins*], and Derrida comments, "The 'we' of this 'our' is the German people. . . . geopolitics conducts us back . . . to the world as a world *of spirit.* Geopolitics is none other than a *Weltpolitik* of spirit."[13]

The Politics of the Spirit: Strauss

"Richard Strauss and the Question" must be read as more restricted and less elegant a formulation than Derrida's. It refers only to *the* specific question of Strauss's politics. What we cannot speak of is the relationship of politics *to* music. Rather, the formulation must be more integrated; it is a question of the politics of the man's musical imagination. The common denominator between politics and music is the same as in Derrida's Heidegger analysis, and that is the politics of the spirit. Once politics becomes a dimension of the imagination and thus internal to the creative process, the defensive claim of apoliticality becomes spurious.

As with Heidegger, the biographical elements in Strauss's associations with National Socialism have recently been elaborated. The parallels are illuminating. As with Heidegger, the limitations of the association in delimiting ideological commitment are striking. Against

Heidegger, Strauss's personal decency is not placed in question. Neither did he ever join the National Socialist party. As for his understanding of the internality of politics to the spirit of music, a 1934 passage that Strauss added to a text of 1903 speaks for itself:

> Kunst ist ein Kulturprodukt. . . . Zeugnis abzulegen von der Kultur der Zeiten und Völker. . . .
>
> So erscheinen uns denn als Vertretern des Musikerstandes die Reformen der Gegenwart auf kulturellem Gebiet von ganz besonderer Wichtigkeit. Wir können ja nur dann mit einer neuen Blüte unseres musikalisches Leben rechnen, wenn es uns gelingt, das gesamte Volk wiederum für unsere Musik zu gewinnen, es mit unserer Musik zu durchdringen und im Herzen jedes einzelnen Volksgenossen wie einen Keim die Liebe zu seiner deutschen Musik einzupflanzen, der nachher aufblühend ein immer grösser werdendes Musikbedürfnis zeitigt, das mit bester Musik zu befriedigen unsere vornehmste Aufgabe sein wird.

> [Art is a cultural product. . . . The bearing of witness of the culture of times and peoples. . . .
>
> For this reason the current reforms in the area of culture appear to us, as representatives of the musical world, of immense importance. We will be able to count on a new blossoming of our musical life only if we succeed in winning over the entire people to our music, saturating them with our music, and implanting within the heart of every individual fellow citizen a love for his German music. Thus the need for music will always increase, and it will be our highest task to satisfy it with the best music.][14]

In the Heidegger year of 1987, Gerhard Splitt published a monograph on Richard Strauss and the politics of music between 1933 and 1935.[15] The book's cover displays a photograph of the smiling Strauss shaking hands with a smiling Joseph Goebbels at the opening of the *Reichsmusikfestwoche* in Düsseldorf in 1938. The image extends Splitt's argument, both chronologically and substantively.

First, Splitt suggests that the insistence on the apoliticality of music had been foreclosed early by the Nazis. In April 1933 Joseph Goebbels had published an open letter to Wilhelm Furtwängler in the *Deutsche Allgemeine Zeitung* insisting that German music could not be considered unpolitical. (On the establishment of the *Reichsmusikkammer* in November 1933, Furtwängler, we can recall here, would be named deputy to President Strauss.)[16] This charge poses an important question in aesthetics and ideology. Once an authoritative agent of the state has declared all art—or an entire art form—to be political, what kind of resistance makes the most sense, assuming resistance is in question? The most common German strategy, invoked by those who cooperated with the Third Reich and then defended that decision after 1945, was to continue to insist on the apoliticality of art. Artists and critics who resisted National Socialism in general also resisted this defense, holding that once art was declared political by the state, this and other views of the state could only be challenged through political consciousness, in other words through insisting that valid art challenge the politics of the state through a different politics. Politics can be fought only with politics. In this vein, Walter Benjamin insisted in a well-known statement of 1936 that fascism, which aestheticizes politics, must be resisted by the politicization of art.[17] Goebbels's charge of April 1933 made it clear that the continued insistence on art's apoliticality amounted to a denial of overall political reality. In the phrase of a Hindemith scholar, "in the Third Reich there was no unpolitical culture."[18]

Strauss was installed as president of the *Reichsmusikkammer* in a cermony at the Berliner Philharmonie on 15 November 1933. His *Festliches Praeludium* was played. In early February 1934 he chaired the opening meeting of the music chamber, journeying to Berlin with his son. A letter to his wife records friendly private meetings with Goebbels and Hitler—"in the most intimate circle."[19] On 13 February he gave a public address celebrating the compatibility between Hitler's cultural goals and the musical goals of the *Reichsmusikkammer*. He spoke of the grounding of a "new German musical culture"; of a "community of destiny" [*Schicksalsgemeinschaft*] that united German music under the authority of its designated leaders [*verantwortlichen Führern*]. The term *Führer* efficiently intermingled musical and political authority, Strauss and Hitler. He promised that the *Reichsmusikkammer* would not hesitate to effect reforms, some of which would be announced in the coming weeks. Even if Strauss had in mind here the technical and economic reforms—such as revision of copyright laws—for which his defenders remember his service to the *Reichsmusikkammer* and to German musicians in economic crisis, it is clear that he slipped easily into the minor chords of ideological service. Thus the music chamber, he intoned, would act as "an organic, essential part" of "our people and our National Socialist state."[20] Strauss thus dedicated himself to the ideology of *Gleichschaltung*, or coordination, of cultural life with politics and National Socialist ideology.

Back at home in Garmisch, on 3 December, he composed a song called "The Little Brook," *Das Bächlein,* and dedicated the piano score to Goebbels, in memory of the fifteenth of November. (The orchestral version was premiered in Berlin in June 1942, with the dedication dropped.) The song's text, as Gerhard Splitt has discussed, has consistently been misidentified as a poem of Goethe's. The text reads as follows:

> Du Bächlein silberhell und klar,
> du eilst vorüber immerdar.
> Am Ufer steh' ich, sinn' und sinn':
> wo kommst du her, wo gehst du hin?
>
> Ich komm' aus dunkler Felsen Schoss,
> mein Lauf geht über Blum' und Moos.
> Auf meinem Spiegel schwebt so mild
> des blauen Himmels freundlich Bild.
>
> Drum hab' ich frohen Kindersinn,
> es treibt mich fort, weiss nicht wohin.
> Der mich gerufen aus dem Stein,
> der, denk' ich, wird mein Führer sein!
>
> [Little brook, light and clear as silver,
> you hurry along forever.
> I stand on the bank and ponder:
> from where do you come, where are you going?
>
> I come out of a dark rocky cave (womb),
> my path takes me over flower and moss.
> The smiling image of the blue sky
> Hovers gently on my mirror.
>
> I therefore have the happiness of a child.
> It drives me along, I know not where.
> He who has called me forth from stone,
> he, I think, will be my leader!]

The text itself uses romantic images and clichés to celebrate a political call to consciousness that at the same time preserves innocence. Strauss was not ambivalent about the connotation of "mein Führer." For the song's final musical line, he repeated the words twice:

> der, denk' ich, wird mein Führer,
> mein Führer, mein Führer sein![21]

Thus Strauss accords a specific political program to a metaphor of personal transformation of the kind Hofmannsthal had favored. Ariadne had also been restored to life from a long period on a rock, if not in one. The Strauss-Hofmannsthal treatment of the Ariadne story had in turn recalled the awakening of Brünnhilde from her more explicitly German rock, located not too far from Garmisch. Strauss's sanguine attitude, in late 1933, toward the Third Reich obviously controls the song, and it can be juxtaposed with his less sanguine attitude of a few years later. The central metaphor of *Daphne* will be the reverse transformation: that of a woman into an inanimate natural object (a tree).

This issue is crucial. From Hofmannsthal, Strauss had developed an intimacy with dramatic and musical metaphors of consciousness, representations of the spirit. These had given a subtle and differentiated dramatic and musical vocabulary to the initial thematics of transformation already apparent in the young Strauss. The programs of virtually all the early tone poems flow back and forth between life and death, innocence and self-assertion. But the personalities painted through music are not psychologically differentiated. Hofmannsthal nurtured in Strauss the art of portraying psychological differentiation, and Strauss responded with a more subtle palette. The post-Hofmannsthal phase is, of course, chronologically, the National Socialist phase.[22] The coincidence becomes meaningful when we discern Strauss's return to bluntness, in his relation to dramatic metaphors, musical-dramatic writing, as well as in his internalization of politics. One equation seems to hold in this period, in biography and in creative work: the active spirit is the political one; the withdrawal of the spirit is the withdrawal from communicative life.

The spirit is political: this assertion must be looked at more carefully. What is the spirit for Richard Strauss? When we look at the pre-, non-, and post-Hofmannsthal works, we begin to discern a pattern. First, there is the question of Strauss's Nietzscheanism: music as materialization of spirit. According to this principle, Strauss's musical modernism is compatible with ego assertion. In the operas, *Salome* and *Elektra* follow in this pattern. With *Der Rosenkavalier,* the musical style begins to reflect the overdetermined social, ritual behavior of the characters. Strauss does not give up on musical modernism, but he does break the association of modernism and ego assertion—his own or his characters'. Like the Marschallin managing her emotions, he modulates the music to negotiate within the intricate behavioral codes of the operas' dramatic contexts. There are exceptions to this tendency, as in *Die Frau ohne Schatten*, where social classes are portrayed to whom behavioral codes are apparently irrelevant. Thus the modernist energy is refocused and tamed in the collaboration with Hofmannsthal and his baroque culture of form: of images, image making, and cultural correctness. The Marschallin captures this baroque ethic with her line "und in dem wie, da liegt der ganze Unterschied" [and in the how, therein lies all the difference]. The social actor, according to this ethic, has a role to perform within the *theatrum mundi*. Within this frame, the aesthetic and moral life comes from the way the role is played, not from the extent to which either the role or the frame is questioned or changed.[23]

The stylistic alternatives of modernism and neoclassicism may not be adequate or accurate in describing the two stylistic tendencies of Strauss. Musical modernism persists. It is perhaps the modernism of the spirit, of ego assertion, which has been defined as Strauss's modernist style *tout court*. But the two tendencies of modernism as the assertion of the spirit, indistinguishable from the will, and an ascetic withdrawal from the world, may be more to the point. The later musical modernism suggests a withdrawal into the security of sensibility, first in the Hofmannsthal operas and then in the works that claim a withdrawal from politics.

Away from Hofmannsthal, the assertion of the spirit prevails. The definition of the spirit involves politics. A strong example is the group of three hymns to texts of Hölderlin (Op. 71), to which I will refer according to the principle of nostalgia for the spirit. They were composed in early 1921, in Vienna, during the period of Strauss's administration of the Staatsoper. The songs stand as a significant exception to the relatively unproductive five-year period between *Die Frau ohne Schatten* in 1918 and *Intermezzo* in 1923. (The ballet *Schlagobers* is the other exception.)

Friedrich Hölderlin, who lived from 1770 to 1843 but spent the years after 1804 in a condition of dysfunctional insanity, had been rediscovered by Nietzsche. By the *young* Nietzsche, more precisely— the Nietzsche of *The Birth of Tragedy* (1871). At this time a young professor of classical philology, Nietzsche sought in Attic tragedy the model of cultural cohesion and rebirth for German culture. The performance of a tragedy amounts to a ritual occasion in which cultural conflicts are worked through and the participating community (actors and audience together) reaffirms its communitarian identity. The music drama of Wagner, as a mirror of ancient tragedy, was of course the contemporary scene of this rebirth. Nietzsche found the same spirit in Hölderlin. Martin Heidegger, in the 1920s, regarded Hölderlin and Nietzsche as the founders of the idea of Greece as the model for an authentic Germany.

It was clearly the Nietzsche in Richard Strauss that led him to

Hölderlin: specifically, the early Nietzsche for whom classical Greece served as a model for Germany. In recalling the young Nietzsche, the aging Strauss also recalls his own youth and its Nietzschean inspirations, spiritual and musical. The music to the three hymns is replete with quotations of youth: of the childhood theme in *Death and Transfiguration* and of natural depictions in the *Alpine Symphony*. The titles of the individual hymns are *Hymne an die Liebe* [Hymn to love], *Rückkehr in die Heimat* [Return to the homeland], and *Die Liebe* [Love]. Thus we have a middle song on fatherland surrounded by two hymns to love. Within each song, the thematic relationship between love and love of country is asserted and organized.

Among the rich natural metaphors at work in the first song, that of the ocean appears twice. At first, the image is of the still ocean:

> . . . die entbrannte Sonn' erfreuet
> sie [die Liebe] im stillen Ozean.
>
> [. . . it (love) delights the blazing sun
> in the still ocean.][24]

The metaphor of the ocean controls the text's shift from a still to a dynamic nature, a transformation effected by the power of love:

> Liebe wallt durch Ozeane,
> höhnt der dürren Wüste Sand;
> blutet an der Siegesfahne
> jauchzend für das Vaterland.
>
> [Love surges through oceans,
> scorns the arid desert's sand;
> bleeds on the flag of victory
> jubilant for the fatherland.]

The activation of love is identical to patriotic fervor. It is portrayed here not only as capable of human sacrifice for love of country but as identical to it. The "Hymn to Love" is thus identical to the hymn to fatherland. In the penultimate stanza, the power of love becomes that of political liberation:

> Mächtig durch die Liebe winden
> von der Fessel wir uns los,
> und die trunknen Geister schwinden
> zu den Sternen frei und gross!

[Mightily through love
we shake our fetters loose
and the ecstatic spirits great and free
vanish to the stars.]

The second song addresses the patriotic theme directly, and here Strauss matches the textually explicit passage from love to patriotism with music. The song begins with light and delicate orchestration, as the text invokes private memories of the homeland. But in the second half of the song's third stanza a strong pulse carried by the strings restores the spirit of affirmation:

Wie lange ists, o wie lange! Des Kindes Ruh
ist hin, und hin ist Jugend und Glück und Lust;
doch du, mein Vaterland! du heilig-
duldendes! siehe, du bist geblieben!

[How long it has been, oh how long! Childhood peace
is gone, and gone are youth and joy and pleasure;
but you, my fatherland! holy-
enduring! see! you have remained!]

The final song, "Love," ends with the following declamation:

. . . Sprache der Liebenden
sei die Sprache des Landes,
ihre Seele der Laut des Volks!

[. . . May the language of lovers
be the language of the land,
their soul the sound of the people!]

In these last lines, the translation choices are clear, but the valences of the terms in English and German are different. *Sprache* means language but in the sense of speech: what is actually spoken rather than the overall linguistic system. It thus connotes an act rather than a potential act. On this principle, the aura and meaning of the term inform the line of reception from Hölderlin to Heidegger and Derrida. The German *Volk* means people in a strongly collective and coherent sense; the nationalization of the term coincides with the nationalization of German cultural consciousness in the nineteenth century. Thus the word's cultural and semantic context is different for Strauss from what it had been for Hölderlin, and more explicitly national in connotation. In the combined textual and musical vocabulary of these Hölderlin songs, we have a rhetoric of musical nationalism. Put another way, music is the representation of the spirit that transforms passion into politics.

Myth and Mediocrity

Strauss's politics of the spirit were strongly affected by the collaboration with Joseph Gregor following the death of Hofmannsthal and the persecution of Stefan Zweig. Strauss recognized Gregor's literary mediocrity and did not hesitate to abuse him for it. But in questions of political ideology and the political ideology of mythical subjects both men were equally incompetent. Gregor is the librettist of record for three of Strauss's last operas: *Friedenstag* [Peace day], premiered 24 July 1938 in Munich; *Daphne,* premiered 15 October 1938 in Dresden, as "curtain-raiser" to *Friedenstag;* and *Die Liebe der Danae* [The love of Danae], performed in the composer's lifetime in a dress rehearsal in August of 1944 at the Salzburg Festival, after which Goebbels's total mobilization order shut down all German theaters. (The official premiere took place also at the Salzburg Festival, in 1952.) *Danae* developed from an idea of Hofmannsthal, first sketched in December 1919 after the premiere of *Die Frau ohne Schatten. Friedenstag* and *Daphne* are most significant as works of the 1930s.

Commentators have sustained the pacifist and hence the ethical legitimacy of *Friedenstag* with the reminder that the original idea and much of the text's development came not from Gregor but from Stefan Zweig. Zweig and Strauss discussed the proposal for an opera on the Peace of Westphalia, first carrying the title *1648,* at the Salzburg Festival in 1934. Zweig's pacifism was earnest and had gained momentum during the First World War, which he did not support and during which he corresponded with French writer and pacifist Romain Rolland. Both men's pacifisms were grounded in a sentimental idea of universal community, a notion intellectually indefensible and politically dangerous. Sigmund Freud, it will be recalled, opened his 1930 diagnosis of *Civilization and Its Discontents* with a respectful but urgent rejection of Rolland's paean to the "oceanic feeling" as the affective signal of world community.[25] For Freud, such emotion achieved political reality in the guise of the manipulative ideology of fascism. Communitarian ideologies are dangerous because the substantive ethic of community is defined according to the interests of the speaking subject. In *Friedenstag,* an ideological slippage occurs from Zweig's sentimentality to the *völkisch* positions of Gregor's politics and Strauss's *neo*-neo-Wagnerism.

Its happy ending notwithstanding, *Friedenstag* resembles the host of hackneyed baroque lamentation plays that Walter Benjamin analyzed with condescension and great contextual insight in *The Origin of German Tragic Drama,* which he submitted unsuccessfully for his habilitation at the University of Frankfurt in 1925 and subsequently published as a book in 1928.[26] Fundamental to Benjamin's question—and to the academic failure of the project, which his teachers could not place within the disciplines of philosophical aesthetics or literary history— is the politics of baroque cultural understanding. The actual plays are interesting to him as representations of cultural practice, not as texts or as works of art. The political problem they engage is that of sovereignty and legitimacy. The cultural problem engaged in turn by this political discourse is that of the dissolution of coherence engendered by the Reformation. The princes who are the plays' protagonists must therefore assert power and legitimacy through new means, principally, power and ideology. The grim historical circumstances of this dramatic tradition—strife, cultural and moral fragmentation, and war, including, of course, the Thirty Years' War—endow it with a certain realism and truthfulness. No new order is available in it or to it. For this reason, Benjamin argues that the greatest figure in the tradition of the lamentation play is Hamlet. The lamentation play *(Trauerspiel)* stands opposite from the tragedy, where cultural coherence, reaffirmed through catharsis, is restored.

If Zweig or Gregor knew Benjamin's work, I am not aware of it. But Gregor certainly knew the baroque dramatic tradition and certainly did not understand it with the historical incisiveness that Benjamin brought to it. For Gregor, as for the late Hofmannsthal, the baroque represented the idea of Austria and of the Austrian claim to a place on the world stage. He had made this view clear in his 1922 book *Das Wiener Barocktheater,* in which he hailed the city of Vienna as the center of the baroque world and the place of the potential rebirth of its "universal, festive spirit."[27]

Benjamin's insight began with his identification of a North German baroque recognition and representation of cultural, religious, and ideological fragmentation and dissipation, as opposed to southern baroque theater of totality—the theater of the world. In the realm of the Hapsburgs, baroque theater and the representation of imperial totality depended on each other more than ever after the resolution of foreign threats both from the North in the Thirty Years' War and from the Southeast with the Turkish invasions. Austrian baroque theater—literally and as a principle of politics—was the instrument of political self-representation. Benjamin in fact recognized a revival of this southern baroque world theater in Hofmannsthal's *The Tower*. This southern baroque ideology was the one Gregor prized.

In *Friedenstag* (or in whatever his contribution to it actually was), he took the pieces of a North German baroque dramatic structure and molded them into southern baroque theatrical holism. Where the actors in the baroque plays are princes, the Zweig-Gregor characters are military commanders. The action takes place on the last day of the Thirty Years' War: the notion that warfare had raged uninterrupted for the full thirty years is one of the text's historical inaccuracies. A town loyal to the Hapsburg emperor and mysteriously prized by him is under impending siege by the northern armies under a Holsteiner general. The commandant of the town has sworn an oath of honor to the emperor and prepares a mass suicide of himself and his troops. As he issues the order, townspeople enter, embracing the enemy soldiers in the joint exclamation that peace has been declared. The commandant's loyal wife, prepared to die with him but also mystically optimistic that a better alternative may present itself, sings repeated invocations to the sun, and in her joy at the miraculous outcome remains rational enough to save her husband from spoiling things when he draws his sword against the Holsteiner general in a confrontation quickly reduced to trivial bickering.

Musically, the work hardly amounts to the successful reappropriation of youthful modernism for which it is occasionally hailed. The score is a pastiche of Wagnerian clichés with all Wagner's psychological depth removed. The commandant and Maria, guarding the citadel, are indeed decayed ghosts of Wotan and Brünnhilde inhabiting Valhalla. Brünnhilde and not Fricka, because Maria's sole tone is exalted—a character in search of an immolation scene. Within the unintentional Wagnerian parody travels an equally unsuccessful pattern of Straussian self-quotation. In view of the prevalence of impressionistic self-quotation in the late Strauss, the practice's peculiar failure in *Friedenstag* may result from its lack of conviction, the musical result of Strauss's disdain for Gregor's text. You are not Hofmannsthal, the music seems to say, and I cannot be Strauss. On 31 October Strauss wrote to Zweig: "For several weeks I have been busy composing, but I have not found the music that I expect of myself. The whole subject is, after all, a bit too commonplace—soldiers, war, famine, medieval heroism, dying together—it isn't quite my dish, with the best of good will."[28]

A momentary evocation of *Die Frau ohne Schatten* serves as an example. The instant of Maria's highest readiness for self-sacrifice is transformed into the instant of miraculous peace. To represent the highest tension and its sudden resolution, Strauss invokes the moment of the Empress's ethical declaration of self-sacrifice at the fountain. By refusing to drink the enchanted water and so to procure a shadow for herself and salvation for her husband, the Empress refuses to profit at the destruction of the Dyer and his wife, who would be lost to each other by her action. Her moral resolution is rewarded at this moment by a miraculous happy end for all concerned. In both operatic moments, Strauss increases and resolves musical and dramatic tension with a conspicuous orchestral silence, slowly broken by the return of musical sound. The moment's success in *Die Frau ohne Schatten* emanates from its resolution of the psychological tension and moral resolve of the (now-) heroine. In *Friedenstag,* the character Maria is entirely unconnected to the circumstantial resolution that bursts upon the scene. The result is an effect, a trick, with no underlying dramatic logic.

The incoherent intentions of Zweig and Gregor and the incompetent text notwithstanding, the allegorical import of this opera is informed by the temporal context of 1938. The status of the Thirty Years' War as an archetype of North-South, Protestant-Catholic, Prussian-Austrian division was of course clear, and the example had been invoked with increasing intensity in conservative discourse after the First World War. The commandant is clearly identified with Austria; his wife, Maria, with a notion of Catholic femininity. The commandant is old; the Holsteiner general is young and vigorous. What is the opera's promise, through its cliché-ridden words and music, its wooden characters, and its hackneyed plot?—peace with the North German invaders, with the new and younger Germany.

An early commentator on *Friedenstag* remarked that it was "the first opera to be born out of the spirit of Nazism."[29] The consensus has been to dismiss this reaction entirely, as peace and Nazism are difficult for the contemporary observer to reconcile. But in 1938, peace and the National Socialist state seemed a reasonable partnership to most Austrians.[30] Not to weigh this historical fact is thus wishfully to ignore how Strauss the Bavarian fell under the spell of the different but compatible pieties of his two Austrian collaborators. Obviously for Stefan Zweig there was no question of sympathy for the *Anschluss.* But like his antagonist Karl Kraus, he was intellectually entirely incapable of understanding the ideological ramifications of the Austrian-German confrontations. For Zweig, as for *Friedenstag*'s Maria, peace was a state that sentimentality and the "oceanic feeling" could define. For Gregor, on the other hand, Anschluss with Nazi Germany was a fine alternative in its promise of peace and prosperity for Austria. In the years following the Anschluss, Gregor sought to place the tradition of Austrian baroque theater into the service of the new German totality, of which Austria, now the *Ostmark,* was a part. In 1942 he published a volume called *Das Theater des Volkes in der Ostmark* and dedicated it to Baldur von Schirach, leader of the Hitler Youth and *Reichsstatthalter* in Vienna. The book's argument hailed the immanent applicability and service of Austrian baroque theatricality to the new totalizing myth of the German Reich.

There are, to be sure, no grounds and no need to declare the peace achieved in the opera an allegory of the Austrian Anschluss. The point is that it could be: aesthetically, text and music fit such a reading perfectly. If not necessarily a mark of the work's evil, it is the mark of its ideological incompetence.

·

Daphne, the second collaboration with Gregor, represents a toggle for Strauss from the heroic modernist mode—or more accurately, in the case of *Friedenstag,* pseudo-neo-modernist mode—to the mode of inner sensibility. But the ideology of myth and the politics of spirit inform both. It is often pointed out that *Daphne* is Strauss's first single-act mythical opera since *Elektra* and that it represents therefore some kind of return. But where *Elektra,* thanks both to Strauss and even more to the young, modernist Hofmannsthal, invoked mythology as the expressive foundation of contemporary cultural conflict, *Daphne* returns to the ceremonial conceits of court masques and baroque evocations of Arcadia. It is a baroque costume play, what the opera seria *Ariadne auf Naxos* would be if it were not a play within a play. The rejection of the Greece of Nietzsche and Freud in favor of that of Winckelmann had begun with Hofmannsthal and *Die ägyptische Helena.* In a February 1945 letter to Gregor, Strauss commented on this Greek duality as follows: "a propos *Elektra* and *Helena* one might comment that in the former I envisaged the daemonic Greece of the fifth century before Christ, whilst the style of *Helena* approaches the resounding ideal beauty of the Goethe/Winckelmann hellenism of the fourth century."[31]

Although *Daphne* is the only one of the "Gregor operas" to carry a text original to its librettist, the work's dramatic momentum was claimed for the music. Daphne, in William Mann's expertly sardonic note, "is fulfilled by metamorphosis into the laurel tree that she should always have been."[32] Daphne's metamorphosis is painted by the orchestra, in an effect to whose benefit Strauss banished all words that Gregor sought to provide. In the case of the imaginary composer-librettist relationship that Strauss was shortly to portray in *Capriccio,* the compromise is "prima la musica e poi le parole"; where Gregor was at hand, Strauss's principle for his denouement was "sola la musica."

But there is a musical-dramatic logic to this dismissal of words—and it has even a precedent in Wagner's banishment of his own text to Brünnhilde's immolation scene. The full heroic consciousness that Brünnhilde masters at the end of the *Ring* ("Alles weiss ich; alles ward mir nun frei" [I know all; all has become clear to me] had to be subsumed by the orchestra in order to emanate as absolute truth. In *Daphne,* the dramatic principle is the same but the content is the opposite. The orchestra alone portrays Daphne's transformation, but the point is the achievement of ecstasy, harmony with nature, and the total relief from the burdens of consciousness: the liberation from the spirit. Daphne becomes a vegetable, but a happy one; "I know nothing" would be the motto of her fulfillment.

Daphne ends with a dehumanization. This prospect has never been a cheerful one for the defenders of consciousness as the measure of humanity. Here is Derrida, ending the chapter in which Heidegger's conception of the spirit as a phenomenon of 1933 is introduced: "On the earth arrives an obscuring of the world (*Weltverdüsterung*): the flight of the gods, the destruction of the earth, the massification of man, the preeminence of the mediocre."[33]

In the case of *Daphne,* the pastoral calm and gentle luxuriance of the final orchestral transformation music cannot be confused with ideological innocence. At stake is the abdication of the spirit, which has not been able to liberate itself from ideology. In the end, the massification of Daphne is a neobaroque conceit, a relic from the nineteenth-century practice of the *tableaux vivants* or *lebende Bilder:* a pastime in many cultural milieus but especially dear to the neobaroque Viennese burghers who could represent themselves as perfect specimens of a static and secure culture by dressing up as characters in Renaissance paintings and "performing" still-life poses. (The young Hofmannsthal had participated in at least one such an event, and a photograph survives.)[34]

The Meanings of Metamorphosis

With his Salzburg morality plays and his well-intentioned but misguided cultural criticism, Hofmannsthal had elevated the baroque gestures of his youth—from lyric poetry to the *lebende Bilder*—into a cultural vocabulary and ideology for Austrian renewal. Such is the agenda of *Jedermann* (written in 1911, revised for the opening of the Salzburg Festival in 1920) and *Das Salzburger grosse Welttheater* (written for the Salzburg Festival in 1922). He thus ended his career with staged, neobaroque blueprints for a reauthenticated Catholic Austrian culture. Strauss collaborated with similar results in his final, post-Hofmannsthal operas, in more dangerous times, in the service of a far more dangerous mythology of cultural identity. In their different ways, *Friedenstag* and *Daphne* suggest a convergence of the ideology of baroque theatricality of the South and the ideology of the spirit of the North. For the final Strauss, after 1945, there is no chance of kitsch stopping and opera beginning again. The promise for music itself, however, remained more potent and more open. Whether or how this inclination related to the path of the Second World War is difficult to know. The wartime cataclysm that occasioned Strauss's articulated grief was the destruction of the cultural centers of Dresden and Munich. When he spoke of the crimes of the Nazis, he referred to the destruction of German theaters. Strauss's postwar mourning appears sincere but characteristically narrow-minded.

Nevertheless, the last music does possess a self-conscious quality. Did Strauss strive to recapture the aesthetic of absolute music, or did he recede into its nonrepresentational security? Like Brahms, Strauss continued to write songs. But the ideology of representation, the Austrian ideology par excellence, receded in the late song literature as in the late "absolute music," where the aesthetic of the tone poem is not revisited. In the *Metamorphosen,* the impression of an ascetic self-consciousness is reinforced by the thematics of quotation, in particular of the funereal theme in Beethoven's *Eroica* Symphony. Can this late neoclassicism be redefined as a music self-conscious about its own practice of representation? The quality and conviction in the *Metamorphosen* and the compositional invention and fluency of the final songs belie the alternative notion that rhetorical shrinkage is a function of attrition in the old man's creative powers. But the general narrow-mindedness mentioned above has its counterpart in the definition of the final music. Its clarity strives for consolation, not understanding. In its contextual implications, the music is neo-Biedermeier more than neoclassical. The late Strauss parts company with the late Beethoven as well as with Mahler and Schoenberg.

My final question is the following: how do we move, interpretively, from *Friedenstag* and *Daphne* to the *Metamorphosen?* Is this last work truly a work of summational wisdom and cultural mourning? If so, on what terms does consciousness return to a music where previously it had been bound up with ideology and then released altogether? Or, where does kitsch end and music begin?

.

In the concluding words to his recent collection of essays on music, Edward Said chose the *Metamorphosen* as the paradigm for enlightened and ethical musical experience, shared by composer and listener:

> In the perspective afforded by such a work as *Metamorphosen*, music thus becomes an art not primarily or exclusively about authorial power and social authority, but a mode for thinking through or thinking with the integral variety of human cultural practices, generously, non-coercively, and, yes, in a utopian cast, if by utopian we mean worldly, possible, attainable, knowable.[35]

This laudatory view of the *Metamorphosen* is widely held though rarely so eloquently expressed. But it was not always so apparent. In November 1947 an article in an Amsterdam newspaper accused Strauss of having written the work as a memorial to Hitler. The Swiss Strauss scholar Willi Schuh quickly responded with the archetypical argument of Strauss's apoliticality.[36] For reasons suggested above, this is the wrong argument. Strauss had written the first sketches for the *Metamorphosen* on the day the Munich Staatstheater was bombed in October 1943 and had given them the name "Mourning for Munich." The final work, completed in a month in March and April of 1945, indeed amounts to a lamentation for German aesthetic culture. To conflate this gesture with Nazi loyalty makes no sense. If in the 1930s Strauss was unable to distinguish between German and National Socialist ideas of culture, it is not to be assumed that he maintained that association. Neither music nor context supports this latter interpretation in any way.

Wisdom remains another matter. First, although the work identifies itself rhetorically, through extensive self-quotation, as a late and pensive work, we cannot automatically define it as summational. Why is not the return to musical hedonism and luxuriance in the postwar *Four Last Songs* necessarily any less summational? Second, the work's inherent qualities of mind and sensibility are not self-evident or straightforward. This problem is reinforced when the work's internal inscriptions of autobiography and history are heard through its patterns of authorial self-quotation. The work is about the past and about what kind of perspective on the past its own sense of history provides.

The work's title recalls Daphne's transformation as well as the multiple other psychological transformations conceived by Hofmannsthal and rendered musically by Strauss. The version of the Daphne myth used by Gregor is that of Ovid, author of the *Metamorphoses*. Thus the first self-quotation in the work is the reference to Daphne. The continuing appearances of quotations are open to interpretation. From works of other composers, there is first of all the quotation of Beethoven, which Norman Del Mar describes as the "motto theme," as underneath one of its appearances Strauss inscribed in the score the words "In Memoriam."[37] Less certainly, there is a possible quotation from King Marke in *Tristan und Isolde*, another commentator on surrounding cultural chaos.[38]

The *Metamorphosen* do not inscribe a return or regrounding of the spirit. The spirit's subjectivity is not recaptured, and thus a new ideological formation is avoided. The same is true for a new cultural ground. Spirit, ground, and the stable communication between the two have been relinquished in a loss that equals the loss of German culture. This attitude, inscribed in the *Metamorphosen,* is also Thomas Mann's attitude in the wartime novel *Doctor Faustus.* Mann uses music as the paradigm for the history and collapse of German aesthetic culture, aesthetic culture meaning here an aesthetic understanding of culture contained within art but not limited to art. The demise of the composer Adrian Leverkühn, into whom Mann invested a solid and conventional postromantic understanding of Nietzsche's personality and Schoenberg's twelve-tone system, reflects the demise of German culture. (Mann was tutored in the basics of twelve-tone composition by Theodor Adorno, who was not concerned with the novelist's conflation of Schoenberg's musical principles with the kind of romantic personality those principles were intended to defeat. Schoenberg, as is well known, was not amused.) But Mann implicates himself, as a German writer, in this very process. As such, he does not command a legitimate or authentic narrative position. Rather, he places the narrative voice within the unreliable and philistine voice of Dr. Serenus Zeitblom. In a far more conscious and articulated fashion, but with similar effect, Mann in *Doctor Faustus,* like Richard Strauss in the *Metamorphosen,* shapes a cultural commentary without subject, spirit, or ground. We might speak of these tendencies as de-Heideggerization.

Loss of ground is also the loss of spirit. This is a necessary association, a result of spirit's ideological claim to have been grounded in cultural authenticity. The *Metamorphosen* are built on structural differentiations, but their unfathomable quality may still lie in the question of linkage between structural variation and the inhabitation of consciousness. Where is Strauss in this work, and who is he?

Norman Del Mar has argued for a literary source for the *Metamorphosen* in the *Zahme Xenien* of the old Goethe. Strauss had spent the final years of the war reading Goethe's complete works. The verses that Del Mar links to the *Metamorphosen* are the following:

Niemand wird sich Selber kennen
Sich von seinem Selbst-Ich trennen;
Doch probier' er jeden Tag,
Was nach aussen endlich, klar.
Was er ist und was er war,
Was er kann und was er mag.

Wie's aber in der Welt zugeht,
Eigentlich niemand recht versteht,
Und auch bis auf den heutigen Tag
Niemand gerne verstehen mag.
Gehabe du dich mit Verstand,
Wie dir eben der Tag zur Hand;
Denk immer: "Ist's gegangen bis jetzt,
So wird es auch wohl gehen zuletzt."

Del Mar provides the following judicious free translation: "No one can really know himself, detach himself from his inner being; yet he must daily put to the test whenever he can see clearly from without— what he is and what he was, what he can do and what he cares for. . . . But what goes on in the world, no one really understands rightly, and also up to the present day no one gladly wishes to understand it. Conduct yourself with discernment, just as the day offers itself to you; always think: 'It's gone all right till now, so it may well go on to the end.'"[39]

In accepting the presence of these thoughts in the music of the *Metamorphosen*, we can perhaps understand what we hear as a moment of unparalleled rhetorical honesty in Strauss's work. Strauss seems here to inscribe a self-portrait stripped of all the posing of the tone poems and of the costumes of the operas, and stripped as well of the sonic security to which he will return in the *Four Last Songs*. Taking, however, the first of Goethe's lines to heart, the composer and his music do not uncover a true self, a personal or a musical subject. We do not have a musical representation of a struggling or confessional consciousness, as we do in a Mahler adagio, for example. We do have a series of perfect musical forms, hovering between composer and world. There is little true thematic development, variation, or metamorphosis. Themes lead into one another with expert fluidity, and without authorial commentary. There are almost no pauses in the music, no moments of Mahlerian silence in which the composing subject stands back, takes stock, ponders the legitimacy of his own mode of expression, questions the possibility of music—and decides whether and how to continue. Strauss does not ask, in music, *the* question that musical modernism asks, and that is whether a musical subject can engage in dialogue with the world legitimately. What remains is not a soul or a subject but a mode of movement and interaction with the world. Neither Strauss nor the restless music finds a self but only continued and ever-ingenious movement—belated and inadequate confrontation with self and history, in other words, but an honest one, in which self and world remain ill-defined and dynamic, distant from the aesthetic and political temptations of cultural myths: the myth of the spirit and the myth of the theater.

NOTES

1. This is Gerhard Splitt's *Richard Strauss 1933–1935: Ästhetik und Musikpolitik zu Beginn der nationalsozialistischen Herrschaft* (Pfaffenweiler: Centaurus Verlagsgesellschaft, 1987). Splitt was not allowed to consult materials in the Strauss-Archiv in Garmisch. In the introduction, he reprints a letter of rejection to his initial query from Alice Strauss, the composer's daughter-in-law. Since Splitt is highly aware of the controversial status of his research in Strauss scholarship and musical taste, he intersperses his narrative with accounts of the difficulties he had in conducting his research. This historian's research is thus an internal part of the story he is telling and a measure of the book's significance.

2. All citations will be to the English translation, *Of Spirit: Heidegger and the Question,* trans. Geoffrey Bennington and Rachel Bowlby (Chicago: University of Chicago Press, 1989).

3. Theodor Adorno, *Jargon der Eigentlichkeit: Zur Deutschen Ideologie* (Frankfurt: Suhrkamp, 1964), translated by K. Tarnowski and F. Will as *The Jargon of Authenticity* (Evanston: Northwestern University Press, 1973).

4. The importance of Heidegger in France and French intellectual life is an important story in its own right. Through his essay "Letter on Humanism" (1947) and his championship by Jean Beaufret, Heidegger can be understood to have grounded the principles of deconstruction, as developed later by Jacques Derrida. The "Letter on Humanism" contains the phrase "Language is the house of Being," and thus the kernel of deconstruction's location of the thinking subject and the process of meaning making within the cultural life of language. The "Letter on Humanism" can be found in English translation in Martin Heidegger, *Basic Writings* (San Francisco: Harper Collins, 1977), pp. 193–242.

5. Victor Farias, *Heidegger et le nazisme* (Paris: Verdier, 1987); Hugo Ott, *Martin Heidegger: Unterwegs zu seiner Biographie* (Frankfurt: Campus Verlag, 1988).

6. See for example Pierre Bourdieu, *L'ontologie politique de Martin Heidegger* (Paris: Minuit, 1988); Jean-François Lyotard, *Heidegger et "les juifs"* (Paris: Galilée, 1988); and Philippe Lacoue-Labarthe, *La fiction du politique* (Paris: Bourgois, 1987). The last has been translated as *Heidegger, Art, and Politics: The Fiction of the Political* (Oxford: Basil Blackwell, 1990).

7. On the American side, see Richard Rorty's review of Farias, "Taking Philosophy Seriously," in *The New Republic* (11 April 1988): 31–34.

8. This is not a consistent tone for Derrida. His treatment of Heidegger's essay "The Origin of the Work of Art," for example, in *The Truth in Painting* (*La Vérité en Peinture*, 1978) is naive about the same issue of the jargon of authenticity. His contemporary defense of Paul de Man, determined in 1987 to have concealed a collaborationist past, was wildly irresponsible. See "Like the Sound of the Sea Deep within a Shell: Paul de Man's War," in *Critical Inquiry* 14, no. 3 (Spring 1988): 590–652. A jargon of authenticity appears already in the title.

9. Derrida, *Of Spirit*, p. 31.

10. Ibid., p. 32.

11. Ibid., pp. 31–32.

12. Ibid., p. 83.

13. Ibid., pp. 45–46. I have amended the English version of Heidegger's phrase from the published translation.

14. Gerhard Splitt, p. 1. Translations are my own unless otherwise indicated.

15. Gerhard Splitt, *Richard Strauss, 1933–1935*.

16. The case of Furtwängler and music in the Third Reich has received lengthy discussion in Michael Meyer's recent book *The Politics of Music in the Third Reich* (New York: Peter Lang, 1991). The case of Furtwängler is clearly ambiguous, as he tried consistently to come to the aid of Jewish musicians in the Third Reich years. But Meyer extends this element of personal decency into a revisionist portrait of inner resistance to National Socialism in the interest of an authentic German cultural tradition. For Furtwängler as for Strauss, it was precisely an undifferentiated loyalty to German culture that led to a fundamental assimilation of the patriotic ideology of Nazism. The love of music must not blind us to the more painful subtleties of its political interstices. Meyer on Furtwängler, like so much musicology and musical biography on Strauss, transposes his aesthetic loyalty into ideological and political rehabilitation.

17. Walter Benjamin, conclusion to "The Work of Art in the Age of Its Technical Reproducibility." The passage appears in the standard English translation on p. 242 of Benjamin, *Illuminations*, trans. H. Zohn (New York: Schocken, 1969).

18. Claudia Maurer-Zenck, "Zwischen Boykott und Anpassung an den Charakter der Zeit. Über die Schwierigkeiten eines deutschen Komponisten

mit dem Dritten Reich," in *Hindemith Jahrbuch/Annales Hindemith* 1980 (Mainz, 1982): 65. Cited by Splitt, p. 9.

19. Cited in Splitt, p. 93.

20. Richard Strauss, speech to an open session of the RMK of 13 February 1934, duplicated in its entirety in Splitt, pp. 102–5.

21. See the discussion in ibid., pp. 87–92.

22. To be recalled is that this pattern works in both directions. The late works of Hofmannsthal that were not collaborative with Strauss show a decline in aesthetic subtlety and a monolithic service to an ideology of Austrian Catholic identity. I have examined this pattern in my study *The Meaning of the Salzburg Festival: Austria as Theater and Ideology, 1890–1938* (Ithaca: Cornell University Press, 1990). Thus we cannot simply accept the received notion that the delicate Viennese Hofmannsthal gave subtletly to the coarse Bavarian Strauss. Although Hofmannsthal's poetic and dramatic skills were of a high order before the collaboration began (most notably with the *Elektra* play), the dramatic mastery and subtlety achieved in the operas was the product of both men together.

23. I am grateful to Carl Schorske for this description of the baroque ethic and for the example of the Marschallin.

24. The English translations are by Lesley Bernstein Translations Services, London, as printed in the booklet to the recording of the work by the Scottish National Orchestra, conducted by Neeme Järvi (Chandos Records 8734, Colchester, England). I have altered them slightly for accuracy.

25. It is worth recalling that Rolland, an amateur musicologist, drew his ideology of world community out of the notion of music as a universal language. This is the central idea of his major work, the three-volume Bildungsroman *Jean Christophe.*

26. Walter Benjamin, *Ursprung des deutschen Trauerspiels* (Frankfurt: Suhrkamp, 1928/1963), translated as *The Origin of German Tragic Drama,* trans. J. Osborne (London: New Left Books, 1977). *Trauerspiel* is more accurately rendered as mourning or lamentation play, especially since the distinction of *Trauerspiel* from tragedy is crucial to Benjamin's argument.

27. See Kenneth Birkin, pp. 39–40.

28. *A Confidential Matter: The Letters of Richard Strauss and Stefan Zweig, 1931–1935* (Berkeley and Los Angeles: University of California Press, 1977), p. 104.

29. See Paul Suits, "The Genesis of *Friedenstag,*" in the libretto to the Koch International recording of the concert of 19 November 1989. In an article called "Strauss's *Friedenstag:* A Pacifist Attempt at Political Resistance" (*Musical Quarterly* 69 [1983]: 408–24), Pamela M. Potter argues that Strauss and Gregor deliberately padded the opera with Germanic and militaristic stereotypes as a way of confounding the Nazis about the work's true pacifist message. The argument is interesting but unconvincing for three reasons. First, it clearly emanates from a desire to defend Strauss at all costs. Second, in doing so, it reveals that the Germanic stereotypes are present and need to be accounted for. Third, such alleged instrumental usage of such stereotypes does not account for the mythical weight they have, in the work itself and beyond it.

30. Andrew Porter, commenting on the succesful concert performance in New York in November 1989, in which its message of German peace coincided with the breaking of the Berlin Wall, imbibed the work's pacifism and judged it "noble." At the moment of peace, a chorus celebrates the crumbling of old walls—the motif that, by coincidence, generated the New York audience's enthusiastic reception of the work and its alleged message in the fall of 1989. The events of 1989 thus blinded Porter and the audience to the more relevant context of 1938. See Andrew Porter in *The New Yorker*.

31. *Richard Strauss–Joseph Gregor: Briefwechsel* (Salzburg: Otto Müller, 1955), p. 275. Cited in Kenneth Birkin, *Friedenstag and Daphne: An Interpretive Study of the Literary and Dramatic Sources of Two Operas* (New York: Garland, 1989), p. 19.

32. William Mann, program note, DGG *Daphne*.

33. Derrida, *Of Spirit*, p. 46.

34. See Mara Reissberger, "Zum Problem künstlerischer Selbstdarstellung in der zweiten Hälfte des 19. Jahrhunderts—Die Lebenden Bilder," in H. Zeman, ed., *Die österreichische Literatur: Ihr Profil im 19. Jahrhundert* (Graz: Akademische Druck- und Verlagsanstalt, 1982), pp. 741–69 with appendix and photographs.

35. Edward Said, *Musical Elaborations* (New York: Columbia University Press, 1991), p. 105.

36. See Gerhard Splitt, pp. 26 and 240. As the dean of Strauss scholars and as his biographer, Schuh remained in a position to camouflage Strauss's cooperation with the National Socialist regime. For example, as editor of a volume of Strauss's memoirs, *Betrachtungen und Erinnerungen,* published in three editions in 1949, 1957, and 1981, Schuh deleted (without so indicating) from Strauss's 1933 essay on secondary music education *(Zeitgemässe Glossen für Erziehung zur Musik)* all references to the Nazi propaganda and cultural ministries, which Strauss praised as the most eminent in the world. See Splitt, p. 66.

37. Norman Del Mar, *Richard Strauss: A Critical Commentary on His Life and Works* (Ithaca: Cornell University Press, 1986), 3 vols., vol. 3, pp. 428–31.

38. See the discussion of this possibility in ibid., pp. 429–30.

39. Ibid., p. 426.

PART II

LETTERS

Selections from the Strauss-Thuille Correspondence: A Glimpse of Strauss during His Formative Years

TRANSLATED BY SUSAN GILLESPIE

Of all Strauss's childhood acquaintances, Ludwig Thuille (1861–1907) stands out as the most influential and beneficial to his musical development. Thuille, a composer and theorist of the late nineteenth and early twentieth centuries, was a leading member of the so-called Munich School. He composed chamber, symphonic, and choral music as well as three operas—*Theuerdank* (1897), *Lobetanz* (1897), and *Gugeline* (1901). In 1903 he succeeded Joseph Rheinberger as professor of composition at the Königliche Akademie der Tonkunst in Munich. Shortly thereafter Thuille collaborated with Rudolf Louis on a *Harmonielehre* that was published in 1907 and remained an important theoretical source for decades. The following year Thuille suffered a fatal heart attack.

The two boys first met in 1872; Strauss was eight and Thuille was eleven years of age. Strauss's mother had heard about the musically gifted Thuille—an orphan—through a friend, and the boy became a regular visitor to the Strauss home; indeed, he was treated like a member of the family. Together the two boys explored music with equal enthusiasm. However, Thuille left for Innsbruck in 1876; there he was enrolled in the *Gymnasium* and also undertook musical studies with Joseph Pembaur. This period is important for Strauss scholars interested in the composer's early years because it witnessed the beginning of a correspondence that would span almost three decades. For this volume, the letters from the early Innsbruck period (1877–79) were chosen. Thuille returned to Munich in 1879, and their correspondence does not resume until 1884, when Strauss went to Berlin.

Unfortunately, the letters from Thuille during the Innsbruck years are not extant; however, the numerous surviving letters of Strauss represent the closest thing we have to a childhood diary of the composer, and they appear in English here for the first time. In them Strauss reports on his own composing, his musical education, and concerts that he attended. Strauss's lengthy concert reviews, in which he often cites specific musical passages from memory, may be the most interesting aspect of these early letters. The influence of his conservative father is apparent throughout. Above all, these letters reveal Strauss's profound regard for the classic masters: Haydn, Beethoven, Schubert, and especially Mozart. Strauss's love of Mozart forms an important thread connecting boyhood, adulthood, and old age. But Strauss was also quite fond of Mendelssohn and, to a slightly lesser extent, Schumann, who possesses the "inevitable tendency to ride his figures to death." Strauss's respect for Weber, Louis Spohr, Franz Lachner, Gustav Albert Lortzing, Karl Heinrich Graun, and Heinrich Marschner is apparent throughout the correspondence, but perhaps more surprising is his regard for François-Adrien Boieldieu and Daniel-François-Esprit Auber. The older Thuille chided Strauss right away for his praise of Auber, to which Strauss replied somewhat facetiously, "Go ahead and be amazed that I write 'Master Auber,' and tremble at my revenge at you for insulting him . . . tremble and fear my wrath!" Strauss's opinion, of course, changed within a matter of years.

According to Schuh, Strauss—in his old age—was often annoyed at seeing excerpts of this correspondence cited in print. Perhaps some of his irritation stemmed from being reminded of his intense boyhood hatred of Wagner—an animosity no doubt fueled by his father. One letter is written entirely in cleverly parodied Wagnerian verse (complete with *Stabreim*): "Nach langem und *s*ehnlichen, *s*auren Warten / *h*ielt in *H*änden ich endlich die neidliche Post; / ich *w*artete *w*eiland auf *W*alhalls Zinnen / vor *S*ehn*s*ucht verzehrte mich beinahe der Rost . . ." His negative comments after hearing *Siegfried* for the first time were unequivocal: "I was quite frightfully bored, so horribly that I cannot tell you."

Strauss and Thuille remained in fairly close touch with each other throughout the 1880s and 1890s (Strauss dedicated *Don Juan,* among other works, to Thuille), but by the turn of the century their correspondence fell off significantly. By then they were traveling different aesthetic paths and both had become preoccupied with their own careers—Strauss as conductor in Berlin and Thuille as music professor in Munich. Strauss became the more famous composer yet always regarded Thuille highly as composer and musician, and he worked hard to get Thuille's compositions performed. And despite Strauss's great successes with such works as *Don Juan, Tod und Verklärung, Till Eulenspiegel,* and *Heldenleben,* he still deferred to Thuille's theoretical knowledge. In a letter from 1902 Strauss, in the midst of composing *Symphonia Domestica,* sent Thuille a fugue statement for the finale, asking him if he could come up with a *schulgerecht* fugal answer as well as a felicitous two-voice counterpoint. Thuille's response has been lost. Five years later, after receiving news of Thuille's sudden death, Strauss wrote his wife, Emma Thuille, that "with him yet another part of dear youth sinks into the grave" [ed.].

[Source: *Richard Strauss–Ludwig Thuille: Ein Briefwechsel,* ed. Franz Trenner (Tutzing: Schneider, 1980), pp. 25–72]

.

[blue monogram] RS   Munich, 5 October 1877

My dear Ludwig,
   It is already two weeks since we left beautiful Innsbruck, since we left the neighborhood of the big lake near Lans.[1] At the moment it is very pleasant here, too, since it is Oktoberfest, during which a bunch of booths, circuses, magic theaters, a dog theater, shooting galleries are set up on the big *Theresienwiese* outside the city, and on the seventh and fourteenth of October are two great races, before which they always have a ceremony and give prizes for livestock and horses. I am now taking piano lessons again, harmony lessons, violin lessons, and am (now) playing Czerny's *Schule der Fingerfertigkeit* [School of finger dexterity], nocturnes by [John] Field, the D-minor concerto of Mendelsohn,[2] and the *Well-Tempered Clavier* of J. S. Bach. In the harmony lessons I have double counterpoint and in the violin lessons the études by Kreutzer and the duets of Viotti. We will all be very happy if you keep your promise and come for vacation at Easter. For now only the most cordial greetings from all of us to you, dear Frau Nagiller,[3] and all the Marquesanis,[4] especially from

                                               Your
                                               loyal friend
                                               Richard Strauss.[5]

.

                                               Munich, 5 October 1876[6]

My dear Ludwig,
   Your dear letter brought me great pleasure, and I hasten to answer you as soon as possible. Your question in the letter whether I

am busy making music and have composed something again I can answer with *yes*. I am now playing the *School of Finger Dexterity* of Czerny, the D-minor concerto of Mendelssohn, the waltzes of Chopin, and whatever else gives me pleasure. I have now completed three movements of my serenade for orchestra[7]—*Adagio, Scherzo,* and *Finale*—and have already finished the orchestration.—Also I have already attended several concerts: a big subscription concert in which Haydn's splendid *Creation* was performed. The loveliness of the melodies, the magnificent choruses, the beautiful arias, recitatives, and duets, the splendid orchestration carried out down to the finest details, all this is thrilling and made my heart leap up in my chest, so to speak. One of our Viennese singers, Frau Schimon Regan,[8] sang the difficult coloratura arias truly masterfully, even if her voice is a bit weak. I say only, she is an artist, more I do not need to tell you, the word *artist* is enough for YOU. The tenor part was sung very well by our opera singer Herr Vogl[9] and bass by a Herr Staudigl[10] from Carlsruhe, whose voice is a bit harsh but who definitely *can* SING!! I was also in a quartet evening in which a quartet of Haydn in G major, one of Mozart in E♭ major, and the last quartet of Beethoven, in F major, was played. One can scarcely decide which of these three heroes one should give first place to; all three quartets were equally beautiful, each in its own way, Haydn with his pleasantness, Mozart with his serious and yet so lovely and fresh composition, Beethoven with his deep seriousness and his gloom.— I hope that you are well and also dear Frau Nagiller, Marchesanis; to all the most cordial greetings from my parents and my sister, but especially to you from

Your
loyal friend Richard.

In my harmony studies I am already far advanced in double counterpoint.

•

Munich, 21 December 1877

Dear Ludwig,

Your dear letter made me very happy. I now have time enough for letters, for I have been lying in bed for seventeen days now with an intestinal cold and must ask you for that very reason, however, to excuse my penmanship, since this letter is also written in bed. You mention in your letter that you are not clear about the way to write transitions and included two modulations with the question which of them is right: both of them are right, for in this case—that is, with modulations—it is quite irrelevant how you mark the key into which you are moving, for between C♭ major and B major is no difference at all, for here you have only an *enharmonic exchange.* I have recently composed four songs:[11] "Der Fischer" and "Lust und Qual" by Goethe, "Die Drossel" by Uhland,[12] and "Lass Ruhn die Todten" (a rather odd title) by Chamisso.[13] Then I completed my serenade in G major for orchestra and, in one and a half days (the day before yesterday and yesterday morning), a trio in A major for piano, violin, and cello.[14] Your request that I send you my piano compositions [is something] I have been thinking about for a long time; my sonata[15] I sent out for copying right after your second letter but have not gotten it back as yet; you will receive it as soon as I get it back. That you have now also finally gotten instruction in harmony makes me very happy; I am still at double counterpoint, for this must be studied diligently, since it is the basis for the fugue.—At our house the Christmas holidays begin on the twenty-second of December and continue until the second of January.—As far as what you mentioned about the *Faust* Overture of Wagner,[16] I can tell you, since I have already heard it, that it is a mess and jumble that is without comparison in the world. The B♭-major symphony of Beethoven, if it comes *after* the mess, will repay you richly for the feast your ears have just endured. But if it is *before* it, then I advise you, since the overture then probably comes at the end, to leave before it, since it would spoil the whole impression of the splendid symphony for you. The ballet music from *Rosamunde* I have not heard yet, and therefore I can't judge it, but in any case as Schubert's work it will be very beautiful.—

With many cordial greetings for you, dear Frau Nagiller, Marquesanis, from my dear parents, my sister, I remain

Your
loving friend Richard.

I enclose with this letter a list[17] of my compositions up to now and you need only write which of them you would like to have and I will send them to you. I promise to dedicate my next piano compositions to you, since I have dedicated them up to now partly to my dear Papa, partly to relatives of mine.

!!!!!!!!!See you at Easter!!!!!!

*I also ask you to send me your sonatas and the two nocturnes.[18]

[green monogram] S   Monday, 31 December 1877

My dear Ludwig,

Prosit tibi annus novus!

Your dear letter, which I received an hour ago, gave me great joy and I hasten to answer it. You will not be able to explain my passion for writing, since Mama told you that I am not a particular friend of letter writing; but quite honestly I write to you with such pleasure that I cannot explain it myself. It may be because I can say everything in the letters to you and can hold forth with essays about the music we both hold dear. As I can see from your letters you compose very quickly, and I am already looking forward very much to your piano pieces and lieder. New, for me, I have composed Op. 16, a Benedictus for four voices.[19] Your statement that Schubert is more recognized than Mozart is not entirely right, for in his own time Mozart was more recognized than now, since he is now no longer understood by most people. If you only knew what he composed in thirty-five years, you would be simply astonished and would exclaim, That is not possible. And yet [it] was completed. It has actually been established that a hard-working copyist could not *write* in thirty-five years what he *composed* in that period. And yet he spent whole days sitting in coffee-houses and went to pubs and played his favorite game, billiards, and he composed the overture to *Don Giovanni* in one night and without having seen a score immediately wrote down the voices, individually, and gave them to the copyist, since next morning the first rehearsal[20] of *Don Giovanni* was supposed to have taken place.—

So far as learning instrumental music is concerned, I can only give you *one* piece of good advice—not to learn it from a book, since this, as my father says, is the worst thing. So I advise you not to buy a book, since even my papa only knows one by Hector Berlioz, who is a real scribbler and hack; instead ask Herr Pembaur[21] for a table covering the range and best position of the various instruments that are used and learn the rest, that is the use and application of the same, from the scores of the great old masters, which Herr Pembaur, if you ask Frau Nagiller to lean on him a bit, will surely lend you.—

Now only the most cordial greetings from all of us to you, dear Frau Nagiller and Marchesanis but especially to you, dear friend, from

Your

loving friend

Richard.

Happy New Year!

·

[violet monogram] S   Munich, 10 January 1878

My dear Ludwig,
    To fulfill your wishes I am hereby sending you the lieder: Op. 7,
no. 2, and Op. 5, no. 1,[22] the E-major sonata[23] is not yet finished;
since I have very little to do at present I composed Op. 17, a new
song, "Spielmann und Zither," by Körner and laid the foundation for
a final movement of my second sonata in D major (variations).[24] I
am more or less cured and since Monday I have been going to school
again, but I must still watch my diet carefully and may not go out
on the ice to skate, on account of cold feet. The three lieder I have
copied myself, while the previous two are written by a copyist. The
boring fellow has had my E-major sonata since the beginning of December and I have still not got it back. I am very annoyed with him.
I can't write more, since it is already quarter to one o'clock, we eat
at one, and I still have several chapters of *Caesar* to prepare. With
the most cordial greetings from us all, for you, dear Frau Nagiller
and Marchesanis I remain

                                        Your
                                        loving friend
                                        Richard.

·

[violet monogram] S   Munich, 26 January 1878

My dear Ludwig,
    Your dear letter gave me great happiness and I can only agree with
your opinions about Wagner, (and); my Papa was also quite enchanted
with them. I am very eager to hear your opinion about the splendid
Symphonia Jovis of the master of masters. It is the most fantastic work
I ever heard and I thought I was in heaven when these sounds
reached my ears. *Musica, omnium artium pulcherrima, vivat!* Most recently I am composing a chorus to my drama *Lila* by Goethe,[25] orchestrating it at the same time, and will have it finished soon. Recently my papa received from General Director Franz Lachner[26] a serenade for wind instruments, in print, Op. 14 by Julius Röntgen,[27] also
a young composer, but already twenty years old or so; please tell Frau
Nagiller, who will be very interested in it and will tell you more about
this creative young man if you have not already heard it from her
directly. The serenade seems from the look of it to be quite pretty,
it is very prettily orchestrated.—I have just played your sonata[28] for

my teacher, Tombo,[29] who liked it very much, especially the third and fourth movements, which are the two I like best, too. They are really very pretty and the last movement pleases me especially. The more often I play it, the more I like it. Since on account of my illness I am only allowed to work as little as possible, I have not yet completed the chorus,[30] which would probably long since have happened otherwise, and started something new.—In math I wish you good luck and will keep my fingers crossed that you pass.—With the most cordial greetings I remain

>Your
>eternally[31] loving friend
>Richard.

The most cordial greetings from all of us to dear Frau Nagiller and Marchesanis.

·

[violet monogram] S   Munich, 6 February 1878

My dear Ludwig,

   Your dear letter makes me very happy except I find your criticism not entirely correct, for the *Leonore* Overture, as wonderfully beautiful as it is, is *never* greater than the *Jupiter* Symphony. For me Beethoven is *never* greater than Mozart, the two of them are at the exact same level in their own way; Mozart is even more many-sided than Beethoven; wait until you come here, and your eyes will be opened about Mozart, for sure. I have been composing some things for piano lately and am now at Op. 20, some songs, of which one— "Im Walde!" by Geibel—is already finished. Only the text of the next one—"Der Spielman und sein Kind" by H. Fallersleben[32]—is done so far. My trio[33] has been performed several times already at my uncle's, Anton Knözinger,[34] royal chief auditor and prosecutor, to whom I dedicated the piece as cellist, and pleased the audience so much that I had not expected such hymns of praise; my uncle especially was thoroughly enthralled about a transition in adagio from F major to E major and was so pleased about my dedication that as a sign of his extreme pleasure he used one of his army swear words with Mama and called me a "scoundrel." When Mama told me about it the next day I really had to laugh. I'm sorry things are going so poorly for you in class, and I will read a long litany from a prayerbook—for you—Cato said a long time ago: *Ego censeo, Carthaginem esse delendam,*[35] that is, I will pray to the gods for you. *Vale! Ego maneo*

Tuus
(good Latin) tibi
amicissimus
Ricardus Strubico.

N.B. Warmest wishes from all of us for you, dear Ludwig, dear Frau
Nagiller, and the Marchesanis.

.

[small brown postcard] [end of February, 1878]

Dear Ludwig,

Forgive me that I can't write you a longer letter just now, it is really quite impossible, since by next Tuesday I must finish three songs
for the fortieth anniversary of a famous singer here[36] and I still
haven't even copied the third (eight pages long).

In the greatest haste

Your
loving Richard. —

My health improves every day.

Ask your guardian very, very, very much to let you come; otherwise
I will go crazy.

A letter will follow, when I have the songs done, soon!

.

[green monogram] S Munich, 1 March [1878]

My dear Ludwig,

You are probably quite angry at me that I have not written to you
in such a long time, but you will have to excuse me, I had so little
time until now that it was quite impossible for me to send you a few
comforting words, as I wanted so much to do. I am really very sorry
about your accident and I find it dreadful of your relatives that they
fall upon you like crows and vultures and refuse to help you; I beg
you to write to me if you should be in need in any way and your
relatives do not support you. I would be seriously angry if I should
find out later that you had been in need. I am very willing you [*sic*]
support you in whatever you need. If this is the case, then write to
me, otherwise . . . ! This can happen to the best students, that they
have bad luck once, and you didn't waste the time when you were
supposed to be studying but spent it on noble *musica* and made
progress in composition during those hours that will later stand you
in better stead than empty career studies. That does not mean that I

want to keep you from studying, on which you now, like me, must spend the most time, for that is our profession for now, and Greek and Latin and so on advances your education significantly, and a good musician must also be educated! I can write nothing about concerts and theater since I haven't been anywhere yet; but this evening I am allowed to go to see the *Jungfrau von Orleans*.[37] Recently we had a Greek exam, a Greek quiz, a Latin and a math exam, of which [I] passed the first with a one/two, the second with a one, the third with a two; we haven't gotten the fourth back yet. We have geography and history exams next, for which I have to study conscientiously.—With cordial greetings from us to all acquaintances and friends in Innsbruck,

> Your
> loving, ever faithful friend
> Richard.

* My health is getting better and better. (But don't show this letter to your guardian but ask him to let you come for Easter.)[38]

·

[green monogram] S   [end of March, 1878]

My best Ludwig,

Your dear letter gave me great pleasure, especially as I learned that your guardian has allowed your visit here at Easter. Your criticism I more or less agree with, I am only surprised that you don't mention anything about the splendid Samson aria and its composition and you shouldn't call Saint-Saëns[39] a dolt or an ass; on the contrary he is a genius. Even if the *Marche héroique* was not to your taste—as I can well imagine, for he has to make something for "his Parisians" that suits their taste!—I have heard very nice things by him, for example a very pretty piano quartet, and a G-minor piano concerto of his that he performed here himself this winter was very much praised *by my father,* which says a great deal in the case of a new composer. (I couldn't go myself on account of my illness.)

II. Subscription Concert [20 March 1878] (Criticism)

1. A wonderful symphony in D major[40] by the divine Mozart. The first movement was passionate and dashing, the second *(Andante)* wonderful; these lovely strains delighted my ears and [I] could have heard this wonderful *Andante* ten more times; then came a friendly, easygoing minuet and then a graceful *Presto.* The symphony was ravishingly beautiful.

2. Three tasteless, affected songs from the *Trompeter von Säckingen*

by Scheffel, sung by the Munich *Kammersänger* Vogl, a comedian by trade; they are composed by a certain Max Zenger.[41]

3. "Le Roué d'Omphale,"[42] a light, racy spinning song (not much substance) by Camille Saint-Saëns for "his Parisians."

4. Three duets (very pretty) by Schumann, sung by M. and Mme Vogl, who compete with each other in their thespian antics in concert. The text of the two last duets, "Liebhabers Ständchen" [Lover's ditty] and "Unterm Fenster" [Under the window] by Robert Burns,[43] are quite vulgar.

5. A very beautiful symphony by Mendelssohn[44] with an extraordinarily original scherzo and a very fiery, magnificent finale.

That the program you are planning to play for us at Easter is lacking Mozart surprises me very much, for it is mainly in his works that one recognizes a fine pianist. Mendelssohn's piano works have also attained a significant level and his things for piano are very beautiful.—

With a request for information about the day and hour of your arrival, I remain

> Your
> warmly loving
> Richard.

N.B. The most cordial greetings from all of us for you, Frau Nagiller, and Marquesanis.

·

[blue monogram] S

Dear, best, most beautiful and splendid Ludwig,

I kept thinking, Why doesn't Ludwig write for such a long time, it is quite contrary to his usual habit. Then I come home today and find a package from Innsbruck and discovered the reason for your long and for me painful delay, since I was already beginning to believe you were prevented from writing, finally, by a serious illness. Thus I spy the package. Cutting the strings and tearing off the paper was a matter of ten seconds. I unrolled the paper and—could scarcely believe my eyes—a quartet for two violins, viola, and cello, dedicated to me![45] The joy that I felt at this is something you cannot possibly imagine, first to read the long-awaited letter, then to the piano to play it through. I found the work exquisite, rich in melodies, very beautifully composed, brilliantly done, full of heightened intensity, splendid form. Papa's judgment I will write to you later, since I am answering the letter at once and Papa is not at home. My

most cordial, warmest, best, best thanks for your generosity and friendliness and love.

Concert criticism

Last Friday the students at the music conservatory here put on a so-
called musical evening, at which were performed:

1. Suite (D major)[46] for orchestra by our master Bach. This is a
splendid work; the first movement *(Vivace)* is fiery and full of spirit
and the D trumpets that Bach and Handel loved so much sound very
beautiful with their passages:

Second movement was a devotional air, in which the first violins carried the melody without mutes, while the second violins and violas
accompanied them with mutes and the basses and cellos provided the
bass in pizzicato in the following way:

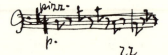

The third movement was a fiery gavotte with trumpet passages similar to the first movement.

2. First movement from a violin concerto of the divine Mozart. All
the compositions by this "hero"[47] are so clear and transparent and
so rich in melodies and so lovely that with every composition by
Mozart I revere him more, and even adore him. The first movement
of the above-named violin concerto was played quite skillfully by a
certain Presel.

3. Aria for bass from *Hans Heiling* by Marschner.[48] The beautiful
aria, which contains significant buildup and passion, was screamed by
a "bawler" named Maximiliano Heitel.

4. A certain Giehrl[49] played the splendid first movement of
Beethoven's G-major piano concerto. This brilliant work is distinguished primarily by genuine virtuoso piano passages and refinement
of the accompaniment, virtues that the earlier violin concerto shares
in equal measure. These two, Mozart and Beethoven, *hi duissimi* (su-
perlative of duo!) "heroes"[50] grab hold of the violin and the piano
in just the right way, and everything is genuinely violin- and pianolike.
The pianist played the movement excellently.

5. Quintet from *Cosi fan tutte* by Mozart. This splendid quintet was so wrecked by five bleaters that it [turned] into a caricature.[51] You can imagine how the five sang if in regard to *Mozart* I use the word "caricature."

6. Evening song for organ, cello, and harp by C. Matys;[52] it is sentimental, boring stuff that I don't want to waste a word on.

7. An airy, fine, graceful, sweet overture by our master Haydn, who, with Mozart, Beethoven, and Schubert, occupies the top level in music; but for the overture the title first or last movement of a symphony would fit better than overture, since it is entirely in symphonic form.

Last Sunday I was in the imposing *Freischütz,* which I have insufficient time and paper to describe. About it at Easter, an oral report!

Last Monday was "quartet soirée." First a *splendid* E♭-major concerto by the *splendid* Haydn.[53] The first movement was made up of variations, of which one, in particular, pleased me; here the first violin had the melody, while the second violin and viola had the figure:

The third movement was an extremely original minuet, which ends very unexpectedly as follows:

The fourth movement is very fresh and passionate. Then came an E-minor quartet of our local contrapuntist and important composer Franz Lachner. This work is as original as it is beautiful and rich in melodies and composed in strict counterpoint. I especially liked the original figures of the cello in the *Adagio.* This repeatedly brings the figure:

which sounds extremely interesting. Especially pretty was the third movement, an airy scherzo, à la Mendelssohn (fairies) *Midsummer Night's Dream,* with a comical trio in $\frac{5}{4}$ rhythm.

[new sheet of paper, blue monogram] S (continued!)

Then came an exquisite quartet (A major) by our master Beethoven.[54] Particularly beautiful and interesting [were] the variations *(Andante)* in the third movement. You could tell right away whose composition you had before you.

IV. Subscription Concert

1. Overture *Abencérages* by Cherubini.[55] As he loves to do, the D-major overture starts with some *all' unisono* passages in the introduction and in it an extremely funny figure appears:

and the instruments of the quartet enter this figure one after another: first cellos and violas, then "second" violins, then "first" violins. The overture itself, that is, the *Allegro,* is very beautiful, and I particularly liked the coda; here the flutes and oboes and then the violins have approximately this figure:

2. A lightening-quick Jew, name of Josephy,[56] from Vienna, played the splendid E-minor concerto by Chopin, in which I especially liked the *Adagio,* in which the bassoon has very pretty obbligato passages; Jospehy is a good pianist but (says Papa) a Jewish slob;

3. Scherzo by Goldmark,[57] another Jew. Junk, I will skip the details.

4. Josephy played 1) Chromatic Fantasy by J. S. Bach, which is very dry and long, but still beautiful; and 2) the well-known Gavotte by Martini:[58]

3. A self-composed study on Chopin's D♭-major waltz, which is a genuine little virtuoso gem; but Josephy would have done better to leave the waltz the way Chopin wrote it;

4. B♭-major symphony by Beethoven[59] (magnificent), which you have already heard in Innsbruck.—

I beg you again most urgently to write me the day and hour of your arrival, and remain, again expressing my warmest thanks,

Your

warmly loving, forever

faithful friend Richard.

Thursday, 4 April 1878
N.B. Most cordial greetings from all of us to you, dear Ludwig, good Frau Nagiller, and Marquesanis.

.

[twenty-four-rule note paper with motto printed above left:][60]

Wenn du fein fromm bist, will ich

Dear Ludwig,

So recently I was in *Siegfried* and I can tell you, I was bored stiff, I was quite frightfully bored, so horribly that I cannot even tell you. But it was beautiful, incredibly beautiful, this wealth of melodies, this dramatic intensity, this fine instrumentation, and clever it was, eminently beautiful! You will think he's lost it, well I will make it all right again and tell you it was dreadful. The introduction is a drumroll with bass tubas and bassoons, shouting in the deepest tones, which sounds so stupid that I laughed right out loud. Suddenly it breaks off and all alone the French horn goes:

Another muffled roll of the drums with bass tubas and potatoes à
~~~ bassoon: the growling goes on for a long time until the curtain rises, then this starts:

This goes on in sequences interminably: When Siegfried comes, it
starts to go:

and so on for a long time. Of coherent *melodies* not a trace: two measures go together, two measures, then it suddenly stops and this comes:

or the original growling again, I say a disorder is in there, you cannot possibly imagine it. I also heard:

from *Rheingold*. Then in the first act comes a frightful passage composed likewise [of] many sequences (in general Wagner is very fond
of sequences) of diminished and augmented triads and seventh
chords. At this point cats would have died and the dissonances were
so horrible that even rocks would have turned to puddles. The vio-
linists exhaust themselves with endless tremolos and the *brass* in VIO-
LIN PASSAGES and Wagner even used the trumpet mute in order to
make everything completely horrible and disgusting. My ears were
ringing from these cripples of chords, if one may even call them that;
and the last act is so boring you could die. The scene between
Siegfried and Brünnhilde all in adagio; I thought, Won't there ever
be allegro; but no, this terrible howling and whining from a seventh
down to a ninth, then back up again like this:

and so on and on; this last scene is ～～. Find no words to write all this horribleness to you; and when you have heard the first scenes of the first act you have heard the whole nonsense, for everything repeats itself again. The only thing that at least *made sense* was the song of the wild bird. The beginning of the third act is a noise that just about destroys your ears, brass instrumentation as follows: four French horns, four trumpets, four trombones, four tubas, four bass tubas, with violins and woodwinds it makes a frightful racket. The whole ——[61] can be expressed in a hundred measures, then always the same thing and always the same thing and always the same thing and always equally boring and always equally boring and always equally bor . . . ～～～, etc., etc., horrible, miserable, etc., etc.

But clever!!!

Sunday I was in *La Muette de Portici* by Auber,[62] a very dramatic, extremely beautiful opera. Although his other operas are more *Spielopern* (not to be misunderstood), this one is highly dramatic. Splendid, truly noble, beautiful melodies, strict forms, enormously beautiful instrumentation, splendid harmonies. Especially the pantomime music; when the mute does her pantomimes, the music expresses her feelings, and it is sometimes wild, sometimes melting and mellifluous, exactly what the mood calls for. Accompanying the postlude of the extremely beautiful fisher's song, the bassoon even goes through a beautiful chromatic scale down three octaves; all in all the whole opera is so rich in splendid melodies; I especially liked the finale of the fifth act with the mad scene; magnificent, I was completely charmed; you would certainly have liked it a great deal too. In general I am learning little by little to appreciate Auber as an extraordinary fellow. There is a prayer for a chorus in four voices in it, it is so contrapuntal, you would think one of the oldest counterpoint masters had written it. *Vale!*

> Your
> eternally and warmly
> loving
> Richard.

(Excuse the laconic *tone I have assumed*.)

[twenty-four-rule notepaper with motto printed upper left:][63]

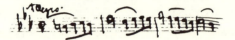

Treibt der Champagner

Dear Ludwig, who insults Master Auber,

Go ahead and be amazed that I write Master Auber, and tremble at my revenge at you for insulting him, a capital offense, for the passage, even if it is not as noble as:

from *Freischütz,* still sounds quite nice, and especially for three trombones. Have you ever heard it for three trombones, or for a full orchestra? No, and so you can't judge it; I, however, have heard it and I am telling you that it is, as I already said, if not particularly noble, still quite pretty. (Now I have told you, you miserable doggone . . . !) Tremble and fear my wrath . . . ! That you advise me to give up Shakespeare surprises me very much; perhaps you think I don't understand the half of it; but there I can tell you without fibbing that up to now (I have read *King John, Richard II,* and *Henry IV,* parts 1 and 2) not a speck has been unclear to me and I like him enormously especially in *Henry IV* the great scene between Henry IV and the Prince of Wales in the fifth act of the second part. I have now also gotten *Ivanhoe* by the splendid Walter Scott[64] to read, and I am looking forward to it very much. Soon the

will be performed here (= XYZ).[65]

Most recently I was in the oratorio *Tod Jesu* by Graun,[66] an old-time composer, which I liked extraordinarily well and is really also very beautiful. I expected an old-fashioned thing but got to hear very beautiful recitatives, arias, and choruses. Too bad you weren't there. (The text is frightful.) The music is *very* beautiful; [I] was completely surprised.—Also I was in *La Dame Blanche,* opera by Adrien Boildieu[67] [*sic*], which I liked a great deal. Such noble melodies, such magnificence and drama and such beautiful instrumentation! In the opera there is a great French horn solo and after that an aria for tenor that goes like this:

This solo (the theater is quiet as a mouse) makes a magnificent impression on the audience. (The accompaniment must naturally be very delicate.) Then the finale of the second act, the great auctioning off of the palace, the rage of the evil ex-owner of the palace who wants to seize it for himself, but is continually outbid by an unknown officer and the cheers of the populace that the bad guy doesn't get the palace; all that is magnificent and dramatic in the highest degree and if [I] wanted to count up everything that is beautiful in the opera I would have to write much more than this sheet of paper.

(!)But now I must write something to you that I would rather not have written. Namely, the whole Pschorr cellar,[68] with the exception of the little house, burned down to the ground. Two big buildings, one of which—a large, new hall—my uncle had just built, a huge amount of empty casks burned up and the two younger Pschorr boys, whom you know, barely escaped the flames, which burned up their bedroom in one building of the two that burned up. The fire started at 2:30 in the morning, but they were still putting it out through the entire day that followed; could see nothing but the four walls and burned-out timbers, bent hoops from the casks, stones, and blackened debris four feet high—made a sad and terrible sight! But enough of that . . . !

Cordial greetings to you, dear Frau Nagiller, Marchesanis from us all, I remain

> Your
> warmly loving friend
> Richard.

6 June 1878!

WRITE SOON!

.

[blue monogram] LD
Dear Ludwig,

When I received your last letter I had sworn to keep you waiting quite a long time because you took so long, so that you too will know what it is like to have to wait quite long and longingly for a letter. Now finally I shall take pity on you and send you news of me from Sillian.[69] We are all very happy and healthy, I drive out a lot, take walks, and amuse myself exquisitely. You will forgive me for not writing much; you know what it is like in the country. I brought the tobacco, just as I bought it, it seemed like an awful lot, but as a result of the packing it got so pressed together that I was quite taken aback when I saw it, and I am embarrassed to send you so little, so I bought some Austrian in addition, which I am sending you separately from the Bavarian.

With most cordial greetings,

> Your
> warmly loving friend
> Richard.

I am playing organ sonatas by Mendelssohn[70] on the organ here, we play trios and quartets, which I enjoy a great deal.

.

[blue monogram] JS[71]   Munich, 28 October 1878

Dear Ludwig,

Long I listed, in painful delay;
Here I hold your mail at last in
  my fist
Woeful I waited on Valhalla's
  walls,
Yearning I was almost devoured
  by rust;
When at last clove through
  clouds the sun
They delivered the letter from a
  faraway zone;
Then I leapt up; jumped for joy
  in the breeze
What was inside the letter—full
  forty (fleas)
  (in Goethe full forty—)

Don't take the verse as an insult. It is a piece of foolishness.[72]

I am in a very serious mood, you will recognize that from the poem, my face is dark; I am a strange person, now serious, full of profound dignity, now cheerful; today I am in the most stupid mood, half-fool, half-man.

I have become a Wagnerian; I was in *Die Walküre*, I am enraptured; I don't even comprehend people who can claim a Mozart might be beautiful, who can go so far as to do harm to their tongue and their gullet by expressing such a thing; if we compare M—— (I prefer not to say it out loud) D.G.,[73] with Wagner's, *The German Herolds* (heros)[74] (a miserable new made-up journal, *Deutscher Herold*), *Walküre.* How characteristic this introduction is: the violins continually tremolate on the splendid D, while the basses thrill the listener with the continually repeated reflective figure:

M—— merely doodles a completely trite march in $\frac{4}{4}$ rhythm with a couple of fiddles, a horn player, and half a kettledrum, only in a faster tempo; tell us, is that artistry, making something with a couple of instruments—five or six; and then the same kind of bagpipe melody only pianissimo; no; but in Wagner this power, this heroldism (-roism), the violence; then the beginning, how much meaning one always hears in the sounds of the cello descending from the third to the fifth and into the seventh and down to the ninth; then the ten horns, the six splendid bass tubas, the imposing thirteen trombones with the grave:

then the beautiful narrative of Wotan, the bass holds a solemn, deep note, Wotan sings the narrative in the low notes (six pages); that is seriousness, that is grief, but M——, if he wants to do something serious, writes down G minor and then invents a melody off it like Augustine; but in these notes in Wagner one doesn't even recognize the key; that is imposing, that is elevating. Then the so-called modulations, pooh—; M—— takes ten measures to get from E♭ major to A major, so that the audience doesn't notice a thing; is *that* what you call music? no; but Wagner simply composes A major = E♭ major; G major = C♯ major; so that the audience notices immediately; then the Ride of the Valkyries, the wild daughters of Mother Nature, characterized in their free state among thunder and lightning; the horns and trumpets blast into the wild night, the violins run around wildly; the conductor, in his enthusiasm, throws the baton at one of the Valkyries' heads, causing her to fall to the ground in a swoon, that is splendid, imposing, elevating. But that one (the listener, that is) at a couple of points in the first act, for example Wotan's Farewell and Magic Fire, can still tell what key one is in—I can never forgive Wagner for this outrage against his own music. With Mozart you always know that, the author's thoughts are not swimming vaguely in front of one's eyes; so damn the simpleton and peasant M——, impudent that he is; and may Wagner, in his splendor, be raised to his magnificently portrayed Wotan as a god in Halvalla.

Seriously:

Also I was in the splendid *Egmont,* in which the poet and the composer compete for the greater honor; this splendid overture with the magnificent victory march; how effective the trumpets and horns are there, what power, what essence it contains, what softness in the splendid intermezzi (not to mention the instrumention); how characteristic the music is at the death of Clärchen, you think [you] hear Clärchen's pulse as it becomes weaker and weaker until it stops altogether. I was also in the *Piccolomini* [by Ernest Guirand, 1876], which I liked very much, especially the banquet with the drunken Illo. I have now gotten [lessons] from an excellent piano player and teacher, Herr Niest,[75] who otherwise only gives lessons to grown-up persons, not boys like me. Great honor. Well now, be well, dear Ludwig; I will tell you more in my next letter. Write *soon.*

Your Richard;

Most cordial greetings and my best, best thanks to *dear* Frau Nagiller for the lovely book: Tegnér's *Frityofsage.*[76]

·

[blue monogram] JS   [early December, 1878]

Dear Ludwig,

Received your dear letter, which gave me as much pleasure as the other one displeasure. I am now reconciled with you again, since I have recognized your obligingness; the last subscription concert [30 November 1878] brought quite a pretty symphony in C major by Schumann[77] in which, however, there is also Schumann's inevitable tendency to ride his figures to death; the brisk scherzo and the pretty *Adagio* are the better movements of the symphony; the last movement, with the exception of the passage

which, as my Papa says, is from one of Lortzing's operas, *Undine,* [is] almost nothing but repetitious figures.

When I said I thought the orchestration was quite tolerable Papa declared that it was very clumsy, they were all blowing and bowing at the same time.

After this Frau Clara Schumann,[78] the wife of Robert Schumann, played the magnificent G-major concerto by Beethoven, with a technique, an attack, and an artistic interpretation the likes of which I never heard before. Every note she struck was pure, every phrase she played corresponded to the overall artistic quality of the composition, so that there is probably no one else who would play this concerto the same way as Frau Schumann. Here there is none of the fakery with which piano players of both sexes[79] try to rouse the audience to enthusiasm, and of which even Herr von Bülow[80] cannot claim to be entirely free, as Papa said, though he plays delightfully (I have heard him myself); here the sole concern is for art itself, and that is the thing, in truth, that makes the audience so enthusiastic. And then the enchanting concerto; such lightness, such grace, then the wild *Adagio,* in which the orchestra has all these wild phrases, and the piano responds as if soothing it, the orchestra gets quieter and quieter, until it finally loses itself in murmurs, then the bright, happy final movement that follows is quite enchanting, and then the instrumentation!! Then our singer Herr Reichmann,[81] three lieder by Schumann, which were very pretty; then Frau Schumann played the well-known *Novelette* and *Romanze* by Schumann and the A♭-major waltz of Chopin, and as an encore the E-minor waltz—quite charming!

The finale was Beethoven's splendid, effective *König Stephan* Overture! It is quite magnificent, these trumpet and drum entries are quite magnificent. You should hear it sometime for orchestra, it sounds entirely different from the chopping board (naturally I do not mean the lovely grand piano belonging to Frau Nagiller).—I am now playing the B-minor concerto by Hummel[82] (very beautiful but very difficult), while my teacher mainly pays attention to "finger position" in another sense of the word, not that my fingers are awkward or crooked, but according to the principle "never the thumb on the highest note" (naturally with exceptions) and "breaking the habit of constantly using the pedal." I have also learned the thirty-two variations in C minor by Beethoven by heart and in my harmony lesson I have *imitations and canon.* I was also in *Hans Heiling* by Marschner, an opera that is very rich in melodies, dramatic, and very beautiful.

Your
warmly loving Richard.

Papa advises you to give up playing Chopin and to concentrate ONLY *on classical music.*

About my new compositions next time!

Write soon!!!!

·

[lilac monogram] S   Munich, 21 December 1878

My dear Ludwig,

Your dear letter made me very happy and [I] answer it right away in order to clear up several misunderstandings.

Regarding the accompaniment of the first and last movements of my E-major sonata[83] I am in agreement that I made a serious mistake here and in many [virtuoso] passages, and in my second sonata and my other things I shall break my old habit

and make a solider accompaniment. I am very grateful to you for drawing my attention to this and would not have dared, if I had seen these serious defects earlier, to appear before you with such a shoddy piece of work, much less to dedicate it to you, in contrast to your sonata,[84] which [is] on a much higher level than mine. Regarding the second part of the first movement I did not dare to do a development so I only wrote a short transition. I don't find at all that the construction of your rondo is all wrong, except that this movement does not deserve the name "rondo." The expression "somewhat form-less" is a little too harsh; and I did not mean formless in the proper sense of the word but only wanted to suggest that quite a few thoughts appear that are "entirely different from one another."

Regarding orthographic errors I would like to mention: first of all, in the fourth measure before the end of the first part of the first movement instead of

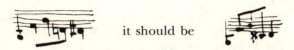 it should be

then in the second measure before the end of the first part of the first movement instead of

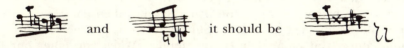 and it should be

Then in the *Adagio:* in the fourteenth measure before the end of the *Adagio,* in the bass, instead of

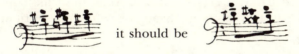 it should be

then in the eighth measure before the end of the *Adagio* in place of

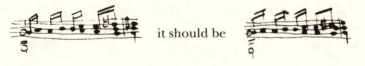 it should be

In the last movement, in the thirtieth measure instead of

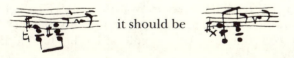 it should be

I don't entirely agree with your change in the "Nachtlied";[85] pre-cisely the G♯ pleases me very much except it would be better if in place of the following C you would put another G♯.

Regarding the book about the theory of musical form I must correct an error—namely, I did not write that I would send this book but rather that musical form theory is treated sufficiently in the book by Richter[86] that I sent you last year, before we knew each other. My health is still not particularly good; I go to class, but I still have to watch my diet very carefully. On account of my measly illness, which I wish were at the other end of the world, I have been prevented this whole time from taking lessons, which naturally makes me very sorry, and my parents would also rather spend money on lessons than on doctors and medicine.

I hope that your fever is better again, too; please let me know in your next letter. So far as math is concerned, I am in complete agreement with you; I get the creeps, too, when I think about it. *Regarding* the saying of twelve rosaries, I am unable to fulfill your request since, first of all, I don't know the rosary and, second, I have no particular desire to learn unintelligent blather. If it is really not possible for you to make the trip before Palm Sunday, then come, as sorry as I would be about it, after Palm Sunday; there is probably a subscription concert on Easter Sunday or Monday. When you enter our living room at Eastertime, the first thing that meets your eyes should be the scores of *Don Giovanni, Fidelio,* and *Freischütz,* and after that, as backup, good Bavarian cigars and beer we keep in the house.

I thank you again with all my heart for your honest critique and remain

Your
warmly loving
Richard.

Most cordial greetings from all of us to you, dear Frau Nagiller, and Marchesanis.

·

[red monogram] R

O thou infatuated Schumann fan!

A Schumann *Adagio* comparable to a Beethoven *Adagio!* ha! ha! ha! ha! ha! ha! That is terrible! What are you thinking! That is the limit! That makes one want to run and hide. Schumann may have beautiful things; but comparable to Beethoven! ha! ha! ha! ha! ha! ha! Then I don't find this

grotesque but rather extremely ordinary. As far as his things for piano are concerned, I find the *Kinderszenen* and some of the *Fantasiestücke* the most beautiful, although once he has a rhythm he rides it so to death that one often can't stand listening to him. (You know stenography.)[87] I am almost finished with the canon now; in a couple of hours the fugue will follow. Up to now I haven't bought any new Richter at all; as you see I am learning everything practically without books. I ask you please to answer my question—do you know stenography (Gabelsberger's)? Also, I promised to send you my critique of *Lohenyellow* (*Lohengreen*); the introduction consists of an A-major rustling of the violins in the highest register, which sounds terribly sweet and sickly like the whole opera; there are beautiful moments in it but then again such boring stuff; they are always doing recitative with the help of musical tones, but now and again there is a melody of two to four to eight, or even (often, in the case of W.) sixteen bars; the orchestration is rough, the whole opera has frightfully much in common with *Euryanthe* (i.e., plagiarized), only the plot is beautiful; the plot, by itself, pleased me, although it, too, is terribly long. If the whole opera, instead of from 6:00 to 10:00, would last from 6:30 to 9:30, it would be considerably better;[88] the whole opera is in duple and quadruple meter, with the exception of a single quarter of an hour, an ensemble (which is quite nice and effective) in $\frac{3}{4}$ time.

Now, dear Ludwig, be healthy, we are all well, most cordial greetings to dear Frau Nagiller: I am your

> Warmly loving friend
> Richard.

Saturday, 22 February 1879

.

[blue monogram] R   [end of March, 1879]

You are a fearfully careless fellow when it comes to writing. First he lets you wait a couple of millennia, then he sends some note he has scribbled in the evening at 10:00 after the theater. It is no longer to be endured. In the meantime there were many concerts and theater performances.

First subscription concert [10 March 1879]

1. Suite (D major) for strings, three trumpets, two oboes, and timpani by Bach. A splendid work; how beautiful and clear the three trumpets sound in the high register; the *Adagio* is a wonderful air for

a solo violin; the second violins and violas accompany it with mutes; the bass pizzicato. Then two wonderfully beautiful gavottes follow and at the end a gigue.[89]

Then came the splendid C-minor symphony by Haydn;[90] a superior composition; what splendid thoughts that master had and in what profusion; how splendid the middle passage in the first movement is:

You know this symphony; then the splendid *Andante* and the splendid minuet

where he suddenly breaks off in the second part and then brings the D♭ chord and then modulates to C minor; then the charming trio with the cello solo.

At the end came Beethoven's splendid *Eroica*.—It is funny how the more often one hears something truly beautiful the more one likes it; but the oftener one hears something bad or mediocre, the more one dislikes it or even finds it quite unpleasant.

Second subscription concert [20 March 1879]

1. The magnificent *Coriolanus* overture by Beethoven, which the conductor unfortunately spoiled so terribly by means of a too-slow tempo [so] that the whole great thrust of it was lost. What is odd is that this overture closes pianissimo, it ends sort of gradually, as he brings the figure

more and more slowly and finally only fragments of the figure, until it gradually disappears altogether.

Then a Herr Sauret (Sow-ret),[91] a musical swine (as Papa also likes to express himself), the virtuoso concerto in F♯ of Ernst,[92] with a sloppiness and looseness that was quite frightful, admittedly the concerto is very difficult, but if he can't do it then he shouldn't play it. Whenever he had high passages one didn't hear a thing except bungling and squawking. Then two female singers from here sang *Due Notturne* from an opera by Berlioz,[93] which is not so bad, at least it sounds good in E major; and what I like about Berlioz in general, all his things are well orchestrated.[94]

.

[green monogram] R

Dear Ludwig,

Forgive me for letting you wait somewhat, but I have so much to do now 1) for the blessed class; 2) I am composing very diligently.

I. I am continuing to work on the orchestration of my A-minor overture;[95]

II. I have recomposed all three songs,[96] this time without any special modulations, ergo to Papa's satisfaction;

III. I have composed four new piano pieces,[97] among them two gavottes, of which the second is quite pretty and original;

IV. I have written—don't be alarmed—variations for flute and piano,[98] at the request of a classmate;

V. I am now working on the last movement of the sonata,[99] I have survived the development section, which is three pages long; consequently it will not be very long now until the end. Aside from that I am going to make a brief melodic *Adagio* in A♭ major, from which I am going to make the transition immediately to a scherzo. So you see that I have had and still have more than enough to do.—Besides that I am diligently writing counterpoint exercises;[100] I am already at the fugue for four voices, that is, the culmination that everything counterpoint strives for. Are you still busy making canons? Are you making a diligent study of *dux* and *comes,* stretto, and so on? What are you composing at the moment? Are you in good health? How is Frau Nagiller?

Papa is still not quite back to feeling well again, and Mama unfortunately has been at the sofa, despite her impatience, as she always wants to be busy with housework. Unfortunately I forgot before to give Frau Diez the *St. Matthew Passion;* please forgive me. Write me if you need it right away. If you do, I shall send it by post in a wrapper; if not I will give it to someone at the next opportunity or to Ernst when he goes home for the summer. The weather here is miserable!—

I have now also read the articles by Schletterer[101] on the

Nibelungenringerl. They are really quite excellent. For he praises what there is to praise and criticizes what deserves criticism (there is, I would say, rather a lot of that), with such remarkable brevity and such justice that after every paragraph I thought, That is exactly the opinion of yours truly. Other than that I really don't know what else there is to write to you.

Stay in good health and write as you should,

Then you'll come to a great big wood. (Clever trochees.)

Your

warmly loving

Richard.

8 May 1879

N.B. Cordial greetings to dear Frau Nagiler [*sic*].

And to the Diezes[102] from Papa, Mama, Hanna,[103] and me.

·

[blue monogram] JS   [end of May, 1879]

Dear Ludwig,

Excuse me for making you wait; I am dreadfully busy.—

I have been composing diligently, namely the last movement of the sonata[104]—finished (immensely long!).

Besides that I have composed two new songs by Geibel: "Die Sonne hebt an vom Wolkenzelt" (no. 37) and "Das rothe Laub,"[105] which last one really turned out so well that I think it is my best one. The first stanza is a gloomy E♭ minor with a modulation to B♭ minor. The second stanza is a friendly passage in B♭ major that gradually goes back into B♭ minor, the last stanza again in E♭ minor similar to the first, but with a somewhat more extended closing.—In addition, I am working hard on four-voice fugues and have a vocal fugue in progress to the text "Der Herr ist König, des freue sich das Erdreich"[106] with a theme I made up myself; it goes like this:

[der Baß fängt an.]

The first statement consists in continuations of the theme. In the second statement, however, the tenor sings:

The alto then [comes in] just like that, while the tenor continues the figure. Then these two come together, then the second statement ends. Then stretto, conclusion and pedal point in the usual manner.—

Excuse me for closing already. (We are all well) but I am really not in the mood for a long letter. Preferably more of them!

Your
loving Richard.

Cordial greetings to dear Frau Nagiller.

Loving friend!
(Has lost his way)
Good morning!
I'm off my rocker!
Good afternoon!
You're off your rocker!
Good evening!
We're off our rockers!
Good night!
Let the bedbugs bite!
Good morning!
Not me!

Nonsense. There is sense in all this!!!
Now I almost think myself that I'm off my rocker!

[at the top of the first page, upside-down:]
Where are you living?

.

[blue monogram] JS   [middle of June, 1879]

My dear, good Ludwig,

How blessedly happy you have made me by sending your little book, you can scarcely imagine; you have my warmest, best thanks for it. Today I also received Scheffel's *Ekkehard*,[107] which is supposed to be very beautiful.—But as regards Dengremont,[108] I am quite delighted. The fellow is a charming phenomenon. The technique, tone, interpretation, and the tranquility (he does not betray even the slightest effort) with which he plays are really something to marvel at. Here he played Beriot's concerto no. 7 (G major),[109] which is very pretty, then Beethoven's Romance in F major with an artistic interpretation that completely suited the beautiful romance. It is really a great deal when one can say this about a twelve-year-old boy (I don't believe he is much older than that). I heard him in both the concerts he gave here. In the second one he played the splendid Mendelssohn concerto.

Are you not also quite enthused about the concerto? Next to Mozart's and Beethoven's it must be reckoned among the most beautiful violin concertos that Germany has produced. Spohr's concertos are also splendid.[110] In these there is a very particular technique that is quite noticeable and that one does not find in the other German violin concertos. The Spohr concertos are as beautiful as they are original.—Also on this occasion I heard three very nice comedies: *Der Zerbrochene Krug* by Heinrich Kleist; *Einer Muss Heiraten* by Wilhelmi,[111] and *Eine Partie Piquet,* after Fourrier, by Friedrich. There is plenty to laugh about and they are also—especially the last one—very fine and nice.

Also *König Renés Tochter* by Henrik Hertz,[112] a poetic lyrical drama, which pleased me a great deal with its atmospheric moments and well-made plot. Yesterday I also saw Lortzing's *Zar und Zimmermann,*[113] which I liked very much because of its charming text and the very pretty music. Music and text are comical, quite hilarious, and yet they don't become vulgar. They may not be exactly what you would call noble, but yet you can never call them common. Thus it is hilarious when the fat, stupid mayor goes as fast as he can through the text "Just look how the verses flow now / Like a stream through the laughing meadow," in sequences with perfect precision. And then the mayor's pretty aria:

Then the song of respect that they pay to the supposed Czar, who is only a carpenter's apprentice; it is extremely stupid, it is supposed to be stupid; for the mayor has made the text and the Cantor of Saardam the music for it.—And then they want to rehearse it, some of them sing off key and miss their entrances, that makes for a very nice dissonance:

The opera is very nicely orchestrated; altogether charming.

—I now have the sonata[114] finished; the *Adagio,* with which I combined the scherzo, turned out very well, and I have been much praised, both by Papa (which is saying a lot) and by Herr Meyer, the conductor;[115] he said it was very tasteful and beautiful. Now I am working on a romance for clarinet with orchestra,[116] in which a fugato also turned out very well. The romance will be played in the year-end concert of our *Gymnasium* by one of my fellow students.

Cordial greetings to Frau Nagiller from all of us.

Your

warmly loving, *grateful*

Richard.

D. also played two insignificant virtuoso pieces by Leonard (his teacher), in which he nevertheless was able to display his brilliant technique.

.

[hand-colored vignette: horse with wagon and pair in the coachman's box]

Munich, 22 July 1879

My dear Ludwig,

In order to put you quite to shame, I am writing immediately; for you are quite miserably bad at writing and it is slower than the post wagon drawn on this card when there is no horse attached to it, when there is no hand pushing it, in other words when it is *standing still.* Even slower! At the moment I am all alone in the apartment. Papa is in the country, Mama two hours away from Papa at a beach resort with Hanna; ergo I am alone at home. I am diligently composing 1) I have composed a romance in E♭ major for clarinet and orchestra—perhaps I already wrote you about it—which turned out quite well; after the first cantilena there develops from the theme, which remains throughout, a six-voice orchestral fugato; 2) yet another new gavotte, no. 4[117] in D major, with a bagpipe melody (musette) for a trio; for smaller piano pieces the form of the gavotte is extraordinarily comfortable for me; 3) I have composed a comical wedding march for the wedding of my cousin Linda Moralt[118] for piano and children's instruments (cuckoo, quail, cymbals, triangle, drum, rattle, nightingale),[119] with a church scene. I am going to perform it on the wedding day with my choir: Hanna and the four Pschorr boys;[120] the whole thing is only a joke; 4) I have finally finished the A-minor overture;[121] I tell you, it makes a hellish noise, but I believe it would be effective; beyond that I have a quartet[122] in mind, which will soon break the vessel in which it is now contained and suddenly appear on sheets of paper. First, though, I have to make changes to the variations for horn in E♭ major[123] and write for *human* lungs and lips; for they are practically impossible to perform as they are. I am now playing Mozart piano concertos diligently from our Mozart edition,[124] and I tell you, it is splendid, for me it is the greatest enjoyment. This wealth of ideas, this richness of harmonies and yet moderation in everything, the splendid, graceful, tender, delicious thoughts themselves, this fine accompaniment! But to play anything like this is not possible anymore! Now nothing but smarminess will do—either sweet rustlings or harsh booming and thundering or uninteresting musical nonsense! While Mozart, using few means, says everything that can refresh and truly please and improve a listener, those others, applying all the means, say nothing at all, or practically nothing. This is precisely the world turned upside down! Enough to make you want to run away! But what I have sworn is that when some day I perform in a larger concert, and can be accompanied well, in a fine manner, then I will play a Mozart concerto.[125]—Recently I found [in] Heine's *Buch der Lieder,* in a kind of addendum, a marvelously beautiful but very sad song.[126] I will not tell you the title, otherwise you will snap it up before I do. In the near future I shall also take a look at Lenau,[127] who appeals to me.—But now farewell! Yes, yes, we are all in good health, the most cordial greetings to you and dear Frau Nagiller from

> Your
> warmly loving
> Richard.

Write *soon* and *a lot!* About musical writings or other reading or scientific matters—I am interested in every line that comes from your hand.

·

[silver monogram] JS   Tuesday, 26 August [?1879]

Dear Ludwig,

My most cordial congratulations on your name day;[128] forgive me
if I come too late, but we had so much we had to do yesterday and
the day before yesterday that I didn't get to writing letters. But here
in Murnau I am diligently going to the lake, where I swim, go boat-
ing and crabbing (climbing around in the lake with bare feet), and
fish for pike with a trolling line. Recently we made a great hiking
party to the top of the Heimgarten,[129] on which day we walked for
twelve hours. At 2:00 in the morning we rode on a handcart to the
village, which lies at the foot of the mountain. Then we climbed by
the light of lanterns in pitch-dark night and arrived at the peak after a five-hour march. There one has a splendid view. Lake Staffelsee
(Murnau), Riegsee, Ammersee, Würmsee, Kochelsee, Walchensee.[130]
Then the Isar valley with mountains, Ötz and Stubeir glaciers.
Innsbruck mountains, *Zugspitze,* and so on. Then we hiked down the
other side to get to Lake Walchensee, but we took the wrong trail
and had to climb around in the midday heat for three hours with
no path. Lake Walchensee is a beautiful lake but makes a melancholy
impression, since it is enclosed by forests and high mountains. It has
splendid, bright crystalline and bright green water. Then we took a
boat across the lake to Uhrfelden.[131] It lies at the foot of Mount
Herzogstand, which is next to the Heimgarten. From there an hour
over Mount Kössel,[132] an hour to Lake Kochselsee (Kösselberg Inn).
On the way there a terrible storm had overtaken us, which uprooted
trees and threw stones in our faces. We hardly had time to find a
dry spot before the storm broke. Lake Kochelsee, a very romantic,
beautiful lake, made huge waves so that it was impossible even to
think about crossing it. After the storm had passed, we had to settle
for walking all the way around the lake, whether we wanted to or not.
On the way the rain came again and that is how we arrived in
Schlehdorf, after a breakneck march (we did not rest for a single
moment)—tired, soaked to the skin—and spent the night, then the
next morning we rode as calm as could be in the hay wagon to
Murnau. The hike was interesting, unusual, and original in the highest degree. The next day I described the whole hike on the piano.[133]
Naturally huge tone paintings and smarminess à la Wagner. Recently
I was in *Götterdämmerung.* Now farewell: with the most cordial best
wishes and greetings from all of us to Frau Nagiller and you, I am

                                        Your
                                        warmly loving
                                        Richard.

NOTES

1. Popular excursion from Innsbruck to the Lanser mountains and the small, round Lake Lanser [Trenner].

2. Throughout his life Strauss remained oblivious to the correct spelling of Mendelssohn [Trenner].

3. Pauline Nagiller (1832–81) was the widow of the Tirolean composer Matthäus Nagiller (1815–74), who worked in Paris, Limburg, Munich, and Bozen before becoming director of the *Musikverein* in Innsbruck in 1866. He wrote the opera *Herzog Friedrich von Tirol,* symphonies, masses, choruses, and lieder. The acquaintance with Johann Thuille, Ludwig's father, began during Nagiller's sojourn in Bozen. There, in about 1865, he married Pauline Cruse, the daughter of a spice merchant from Hamburg. Thus it seems quite certain that Pauline Nagiller met Ludwig Thuille there, when he was already fourteen years old. At any rate, she made sure that Ludwig Thuille was able to attend the *Gymnasium* in Innsbruck during the years 1876–79 and made it possible for him to study in Munich afterward. On 16 May 1876, Richard Strauss dedicated his Twelve Variations (D major) for piano (WoO 50) to her [Trenner].

4. Frau Marchesani (also Marquesani) was the oldest half-sister of Ludwig Thuille, from his father's first marriage. Ludwig lived with her during his years in Innsbruck [Trenner].

5. Only in this first letter did Strauss write his name with the German form of *sz* [Trenner].

6. Richard seems to have erred in the date of the first or second letter [Trenner].

7. Serenade (G major) for Orchestra (WoO 32) [Trenner].

8. Anna Schimon-Regan (1841–1902), soprano, was in Hannover from 1864 to 1867 as understudy, then concert singer, and from 1886 to 1891 was a voice teacher at the Royal Conservatory in Leipzig and then at the Royal Music School in Munich [Trenner].

9. Heinrich Vogl (1845–1900), tenor, and his wife, Therese (1845–1921), at the Munich Hof- and Nationaltheater, since 1865 were famous as interpreters of Tristan and Isolde. In 1870 they appeared as Siegmund and Sieglinde in the premiere of *Die Walküre.* Heinrich Vogl sang at the Bayreuth Festivals from 1876 to 1897. Richard Strauss dedicated the Eight Lieder, Op. 10, to him [Trenner].

10. Joseph Staudigl (1850–1916), bass, son of the more famous father of the same name. He spent 1874–84 in Karlsruhe and his guest appearances as opera, oratorio, and concert singer included the United States. He was later professor at the Vienna Conservatory [Trenner].

11. *Der Fischer* (WoO 33), *Lust und Qual* (WoO 36), *Die Drossel* (WoO 34), and *Lass ruhn die Todten* (WoO 35) [Trenner].

12. Ludwig Uhland (1787–1862) was a popular poet, dramatist, and philologist. He wrote folk songs, ballads, and lyrics of many kinds as well as pro-

gressive, patriotic dramas. His first volume of collected poems, published in 1815, was one of the most popular literary books of the century [trans.].

13. Adalbert von Chamisso (1781–1838), a French nobleman, fled with his family to Germany during the French Revolution. He became a noted poet, later a respected botanist, and one of Germany's first social historians. His most famous publication was the *Wundersame Geschichte des Peter Schlemihl* [The strange history of Peter Schlemihl] (1814) [trans.].

14. Trio no. 1 in A major for piano, violin, and cello, Op. 15, is the autograph title (not WoO 37) [Trenner].

15. Sonata no. 1 (E major) for piano (WoO 38) [Trenner].

16. Wagner's name has been made unrecognizable by means of circles drawn over it [Trenner].

17. The list is not extant [Trenner].

18. Probably lost [Trenner].

19. In May 1877, Richard Strauss had composed a Kyrie, Sanctus, and Agnus Dei for four-part chorus and designated it as Op. 12. With the Benedictus, which was written half a year later and leads up to the Hosanna and Sanctus, these four movements of a mass for mixed a capella chorus (Op. 31) constitute the only example of a sacred work by Richard Strauss [Trenner].

20. Crossed out: performance [Trenner].

21. Joseph Pembaur (the elder) (1848–1923), Tyrolian composer, student of Bruckner (in Vienna), Rheinberger, and Wüllner, among others. He wrote an opera, *Zigeunerliebe*, a symphony, masses, works for chorus, organ, and piano, as well as lieder. From 1875 to 1918 he was director of the music school of the Piano Society of Innsbruck and there was Ludwig Thuille's teacher of piano, organ, and music theory; he recommended Thuille to Josef Rheinberger in Munich. Joseph Pembaur the younger (1875–1950), pianist, was Thuille's student from 1893 to 1896 at the Munich Academy [Trenner].

22. The young Richard Strauss variously altered the opus numbers of his early compositions until 1881, with the printing of the Festival March, when he began to count definitively from Op. 1. WoO 14, *Husarenlied* [Hussar's song] (probably composed in 1873) bears the original identification Op. 7, no. 2, and appears in a copy as I [4]. WoO 2 *Weihnachtslied* [Christmas song] (composed in December 1870) should be identified, according to Steinitzer, with Op. 5, no. 1, later Op. 1 (see Max Steinitzer, *Richard Strauss* [Berlin and Leipzig, 1911; reprint, 1927]) [Trenner].

23. Sonata no. 1 (E major) for piano (WoO 38) [Trenner].

24. The sonata composition does not seem to have been pursued further. The variations (WoO 50) were dedicated by Richard Strauss on 16 May 1878 to Frau Pauline Nagiller [Trenner].

25. After Almaide's aria from the second act (WoO 44), Richard Strauss wrote the chorus from the fourth act (WoO 45); other compositions belonging to this singspiel are not known from this time. Not until 1895 did he write to Cosima Wagner that he had written "three acts of the things that were to be composed in 'modern' music" (see *Cosima Wagner–Richard Strauss:*

A Correspondence, ed. Franz Trenner with Gabriele Strauss [Tutzing: Schneider, 1978]). However, difficulties with the fourth act and symphonic plans *(Also sprach Zarathustra)* persuaded him to drop the work [Trenner].

26. Franz Lachner (1803–90), composer, organist, and director. From 1836 until 1868 he was at the *Hofoper* in Munich (music director after 1852). He published eight symphonies, eight suites, operas (*Catherina Cornaro,* among others), masses, chamber music, and vocal works. Richard Strauss prepared an arrangement for four hands (1880–81) of his nonet in F major (1875) [Trenner].

27. Julius Röntgen (1855–1932), Dutch composer (student of Lachner, Hauptmann, and Reinecke), also a composer and pianist. Co-founder and leader (1914–24) of the Amsterdam Conservatory. A friend of Brahms and Grieg [Trenner].

28. Lost [Trenner].

29. August Tombo (1842–78) was harpist at the *Hof-* and *Nationaltheater* beginning in 1861 and a teacher at the Royal Music School in Munich. He had been giving piano lessons to Richard Strauss since 1868 [Trenner].

30. From *Lila* [Trenner].

31. "Warmly" changed to "eternally" [Trenner].

32. *Im Walde* [In the forest] (WoO 43); *Der Spielmann und sein Kind* [The minstrel and his child] (WoO 46) [Trenner].

33. Trio no. 1 (A major) for piano, violin, and cello (WoO 37) [Trenner].

34. Anton Ritter von Knötzinger (1823–1913), auditor general to the Emperor, was married to Amalie Pschorr (1837–71), the sister of Richard Strauss's mother [Trenner].

35. "It is my opinion that Carthage must be destroyed." Cato's habit was to end every public pronouncement with this sentence [trans.].

36. The songs *Im Walde* (Geibel), Op. 15, no. 1 (WoO 43), and *Der Spielman und sein Kind* (Hoffman von Fallersleben), Op. 15, no. 2 (WoO 48), the orchestral accompaniment of which Richard Strauss had "arranged for piano," was "dedicated in profoundest respect to Frau Caroline von Mangstl, Royal Bavarian Chamber Singer, on the occasion of her fortieth anniversary as a member of the Royal Bavarian Court Chorus." The third song is unknown [Trenner].

37. Friedrich von Schiller's play [trans.].

38. On the reverse of this letter is a sketch (four measures) of a composition by Ludwig Thuille [Trenner].

39. Camille Saint-Saëns (1835–1921), French composer and organist. Composed operas (including *Samson and Delila,* premiered 1877 in Vienna), five symphonies, symphonic poems, concertos (five for piano, three for violin, two for cello), choral works, and chamber music (including the piano quartet in B major, Op. 41) [Trenner].

40. KV 385 [Trenner].

41. Max Zenger (1837–1911), a Munich composer and director; after Regensburg he was music director of the Munich Royal Opera, royal conductor in Karlsruhe, and chorus director and teacher at the Royal Music

School in Munich until 1897. He wrote operas, ballets, symphonies, choral works, and songs. The *Drei Lieder Jung Werners* [Three songs of young Werner], Op. 21, are dedicated to Heinrich Vogl. Theodor Kroyer published his posthumous *Geschichte der Münchener Oper* [History of the Munich Opera] [Trenner].

42. *Recte* "Le Rouet d'Omphale" [Trenner].

43. Robert Burns (1759–96), English [should be Scottish] folk-song poet. The text of the first duet, *Familiengemälde* [Family portrait], is by Anastasius Grün [Trenner].

44. Symphony no. 3 in A minor, Op. 56 (Scottish). All subscription concerts from 1877–88 were conducted by Hermann Levi, whose name did not appear in the program [Trenner].

45. The string quartet that Ludwig Thuille dedicated to Richard Strauss is lost [Trenner].

46. Johann Sebastian Bach, suite no. 3 for two oboes, three trumpets, timpani, two violins, viola, and continuo [Trenner].

47. Strauss writes the Greek word *hérōs* [trans.].

48. Heinrich Marschner (1795–1861), composer and conductor. Royal chorus director in Hannover for twenty-eight years. Among his operas the following were successful: *Der Vampyr* [The vampire], *Der Templer und die Jüdin* [The templar and the Jewess], and *Hans Heiling* (1833) [Trenner].

49. Joseph Gierl (1857–93), Munich pianist. Richard Strauss dedicated the Sonata for Piano (B minor), Op. 5, to him.

50. Again Strauss uses the Greek term [trans.].

51. Misspelled in Strauss's original [trans.].

52. Carl Mathys (1835–1908), cellist with the Hannover Opera and composer [Trenner].

53. *Recte* E♭-major quartet, Op. 17, no. 3 [Trenner].

54. Op. 18, no. 5 [Trenner].

55. Luigi Cherubini (1760–1842), Italian composer, since 1788 in Paris. Wrote operas (including *Medea*, *Der Wasserträger* [The water-carrier], *Anacreon*, and *Les Abencérages* [1813]), and sacred and chamber music [Trenner].

56. Rafael Joseffy (1853–1915), Hungarian pianist, student of Tausig in Berlin and of Liszt, later a teacher and conservatory director in the U.S.A. [Trenner].

57. Karl Goldmark (1830–1915), Austrian composer. Wrote operas (including *Die Königin von Saba* [The Queen of Sheba]), the scherzo, Op. 19, two violin concertos, and choral and chamber music [Trenner].

58. Padre Giambattista Martini (1706–84), a Franciscan monk, composer, conductor, and music theoretician. He wrote oratorios, masses, sonatas, and pieces for piano and organ, a three-volume history of music, and a two-volume textbook on counterpoint [Trenner].

59. Beethoven, Symphony no. 4 in B♭ major, Op. 60 [Trenner].

60. Motto: beginning of Zerlina's aria (no. 19) from Mozart's *Don Giovanni* [Trenner].

61. Illegible, perhaps stenography [Trenner].

62. Daniel-François-Esprit Auber (1782–1871), French composer. The best-known of his forty-five operas are *Le Maçon, La Muette de Portici, Fra Diavolo, La Part du diable,* and *Le Cheval de bronze* [Trenner].

63. Motto: beginning of Don Giovanni's aria (no. 12) by Mozart [Trenner].

64. Walter Scott (1771–1832), Scottish writer; among other things he wrote the novels *Waverley, Ivanhoe, Quentin Durward,* and *Kenilworth* [Trenner].

65. Smith motive from *Siegfried,* a sentence that probably referred to Richard Wagner crossed out repeatedly, replaced with = XYZ [Trenner].

66. Carl Heinrich Graun (1704–59), composer. Supported by Frederick the Great, he wrote Italian operas for Berlin, and concert and chamber music. The cantata *Der Tod Jesu* is the best-known of his sacred works [Trenner].

67. François-Adrien Boieldieu (1775–1834), French composer, known for his operas *Le Calif de Bagdad, Jean de Paris,* and *La Dame blanche* [Trenner].

68. The Pschorr cellar was located on the Theresienhöhe. The two young Pschorr boys were Richard's cousins Joseph Pschorr (1867–1942), later head of the New York sales office of the brewery, and Robert Pschorr (1868–1930), later a professor of chemistry in Berlin [Trenner].

69. Sillian on the Drau in the Pustertal, East Tyrol, between Lienz and Innichen, near the Italian border, a frequent vacation spot for the Strauss family [Trenner].

70. Felix Mendelssohn Bartholdy (1809–47), six organ sonatas, Op. 65 (1845) [Trenner].

71. JS = Johanna Strauss [Trenner].

72. The German text, complete with *Stabreim,* reads as follows:

> Nach langem und *s*ehnlichen, *s*aueren *W*arten
> *h*ielt in *H*änden ich endlich die neidliche Post;
> ich *w*artete *w*eiland auf *W*alhalls Zinnen
> vor *S*ehn*s*ucht verzehrte mich beinahe der Rost;
> *d*och *d*a nun *d*urchbrach *d*as Gewölk *d*ie Sonne;
> man *b*rachte den *B*rief her aus ferner Zonne;
> da jubelt ich auf; ich sprang in die Höh;
> *w*as *w*ar in dem Brief—gleich 40 (Flöh) [ed.].

The two sentences of apology are written in the right-hand margin next to the salutation [Trenner].

73. Mozart's *Don Giovanni* [Trenner].

74. Again Greek: *hērōs* [trans.].

75. Friedrich Niest (1816–92), pianist and pedagogue, teacher of Sophie Menter. In the Strauss literature the first name Carl is given. A Carl Niest (1804–70), Friedrich's stepbrother, was a horn player in the Royal Orchestra and a colleague of Strauss *père.* The beginning of Strauss's study with Niest, which is given since Steinitzer as 1875, seems, according to this letter, not to have been before 1878 [Trenner].

76. Esaias Tegnér (1782–1846), author of the Swedish national epic *The*

Fritjof Saga [Trenner].

77. Robert Schumann (1810–56), Symphony no. 2 in C major, Op. 61 [Trenner].

78. Clara Schumann *née* Wieck (1819–96), pianist and composer [Trenner].

79. Strauss puns on the German words for piano player and a phrase meaning "empty . . . inside" [trans.].

80. Hans von Bülow (1830–94), pianist, conductor, and composer, student of Richard Wagner and Franz Liszt, married to Cosima Liszt, royal chorus director (*Tristan und Isolde* and *Die Meistersinger von Nürnberg,* among others), and director of the Royal Music School in Munich. After his separation from Cosima in 1878 he was director of the Royal Chorus in Hannover, from 1880 to 1885 royal music director in Meiningen, a friend of Johannes Brahms and patron of Richard Strauss, the director of the subscription concerts in Hamburg, and at the same time conductor of the Berlin Philharmonic. His second marriage was to Marie Schanzer, who edited eight volumes of his letters and writings. Wrote works for orchestra (including the symphonic poem *Nirwana*) and instructive editions of classical piano works. See "Hans von Bülow–Richard Strauss: Briefwechsel," ed. Willi Schuh and Franz Trenner, in *Richard Strauss–Jahrbuch 1954* [Bonn, 1953]) [Trenner].

81. Theodor Reichmann (1849–1903) baritone; after various engagements, including Hamburg (1873) and Munich (1875), was a member of the Royal Opera in Vienna from 1882 to 1889 and again from 1893 on. Sang as a guest performer in New York and London as well as at the Bayreuth Festival, where he appeared in the role of Amfortas in the premiere of *Parsifal,* among others. In an academy concert he sang the Schumann songs *Waldgespräch* [Forest conversation], *Die Alten Bösen Lieder* [The old bad songs], and *Ich grolle nicht* [I don't complain] [Trenner].

82. Johann Nepomuk Hummel (1778–1837), Austrian pianist and composer and student of Mozart, Albrechtsberger, and Salieri. Made concert tours as a wunderkind, followed Haydn as Choirmaster of Prince Esterhazy (1804–11), and after 1816 was Royal Choirmaster in Stuttgart and 1819 in Weimar. Works included operas, ballets, masses, and for piano, among other things, seven concertos (the fourth in B minor), and chamber music [Trenner].

83. WoO 38 [Trenner].

84. Lost [Trenner].

85. From *35 Klavierlieder,* manuscript [Trenner].

86. Ernst Friedrich Richter (1808–79), music theoretician and composer who published *Die Grundzüge der musikalischen Formen* [The fundamentals of musical forms] in 1852 and later three textbooks on harmony, fugue, and counterpoint, collected as *Die praktischen Studien zür Theorie der Musik* [The practical studies on the theory of music] [Trenner].

87. Franz Xavier Gabelsberger (1789–1849) succeeded in 1834 with the general breakthrough of stenography, among hundreds of systems of abbreviation; the system that is in general use today is based on it. Richard Strauss had learned stenography during the 1878–79 school year and occasionally

made use of his new acquisition in his letters to Ludwig Thuille. The passages, which are brief, have been converted without special note for this edition [Trenner].

88. There is an illegible word here [Trenner].

89. The movements of the Suite no. 3 by J. S. Bach are Overture, Air, Gavotte, Bourrée, and Gigue [Trenner].

90. Haydn, Symphony in C minor, Hob. I: 95 (the fifth "London" symphony, 1791) [Trenner].

91. Emile Sauret, French violinist and composer, student of Beriot; from 1877 a teacher at Kullak's Academy in Berlin and from 1891 at the Royal Academy in London. He wrote a violin concerto in G minor and solo pieces.

92. Heinrich Wilhelm Ernst (1814–65), Bohemian violinist and composer, Concerto Pathétique in F♯ major, Op. 23 [Trenner].

93. Hector Berlioz (1803–69), duet no. 8 (Hero and Ursula) from *Béatrice et Bénédict* (sung by Schefzky and Schultze) [Trenner].

94. Continuation and end of the letter are missing [Trenner].

95. WoO 62 [Trenner].

96. Strauss refers to three songs by Emanuel Geibel: *Waldgesang* [Forest song] (WoO 55), composed on 6 April 1879, and the two lost songs *O schneller mein Ross* [O faster my steed] (AV 159), composed on 9–10 April 1879, and *Die Lilien glühn in Düften* [The lilies glow with perfume] (AV 160), composed on 12 April 1879. They are "dedicated to Frl. C. Meysenheym, R. B. Court Singer, with Gratitude"; she sang them for the first time in public on 16 March 1881, in the Hall of the Munich Museum. Cornelie Meysenheym (1853–1923), soprano, student of P. Viardot-Garcia, among others, was already active in the 1870s in Munich, in 1880–85 in Karlsruhe, and 1885–96 at the Munich Hoftheater and traveled as a guest artist to the U.S.A., among other places [Trenner].

97. 1. *Allegro* in E major; 2. *Andante* in G major; 3. Gavotte II, *Allegretto* in D major; and 4. Gavotte III, *Allegro* in G major; subsequently expanded by the addition of Gavotte IV, *Allegro molto* in D major, and referred to by Richard Strauss as *Skizzen: 5 kleine Klavierstücke*, Op. 24 [Sketches: 5 little pieces for piano, Op. 24], now WoO 59 [Trenner].

98. Introduction, theme, and variations for flute and piano, WoO 56 [Trenner].

99. Great sonata no. 2 (C minor) for piano, WoO 60 [Trenner].

100. *Kontrapuntische Studien II*, WoO 54 [Trenner].

101. Hans Michael Schletterer (1824–93), conductor, composer, and writer on music, was music director of the University of Heidelberg, among other places, and after 1858, church choirmaster in Augsburg and founder of the oratorio society and the conservatory. He wrote operettas, choral works, and church music and published *R. Wagners Bühnenfestspiel: Nachklänge an die Aufführung des Jahres 1876* [R. Wagner's theatrical festival: reminiscences of the performance of the year 1876]. On 12 March 1884, he conducted the second performance of the *Concertouvertüre* in C minor, WoO 80.

102. Ernst Friedrich Diez (1805–92), tenor (student of Conradin Kreutzer in Vienna), who sang in Pressburg, Triest, Berlin, and from 1830 to 1837 in Mannheim, then until 1849 at the Munich Hoftheater. His wife Sophie Diez *née* Hartmann (1820–87), soprano, began as a member of the chorus at the Munich *Hoftheater* in 1837 and advanced, under Lachner's patronage, to Royal Bavarian Chamber Singer. She stepped down in 1879 as an honorary member of the Royal Opera. Richard Strauss dedicated the song *Für Musik* (Geibel), AV 158, which he composed on 7 April 1879, to her. On 10 June 1879, he dedicated the three songs *Friede* [Peace] (K. Domanig), *Unter blühenden Bäumen* [Under flowering trees] (O. Genischen), and *Am Strande* [At the beach] (Geibel) [Trenner].

103. Berta Johanna Strauss (1867–1966), the sister of Richard Strauss, married Otto von Rauchenberger (1864–1942), who later advanced to Royal Bavarian Lieutenant General, Knight of the Order of Max-Joseph after 1917 [Trenner].

104. WoO 60 [Trenner].

105. *Frühlingsanfang* [Early spring], AV 162 (*Die Sonne hebt vom Wolkenzelt* [The sun shines forth from the tent of the clouds]), composed 21–24 May 1879; and *Das rote Laub* [The red foliage], AV 161. Both are lost [Trenner].

106. *Kontrapunktische Studien II*, WoO 54 (no. 8, a four-voice fugue; no. 9, a four-voice vocal fugue) [Trenner].

107. Victor von Scheffel (1826–86), famous in his time for *Der Trompeter von Säckingen* (1854), *Ekkehard* (1855), and *Gaudeamus igitur* (1868) [Trenner].

108. Maurice Dengremont (1866–1903), Brazilian violinist, student of the Belgian violinist and violin teacher Hubert Leonard (1819–90). As a twelve-year-old wunderkind he appeared on 6 June 1879 for the first time at the Munich *Hof-* and *Nationaltheater*. The program included Beriot, violin concerto no. 7; Kleist, *Der Zerbrochene Krug* [The broken pitcher]; Beethoven, romance in F major; Wilhelmi, *Einer muß Heiraten* [One must marry]; and Leonard, souvenir for violin. Several other performances followed in the course of the year with similarly mixed programs [Trenner].

109. Charles-Auguste de Bériot (1802–70), Belgian violinist, teacher of Henri Vieuxtemps; wrote ten violin concertos, among other things [Trenner].

110. Louis Spohr (1784–1859), violinist, conductor, and composer, wrote, in addition to ten operas, four oratorios, nine symphonies, more than fifty chamber works, and some fifteen violin concertos [Trenner].

111. Alexander Wilhelmi (actually Zechmeister) (1817–77) published *Lustspiele* [comedies] between 1853 and 1860, among them *Einer muß heiraten*, *Alle Sind Egoisten* [Everyone is an egoist], *Abwarten* [Just wait], and *Zu spät* [Too late] [Trenner].

112. Heinrich Hertz (1798–1870), Danish poet in the tradition of Heiberg. His romantic play in verses *König Renés Datter* [King René's daughter] was translated into German ten times as *König Renés Tochter* [Trenner].

113. *Zar and Zimmermann* (1837) by Albert Lortzing (1801–51) [Trenner].

114. WoO 60 [Trenner].

115. Friedrich Wilhelm Meyer (1818–93), conductor, came from Stettin in 1854 to join Lachner as music director at the Munich Royal Hoftheater and in 1858 became Royal Music Director and in 1869 Royal Court Conductor. In 1879 he received the Ludwigs-Medal for Art and Science. At the beginning of the year 1882 he retired. He taught Richard Strauss music theory from 1875 to 1880. Dedicated to him are *Serenade* (G major), WoO 32; *Overtüre* (A minor), WoO 62; and *Serenade* (E♭ major), Op. 7 [Trenner].

116. *Romanze* (E♭ major), WoO 61 [Trenner].

117. WoO 59, no. 5 [Trenner].

118. Julie Theodolinde (Linda) Moralt (1852–1932), married the businessman Johann Friedrich (Jean) Mayer (1849–1907) on 11 August 1879. Her parents were the head cashier of the *Hoftheater,* Theodor Moralt (1817–77), and Maria Elisabeth *née* Pschorr (1834–89), a sister of Richard Strauss's mother [Trenner].

119. *Hochzeitsmusik* [Wedding music], AV 163 [Trenner].

120. The four Pschorr boys: August (1862–1935), Georg Theodor (1865–1949), Joseph (1867–1942), and Robert (1868–1930), sons of Georg Pschorr, Jr. (1830–94) and Marai Johanna *née* Fischer-Dick (1838–1918) [Trenner].

121. WoO 62 [Trenner].

122. Probably Op. 2 [Trenner].

123. *Introduction, Thema, und Variationen für Waldhorn und Klavier,* WoO 52. The new version is lost [Trenner].

124. Franz Strauss was one of the few private subscribers to the first edition of Mozart's collected works [Trenner].

125. Richard Strauss was able keep his pledge on 20 October 1885 in Meiningen, when he performed the piano concerto in C minor, KV 491, under the baton of Hans von Bülow, with his own cadenzas (AV 179) [Trenner].

126. Strauss did not write down the song *In Vaters Garten heimlich steht* [In father's garden secretly there stands] (from *Junge Leiden,* lieder section) until December 1879 [Trenner].

127. After the song *Nebel* [Fog], WoO 47, a year before this letter, Nicholas Lenau was not set to music again by Richard Strauss until *Don Juan,* Op. 20, and in 1891 with *Zwei Lieder,* Op. 26 (*Frühlingsgedränge* [Spring bursts forth] and *O wärst du mein* [O if you were only mine]) [Trenner].

128. Ludwig's name day on 25 August [Trenner].

129. Herzogstand (1,731 meters) and Heimgarten (1,730 meters), the high ridge that stretches from east to west between Murnauer Moos and Walchensee [Trenner].

130. Names of lakes [trans.].

131. *Recte* Urfelden [Trenner].

132. *Recte* Kessel [Trenner].

133. The sentence is underlined in pencil, probably added later by someone else [Trenner].

Selections from the

Strauss-Gregor Correspondence:

The Genesis of *Daphne*

TRANSLATED BY SUSAN GILLESPIE

When one thinks of Strauss opera, the name Joseph Gregor (1888–1960) does not immediately come to mind. Rather, one thinks of Hugo von Hofmannsthal, who had been Strauss's sole librettist from 1908 until the writer's death in 1929; together they produced five operas. Strauss's brief collaboration with Stefan Zweig, which produced only one opera *(Die schweigsame Frau)*, is likewise well known—due, in part, to its colorful political context. Letters between the composer and both librettists have long since been published and are available in English translation. By comparison, Strauss's most important post-Hofmannsthal librettist, Joseph Gregor, has been largely ignored, despite the fact that—as Zweig's successor—he contributed no fewer than three operatic texts. Part of the reason stems from Gregor's modest gifts as librettist, for he was not, in essence, a playwright but a theater scholar (indeed, director of the Theater Collection of the Austrian National Library) who fancied himself a stage poet.

With the rise of National Socialism, Zweig, a Jew, realized he had no future as a Strauss librettist. By early summer 1934, he began suggesting various possible successors (Rudolf Binding, Robert Faesi, Alexander Lernet-Holenia), but the composer stubbornly refused each one. In fact, Strauss initially rejected Gregor as well, but Zweig held his ground, declaring that he would be willing to assist Gregor with any text draft "page by page" if necessary. By then nearly a year had passed, and Strauss, no doubt, had begun to realize the improbability of another Zweig libretto and the inevitability of one by Gregor. Zweig proved to be true to his word, for he faithfully advised Gregor throughout much of his collaboration with Strauss. He helped Gregor extensively in the drafting of *Friedenstag*, which was, after all, Zweig's idea in the first place, and he provided assistance on *Daphne* and—to a lesser extent—on *Die Liebe der Danae* as well. For political reasons, Zweig is rarely mentioned by name in the Strauss-Gregor letters, but rather as "our friend" or, less often, "Z."

The Strauss-Gregor correspondence reveals a unique working relationship in which the composer assumed almost total artistic control. Strauss could be blunt and occasionally downright insulting in order to achieve the desired results; sometimes he would rewrite particular passages of text himself. Moreover, he never hesitated to seek outside advice, principally that of the conductor Clemens Krauss, who would serve as collaborator for Strauss's final opera, *Capriccio*. The Strauss-Gregor correspondence represents an indispensable source for anyone interested in late-Strauss opera, and it is a pity that these published letters have never been translated. What follows is a sampling, a series of letters pertaining to *Daphne*, Gregor's only original libretto subject. In them one finds Strauss constantly urging Gregor to avoid "schoolmasterly banalities" and to resist becoming "intoxicated by [one's] own verses." "Consider the following," Strauss urges at one point, "Elsa's dream [in Wagner's *Lohengrin*], an aria lasting three pages in piano reduction = twelve lines [of text]!" These letters reveal Strauss as the seasoned, practical man of the theater who tried his best to communicate this experience to a collaborator who all too often failed to comprehend [ed.].

[Source: *Richard Strauss–Joseph Gregor: Briefwechsel* (1939–49), ed. Roland Tenschert (Salzburg: Otto Müller, 1955), pp. 32–89, passim]

•

[Vienna, 3 September 1935]

Most honored Doctor Strauss:

I thank you cordially for your kind letter from Garmisch and am very happy that the *Friedenstag* now meets with your general approval. Please just tell me what you wish to have changed; I have a few more minor revisions to make, myself, as well.

In the meanwhile I have also written *Daphne,* and am sending you the text. Stefan Zweig, who is staying in Vienna at the moment, was nothing short of enthusiastic about this text and wrote me a long letter about it, which I send you in the enclosure. I have made notes in the manuscript of *Daphne* to indicate those passages that Zweig would like to see expanded. Zweig has some wishes regarding the *Friedenstag,* too, which are easily fulfilled. Otherwise we are in the best of agreement, as you see; he prefers *Daphne* to the *Friedenstag* by far.

I am extraordinarily eager to know your reaction, as is Zweig. He reminded me again when we last spoke to pass along his most respectful greetings. He will be here through about the middle of this month and thus I would be in a position *to inform him if Doctor Strauss should desire anything?* I would have to receive word from you soon, however.

I hope that Vichy agrees with you and ask you to convey my greetings to your esteemed wife. With profound regards, I remain your most devoted

Encl.[1]

Gregor

·

Hotel Meurice
228, Rue de Rivoli, Paris

15 September [1935]

Dear Dr. Gregor:

Daphne pleases me quite well, although I would have preferred a tighter dramatic focus in plot and language. We will discuss it further (first half of October in Garmisch, I hope) in person. I strongly urge you to adopt our friend's [Zweig's] suggestions. . . . The figure of the swineherd Zeus is not good: a poor version of Wotan. Also, the pantomime with Medusa would probably be impossible to stage: please create something else here. From the sixteenth I am in Kissingen (Dr. Dapper's sanatorium). In haste, cordial greetings from your sincerely devoted

Dr. Richard Strauss

·

Sanatorium
Professor Dr. C. von Dapper-Saalfals
Bad Kissingen

25 September 1835

Dear Herr Gregor:

Yesterday I finally received word from my son that the matter before the Foreign Exchange Bureau is going forward, and thus I hope we will soon be able to give you complete satisfaction. In the meanwhile I have taken a more intensive look at *Daphne* and must, in contrast to the opinion of our friend, regretfully confess that the more I read it the less I like it. It is nothing more than a sequence of events, not a trace of any dramatic climax; seriously lacking is a major confrontation between Apollo, Leukippos, and Daphne in which Daphne explicitly expresses her virginal stance toward both of them: awe of the god, whose presence she senses, sisterly love for the friend of her youth. This should be a *Kleistian scene,* dark and rich in secret forebodings. Nothing must take place behind the scenes, not even the murder of Leukippos—the catastrophe [would be] much more elemental without the schoolmasterly *Weltanschauungs*-banalities of the completely superfluous Jupiter—in short: the whole thing in its current form, as it simultaneously unfolds in a not particularly felicitous imitation of Homeric jargon, would not draw a hundred people to the theater. In any case, we must also have a very extensive conversation about it. Perhaps you would be so good, before we discuss it, as to make the changes we recently discussed to the other piece. *Theater* and not literature!

With best greetings, your always devoted

Dr. Richard Strauss

·

[Bad Kissingen] 29 September 1935

Dear Herr Gregor:

I leave tomorrow for Munich and am in Garmisch from 2 October on (except for the twelfth and thirteenth, when I again have business in Munich). Please write soon to let me know when I may expect to see you again in Garmisch.

About *Daphne,* we must talk in person. But on *1648* I ask you, if possible, to go ahead and make the changes we discussed: regarding the moment when the bells begin to chime following the cannon shot—also the conversation of the two commanders, which must be given a much sharper dramatic form and in which the woman must also play a role.[2] All your dialogues are much too literary, not theatrical enough. Do you understand my point? In *Daphne,* too, everything is *written* and not *visualized on stage!*

I hope to see you soon! With cordial greetings from my wife, as well, your always sincerely devoted

Dr. Richard Strauss

·

[Vienna] 5 October 1935

Most esteemed dear Doctor Strauss:

I thank you for the kind letter, just received, and send you herewith the requested changes. I would like you to remove from the copy I sent you at the end of August pages 2, 3, 13, 21, 22, 23, and 25–

28 and insert the enclosed pages in their place. If further changes should be necessary, please send me the pages in question with your comments.

I thank you for the most especially kind invitation and have no greater wish than to spend time with you once more in fruitful work. . . .

I ask you to convey my greetings to your dear gracious wife and [let her know] how delighted I would be to spend time in your lovely home again!

With most devoted respects always, your

Gregor

.

[Vienna] 10 October [1935]

Most esteemed dear Doctor Strauss:

I am in possession of your two last letters. You can be reassured that I am not offended by the *Friedenstag* business, for in your first letter I immediately recognized your momentarily depressed mood. Our friend would be able to corroborate that. Your second letter, which I received today, merely confirms what I already knew.

I could not imagine that *everything* I had accomplished in those many months, often in your presence and with your so valuable advice and directions, should suddenly be worthless. I am glad that the last package has been able to modify this judgment.—

The very lovely ideas that your letter of today develops concerning the conclusion of the piece are very easy to implement. I would like, however, at least with regard to some portion of the work, to arrive at a *lasting* judgment and have therefore sent the work to our friend and asked him, beginning with the passage where the first cannon shot rings out, to carry out the "practical and active super-revision" that you have requested. I am also sending him for that purpose a copy of your letter of today and am quite sure that the improvements and revisions that he will, as I hope, carry out, will be very much to your liking.—

Since you, honored Doctor Strauss, always emphasize your particular straightforwardness, which I very much appreciate, you will surely allow me to express myself straightforwardly this once. I am not speaking of the *Friedenstag*—there I see quite clearly and am convinced that we will reach the goal. It has to do, rather, with *Daphne*. I wrote this piece in true and genuine inspiration, and it also earned the enthusiastic applause not only of our friend but also of a number of very serious people whom I have occasion to hold in high regard. And

· 241 ·

there I must tell you that your opinion, which had nothing better to say about it than "not particularly felicitously imitated Homeric jargon" and "*Weltanschauungs*-banalities," has caused me considerable pain. The matter is now behind us and I shall never come back to you again with this plan—but I had to tell you, for you yourself would not want the person who works with you to be an insensitive, unartistic bloke.

I would like to express my most sincere and heartfelt hope that the unfortunate mood of which you write has meanwhile evaporated in the brightness of these magnificent fall days. How much I would like to be there with you! How keenly I remember those summer days in which I had the good fortune to work in your presence and under the general influence of your esteemed person!

In cordial devotion, your

Gregor

Allow me to send you another piece of mine for you to take a look at.[3]

·

[Garmisch] 15 October 1935

Dear Herr Gregor:

Many thanks for the manuscript and friendly letter. I am naturally sorry that I hurt your feelings: but the surgeon's saw also hurts, when it is used without anesthetic. So please do not be annoyed if I find your *Daphne* in its present form unusable, above all untheatrical, and not interesting for any public in the world. That is not to say that the pleasing subject and many pleasing details of its execution couldn't become a nice one-acter. Give my objections a parliamentary form, in which you are invited to think them through—above all be mistrustful of this dangerous

"TRUE AND GENUINE INSPIRATION,"

in which you claim to have written the little piece. Such products neither stand up to sober artistic judgment nor awaken the same sentiments in the observer. So I ask you again: consider without rancor what I wrote to you about *Daphne*.

The dramatic focal point is lacking, one that consists in a Kleistian scene involving Daphne, who is a very colorless marionette, Apollo, and Leukippos. Zeus with his truth preaching is impossible, also the ballet of Medusa, and the language, which copies too much from Johann Heinrich Voss.[4] If you can manage it, communicate my bru-

tal criticism to our friend in all its nakedness. His "corrosive"[5] intellect should make the shortcomings I have criticized more evident than
they have been up to now.

No reason to despair! What is not yet can still become! If you value
corroboration from third parties, the enclosed recognition should give
you pleasure.[6] My wife, without my knowledge, sent that shrewd man of
the theater the *next-to-last* version. I hope you can come out this way
soon! Finally, only face-to-face conversation is conducive. Always your

Dr. Richard Strauss

·

[Garmisch] 19 December 1935

Dear friend Gregor:

For the Holsteiner [a character in *Friedenstag*] (page 26), after "Du
böser Schirmer uralter knöcherner Macht" [You evil protector of ancient, ossified power], I need four similar lines—for Maria, page 28a,
about another eight incantatory lines—you also wanted to reformulate the negative "Noch fehlt das Wort" [the word is still lacking] into
a positive idea! The whole thing at least sixteen lines long, so I can
spread myself out in rather arialike expansiveness at this point!

Please also send the conclusion soon!

At New Year's I hope to be done with the first draft!

Regarding the *Schweigsame*-Salzburg,[7] yesterday I made a tentative
inquiry of Dr. Böhm in Dresden! I am afraid, however, that it will
not be able to be realized.

With best wishes for good *Daphne* and a happy holiday. Cordial
greetings from your

Dr. Richard Strauss

·

[Vienna] 24 December 1935

Most esteemed Doctor Strauss:

I received your kind letter and warm wishes and am delighted that
everything is going so well. I am therefore sending off the changes I
made on Christmas Eve day immediately.

I await the result in your inquiry regarding Salzburg (*Schweigsame*).
I, too, believe that it will not be without its difficulties, the people
there are so narrow-minded in what they undertake. Always *Jedermann*
and *Faust*—to me they say that these works must "earn a return" and
that my *Cenodoxus*,[8] which they also want to perform, must therefore
wait . . . To my surprise I hear that your friend has approached the
directors of the Opera all on his own, on behalf of the *Schweigsame*.

He did not consult with me ahead of time, and I am familiar with your position. I am curious what kind of an answer he will receive there?

On the other hand things seem to be going well regarding the chances for a big concert. As soon as the holidays are over and Burghauser (Philharmonic)[9] returns—he is with Toscanini at the moment—I will pay a call on him.

I hope you are having lovely, work-filled days. There will be time for the final choruses of the *Friedenstag* . . .

Once more, esteemed Doctor Strauss, all the best for the holidays. I look forward to *Daphne* and remain your

Gregor

.

[Garmisch] 1 January 1936

Dear Herr Gregor:

Prost for the New Year! *Daphne* promises, if the two main scenes succeed, to be outstanding. Congratulations!

The trouble our friend has caused at the Vienna Opera is unbelievable. I have written him a distinctly indignant letter, for he has created a very awkward situation for me with W.[10] At any rate he should cease all further propaganda for the piece!—

Continue to work on *Daphne* at any rate!

With best greetings, your

Dr. Richard Strauss

.

Vienna, 6 January [1936]

Most esteemed Doctor Strauss:

I have received your friendly letter and am delighted with your opinion about the *Daphne* draft. Your comments were most excellent and insightful.

I am sending you the rest of the piece up to the principal scenes and [ask you to] be kind enough to write to me about it. I would like to mention that I have introduced Gäa, because otherwise there is no low female voice. The figure will later gain more significance through the fate of her daughter. If you don't like her, she can disappear. . . .

I am in the midst of the work and would be very happy if you could write to me soon.

With most devoted respects, your

Gregor

.

[Garmisch] 7 January 1936

Dear friend Gregor:

Daphne is superb—more in this vein! Do you know a short, popular French history of the period from Henry II to Louis XIV for my wife, who would like to inform herself about it in a superficial way?

With cordial thanks and best greetings, your always devoted

Dr. Richard Strauss

.

[Vienna] 13 January [1936]

Most esteemed Doctor Strauss:

I thank you for your dear, encouraging letter and send you the next "delivery" in the enclosure. The piece will probably be finished this week.

As to a history of France, this is not so easy. The best is in French: Jacques Bainville, *Histoire de France,* Paris 1928 (this is shorter), or ibid., in two volumes (large, illustrated). Both works were published by Tallandier in Paris.

In German, I would be most inclined to recommend volume 5 of the Propyläen world history: *The Age of Religious Revolution.* It includes sections on France during that epoch.

If I should obtain any of these books for you, please write.

With many most devoted regards and greetings to your wife, your

Gregor

I noticed that in the *Daphne* manuscript on page 2, during the copying "First shepherd" and "Second shepherd" have been reversed. No doubt you noticed it too.

.

[Garmisch] 13 January 1936

Dear friend Gregor:

I am sending *Daphne* once more for linguistic super-revision! My *hasty, not at all* final or absolutely decisive corrections are only to suggest what I would like to see improved: more evenness in the lines, avoidance wherever possible of feminine endings, avoidance of the little usually superfluous expletives, avoidance of subordinate clauses that begin with "while" and "although"—you see what I mean—I declaim everything out loud for myself, to see what is the best way to compose it. But please don't hold me strictly to my textualization!

Make your own improvements according to the scheme I have suggested!

In content and dramatic structure everything is excellent!

With best greetings, your sincerely devoted

Dr. Richard Strauss

•

[Garmisch] 13 January 1936

Dear friend Gregor:

Thanks for the package: it is splendid and has lovely *clair-obscur*.[11]

Reporting as directed that no. 1 is already finished in rough draft and will be done in final draft in about two weeks. I think the final hymn [of *Friedenstag*] turned out particularly well.

With cordial greetings, your grateful, devoted

Dr. Richard Strauss

•

[Vienna] 17 January [1936]

Most esteemed dear Doctor Strauss:

I am delighted at your good news that you have completed no. 1 [of *Friedenstag*] in rough draft and, as I see, are in the midst of such a brilliant period of work.

I send you enclosed the conclusion of no. 2 [*Daphne*] and ask you once more to make changes, deletions, and so on, to it just as you did with the beginning. I have received the return package and find your remarks extraordinarily insightful. When I have received this conclusion back again, as well, then I will begin with the revision of the whole.

As always happens when one is working concentratedly on something, new themes and materials are constantly occurring to me. If you wish and have a break in your work, I will come to see you again to talk about them. Perhaps then I could already listen to some of the *Friedenstag* music, which I am understandably longing to hear.

With the most cordial admiration, your

Gregor

•

[Vienna] 18 January 1936

Honored dear Doctor Strauss:

Upon rereading the conclusion of *Daphne*, which I sent off yesterday, a change occurred to me that I will make during the revision, but would like to tell you about now, for your orientation.

The way it is now written, the catastrophe on pages 40 and 41 is unclear. I am going to rework it as follows: Apollo rhapsodically celebrates the sunrise in song—that seems good to me, as a means for him to declare and fully express himself again. Daphne: "Wie längst Gehörtes rührts mich an . . ." [Like a long-lost melody it moves me . . .] is also good and suits the natural predisposition of the character. But from here on Daphne should be completely rooted to the spot by the nature vision of Apollo, spellbound, as it were, while in contrast the jealousy of Leukippos is excited to such a point that he repeatedly attacks Apollo. Leukippos will exclaim, "So hilf mir doch, Daphne, Du hasst ihn ja . . ." [So help me, Daphne, after all you hate him . . .], while Daphne will answer, "Ich kann nicht, die Sonne, die ich rief, hat mich festgebannt . . ." [I can't, the sun, which I invoked, transfixes me . . .] or something of the sort. In this way it is better motivated when Apollo, one last time, pleads with Daphne: "Folge mir in den goldenen Wagen" [Follow me into the golden chariot]—that seems good to me. But Leukippos, whom Daphne does not protect, becomes so wild as a result that he hurls his curse at Apollo and as a result can be struck down by the latter.—On the other hand I think it is good that on page 42 Apollo leaves so quickly, after the deed, because every bridge between him and mankind has been broken off. He will perhaps be given a line of regret or melancholy.

As a result of this change, which corresponds better to the character of Daphne, the line on page 39, "Ganz wie du ihn wollt ich Dir tun!" [As you did unto him I would do unto you], is deleted. That is something Daphne cannot say. On the other hand, on page 40, "Bekenne, bekenne! Die Wahrheit!" [Confess! Confess! The truth!] remains. For this is precisely what unleashes the catastrophe.

This will be better, I think, and I at least wanted to let you know this new idea, with the most devoted greetings, your

Gregor

•

Hotel Vier Jahreszeiten
Restaurant Walterspiel
Munich

21 January 1936

Dear Herr Gregor:

The second part is also good in its plan and structure, but linguistically very much in need of revision and the thoughts sometimes unclear, many empty phrases and cheap commonplaces like clarity—

truth—repentance—regret—confession—manliness—*culpable* passion—eternal—a just (?) and kindly tree?

Please think it all over carefully and check over those passages I have marked with question marks for all possibilities of improvement! It all seems to me a bit hastily composed, not clearly thought through or polished. Give yourself plenty of time to finish it and check it carefully!

With best greetings, your most devoted

Dr. Richard Strauss

·

[Garmisch] 24 January 1936

Dear friend Gregor:

The clean copy of the draft will be done tomorrow. I would be happy to see you again before my trip to Italy and hear about your new plans.

I am in Munich 5–7 February *(Rosenkavalier)*,

11–12 February *(Frau ohne Schatten)*,

17 February *(Lohengrin)*, and

the rest of the time here. Around the twentieth I will be leaving for Genoa for *Arabella*. . . .

Please send the beginning of *Daphne* back to me again soon, up to the appearance of the god, or thereabouts, so that I may gradually begin to get to work!

With cordial greetings, yours!

Dr. Richard Strauss

·

[Garmisch] 26 January 1936[12]

Dear Herr Gregor:

Through an accident I did not receive your letter of the eighteenth until yesterday; therefore I have not responded to it, but hasten to tell you at once that the new line that is suggested in it is absolutely the right way to give the figure of Daphne the *twilight* she needs, in order to give visual expression to her fateful bond with nature and her failure toward the human being and toward the god who approaches her in human form and with human feelings.

Thus my antipathy, in my last letter already, to all-too-precise wording—like "truth"—"confession"—"regret"—"repentance." More *clair-*

obscur—I don't know whether I express myself clearly enough—whether you understand me! If so, then I ask you to review *every* thought and every word exactingly—there is too much that is hasty and banal in it, the way one dashes something off in the first flush of enthusiasm!

But your very letter of the eighteenth gives me hope that you already sense the weaknesses yourself and have already clearly recognized some of them, and [I] merely want to send you my quick encouragement to continue reviewing, polishing, and adding so that something really quite special will result.

With best greetings, your

Dr. Richard Strauss

.

[Vienna] 17 February 1936

Most esteemed, dear Doctor Strauss:

Back in Vienna, my first act is to thank you again most cordially for receiving me before your departure and for having given me the great impression of your new work.

The great simplicity and monumentality of the *Friedenstag* will make this work shine lastingly among all your works. The soldiers at the beginning with the wonderful contrast of the Italian, the funeral march of the deputation, the soldiers' songs, and the great duet of the *Kommandant* and the woman are the four simple structural pillars upon which the second part, beginning with the bells, rises like a huge cupola. If the first part belongs to the actual reality of war, the ideal world of peace in the second part is made with a generosity of such ideal proportions that I am at a loss to find anything so completely entrancing among even your works. I can't help recalling the *Death and Transfiguration* and my beloved *Zarathustra*—it has its roots there. But the perfection you have achieved in the final choruses will be compared with the greatest models. I can compare only the conclusion of Beethoven's Ninth, but the conclusion of the *Friedenstag* is even simpler, more monumental, more domelike, whereas the conclusion of the Ninth, as I feel it, is disturbed by the audible strains of the solo [vocal] quartet. In the *Friedenstag* everything is simple, monumental, C major really clear as a dome, not refracted from B, as in *Zarathustra*.

What an unheard-of effect is the coming together of the choruses, through which the tower is neutralized, immaterialized, destroyed!

What a different kind of destruction from that brought about by gunpowder! This ideal effect of two choruses coming together (*St. Matthew Passion,* opening) is something I have *always wanted to see in the theater as well*—you have accomplished it in the most sublime way!

Please accept, revered master, the early congratulations of the one who is privileged, as a modest servant of your music, to take part in your work. Here one must not say *Prima le parole, dopo la musica* but *First the words, but then* only *the music.* You will undoubtedly hear what I have said here reiterated in all serious and informed music criticism!

It was endlessly valuable for me to hear the magnificent work, since I am still laboring on the pedestal upon which this gigantic structure will stand, *Daphne.* If the *Friedenstag* expresses the highest idea of man, *Daphne* sings the peace of nature. The two works quite naturally belong together.

I hope this letter will find you still there and thank you again. Please send me your next address, too, since I would naturally like to report to you on the explanation that I plan to give the officials here.

With warmest admiration, your

Gregor

·

[Genoa] 29 February 1936

Dear friend Gregor:

In order to make your work easier I have now cut brutally whatever already seems expendable to me at this time. Please consider carefully and delete and abridge as much as possible and condense down to only what is absolutely necessary for the plot.

If possible, send me the new result in Milan (Hotel Cavour), where I am staying until the eleventh of March! Then I will be making a five-day detour through France by way of Marseille-Avignon; on the nineteenth I am in Antwerp (Flemish Opera); from the twenty-seventh of March, Paris (Hotel Meurice).

With best greetings, your

Dr. Richard Strauss

·

Hotel de Paris
Monte Carlo

4 March 1936

Dear friend Gregor:

Letters and the supposedly cut *Daphne* received today! But my dear friend—we are still a long way from a usable opera text—it is still all too long by half. Consider the following: Elsa's dream, an aria lasting three pages in the piano reduction = twelve lines! The king's prayer = twelve lines, and so on.[13]

I hope you have meanwhile received my cut copy. You yourself still become much too intoxicated by your own verses, of which in the opera the audience scarcely understands a fifth and immediately turns away in boredom if asked to swallow "ideas" coated in music, instead of hearing beautiful cantilenas based on only the bare minimum of text that is immediately necessary for the plot. From my cuts you see precisely what already appears expendable today on the basis of *not overly careful* revision. But I am convinced much more can be cut and above all "condensed"! So cut, in addition, whatever you can. If, in composing, I should actually need somewhat more text, I shall take it from the present copy!

But now a couple of other concerns: Daphne immediately notices the eroticism in Apollo's "brotherly" kiss; why not in the "sisterly" kiss of Leukippos, as well? The disguise does not do it! Pages 35–36 of Daphne's speech are weak. "Betrug ist der Männer ewiges Anteil" [infidelity is the eternal lot of men] is an empty phrase, and can be asserted equally well of women.

The "Gott, der die *Ehre* vergaß" [the god who forgot *honor*] is also impossible.

What is honor of a god?

"Höher scheint mir die menschliche Liebe" [higher, to me, is human love], and so on, is also an empty claim!

In short, the whole speech is not good, or at least very much open to quibbling. Please see to it that something better occurs to you. The present version is too banal!

Please spare no efforts and continue to think about it. Above all it is too simplistic when Daphne, immediately following Apollo's kiss, turns to hate. Even if she is ignorant of human erotic love or despises it, the kiss of the god would still have to awaken other feelings in her besides the simple one of hatred. So the motive from page 34, Daphne, "Festgebannt hat mich der Fremde" [transfixed am I by the stranger], *must begin right after Apollo's kiss.*

What is the meaning of "Er weiß mein Geheimnis, er kennt mein Herz" [He guesses my secret, he knows my heart]?

Is unclear in this form! If they [her secret and feelings] *are to be found in the fact that she worships the light and "he himself is light," then this theme must already sound in the first scene between Apollo and Daphne and play into it.* You see, psychologically everything must become much more subtle and complex! I can only repeat: Kleist![14] Please review the whole thing once again with care and when you have found a new form that corresponds better to my wishes, then have it read by a very acute, fastidious critic and discuss it with reference to my demands!

It may turn out lovely—but not on this simple path!

Am in Milan on the seventh!

With best wishes, your

Dr. Richard Strauss

And as always: Don't take it amiss!

Friends in Vienna suggest that you should discuss my concern with the chancellor Kurt Schuschnigg himself!

·

[Monte Carlo] 6 March 1936

Dear Herr Gregor:

Apollo's kiss cannot engender hate in Daphne. A natural being like Daphne must be completely incapable of hatred.

The feelings that Apollo's kiss arouses in her can only be alarm, astonishment, and pain, that the light, which she worships and whose disappearance she has just been lamenting, which she has heretofore only seen—she now feels inside herself as *passion!* So after the kiss— nearly swooning—"the light—the sun—woe is me! I cannot bear it!"

Just as from the very beginning she has divined the higher being in Apollo—now gradual recognition that she is unworthy of the god and as his natural creature cannot be raised up to him. The entire inner plot must therefore proceed in such a way that she develops from her presentiment of the god to full knowledge,[15] which can only end tragically or, as here, through transformation!

So no deceit! Perhaps not even on the part of Leukippos! The latter may not under any circumstances kiss Daphne! Couldn't the catastrophe be brought on by the fact that during the festival the two divine elements Apollo and Dionysos come together in such a way that Daphne, in her fear of the god, flees, as it were, to Leukippos, whom she can perfectly well *recognize in his disguise,* perhaps letting herself be drawn into a dance that intensifies under the influence of wine, and that proves that for the *human being Daphne*—Dionysos remains nearer than the unapproachable sun god? Therefore jealousy of Apollo toward Dionysos, to which Leukippos is sacrificed!

Here, too, no motive of deceit, or at most touched on in such fashion that it would appear rather more sympathetic to Daphne, since it permits her to flee from the god, whom she worships but cannot endure, to the human Leukippos! Do you follow where I am headed—to the most intimate feeling and refinement?

And when Apollo shows himself as a cowherd, that is never deceit but merely one of the forms in which the god is able to present himself to human beings. And do not attach too much importance to the "brother" he appears to be when gives her the first kiss: at any rate, not a principal motive. This would have to be the fact that the divine, when it wishes to approach human beings, only finds weak beings who cannot endure it—except in the genius of the artist, some of which we might ascribe to Peneios, who must not, at the end, be an old, infirm man, but sees, in the symbol of Daphne's transformation into the beautiful, perfect tree, the true fulfillment of his artistic dream.

I believe that in this way the various elements embodied in the material could be brought into halfway decent accord!

With best greetings, your

Dr. Richard Strauss

Best congratulations on the success of Calderon![16]
For me no more!
Prima la parole, dopo la musica![17]
Or, better yet, *Cölestine!*

.

Hotel Cavour
Milan

8 March 1936

Dear friend Gregor:

Could one not interpret Daphne thus, that she represents the human embodiment of nature herself, who is touched by the two godheads, Apollo and Dionysos, the elements of the artistic, who senses but does not comprehend them and can only be resurrected in death into a symbol of the eternal work of art: the perfect laurel [tree]? Apollo's kiss on the one hand, and on the other hand a hieratic dance with Leukippos, who bears the Dionysian within himself in the theatrical mask of his disguise, would be the two motives of a receptive mankind moved by artistic genius. Alongside them the contemplating, inspired Peneios! Please give this some thought!

Best greetings! Your

Dr. Richard Strauss

.

[Milan] 9 March 1936

Dear friend Gregor:

Yesterday I gave Wallerstein *Daphne*[18] to read. In the evening after the dress rehearsal we discussed the following at Biffi's:[19] Apollo betrays his godhead by approaching Daphne with Dionysian feelings; she feels this betrayal in his kiss and denies the impure god as a purely instinctual and natural being, when, with vacillating emotions, she senses his presence but cannot fully apprehend him. After this adventure, Apollo, before he can mount his sun chariot again, must also undergo a purification within himself, which has its dramatic climax in his killing, in Leukippos, *of the Dionysian element within himself.* The symbol of his own purification would be Daphne's salvation through her transformation into the laurel!

We gave a lot of thought to the very ticklish figure of Leukippos in girl's clothing—already quite discomfiting in itself. The disguise can only play a very secondary, transitory role, if only because the all-knowing god must immediately see through it.

Daphne, too, must recognize and reject him at once, or at least soon after their first touch—possibly after a brief dance (?)—at once Leukippos himself must tear off the disguise and challenge the god to a fight over his beloved Daphne, who naturally, according to her essential nature, can belong to neither of them.

The most important thing would consequently be Daphne's lament for Leukippos, which is now very weak and which is the principal medium of Apollo's self-purification.

Wallerstein also remarked quite rightly that Gäa, if she is to be on the program, should play a much more significant role. There should be a short, meaningful conversation between Mother Earth and Daphne, who now, as a tree, is eternally rerooted in the Earth!

These are brief prefatory suggestions! I have asked Wallerstein to discuss the material with you immediately following his return to Vienna (I believe Saturday)! Trust him: he is a fine, clever, highly educated man, has very good ideas, knows my life's work in minute detail, and understands a great deal about theater!

With best greetings, your

Dr. Richard Strauss

·

[Vienna] 10 March [1936]

Esteemed dear Doctor Strauss:

I received the copy of *Daphne* as revised by you, which crossed in the mail with my cut draft, along with your most interesting letters regarding the text, and thank you very much. I must tell you that I am *enthusiastic* about your letters, since they reveal to me the most intensive and productive preoccupation with the material and are endlessly stimulating to me.

I am completely in agreement with everything of importance to which you refer. In particular, I completely agree to have the play take place in the shadow of the great contradiction between the Dionysian and the Apollonian and to have Daphne incline, through a hieratic dance, to the Dionysian side. This naturally offers much finer but naturally also more effective spiritual motives than the old deceit motive. I am also completely enthusiastic about the idea of giving Peneios more profundity as a prototype of the artistic nature.

It is only implicit in my own most deeply felt wishes to reformulate the piece with this in mind. Simple condensation or mere deletion will no longer suffice here; a number of scenes must be entirely rewritten, all the others revised line by line and brought into harmony with the singular meaning that you wish to convey. It is quite self-evident that then certain details, such as the long speech by Daphne, will turn out quite differently. . . .

Certainly it is my intention to go all the way to the chancellor.[20] But this is not so easy, since he is surrounded by only his closest colleagues. But my recent success has been very helpful; both the chancellor himself and in particular Baron Hammerstein, a personality who is very close to him, were very enthusiastic. I hope that with patience and firmness of will I will be able to do as you wish.

In admiration and again with great thanks for the magnificent letters, your

Gregor

·

[Milan] 12 March 1936

Dear Herr Gregor:

I . . . ask only that you get in touch with Dr. Wallerstein immediately and revise the material *again with him.* I have discussed the work thoroughly with him and explained to him exactly what I want—

namely something almost entirely new!
In haste, greetings from your

Dr. Richard Strauss

•

Hotel Meurice
Rue de Rivoli, Paris

Sunday, 29 March 1936

Dear friend Gregor:

Many thanks for the new draft, which has already turned into something much closer to what I have in mind! But all the passages where
you write "remains" are much in need of revision in their linguistic
form, if they are to be composable. Above all, much is lacking in the
architecture of the songs. How I imagine it you may deduce from the
enclosed draft of the first Daphne song—naturally still to be polished—how I have combined the various, often scattered ideas and
images and constructed the whole at least in a straight line.

And now I wish you pleasant labors: I am in Garmisch again from
the seventh of April and am, with the most friendly greetings, your
ever devoted

Dr. Richard Strauss

    1. O bleib, geliebter Tag
       Lang weiltest du—
       so bleib für immer!
       Gesegneter Schein
       in dir lebe ich
       mit meinen Brüdern, den Bäumen!
       In dir prangen in Blüte
       die Sträucher, meine Schwestern!
       In dir sehe ich
       mein Zwillingsbild
       die tanzende Quelle!
       In dir folgt mir lachend
       die Pracht der Falter.
       In dir spielen
       der Wiese Blumen mit mir!
       O bleib, geliebter Tag,
       nimm noch nicht Abschied!

       [O stay, beloved day!
       You have tarried long—

So stay forever!
Blessed light
in you I live
with my brothers, the trees!
In you blossoms deck
the bushes, my sisters!
In you I see
the face of my twin,
the dancing spring!
In you bright butterflies
flutter behind me.
In you I play
with the meadow's flowers!
O stay, beloved day,
Do not yet take your leave.]

2. Umgib noch nicht mit sanftem Rot
der Wehmut mein Gesicht,
küß meinen Finger nicht mit süßem Glanz:
ich liebe dich—so geh nicht fort von mir!

[Do not yet suffuse my face with the soft
crimson of melancholy,
do not let your sweet glow caress my finger:
I love you—so don't leave me here alone!]

3. Wenn du entweichest,
geliebtes Licht
sind sie mir ferne,
Bäume und Blumen,
Schmetterling, Quelle,
Brüder und Schwestern,
gehen ins Dunkel vor meinen Blicken,
antworten nicht mehr dem ängstlichen Rufe,
still ist alles, Nacht und leer,
einsam bin ich.

[When you flee from me
beloved light
they are all far away,
trees and flowers,
butterfly, spring,
brothers and sisters,
fade into darkness before my eyes,

reply no more to my anxious calling,
all is still, night and empty,
lonely am I.]

4. Warum, lieber Vater,
   lockst du heute mit deines Hornes Gewalt
   die Menschen,
   die mit schweren Füßen mir die Wiese versehren,
   Mit stumpfem Getier mir die Blumen vernichten,
   die meine Brüder, die Bäume, entlauben,
   meine geliebteste Schwester trüben, die Quelle!
   Ihre verlangenden Blicke quälen mein Herz,
   ihre wilden Lieder bedrängen mein Ohr.
   Fremd ist ihre Sprache, rauh ihr Sinn,
   fremd ist mir alles,
   einsam bin ich!

   [Why, dear father,
   do you call forth today with the power of your horn
   mankind
   with their heavy-shod feet to trample my meadows,
   destroy my flowers with their dumb beasts,
   defoliate my brothers, the trees,
   muddy my dearest sister, the spring!
   Their lascivious glances torture my heart,
   their wild songs assault my ear.
   Foreign their tongue, rough their senses,
   foreign is everything
   lonely am I!]

5. O wie gerne bliebe ich bei dir
   mein lieber Baum,
   mit dem Kinde gepflanzt
   mein teurer Brüder!
   Wenn der Tag uns verlässt,
   die Sonne—Apollo—
   der große Gott
   stolz dahin zieht nach Hause,
   ins Gebirge der Götter—
   bliebe ich bei dir!
   Suchte im Dunkel deinen schützenden Ast,
   umklammerte dich fest,
   liebkoste dich.

Und im feinen Rauschen,
im schweigenden Nachtwind
sängest du mir vom Glanze der Sonne,
den du empfingst auf mächtigen Zweigen,
von der Stärke der Erde,
die dein Fuß umfasst,
sängest ein gewaltiges, stärkeres Lied
als das Lied der Menschen,
o geliebter Baum!

[O how gladly I would stay with you,
my beloved tree.
Planted with the child
my brother dear!
When the day leaves us,
the sun—Apollo—
the great god
departs, proudly returns
to the peaks of the gods—
I'd stay with you!
In the darkness I'd find your protective limb
clasp you fast in my arms,
caress you.
And in the fine rustling
in the silent night wind,
you would sing to me of the glory of the sun,
whom you welcomed with mighty branches
from the strength of the earth,
which your foot embraces,
you would sing a mighty, more powerful song
than the song of mankind
O beloved tree!]

.

[Paris] 1 April 1936

Dear friend Gregor:

Before you start your work: I have thought about it and Cl[emens]. Krauss, to whom I also [gave] *Daphne* to read, is also of the opinion that Leukippos disguised as a girl must not be altered. The transformation into the mask of Dionysos may be more effective theater, but Apollo, as a god, would have to recognize him immediately. Naturally Leukippos may not speak a single word as a girl, since at that every-

· 259 ·

one, not last Daphne, would recognize him in a flash, and thus I have thought up the following: Beginning on page 21 everything must change: already Daphne's last words, "Niemand hat mich so reich beschenkt" [No one ever made me such a fine gift], are not good, dry and banal. Perhaps the words "Brüder, Brüder!" will suffice. Then the kiss follows, from which Daphne extricates herself with a few alarmed, doubting words. Perhaps here, too, it is enough to say, "Du nanntest dich Brüder" [You called yourself brother].

A.: Ich liebe dich, Daphne! [I love you, Daphne!]
D.: Schlichst dich du mir in meinen Traum? [Did you secretly
         steal into my dream?]
A.: Wahrheit bring ich! [I bring truth!]
      Folge mir Daphne! [Follow me, Daphne!]

Now invisible chorus: Gib Dionysos [Give Dionysos], etc.
Then Apollo: Hörst du, Geliebte [Do you hear, beloved], etc.
      Wagst du Verneinung dem Liebesfeste? [Do you dare refuse
         the feast of love?]
D.: Ich kann nicht! Weh mir! [I can't! Woe is me!]

Now at once, entrance of the others: Peneios, Gäa—then dance of the masked men, followed by dance of the maidens, *among whom Leukippos has insinuated himself, wordlessly*. A group of the maidens dances, the others proffer drinking bowls.

Daphne to one side, facing her Apollo, whose glance seems to hold her spellbound, so that every time the maidens or also Leukippos try to pull her into the dance or offer her a bowl of wine, which Gäa, at her side, also urges her to take, she shudders and hesitantly refuses. But finally she, too, is sufficiently affected by the spirit of the festival that when Leukippos offers her the bowl a second time she drinks after all and now enters the dance with him! Perhaps after a few dance movements one could have Leukippos then say: "Follow me, sister!" Then Apollo jumps in and exposes him. Thunder, flight of the shepherds to their herds! Final dispute among Daphne, Apollo, Leukippos—his death!

Thus everything would be deleted up to the bottom of page 31!

She is deceived by both, by "brother" Apollo, by "sister" Leukippos! And cannot go on living, since as a result of the Dionysian draft she has become untrue to her own nature. Then the god finds the miracle of his own purification and her salvation in the transformation into the laurel!

How do you like it?

This final conflict among the three, the parting words of the rue-ful god and her lament for Leukippos must become very beautiful. Please think it through again in a completely new way!

Am in Garmisch beginning 7 April!

Cordial greetings from your

Dr. Richard Strauss

I believe that through my idea the beautiful myth is salvaged and everything compromising in L.'s disguise as a girl is avoided, since the dance scene plays in the darkness of night.

·

[Vienna] 16 April 1936

Very esteemed dear Doctor Strauss:

Enclosed please find a new *Daphne* text. All of the changes desired in your letters from your trip have been taken into account, as I have, in addition, discussed them with Dr. Wallerstein; however with regard to Leukippos it has followed the myth, as you discussed with Clemens Krauss. Along the same lines, Apollo must turn to Zeus to transform Daphne—Apollo himself is incapable of transforming anyone.

I share the opinion that it is better not to stray too far from the myth. One then only hears over and over again that it is different in the myth, because this reference is the cheapest kind of criticism. I thought at first that you would give [the role of] Leukippos to a woman; since, as Dr. Wallerstein tells me, it is to be a male singer, this version with the very discreet costume scene will be more appropriate.

In the hope that the draft pleases you and with the warmest re-spects and greetings to your valued family, I am your ever admiringly devoted

Gregor

·

[Garmisch] 29 April 1936

Dear Herr Gregor:

I am in agreement with the preface to the Mask.[21] Only forgive me that I have not yet confirmed my receipt of the new *Daphne*. She has already gotten very good. My only remaining reservations have to do with the conflict between Apollo and Leukippos; I shall report them in more detail as soon as I have reviewed the whole thing more closely.

With best greetings, your

Dr. Richard Strauss

·

[Bad Kissingen] 20 May 1936

Dear Herr Gregor:

To my horror I have just read the enclosed announcement,[22] which can come only from you. I urgently ask you to give no interviews about our work and to avoid every advertisement. This premature notice destroys several important actions that I was about to undertake myself with the advice of my friends . . . I urgently ask you to maintain silence, no information about content, no encomiums or the like.

With best greetings, your ever devoted

Dr. Richard Strauss

·

[Vienna] 20 June 1936

Most esteemed dear Doctor Strauss:

I am rereading this notice and can tell from it that it comes from another quarter and *not* from me. I would like to let you know that right away. The journalist in London, namely, knows *more than I*, for I myself know nothing of a "Peloponnesian version." I have also told no one, not even my wife, the titles and see now that they have also become known.

This merely for your information, the case is surely not a tragic one; however I attach some importance to emphasizing the fact that I, for my part, have respected your desire for secrecy.—It is now almost a year since the lovely days in which this rewarding work was begun. I would like to continue, either a great Spanish piece, *Celestina,* or— even more eagerly—*Semiramis.* If you can use me, let me know.

To you, dear Doctor Strauss, and all of your esteemed family, wishes for a lovely summer from your very devoted

Gregor

·

[Garmisch] 23 June 1936

Dear friend Gregor:

The first notice came from a Viennese correspondent of the *B.Z. am Mittag,* who could only have his information from a source very close to you. Well, never mind! I would only like to protest against the expression "short operas" [*Kurzopern*]. As far as *Celestina* is concerned, I have been busying myself for the last several days with the two German versions (Zoozman and the exact translation by Eduard von Bülow); already saw a very good act 1 ending (Celestina's solo scene after her first visit to Melibea). Act 2 ending: final uniting of the two lovers—the scene before and including the death of Celestina would be very good, too—but—the conclusion?! At first it didn't want to make sense to me that the lovers should come to a tragic end, and my thoughts went back and forth over whether a happy ending—perhaps flight—might be possible. Normal marriage with permission from the parents would naturally be too banal. I am still reading the very tiresome Bülow and only noticed at the end that in his version Calisto *falls off the ladder* and Melibea throws herself from a *tall tower* and then I had the bright idea that a stage version (*even more* with music than in only spoken dialogue) is possible only if the poetic figures of the play—the parents, Fabio, and the lovers—are treated parodistically.

The gang of scoundrels can remain the same as in the original; they are already near-caricatures—but in the lovers Zoozman found only poetry and he has put really beautiful verses and thoughts into their mouths, without noticing that as a result the murder of the lovers seems unmotivated and brutal, something that has been shocking to me from the very first.

But now I see in Bülow that Calisto, in particular, is treated from the first as quite a buffoon (especially in his conversations with Celestina), and with that the character of the Spanish "tragicomedy" became clear to me; only if it should prove possible to *maintain* this tragicomic style in the love scenes, too, with false pathos in moments that are, in part, really poetic—could Calisto "*fall* from the ladder," and so on. The parents, as well, would have to be drawn as reverse "Capulettis"—the whole thing a kind of satyr play on *Romeo!*

It would be a continuation of the ironic style of *Cosi fan Tutte* and the completion of the joke that began with *Feuersnot*.

In other words, only possible if treated throughout as a grotesque—then the original ending is right, too.

Would you like to have a go at it in this direction? The Zoozman treatment with its condensed selection of the most essential passages has many other good features—only at the end, the resolution, beginning with the death of Don Luis, would have to be tightened up in a great (confusing) ensemble scene and the opponents—parents and Fabio—would have to be involved directly!

Final *Figaro* finale!

I have definitely dropped *Semiramis!* Rather: *poi le parole, dopo la musica!*[23] At least it is amusing and only one act! After *Daphne* I should like to do something cheerful! No more tragedy!—

But now to something else! Are you familiar with Hofmannsthal's opera sketch—*Danae,* published in the journal *Corona* 4, vol. 1, published by R. Olderbourg, Munich and Berlin, which I have just received from Zurich?[24] Charming material, which I would also like to compose—naturally it would have to be handled with a certain precious irony, and there Hofmannsthal himself may have felt that his ending is a little banal, too bourgeois—perhaps the whole thing (as in *Don Giovanni* with the last, always deleted sextet) should end with a merry ensemble of Jupiter's five lovers with their husbands!

Would you like to talk all this over with our friend on occasion? Could I meet with you somewhere in the near future—in Innsbruck? I have free entry into Austria again, could slip into the Pustertal or Kärnten, too! Will be staying here all summer, except in August I am conducting now and again in Munich!

With best greetings, your

Dr. Richard Strauss

The score of the *Friedenstag* is finished!

·

[Vienna] 3 August [1936]

Very esteemed dear Doctor Strauss:

I thank you many times for the kind letter; I am exceptionally pleased that the sketch for *Celestina* pleases you. I will certainly complete it according to your directives.

At the moment I am in the midst of preparations for the great theater exhibition, which I am curating, and which will open on 3 September. As soon as it is over, I would like to give myself a few days of rest and, if you would permit me, get together with you. What do you think of Gastein? It is gorgeous on beautiful fall days, when everyone has left. A town in Tyrol would be possible, too, but I don't want to go very far from Vienna.

Please, if the picture of the Bernini-Daphne is no longer needed, send it back to me; it belongs to my collection of reproductions.

I was enormously pleased to hear about the splendid *Olympia Hymn!*[25] It must have been an exalting feeling for you, on which I warmly congratulate you.

I received an extraordinarily dear and kind letter from your esteemed wife in response to my sending the Danae of Titian and would like to ask you to convey the expression of my most devoted thanks and greetings.

To you, most esteemed Doctor Strauss, I wish a good and satisfying time and am already looking forward to *Celestina,* as your most devoted

Gregor

.

[Garmisch] 2 September 1936

Dear friend Gregor:

Dr. Kerber director of the Staatsoper—a most delightful piece of news! Gastein isn't possible for me to visit—soon I must—perhaps—travel to Venice and am leaving on 20 September again for twelve days in Kissingen. But in mid-October between the eighth and the sixteenth your visit to Garmisch would be quite agreeable to me, and on the eighteenth and nineteenth a rendezvous in Munich could be arranged. Perhaps by then you could send me some worked-out ideas. In the meanwhile I am working continuously on *Daphne.*

With best wishes, your most devoted

Dr. Richard Strauss

.

[Garmisch] 17 October 1936

Dear friend Gregor:

I am in London from 2–7 November, 8–10 in Munich, 11–14 in Garmisch, and will probably leave on the fifteenth by car for Rome, could be in Bozen (Hotel Greif) for lunch on the fifteenth, that evening in Verona, around the sixteenth in Florence, seventeenth Perugia, and eighteenth in the evening Rome (Hotel Russie).

On the twenty-second and twenty-fifth concerts there, on the twenty-sixth beginning of the return trip by way of Orvieto, Siena, bringing me back to Garmisch again on the twenty-eighth or twenty-ninth. It would be nice if you could work something out in one of these places.

Daphne moves ahead. I am reading your reviews in the *N. W. Journal* with pleasure.

With best greetings, your

Dr. Richard Strauss

Do you know of a publisher in Vienna for an Italian (Prof. Errante, Florence), who has written good book about Lenau, translated by Charlotte Rau?

.

[Vienna] 27 October [1936]

Esteemed dear Doctor Strauss:

You will pardon me for I must follow my last letter with another inquiry. As a pleasant consequence of the large exhibition I put together I shall be publishing a major theater journal beginning at Christmas. It is to be a thoroughly serious literary journal, not at all an illustrated magazine of the sort that is now commonplace. This monthly journal will cover the "entire theatrical culture" and have a permanent representative in every great theatrical country.[26]

The thought occurred to me to ask you whether it might be agreeable to you to publish a scene from *Daphne*, the text, in the first volume? This first volume will certainly be widely circulated and the attention paid to the work will, as a result, certainly be very considerable. I would like to choose the scene from the middle of the work in such a way that it will reveal next to nothing—for example, the festival scene.

But I know your caution in this regard and will certainly not be disappointed if you do not wish to give your permission. I continue not to wish to betray anything that you yourself do not want and would not have made the suggestion to you if this case were not an *exception*. The journal, namely, will certainly attract a lot of attention. The fact that I myself am the director will certainly suffice to assure you that it is a very serious publication. I would also like to remark that here—as in the case of the exhibition—I am taking the first official steps to do away with the quite unnecessary tension between the two countries in matters cultural. The journal will have official contributors from the [German] Empire and for this reason, too, it would seem logical to me to begin with a remembrance of the most significant work that connects Germany and Austria, namely our own.

Please give me the decision on this before your departure for England and know that you are, as always, respectfully greeted by your

Gregor

.

[Garmisch] 28 October 1936

Dear Professor:

To Rome I shall travel direct, round-trip, by sleeping coach. From the thirtieth of November on I am in Garmisch again with the exception of *5–8 December* (concert in Munich on the seventh) and *10–16* (two concerts in Berlin).

That the *Josefslegende* [turned out] so beautifully in Vienna makes me very glad; please convey my warm thanks and best greetings to Frau Wallmann. I urgently request you to avoid every type of publication of *Friedenstag* and *Daphne*. Only creates misunderstandings—an uncomposed opera text that no one can understand properly or appreciate in the slightest.

I suggest, however, that you send me the first act of *C[elestina]*. I [will] then, by reading it over and over, reach the point in its treatment where a personal discussion will bring better results. Reading out loud by the author makes too strong an impression.

All best wishes for your theater journal! With best wishes, your

Dr. Richard Strauss

·

[On a postcard bearing a photograph of Bernini's *Apollo e Dafne*]

Garmisch, 1 December 1936

Dear friend Gregor:

Rome was splendid . . . Now I am leaving for Munich (sixth to eighth), then Breslau and Berlin (twelfth to fifteenth), Hotel Adlon, and am not back here until the sixteenth. But perhaps we can meet at the end of the month in Salzburg, where I have promised, at the invitation of Director Wallek, to direct a concert of the Munich *Staatsorchester* in the Mozarteum, without honorarium! The final *Friedenstag* is not yet complete. My children arrive today in Vienna.

With best greetings, your

Dr. Richard Strauss

·

[Vienna] 4 March 1937

Most esteemed dear Doctor Strauss:

I thank you for your so friendly letter and for the excellent suggestions.

Based on these suggestions I shall develop various samples. But then I think it will be best if I show these examples to you personally and can talk things through with you for two or three days, in order to find the poetic form, as was the case at the inception of the *Friedenstag* and *Daphne*.

Toward the middle of the month I have a lecture tour of Yugoslavia ahead of me, which, I believe, will be over just before Easter. During the Easter holidays, and afterward, I could be with you in Garmisch or at any place you wish. I will certainly not take up your time for more than two or three days.

With repeated thanks for the most interesting, very accurate observations, and greetings to your spouse, I am your devoted

Gregor

·

[Garmisch] 12 May 1937

Dear friend Gregor:

On Sunday Clemens Krauss was here and we agreed that after Apollo's *Abgesang* no human being but Daphne must appear on stage, no Peneios, no solo voices—no chorus—in short, no oratorio: everything would only make it weaker. During Apollo's last moments of song Daphne, regarding him in astonishment, arises slowly from the corpse of Leukippos and after Apollo has exited she wants to follow him, but after only a few steps remains as if rooted to the spot and now—in the moonlight, but completely visible—the miracle of transformation occurs: *only with orchestra alone!* At most Daphne might speak a few words during the transformation, which turn into stuttering and then *wordless* melody! Perhaps not [even that]! At most at the very end: after the tree is complete, she might wordlessly—nothing but sounding nature—sing eight beats of the laurel motive! Do you like that?

In any case, however, I would need for Apollo after his concluding words, "I will endow her with the highest honor," another eight to twelve verses—perhaps before that, too—since I wish to be much more expansive in this musical farewell. Please see that something really beautiful occurs to you—perhaps along the lines of Peneios's last song, which is now superfluous!

I am in Vienna on Whitmonday evening in my apartment at the Jacquingasse 10 and hope to hear from you soon.

With cordial greetings, your

Dr. Richard Strauss

·

[Garmisch] 16 June 1937

Dear friend Gregor:

The draft [Daphne?] seems very good to me: I believe you can now—in the best of moods, I hope—begin with the development.

Warmest thanks and best greetings, your

Dr. Richard Strauss[27]

·

San Domenico Palace Hotel
Taormina (Sicily)

25 December 1937

Dear Friend Gregor:

With warm thanks we return your friendly New Year's wishes! *Danae* arrived in good shape and seems to me to have turned out well. As much as I cherish Wallerstein's collaboration and judgment—he is not correct. The material is too light for serious treatment! Besides, I have no more inclination just now for anything serious. The *Daphne* score was finished yesterday. But please tell no one! About *Danae*, too, I ask for deepest silence (from Wallerstein as well)! Would you like to have the list of roles from *Daphne?*

How do you like:

> Apollo—Heldentenor
> Daphne—Soprano
> Peneios—Bass
> Gäa—Alto
> Leukippos—Lyric tenor
> Daphne's two playmates—Soprano
> First shepherd—Baritone
> Second shepherd—Tenor
> Third and fourth shepherd—Basses?
> Place?

With best greetings, your

Dr. Richard Strauss

And *Friedenstag?* Drama or opera? Do we stick with bucolic tragedy?

NOTES

1. A copy of Stefan Zweig's letter may be found among the documents of the Vienna Philharmonic [Tenschert], now the Archive of the Vienna Philharmonic [ed.].

2. *1648* was the original title for *Friedenstag* [ed.].

3. In the possession of Joseph Gregor [Tenschert]. Gregor died in 1960, and much of his estate went to the Theater Collection of the Austrian National Library [ed.].

4. Johann Heinrich Voss (1751–1826) is best known for his translations of Virgil and Homer. He edited the Hamburg *Musenalmanach* and was an early proponent of German cultural purity of a Protestant, egalitarian stripe [trans.].

5. A sarcastic reference to Nazi ideology [Tenschert].

6. Enclosed with the letter was a positive response to the *Friedenstag* text by Clemens Krauss [Tenschert].

7. Inclusion of the opera *Die schweigsame Frau* in the program of the Salzburger Festspiele [Tenschert].

8. *Cenodoxus, Doktor von Paris,* play in three parts adapted from Jakob Bidermann (Munich, 1938) [Tenschert].

9. Hugo Burghauser was at the time director of the Vienna Philharmonic [Tenschert].

10. The reference is to Felix Weingartner [Tenschert].

11. The package is the revised *Daphne* text [ed.].

12. In the original, incorrectly, [19]35 [Tenschert].

13. Both from Richard Wagner's *Lohengrin* [Tenschert].

14. As Stefan Zweig informed the editor, Strauss at one time planned to set Heinrich Kleist's *Amphitryon* to music [Tenschert].

15. In the original the word is "led" [Tenschert].

16. Gregor's version, *Die standhafte Frau* [The steadfast woman], premiered on 27 February 1936 in the [Vienna] Burgtheater [Tenschert].

17. The fundamental idea behind *Capriccio* [Tenschert].

18. Lothar Wallerstein was the senior producer at the Vienna State Opera. Strauss valued his opinions concerning theater and later turned to him for advice concerning *Die Liebe der Danae* and *Capriccio*. They discussed *Daphne* while in Milan, where *Arabella* was being produced [ed.].

19. A well-known restaurant in Milan [Tenschert].

20. Kurt Schuschnigg [Tenschert].

21. The reference is apparently to Joseph Gregor's book *Die Masken der Erde* [Masks of the earth] (Munich: R. Piper, 1936) [ed.].

22. "New Strauss Librettist: Joseph Gregor," newspaper article from the *Österreichische Zeitschrift am Abend* (18 May 1936) [ed.].

23. *First the words, then the music.* Strauss refers to Abbé Giovanni Battista Casti's libretto *Prima la musica e poi le parole,* which Zweig came across while undertaking some research at the British Museum. He suggested the idea to Strauss when the composer was considering new projects to follow *Die schweigsame Frau.* The Casti libretto was the inspiration for *Capriccio* [ed.].

24. Dr. Willi Schuh was the one who reminded the master about the forgotten plan [Tenschert].

25. Gregor refers to Strauss's *Olympic Hymn,* commissioned by the International Olympic Committee for the eleventh Olympiad (Berlin, 1 August 1936) [ed.].

26. In January 1937 *Theater der Welt* [World theater], a journal for the entire theatrical culture edited by Joseph Gregor and published by Franz Leo (Vienna, Amsterdam, and Leipzig) began publication [Tenschert].

27. In Alice Strauss's (the composer's daughter-in-law) handwriting [Tenschert].

PART III

MEMOIRS

Richard Strauss: The Man

ALFRED KALISCH

English music critic Alfred Kalisch (1863–1933) was one of Strauss's earliest advocates outside of Germany. The son of a Jewish theologian of German origin, Kalisch began a career in law before opting for music journalism at the age of thirty-one. He wrote criticism for the *Star*, the *World*, the *Morning Leader*, and the *Daily News*. Critic and composer first met in 1902 at the Berlin premiere of *Feuersnot*, and they maintained friendly relations over the years. In addition to his various writings on Strauss's music, Kalisch translated a number of vocal works into English, including the operas *Salome*, *Elektra*, *Der Rosenkavalier*, and *Ariadne auf Naxos*.

Ernest Newman's 1908 book on Strauss represents the first major English-language study of the composer and his music. From the outset Newman admits that he is "almost wholly ignorant of [Strauss's] private personality and details of his private life." Newman thus asked his friend Kalisch to fill that gap by providing a firsthand character sketch, which appears here. Kalisch succeeds in offering the reader a colorful portrait of Strauss the man, based on various visits with the composer, and he also touches upon some of Strauss's aesthetic views as well. It is the first such essay in English and serves as a worthy companion piece to Romain Rolland's more widely known character sketch of nine years earlier; they are two of the most important examples of foreign reaction to Richard Strauss at the turn of the century [ed.].

[Source: Ernest Newman, *Richard Strauss* (London: John Lane, 1908), pp. ix–xxi]

.

Like all dominant personalities, Strauss possesses in a marked degree the gift of inspiring strong admiration and creating for himself enthusiastic apostles. That he is sometimes not overpleased at their missionary zeal is shown by the story told (with what truth it is impossible to discover) of his remark to a very insistent admirer, who said:

"Master, you are the Buddha of modern music," and to whom he answered: "I do not know about that; but I do know what is the past." It is, of course, part and parcel of his modernity—an objectionable word, but nothing else expresses the idea so well—that he should have a complex mind and be prone to introspection; if he had not been born with it, his training and his surroundings would have created it. But there is a point at which he grows impatient of self-analysis, and at bottom there are in him the simplicity and directness which must be the mainspring of all considerable creative activities in all branches of human endeavour.

He was once asked what were the tendencies of modern music and whither he thought his own music was leading him; and his only answer was: "Ask the writers on music—not the writers of music." This answer is instructive and has a distinct bearing on his whole artistic creed. It means, of course—unless it is a mere heedless epigram, which is not probable—that he recognizes that there is at the root of all musical inspiration something unconscious which the creative artist himself cannot account for; and in so far as it involves a refutation of those who argue that the doctrine of programme music is incompatible with the presence of any superhuman spiritual element in the art. It is in seeming, but only seeming, contradiction to the well-known saying attributed to him: "There is no such thing as abstract music; there is good music and bad music. If it is good, it means something; and then it is programme music." The best exposition of his artistic creed is that contained in his preface to the series of booklets on music published by Bard, Marquardt, and Co., to which reference is made elsewhere; but it contains nothing new for those who have conversed with him on such topics.[1]

One of the cardinal dogmas in his musical faith is his love of Mozart, whom he claims as a "modern" in the sense that his music expresses ideas which appeal to men of this day more than Beethoven's work. His interpretations of Mozart are criticized in some quarters as being too modern because they impart into his compositions these very ideas; but this is not the place to discuss the justice of such strictures. It is more to the point to protest that it is unjust to say, as is so often said, that his love for Mozart is a mere pose. Any one who has been in his society during a good performance of a Mozartian masterpiece can vouch for the sincerity of his worship, at any rate. The writer remembers his saying once, after he had heard the Jupiter Symphony with rapt attention: "We can still all of us learn something from that." In keeping with this is his advice, habitually given to all very young aspirants who come to him with portentous symphonic poems and tell him that *Tod und Verklärung* and the *Symphonia Domestica* have been their models: "Go home and study Haydn's symphonies and then the symphonies of Mozart, and come to me again in two years' time."

Like all great innovators, he has thoroughly mastered the work of his predecessors, and there is no doubt that he could write a "correct" and learned fugue as well as any professor if he wanted to; that is to say, if it should ever happen that a fugue should be the best means of expressing what he had to say. The score of *Also sprach Zarathustra* is sufficient proof, if proof is needed. In a discussion on form he once said—or quoted with approval the saying—that till the time of Liszt and Wagner the utmost that was permitted to a composer was to ask himself: "How much expression can I put into this or that form?" whereas the modern composer says to himself: "How can I modify the form so as to make it the best possible way of expressing all I want?"

This is perhaps the place to mention two little incidents which show his attitude toward the unconscious reminiscences in his works. After the first performance of the *Domestic Symphony* in London some friends pointed out to him that a passage at the beginning of the Nocturne was identical with the beginning of the well-known Gondoliers' Song in the first book of Mendelssohn's *Songs without Words.* Those who were present at the conversation could have no doubt that the discovery was a complete surprise to him. Similarly he was quite taken aback when at one of the orchestral rehearsals of *Salome* at Dresden a member of the band (who was an Austrian) pointed out to him that one of the love motifs is one of the cavalry calls in the Austrian army, which he must have heard hundreds of times. One may compare with this the anecdote of Wagner, who, when he was rehearsing *Die Meistersinger* and came to the passage in the third act when Sachs says to Walther: "Mein Freund, in holder Jugendzeit," remarked, "My friends, this is certainly Nicolai, but I never knew it till today," meaning that the phrase is identical with the principal melody of the overture to *The Merry Wives of Windsor,* with which he must have been familiar.

In his work Strauss is fastidiously methodical, and his writing table is a model of neatness which would put to shame the most precise of businessmen. All his manuscripts and his sketchbooks are arranged, indexed, and docketed with the most scrupulous care, and his autographs are miracles of clearness and musical calligraphy. His wife once said to the present writer: "You may say what you like about his music; but if you don't praise his handwriting he will be cross with you." He dashes off his songs at great speed; often he has composed and

written a whole song during the intervals between the acts of an opera he is conducting; but he never works at his larger works at odd
moments. His usual plan is to compose in the country in the summer; formerly it was at Marquardtstein, now it is in his new house,
which is still more solitary, near Garmisch, so solitary that he whimsi-
cally said building operations were interfered with by the chamois
which came to inspect the site. His method is to allow himself a complete rest for a few weeks and then to begin regular work. He retires
every day immediately after breakfast, which is early, and the writing
of necessary letters, to a summer house, where he remains undisturbed, even by telegrams or urgent messages, till the midday meal,
after which he reads or walks for the rest of the day. Then, when he
returns to Berlin, he completes the scoring. Every evening, when he
is not conducting at the Opera or elsewhere, he sits at his table from
about nine till one, never later; and in this way he gets through a
vast amount of work. The score of a symphonic poem used to take
him not more than three to four months, and there is hardly an era-
sure or correction in it. The manuscript of his first childish composition is as legible and as free from alteration as those of his latest works.

Strauss is very sociable but not in any sense a society man. His
favourite amusement is skat, at which he is a great expert; and he is
almost as proud of his reputation as one of the best skat players in
Germany as of his musical fame. Being himself a man of very wide
culture, he loves the society of his intellectual equals, and his house
in Berlin is the resort of all who are associated with the most advanced movements in art. He is modern in all his artistic tastes, as
the pictures on the walls testify. This love of all that is new and of
this century is part and parcel of himself and is not a mere accidental accretion, as some would have us believe. He is a convinced be-
liever in the *Übermensch,* and respects all who, though they may be
his opponents, display the qualities connoted by this word. Hence his
admiration for the German Emperor, who is, intellectually and artistically, at the opposite pole, and though they can never agree on any
musical topic. The relationship between the two is well characterized
by an anecdote which may be given here for the sake of complete-
ness, though it is very familiar. After a performance of an opera of
Gluck the Emperor asked Strauss whether he did not think such music vastly superior to modern music drama. When he said that he
could hardly be expected to agree to such sentiments, the Emperor
turned to the rest of the company and said: "See what a snake I have
been warming in my bosom!" After that Strauss was for some time
known in Berlin as the "Hofbusenschlange" (i.e., court bosom snake).

One trait in Strauss's character impresses itself on those who see him at close quarters on important occasions, and that is his extraordinary power of keeping, or seeming to keep, absolutely calm when everybody else is on tenterhooks. Of course, it is only by dint of a considerable effort of will that he manages it, but it is none the less striking to see him in the artists' room at a concert, when some work of his has thrown a large audience into a ferment of excitement, sitting down and talking about things in general as if the whole business had no further concern for him. On these occasions he often finds an outlet for his superfluous vitality by sitting down and working steadily through the large pile of autograph albums which generally await him.

There is no point at which he has been more fiercely attacked than his relation to the material rewards of his art. It is very difficult to clear one's mind of cant on this matter, and it is fatally easy to obtain unthinking applause (from the very people who pride themselves on the superiority of their intellect) by raising this cry of "commercialism." Strauss is, at any rate, quite frank, and without holding a brief on one side or the other, one will do well to consider his view of the question. He always says that he is anxious, as quickly as the fates will allow, to acquire a capital which will enable him to live without holding any official post and devote himself to composition and literature. He does not say what the amount is to be, but presumably it is a fairly large one. It must be remembered that he was born with a wealthy grandfather and has been used to comfortable—nay, luxurious—surroundings from his childhood. This is no more his fault than it is the fault of other composers that their grandfathers were poor or worthless. Besides, other musicians have had parents connected with business or finance and have inherited business instincts. One would have more respect for the outcry against Strauss's monetary successes if one had any sort of confidence that those who protest most vehemently would ever refuse a good fee if they had the chance. Not that they are to blame; for it is difficult to see why musicians, of all people, should be expected to do everything for the love of art or the good of mankind. It is all very well, too, to hold up one's hands in horror because Strauss was paid £1750 for the *Domestic Symphony* and say that Beethoven got a paltry twenty pounds for a great symphony, or to simulate noble indignation because *Salome* brings in so many hundreds a year. Those who pay him have not been the losers, at any rate, and do not complain. On the other hand, he sold *Traum durch die Dämmerung* for thirty shillings, and the publisher is said to have made £400 out of it in the first two years. Besides, after all, the unholy profits of the *Domestic Symphony* and *Salome* combined will probably never amount to a tenth part of those won by *Soldiers in the Park* or *The Merry Widow Waltz*. One of the favourite weapons used against him has been that he once in America conducted a concert in a room above a large store in the afternoon while the ordinary business of the establishment was going on downstairs.[2] "Prostitution of art" was the politest thing said about it. The attack has been renewed within the last few weeks, and he was induced to reply, and what he said is instructive. He said that, as a matter of fact, the room was, or was turned into, an excellent concert room with very good acoustic properties, and that it was stipulated beforehand that all traces of business should be removed. Further, he had one of the best orchestras in the States at his disposal and better opportunities for rehearsal than were granted by some of the most prominent artistic institutions. Even if this had not been so, he continues, he might well say, as was said by an eminent actress who was taken to task for appearing in a hippodrome: "Where I appear, there it is a first-class theatre."

Every composer of any importance is accused of not doing enough to help his less prosperous colleagues, and of jealousy of those equally successful. Strauss has not escaped, and the charge is as true, or untrue, in his case as in most others. But all English people should remember with gratitude his almost impassioned advocacy of Elgar in the days when England had not yet learned to admire the *Dream of Gerontius*. His remarks in his speech at the banquet after the Lower Rhenish Festival at Düsseldorf in 1902 were no mere idle after-dinner talk.[3] He spoke them knowing full well that they were, in a sense, spoken ex cathedra and that they would be severely criticized by his German colleagues as unpatriotic. At that time hardly any English authority had dared to speak so enthusiastically of Elgar and his work.

In appearance Strauss is scrupulously neat always—not in the least like the traditional musician—without being in any sense fashionable, and his face is quite unlike that of any other great composer. Indeed, some of his critics have been heard to say that there could be no real music behind a forehead so round and prominent. In his speech he clings tenaciously to the broad Doric of his native Munich; and though (in *Feuersnot*) he has been the partner in a violent satire on his fellow townsmen, he resents attacks on them from other quarters, especially from North Germans. The typical Bavarian naturally looks on the average Prussian much as a Home Rule M.P. looks on the "garrison" of Dublin Castle; and though Strauss is too diplomatic to say much, his friends would not be surprised to hear that he agreed with his legendary fellow countryman who said that Berlin would be beautiful if there were not so many Prussians in it.

NOTES

1. Kalisch refers to the series of short monographs, under the general editorship of Strauss, called *Die Musik. Sammlung illustrierter Einzeldarstellungen,* published by Bard, Marquardt, and Co. in Berlin. The series began in 1904 and ran some thirty-two volumes [ed.].

2. A highly publicized event during Strauss's 1904 American tour was a pair of afternoon concerts that he conducted in a makeshift auditorium in Wanamaker's department store in New York. The German press was particularly vehement in their denunciation of this alleged "prostitution of art." Linda Tyler discussed the incident in a recent study, observing that Strauss was neither the first nor the last famous musician to be involved with a performance in a department store: "The musical life of the stores of the late nineteenth and early twentieth centuries was a surprisingly rich one . . . the musical fare offered by the stores often rivaled that available in traditional concert halls" ("Strauss Plays Wanamaker's: Music, Commerce, and the American Department Store, 1880–1930," a paper read by Linda Tyler at the fifty-seventh annual meeting of the American Musicological Society, 7 November 1991) [ed.].

3. Newman describes the event elsewhere (p. 23) in his book: "After the official toasts had all been proposed Strauss surprised every one by spontaneously proposing another; 'I raise my glass,' he said, 'to the welfare and success of the first English progressivist, Meister Edward Elgar, and the young progressive school of English composers'" [ed.].

Richard Strauss:

Seer and Idealist

PERCY GRAINGER

Percy Grainger's (1882–1961) admiration for Strauss's music is not well known. This early essay on the composer appeared as an introduction to Henry T. Finck's volume on Strauss—the first one to be published in the United States. Born in Melbourne, Australia, Grainger left for musical study in Germany at age thirteen; he stayed there for six years. During those years Strauss was at the height of his career as a composer of tone poems. No doubt Strauss's music made a strong impression on the young Grainger. In 1901 Grainger moved to London and then moved to the United States thirteen years later.

Clichéd views of Grainger's life and works have portrayed him as little more than a virtuoso pianist and composer of folk-song settings. Not only was he a prolific composer in various genres (chamber, symphonic, choral) but he also wrote important music criticism, of which the essay on Strauss is a fine early example. At the time it was written Strauss had completed his final tone poem, *Eine Alpensinfonie,* as well as his most famous operas, *Salome, Elektra,* and *Der Rosenkavalier,* and both versions of *Ariadne auf Naxos.* Grainger's essay is remarkable for a number of reasons. At a time when most critics perceived a composer in artistic decline, Grainger recognized such works as *Rosenkavalier* and *Ariadne auf Naxos* as signs of improvement: "[They kindle] a still warmer glow of sympathy, strike a still deeper note of reverence than even the most splendid and brilliant of his earlier compositions. Strauss appears to me to become . . . more genuine, more effortlessly himself with each successive work." What impresses Grainger is neither Strauss's technique nor his "diabolical cleverness" but rather his affectionate, idealistic side—a side that was becoming more pronounced in works after *Elektra.* Grainger's optimism about

· 280 ·

Strauss's music in 1917 was unique in its time, but his views are remarkably consonant with more recent Strauss scholarship, particularly Leon Botstein's essay, "The Enigmas of Richard Strauss: A Revisionist View," in this volume [ed.].

[Source: Henry T. Finck, *Richard Strauss: The Man and His Work* (Boston: Little, Brown, 1917), pp. xvii–xxv]

.

Among the great composers of our era, Richard Strauss seems to me to stand forth as a type of the gemütlich family man in music; normal, kindly, well-balanced; a genius by reason of attributes of the soul and heart rather than of the head; a seer rather than a pure artist, an emotionalist rather than a craftsman; above all an inveterate idealist, seeking always heroic nobility and spiritual exaltation and able to find them in what may seem unexpected places and subjects.

The generous magnitude of his soul leads him to desire to inclose and depict, as far as possible, all phases of existence, not only those universally considered worthy of artistic presentation but also many that appear merely gruesome, sordid, and "unpleasant" to a less cosmic vision than his own.

I see permeating his music (the songs no less than the tone poems and operas) a humane soul overflowing with the milk of human kindness, a lackadaisically robust personality replete with tender affectionateness and fatherly insight.

Wondrously Bavarian, is he not perhaps the most supremely gemütlich of all composers, past and present?

Brusque and roughshod on the surface at times; careless, uncritical, and unfastidious at all times; not, perhaps, a craftsman of the highest degree: but a *man,* a *human being* of the great order, supremely possessed of the ability to soar above the petty affairs of everyday existence into the eternal realms of cosmic contemplation and religious ecstasy.

No doubt he has an almost childish weakness for tinsel and tricks and is no eschewer of storms, turmoils, and the vagaries of passion.

But it seems to me that it is essentially as a portrayer of "the calm that follows the storm," as a prophet of eternal values, that Strauss reigns supreme among contemporaneous composers. He loves to render the human soul ensconced in the serenity of philosophic calm, looking back over the struggles of life or across the strokes of fate in a mood of benign forgiveness and understanding.

Battles and the myriad manifestations of energy merely serve to usher in this final state of lofty repose, out of which Strauss himself seems to speak in the telling accents of the first-person singular.

This Nirvana, liberally tinged, it is true, with the aforesaid typical South German gemütlichkeit, is the very essence of the composer's own lovable temperament, and it is to this goal, therefore, that he loves to lead his heroes toilsomely, precariously, outrageously, but inevitably.

It is hard to conceive of any other composer possessing to a greater degree the peculiar qualities that go to make for a perfect exposition of this particular soul-state.

Constraining considerations of "style" (such as inclose a Debussy, a Ravel, a Cyril Scott,[1] within the narrow bonds of exquisite choice) exist no more for Strauss than for Frederick Delius. Uncritical and unselfconscious in the extreme, and chastened by no strict standards of artistic morality, Strauss is singularly able to give his inner nature free rein in an ingenious musical language of sweeping breadth. Somewhat commonplace, somewhat sentimental phrases flow forth with a ring of perfect truth and conviction (for they are really typical of the man) and are handled with a sense of bigness that always seems inspirational rather than premeditated. The greater the moment, the more truly does Strauss appear to be himself and himself only.

His inherent propensity for rising above all worldly deterrents to final glory is shown no less strikingly in the last act [*sic*] of *Salome* than it is in the trio in *Rosenkavalier,* or in the great spiritual climaxes of *Tod und Verklärung, Ein Heldenleben, Also sprach Zarathustra, Don Quixote,* and *The Legend of Joseph,* though it is shown in a different way. Here, again, we note Strauss's idealism. *Salome* might have been many things in many men's hands. Through Strauss's vision, we see the purifying white heat of self-effacing passion resulting in a rapt trance of world-forgetting ecstasy, in which are drowned all puny personal considerations of life.

This sublime tragedy of the senses seems to have awakened in Strauss's philosophic intuitions the same universally religious note that it equally would in the mind of an Oriental mystic, and were Salome's swan song put before us as religious music, I feel sure it would not seem to us incongruous in that character, so noble, so cosmically devout is its whole tenor.

No less perfect than Strauss's exponence of the calmly sublime appears to me his ability to voice a certain warm and gentle phase of modern affection: a comradely emotionalism well watered with sentiment but deliciously free from mawkishness. We find lovely instances of what I mean in his song *Mit deinen blauen Augen,* in the ingratiating ariette *Du, Venus' Sohn, gibst süßen Lohn,* in *Der Bürger als Edelmann,* in the breakfast scene in the first act of *Rosenkavalier,* and in the entrancing final duet of the same opera.

It is as if the whole world melts in a motherly mood of gentle loving-kindness and graceful generosity.

It seems to me that in estimating Strauss, too little is usually said of the balmy, sentimental, affectionate, and idealistic side of his nature, while an altogether disproportionate emphasis is laid upon his "diabolical cleverness" as a technician, the daring of his originality, his skill as an orchestrator, and his wizardry as a descriptive programist.

In all modesty I must confess that it is not where technical deftness or abstract musical mastery is concerned that I find Strauss preëminent.

Strauss is not an intrinsically exquisite composer like Delius, the complex beauties of whose scores baffle full realization at first acquaintance but yield up new and ever new secrets of delicate intimacy at each fresh hearing.

Nor is Strauss a born innovator like Debussy, changing the face of contemporaneous music with one sweep, nor a prolific iconoclast like Cyril Scott, Scriabin, or Stravinsky, bringing new impulses and interests to the brotherhood of fellow composers by a thousand versatile experiments.

Strauss is no dream-inspired colorist like Debussy or Ravel, weaving round his musical ideas veil upon veil of subtle tonal enchantment. Though capable of wonderful momentary inspirations as a colorist, I cannot deny that his *average* orchestration seems to me afflicted with a certain dull, flat, stodgy quality that for want of a better term, I venture to call "middle class." Practical it is, and safe; it never sounds thin; but it is often "muddy" in the extreme, and though it covers large surfaces with a magnificent stride, it does so at the expense of charm of detail and evinces but little sensitiveness with regard to the harmonious balance of sound proportions.

Nevertheless Strauss's every score is lit up by occasional flashes of orchestral imaginativeness of a transcendingly original quality, and the more daring these moments are—the more they emerge from the pure flame of Strauss's own whimsical imagination rather than from the nucleus of previous orchestral experiences—the more bewitchingly lovely they are.

Is this not yet another proof of the inborn effortless greatness of the man: a token that his genius is, at its best, at least, of the purely inspirational order; not a built-up laborious product, sullied with "cleverness" and trickery, but a spirit utterance, welling forth in native and inconsidered purity from the soul within?

The imitations of sheep-bleatings in *Don Quixote* appeal to most people's sense of the comical for nonmusical reasons, no doubt. But let us set these considerations aside for a moment and listen to the orchestral bleatings as pure sound; and I ask: Is not this one of the most soothing, mesmeric, opalescent acoustical achievements in musical history?

Here again we see the soaring idealist, the inveterate beautifier in Strauss revealed.

As a mere programist, his purpose would have been amply fulfilled by making the sheep in *Don Quixote* merely sheeplike and comic, by making the chorus of carping critics (high chromatic polyphonic woodwind passage) in *Heldenleben* merely ludicrous and cacophonous.

But in both these cases, as in a myriad others I might name, the instinctive (though possibly unconscious) aesthete in Strauss was not to be denied, in the place of what might have been two emotionally barren descriptive passages we have a precious pair of tonal creations of the most sensitive abstract beauty.

I am myself too little in sympathy with the artistic viewpoint that leads a musician to write program music—I see too little connection between literary plots and music, between everyday events and music—to be in a position to fairly judge of Strauss's "descriptive" powers. Certainly it is not on account of these that I consider him a great genius.

Strauss grew up in a would-be "brainy" age; an irreligious and emotionally impoverished age, curiously susceptible to the cheapest fripperies of intellectualism; and it is just possible that what seem to some of us the somewhat shallow descriptive tendencies of some of his tone poems are the toll he had to pay to that environment. In the later Strauss, however, I seem to note an ever-increasing development of the pure musician at the expense of all side issues, and for that reason the *Rosenkavalier* and *Ariadne* (particularly the latter) kindle, in my case, a still warmer glow of sympathy, strike a still deeper note of reverence than even the most splendid and brilliant of his earlier compositions. Strauss appears to me to become more mellow, more genuine, more effortlessly himself with each successive work; another sign, for me, of the depth and truth of his genius and of the abiding value of his muse.

With the exception of certain exquisite but very rare moments, his resources as a harmonist strike me as lagging sadly behind those of most other great living composers.

Whether as regards harmonic originality or a refined sense for the euphonious and expressive distribution of the component parts in chords, one could not for one moment dream of comparing him with such harmonic giants as Debussy, Ravel, Delius, or Cyril Scott.

But here, again, the later Strauss by far outstrips the younger, and the harmonic beauties of the *Ariadne* overture denote, to my mind, a, for him, quite new sensitiveness in respect to harmonic possibilities, possibly derived from contact with the remarkable life-giving innovations of French and English composers in this field or, equally likely, evolved by himself independently straight out of his own evergreen imagination now, for the first time, focused upon a more purely "chordy" style. Perhaps, however, his supreme harmonic achievement is the cascade of wondrously unrelated triads associated with the silver rose in *Rosenkavalier,* constituting one of the most ravishing chord passages in modern music and certainly something entirely unprecedented in Strauss's own compositional career.

It is interesting to compare with this the no less lovely and epoch-making chord progressions in the middle of Ravel's incomparable "Le gibet," published in 1909.[2] Whether or not both of these emanations of the highest harmonic originality came into being without influence on either side, of one thing we can be certain: that Strauss in his "silver rose" music no less than Ravel in "Le Gibet" has given the world of harmony a new inspiration and impetus from which discerning composers can, if they will, drink a profitable draught of freshness.

To my mind, however, the greatest purely musical quality of Strauss's genius is manifested in the pith and pregnance of his musical ideas, which, though frankly and bravely commonplace at times, burst forth with an almost Beethoven-like explosive inevitability and naturalness that disarm criticism and bear upon the face of them the stamp of the great personality from which they spring.

His themes and motives make their appeal chiefly through their sharply chiselled intervallic and rhythmic physiognomy and not by reason of their adaptability to sophisticated color treatment. They create almost the same vital impression when played on a piano, a harmonium, or a penny whistle that they do in their original orchestration, and this seems to me a conclusive proof of the initial inventive vigor that gave them birth.

On the whole, Strauss does not seem to appeal to the younger generation of composers as much as he perhaps deserves to do, and this, I imagine, is largely due to the somewhat coarse, careless, and uncritical methods of his compositional workmanship.

The general public seems capable of continuing to love a genius chiefly because of his emotional type, but fellow composers have to be able to *admire qualities of craftsmanship* as well if they are not to weary of an art product.

Strauss is not a musician's musician like Bach, Mozart, Schubert, Grieg, or Debussy, capable of turning out flawless gems of artistic subtlety and perfection, but rather is he a great cosmic soul of the Goethe, Milton, Nietzsche, Walt Whitman, Edgar Lee Masters caliber: full of dross but equally full of godhead; lacking refinement but not the supremer attributes; and uniquely able to roll forth some great uplifting message after gigantic preliminaries of boredom and inconsequentialness.

And is not the general public fundamentally right (as usual) in its instinctive response to Strauss? For is not, at least from the nonmusician's standpoint, grandeur and purity of soul of more account than the most exquisite gifts of musical sensitiveness, originality, and culture? Is not, therefore, Strauss's hold upon the general public a good omen? For does not his personal message, like that of George Moore's indescribably significant "Brook Kerith," contain the exact reaction most needed from the present worldwide immersion in strife and commercial enslavement and competition;[3] the message that the seer, however, at all times has to proclaim to the empirical world; that the real gold dwells in the heart within and is not to be captured in any other place, and that the real hero is he, who, turning dissatisfied away from the outer world's illusionary shows of victory and defeat, finds contentment finally within himself in viewing in the mirror of his own contemplative soul the whole universe suffused in a glory of love and understanding?

26 April 1917

NOTES

1. Cyril Scott (1879–1970), an English composer and pianist [ed.].
2. Grainger is referring to "Le Gibet" from Ravel's *Gaspard de la nuit* [ed.].
3. George Moore (1852–1933), an Irish novelist and playwright. The "Brook Kerith" appeared in 1916.

Richard Strauss at Eighty

WILLI SCHUH

TRANSLATED BY SUSAN GILLESPIE

Willi Schuh(1900–86), longtime music critic for the *Neue Zürcher Zeitung*, was Strauss's official biographer and friend for many years. Composer and biographer first met in conjunction with the Swiss premiere of *Die schweigsame Frau* in 1936. Beyond his important essays on Strauss, Schuh was involved with editorial projects that would lay a foundation for future Strauss research. These included the published correspondences between Strauss and his parents, Hans von Bülow, Hugo von Hofmannsthal, Stefan Zweig, and Clemens Krauss, as well as the important collection of Strauss's writings entitled *Betrachtungen und Erinnerungen*, now in an expanded third edition. Schuh, however, did not live to complete his most ambitious project, a comprehensive biography of the composer. Fortunately, he managed to see the first volume to the end, and it serves as a vital source for the study of Strauss's life from his birth to his move to Berlin in 1898.

The following birthday tribute appeared as an introductory chapter to a collection of essays on Strauss's operas. In assessing the life of the eighty-year-old composer, Schuh finds a parallel with Goethe. Both figures, he contends, followed their artistic visions "through all the various phases of their relation to the world . . . leaving the actual discovery of their spiritual heritage to later generations." Schuh's essay explores themes central to Strauss's creative life. Perhaps the most important one concerns the harmony of contrasts in the life work of the composer, especially in the fifteen operas, which range from the tragic *(Elektra)* to the comic *(Der Rosenkavalier)*, from the metaphysical *(Die Frau ohne Schatten)* to the everyday *(Intermezzo)*. "To be steadfast and yet capable of change," Schuh observes, "may also be regarded as the secret of [Strauss's] spiritual experience" [ed.].

[Source: *Über Opern von Richard Strauss* (Zurich: Atlantis, 1947), pp. 9–19]

For 11 June 1944

There is something great and almost strange in the thought that among us lives a master who, looking back on eighty blessed years of life and more than sixty years of creative work, can carry within himself the awareness that he is the heir and final exponent of a music-historical epoch whose roots reach deep into past centuries. The mental circumstance of the eighty-year-old Strauss can only be compared with that of Goethe in 1830: in an environment filled with new ideas and tendencies, both—beyond all misunderstandings and envy that fame inevitably brings with it—became the objects of profound and widespread reverence as commanding figures of their century. In their young years lauded and condemned as "revolutionaries" of their art, in their mature years, on account of their classical posture, suspected of being "reactionaries," both followed their *daimon* calmly through all the various phases of their relation to the world until they reached advanced age, and, "carrying on in their own fashion," created work after work, leaving the actual discovery of their spiritual heritage to later generations. Thus we believe we are justified in naming Richard Strauss in the same breath with that great figure whom he revered, along with Mozart and Wagner, as his intellectual master, and whose collected works, diaries, and letters he undertook, at the age of seventy-six, to read, volume for volume and word for word, in their entirety, in the great Propyläen edition.

For us Richard Strauss forms the bridge to a great past. Father Strauss, the distinguished horn player and fierce opponent of Wagner, once showed the boy from the balconies of the Odeon Hall in Munich (now in ruins) the "Mephisto of Music" in person and thus presented him with a memory that the master still recounts with glowing eyes. The ghosts of an era that has assumed almost mythic proportions walk once more when Strauss retells this and other episodes from his youth or recounts conversations with his esteemed teacher, Hans von Bülow, as if they had occurred only yesterday. But it is not only in such tales that this mythic past lives on: the conductor Strauss, whom we all had the opportunity to experience, knew how to preserve the inheritance of Bülow with deep respect and, in particular, how to preserve his Beethoven interpretations for the present. Our debt to Strauss the interpreter, as significant as it may be for the cultivation of Mozart, Beethoven, Wagner, and Liszt, naturally takes a back seat to the musical works that the creative genius Richard Strauss gave the world. We are scarcely in a position, today, to imagine the storms of enthusiasm and rejection that were whipped up by the young firebrand's first symphonic poems and later *Ein Heldenleben* and, above all—like torches applied to dry timber (of the post-Wagnerian music drama)—by the one-act operas *Salome* and *Elektra*. If the significance of these works, recognized in their own time for their unheard-of boldness, had been limited to what was new and exciting about them, they would hardly be counted among the standard works of the concert and opera repertory today. The power of the extraordinary that inspires them has been able to withstand the turnabout in public taste, which, Stendahl once observed, changes every thirty years. Strauss's principal works have long since survived the trial by fire of the passing of successive generations, and Strauss is the only living German master who occupies a firm place, along with the classical composers, in the concert programs of the world. One can even say that in the consciousness of the world he himself is counted among these classical composers. In the mortal sphere Richard Strauss (following Goethe's advice) extended himself in all directions, so as to reach the immortal. With a visual sense that was almost as developed as the aural, his mind also grasped the entire world of phenomena. Perhaps the most comprehensively educated of all the great masters of music, he shifted constantly, in his creative work, from one subject to another. As he approaches the completion of one score, almost with impatience, a new creative endeavor, usually in a completely opposite world, already begins to take shape in his head. His rhythmic alternation of tension and relaxation, illustrated most clearly in the succession of serious and comic works for the stage, has already been correctly pointed out many times. To be steadfast and yet capable of change—Ariadne's secret, which magically became sound in what is perhaps the most precious of all his scores—may also be regarded as the secret of his spiritual existence. The miracle of transformation was splendidly manifested in his operatic works countless times; no less, however, the power of steadfastness: throughout sixty years Strauss was able to hold fast to the knowledge he had acquired in his Meiningen period under the "whirlwind" influence of Alexander Ritter but also under that of the scores and writings of Richard Wagner.[1] The formalist was transformed, at that time, into the innovative *Ausdrucksmusiker*—able, with the sureness of a sleepwalker, to extract new forms from the poetic idea. And Richard Strauss then defended, with unswerving loyalty and unfailingly active engagement, those masters whose work, he was convinced, represented the only organic and meaningful development of music after Beethoven: Berlioz, Liszt, and Wagner. In his own creation, however, his goal was to carry this line forward toward fulfillment of its inner logic.

The realization occurred in two creative periods, each of which, complete in itself, is now history. The first includes his symphonic works; the second, his works for the stage. Strauss never repeated himself, although he sometimes sought to build further upon something that others before him or he himself had constructed. If he explored new territory in *Salome,* he was accused of being a destroyer of sanctified norms; if he drew on more familiar sources, using the entire magic of his orchestral tone fantasy to transfigure a long-lost world, in *Rosenkavalier,* they spoke of exhaustion. Strauss was never affected by such judgments, and they never influenced his choice of material in the slightest. It is perhaps not entirely superfluous to point this out, since in some heads the image of the savvy "businessman" Strauss still lingers. If there were cases in which a Straussian work met a need of the time, there are also other, much more numerous instances in which the composer placed himself in opposition to the popular taste. Strauss gave form to whatever struck his artistic fantasy—gave it form from the creative distance of the true artist, who does not lose himself in his subject but rather approaches it objectively. This is one of the traits that he shares with Mozart, the musician he loves and respects above all others. The superiority of the artist who senses the forms in the material permits him to compose Oscar Wilde's *Salome* and then to move on to the Marschallin and Octavian, but also the *Frau ohne Schatten* and Barak the Dyer, from whose mouth issues the song of conjugal love for wife and children. Strauss combines glowing enthusiasm with an unerring sense of reality, which lets him see human beings, works, and situations as they are. This sense of reality prevents him from overstepping his own limits—they are broad enough! Will and execution are one for him. Mastery, admittedly, did not come easily even to him: he worked to acquire it step by step. But for his sunny spirit, creative work does not mean suffering and weary struggle but rather the meaning and fulfillment of being.

The symphonic poem, as a genre, found in Richard Strauss the creator of its ultimate perfection. Today we recognize it, along with the composer himself, as a preparatory stage (which retains its own independent value) for his operatic creations. The historic significance of the greater and more comprehensive part of his life's work—that is, opera—consists in the fact that Strauss, picking up where Wagner left off but also drawing essential inspiration from Mozart's dramatic works, completely overcame the style of the Wagner epigones. Strauss once compared his relationship to Richard Wagner with that of Tintoretto to Titian. The extreme, the ultimate of what was possible after Wagner is what he claimed to dare. The comparison is revealing in several respects: it shows, once again, the capacity to see his

own work in historic perspective and to place it within a larger framework; it simultaneously characterizes his relationship to the visual arts
and his unerring sense of proportion. Strauss's operatic works, which
from *Salome* to *Capriccio* encompass a span of nearly forty years, were
met and continue to be met with incomparable, if naturally not always equal success—success that seemed all the more significant because almost every one of his works for the stage requires its own performance style and demands something unfamiliar from performers
and audience alike. The great and splendid task remains for us and
future generations to take full and inalienable inner possession of the
nearly incomprehensible wealth of artistic meanings conveyed in the
opera scores and the unparalleled richness of musical-dramatic relationships concealed within them. Strauss's most important insight was
that "it is only with the invention and utmost differentiation of the
modern orchestra that world theater has ascended to the peak of its
perfection." Strauss, with his operatic work, which in a manner of
speaking realized the final consequences of the development of the
musical-dramatic forms and ideas of the eighteenth and nineteenth
centuries, is an essential aspect of that perfection. His artistic rank,
however, is determined not least by the group of works that form the
innermost circle of his operatic creation and show the greatest poet
of the epoch working in tandem with its greatest musician. We have
reached a point in time at which the broader public, too, is beginning to appreciate Hofmannsthal's late poetic works in the entire fullness of their contents and the pure beauty of their linguistic form.
This should also bring with it greater openness and deeper understanding toward even *Die Frau ohne Schatten* and *Die ägyptische Helena*.
The person who wishes to understand Strauss completely can no more
afford to neglect these works than can the person who would grasp
the entirety of Hofmannsthal's work.

If Strauss's operatic works based upon Hofmannsthal's poetry are
already astonishingly varied in their form, the whole list of his works
for the stage, comprising fifteen operas, embraces an even greater
range, reaching as it does from bourgeois comedy with symphonic
interludes to mythological opera of both a tragic and a comic character; from one-act opera of unheard-of tension and density to great
mystery opera.[2] Early and late antiquity, baroque and rococo, the
Vienna of 1860, and present-day bourgeois society are all reflected
in the bright mirror of Straussian operatic music. And in the process
each work presents itself as something unique and incomparable in
style, technique, and underlying tone. Here, as everywhere in Strauss,
we find variety in unity, unceasing transformation combined with un-

broken faithfulness to his own being. Transformation is also the law under which all his significant operatic figures appear; this is what makes their embodiment such a difficult but artistically intriguing, humanly fascinating challenge. At the center of the symphonic works stands man. The operas, in contrast, revolve around the secret of woman, which Strauss's orchestra explicates in thousand-tongued eloquence on an endlessly fine-tuned scale of colors that is equally capable of giving perfect expression to the most delicate and nervous stirrings of the emotions or to monumental pathos; of mirroring the quotidian reality of a servants' quarrel as clearly as the dreamlike nature bond of the nymph who is beloved of a god. The realism of the little marriage opera *Intermezzo* is balanced by the stylistic masterpiece *Ariadne*, and between the two ends of the scale, Christine and Ariadne, resonate the tones of all the enchanting songs Strauss put into the mouths of his female characters. The whole of Strauss can be grasped neither in Elektra's monologue nor in the final trio from *Rosenkavalier*, neither in the Empress's dream scene [*Die Frau ohne Schatten*] nor in the sisters' duet in *Arabella* or the arias of Daphne. To comprehend it, we must not only add together the sum of all these but also observe their placement and their function in the dramatic structure as a whole. For in nothing else, perhaps, does the superior form-giving power of the master appear so clearly as in the integration of the part into the whole. It is this concern for the whole that lets the formerly much-discussed "illustrative" passages vanish so completely into the great, transporting stream of a music that blends the forces of expression and form into seamless unity.

Strauss has made the opera theater an immeasurable gift, drawn from the fullness of his being, which is strong and healthy, yet sensitive to the most finely differentiated emotional problematics. Generations will have to come to terms with his masterworks. With growing distance, the inner developmental arc that he traversed from *Feuersnot* to *Capriccio* will become all the more clearly perceptible, and it will be recognized how (in the composer's own words) the late works "return to the artistic mean that Goethe describes as the final goal of artistic maturity." Struggling with never-relaxing self-criticism to achieve the ideal relationship between voice and orchestra and ever more successfully overcoming his inclination toward an overindulgence in orchestral polyphony—"it was old Lucifer who put counterpoint in our German cradles," he says in the preface to *Intermezzo!*—Strauss, in *Arabella, Daphne,* and *Capriccio,* has realized the synthesis of "symphonic" and "dramatic" style that he envisions as the highest goal of the opera composer. From the vantage point of these transcendent creations, which unite the tonal wonders of orchestral polyphony with the expressive forms that enable the sung word to come into its own, we can look back on his life's work as a completed whole. We assume the right to do so based on a passage in a letter from the year 1941, in which Strauss responded to his friend and collaborator Clemens Krauss concerning proposals for new works of opera: "Is not this Db major (of the mirror scene in *Capriccio*) the best conclusion of my theatrical life's work? One can, after all, leave only *one* last will and testament!" Thus the great giver of joy, who not only returned to opera the solemnity of its origins but also enriched it with the ultimate in psychological refinement, would leave us with an unanswered question on the lips of a smiling woman—words or music?[3] The eighty-year-old has finally not denied us the "right answer," however: on the manuscript pages designated for his estate, which are even now piling up on his writing desk, there are no more operas in the making but rather small instrumental works—"wrist exercises," he calls them with a serene smile, recalling greater things— works that seem to come full circle back to his origins sixty and more years ago . . . Strauss recently made a note of Goethe's saying that nothing is more miserable than a man in comfortable circumstances without work. In the life of the eighty-year-old, work still occupies the first place. If it is set aside for a few hours, books and paintings take its place. But perhaps one should not even use the word "work," for it is no accident that Strauss quotes the expression Anton Kippenberg once noted down from the mouth of Maillol: "Je ne travaille jamais, je m'amuse."[4]

The portrait of the eighty-year-old recalls an hour I spent in the master's study in Garmisch. During a conversation about our era, he took down a volume of Goethe from the bookcase to read the passage from the last letter to Wilhelm von Humboldt, written five days before Goethe's death: "Confusing conclusions about confusing deeds dominate the world, and I have nothing more pressing to do than if possible to increase that which remains and is left to me and to keep my originality in hand . . ." That the name of Goethe crops up again and again may be justified by a passage in a letter from January of this year, where it says, concluding the self-portrayal of the eighty-year-old, "I am quietly working away for myself (following Goethe's sublime example)."—For us, however, the thing to do is bow our heads in respect before the man whom the world has long since declared a master but who, for his part, does not let up in his striving (resembling a form of serene play) for self-realization and self-perfection, a striving that accepts as the measure of true mastery only the works of the very greatest men.

(1944)

NOTES

1. Strauss served as Hans von Bülow's assistant conductor in Meiningen from 1885 to 1886 [ed.].

2. Schuh probably refers to *Intermezzo, Die Liebe der Danae, Elektra,* and *Die Frau ohne Schatten,* respectively [ed.].

3. The reference is to the central question posed in *Capriccio:* "Wort oder Ton?" [ed.].

4. "I never work, I amuse myself" [trans.].

The Last Visit with Richard Strauss

RUDOLF HARTMANN

TRANSLATED BY SUSAN GILLESPIE

Rudolf Hartmann (1900–88) was a central figure in the last decade of Strauss's life. A bright, young operatic stage director who had held positions in Bamberg, Altenburg in Thüringen, Nuremberg, and Berlin, Hartmann came into close contact with the composer when Clemens Krauss, music director of the Munich Opera, brought him to the Bavarian capital in 1937. There he staged the world premieres of *Friedenstag* and *Capriccio* as well as of *Die Liebe der Danae* in Salzburg.

Hartmann may well have been the last friend to have visited the composer. His account of this last visit offers us a vivid portrait of Strauss in his final days, a composer who understandably reflected on his past accomplishments but also looked to the future with enthusiasm. The opera houses of Dresden, Munich, and Vienna lay in ruins, and their destruction caused the composer great pain—but ultimately Strauss overcame his depression, in part by seeing himself as a kind of creative architect who would help these musical institutions, especially his beloved Munich Opera, to emerge from the rubble. Hartmann was a leading stage director in postwar Germany, and Strauss viewed him as a messenger for his plans. It is surely not coincidental that Strauss, at the end of their conversation, thought of a line—"Grüß mir die Welt"—from *Tristan und Isolde*. At that moment in the opera, Isolde has resolved that she must die, and she asks Brangäne to give the world her final greeting [ed.].

[Source: *Richard Strauss–Rudolf Hartmann: Ein Briefwechsel*, ed. Roswitha Schlötterer (Tutzing: Schneider, 1984), pp. 91–96]

.

On 13 August 1949, just before my departure for a guest appointment as stage director in Zurich, I received from Garmisch the first very grave news about Richard Strauss's condition. The following weeks brought varying reports about the changing state of his health, so that the days, which were occupied with work on *Lohengrin,* were darkened by not a little concern. My thoughts returned to the unforgettable experience of the thirteenth of July, 1949, when Richard Strauss drove to the radio headquarters in Munich and directed the musical interlude for the movie *Capriccio,* which had been created in celebration of his eighty-fifth birthday. In view of his astonishing freshness and the masterful superiority with which he cast his spell over the large orchestra, a sense of breathless admiration spread throughout the building—usually so preoccupied with business—and it would not have occurred to anyone that a few weeks later this brief afternoon was to assume historic significance: it was the last time that Richard Strauss would conduct an orchestra. On the trip home afterward he took the route through the Isar Valley: "Let's say hello to your wife on the way." We sat for a while on the terrace of the little house. As always, he was full of ideas about the musical theater and was particularly interested in the development of the Munich Opera.[1] Although I myself had no direct influence on the matter, I was able to tell him of positive plans, to which he listened attentively. Vividly, he developed his own thoughts, and at his express wish this conversation was continued on 23 July in Garmisch. In conversation with Alois Johannes Lippl, who because of his position[2] was able to describe many details of the development in Munich, Richard Strauss gave new evidence of the unbroken intellectual capacity and clarity of his mind. With heartfelt joy, he observed that the construction plans incorporated a number of suggestions that he had often expressed in the past to no avail. The unusually lively and stimulating conversation concluded with a short walk in the beautiful garden. Richard Strauss walked upright, without any assistance, and in the course of a cheerful conversation that in the presence of family members had turned general, he approached his favorite large flower bed. He stood there in contemplative enjoyment, looking down at the blooming summer splendor, and then said, as if talking to himself, in an aside: "They will still be blooming when I am gone." These words passed over like the shadows of a cloud, then he was already smiling again and took leave of his guests, with genial cordiality, summarizing once more the result and further implications of our exchange of views. Later communications from his family informed me that for several hours each day, stimulated by these conversations, he would work on written plans and that his condition had greatly improved.

All the more dismaying was the news of his worsening state of health that reached me in Zurich.

On 28 August I returned from there, immediately got in touch with Garmisch, and received confirmation that Richard Strauss had been confined to bed since the thirteenth of August. The day before that he had still worked for several hours at his desk. The autograph at the bottom of a page with a sketch from *Daphne,* which he sent me as a gift in Zurich through his grandson Richard, was also written on 12 August, and the lovely words of this dedication are among the last things written in his hand.

On 29 August I receive word by a telephone call that Richard Strauss wishes to see me. In the early afternoon hours of the following day I am picked up in Ebenhausen by Dr. Franz Strauss, the son, and Christian, the second grandson. We drive rather silently through the landscape, in radiant sunshine. Dr. Strauss informs me briefly about the course of his father's serious illness, about the opinion of the doctors, who give his life only a few more days, perhaps hours. I know now that it will be the last visit, and in unceasingly changing images all the encounters with Richard Strauss pass through my mind. Of the journey itself I notice little; everything remains half-conscious, the Bavarian landscape gliding by like a carpet lying before Garmisch. At some point, when we are already past Murnau, Dr. Strauss breaks the silence and says with a smile: "He is looking forward very much to your visit. Since this morning he has been worrying about picking you up on time." We drive through the birch alley of the moors, then, briefly, close along the quickly flowing Loisach, and a few minutes later we are driving in over the familiar garden road. After a brief, cordial greeting by young Richard and his wife Alice, whose face clearly reflects the strain and agitation resulting from her self-sacrificing care of the invalid, we enter the small living room on the second floor. I learn that two days earlier Richard Strauss had survived several serious attacks and that his wife, Frau Pauline, is herself in a clinic, having become indisposed. At the moment the patient is dozing a little; as Frau Alice reports, he had said about an hour earlier, "Now I will sleep a little bit, so that later I will feel quite fresh." We carry on a subdued, halting conversation. The faces are serious and tense. My gaze returns again and again to the white door on the far side of the open sitting room—until Frau Alice then rises to see what the situation is. I agree with Dr. Franz Strauss that I will take my leave after only twenty minutes, so as not to cause the sick man any overexertion; then I am called, and through the door, which Frau Alice has opened, I enter the bedroom. In the room, which seems very bright, stands the white bed, its headboard toward the entrance. Richard Strauss has turned his head a little, stretches his right hand out and greets me: "How good that you are here. Come and sit down near me." While I move the chair close to the bed, my eyes fall on the large oxygen tank that stands ready, close at hand, and with anxiety I think of the report I have just heard concerning the course of the illness in recent days. My cautiously inquiring words about his well-being are answered with a small, expressive gesture. Since he is silent, I would like to say something to him, comfort him; in the excitement of the tense moment I do not find the right words—with a long gaze he looks at me, so that I am compelled to fall silent before the knowing expression of his bright, clear eyes. Then he says, "Death has dealt me the first heavy blow, given me the first signal." But then he immediately changes his tone, asks about personal things, cordially concerned, as always. His facial expression is not much changed; unusual is only the deep pallor and tiredness of his features. Gradually his thoughts turn to the things that always interest him. He lies there peacefully, propped up quite high; his hands glide over the blankets in brief emphatic gestures. I hear the deep, somewhat hoarse voice speaking of the constantly recurring concern for the future of European theater; then after a short pause he says, "Imagine, 140 years ago Goethe and Napoleon shook hands in Erfurt! What a development that would have been: Napoleon as the ruler of a united Europe and Goethe his first minister of culture—and the others, Friedrich Wilhelm, Alexander, Franz, could perfectly well have disappeared and the world would have been spared a great deal." In connection with this thought he tells me that he is working on composing a letter to an important political figure in present-day France, François-Poncet; the dictated draft is half-finished. He speaks more animatedly, his thoughts quite given over to the theme he has chosen, and does not notice when the door opens softly. Frau Alice gives me a brief nod of agreement, goes to the other side of the bed and tries to give the invalid something to eat. He starts slightly when he sees the plate in front of him and waves it away almost violently. But immediately afterward he says a few comforting words to his patient nurse and turns to me, half apologizing: "I am always supposed to eat, and I can't. My stomach is not quite in order." Frau Alice leaves us alone again.—I see in the constantly changing expression of the eyes in the motionless face in front of me how unceasingly the undiminished, lively spirit is working in the worn-out body. Then the voice comes again: "There is so much I would still have to do—but I believe that some of what I wanted and have begun has fallen on fertile ground." He looks half-questioningly over at me. After my assenting reply he speaks of the afternoon visit in July and the Munich plans described on that occasion by Alois Johannes Lippl. He has evidently given much thought to all of it: names come up, little recollections of great personalities from past eras are inserted between them— Bülow, Wagner—but always his conversation returns to matters of the present and the future. With heartfelt words he remembers the worthy contributions made to his work by important opera directors at our theater. Clemens Krauss, whose unforgettably beautiful premiere of *Capriccio* he mentions in particular, Karl Böhm, and others are named. He reviews the formation of the classic operatic performance program with reference to his many years of experience; his own works are included. He speaks fluently, animatedly, and his face no longer shows any sign of fatigue or illness. I have a piece of business to take care of that has been entrusted to me concerning the forthcoming premiere of his opera *Die Liebe der Danae*. At once he is fully concentrated on this question, expresses himself unmistakably to the effect that the work should receive its first performance in Salzburg, and also names the earliest date that seems favorable to him. (He would later repeat these statements to his son.) In the meantime the time has grown longer than I had intended. The door opens once more; his grandson Richard enters to remind me of the scheduled departure time of my train. Richard Strauss is attentive, wants to continue the conversation, and orders that the car should be readied again for the return trip. I am afraid of causing him too much exertion, but he insists energetically: "Who knows when we will be able to talk together like this again?" The interruption has disturbed him. Several heavy, slightly gasping breaths fill me with suddenly rising anxiety. It is nothing—he calms himself again after I have helped him by handing him a few things. Again he begins to speak, attempts to pick up the thread of the earlier conversation, and is distracted again—this time by me: a hasty movement has caused a button to come loose from my jacket; irritated, I am looking around for it. Richard Strauss asks me inquiringly, "What is the matter?" and when he learns the cause of the little disturbance he responds with the domestic practicality of the pater familias: "Stand up, and it will fall on the floor so that you can retrieve it." This happens just as he says it will, and he looks on attentively as I place the disobedient button carefully in my pocket. He nods in satisfaction, then turns his gaze straight ahead in order to pursue his own thoughts once more. After a while he has found the connection and says, "I think I did a good job of conducting Wagner's works. A great deal depends on the conductor

there; he has to hold it all together and at the decisive moment drive
it forward. For example in *Siegfried,* after the Idyll [toward the end
of act 3], a powerful animation must begin and continue through to
the end; all the slow tempi must be taken only in a relative sense,
but hardly anyone does that. Especially in the great concluding scene
with Brünnhilde, where young Siegfried is overcome for the first time
by erotic feelings, that is tremendously important." He becomes very
lively, sits up straight: "You know the passage I mean, after the Idyll?"
Without waiting for an answer, he raises his arms, directs and sings
the orchestra melody in a loud voice, demonstrating with his arms.
The face is slightly flushed; his shining eyes are gazing far, far beyond the walls of the room. Fascinated, I follow the expressive movements of the long, narrow hands, until they sink back down again.
Richard Strauss has leaned into the pillows, his eyes moist with tears.
"You must forgive me," he says, "but when you lie here so alone and
there is so much to think about, you become a little sentimental." I
am unable to answer, compelled by the nearness of this artistic nature, which is expressed down to the very last fibers of his being, and
feel almost relieved when he begins to speak again. He returns to the
well-known personalities of today's theater and asks about the current
artistic activities of each. I give whatever information I can. He is sad
about the many destroyed theaters, speaks of the inner and outer reconstruction that has begun, and turns ever more to eager planning.
He would like to see this person or that working in the appropriate
job, he reviews the possibilities of the remaining great opera institutions, and finally observes with a smile, "With that we would seem to
have divided the world up quite nicely—our world." Then he is silent for a long time and follows his thoughts, which I can feel almost palpably. Quite changed, softly, his voice sounds again after a
while: "Grüß mir die Welt[3]—where does that come from?" I think
fleetingly of the similar words from *Die Walküre,* and say so, but he
shakes his head: "No, no, that's not it; this passage occurs somewhere
else," and repeats, "—Grüß mir die Welt!" He falls silent for a long
time; I see that his face shows signs of fatigue and feel that it is time
to leave him. But it is tremendously hard for me to say the first words
of parting. Richard Strauss is lying there very peacefully. As I remain
with my gaze fixed on him, the names of the external stations of this
successful life pass quickly through my mind—Weimar, Munich, Berlin, Vienna, Salzburg, Bayreuth—then he turns his gaze back to me.
With great effort I maintain my composure. Since my arrival, more
than two and a half hours have passed, and I say that it is now time
for me to depart. He gives me a long look: "Yes, I am tired now. Stay

for another ten minutes, we will talk a little bit more, and then I want to sleep." Once more he summarizes everything that he has confided to me in the course of our conversation regarding his wishes for his work, for the future of his grandson Richard. Insistently, his eyes hold mine fast. Finally he grows calmer and in the engaging conversational tone that is peculiar to him he inquires once more about my next projects. I mention Switzerland and Zurich, and with a heartfelt expression of gratitude Richard Strauss speaks warmly of the deserving activities of his biographer Willi Schuh.

The time has come. I rise to take my leave. He gives me his hand and thanks me for the visit, in a perceptible attempt to deprive this parting of its all-too-palpable weight and significance. Then he grasps my right hand once more in both his and holds me fast: "Perhaps we will see each other again; if not, you know everything." A final squeeze, his hands release me, and quickly I leave the room. As I leave I hear Richard Strauss give a muffled sob and then call loudly for his son.—

Outside darkness has already fallen. The grandson Richard brings me home. We do not speak. I look out into the night landscape, all the while listening to the words whose soft, urgent tone does not want to leave me: "Grüß mir die Welt!"

Written in October 1949

NOTES

1. The Munich Opera had been destroyed by a bombing attack in 1942 [ed.].

2. Alois Johannes Lippl served at that time as *Intendant* at the Bavarian State Theater [ed.].

3. The quotation "Grüß mir die Welt" [Greet the world for me] comes from act 1, scene 4 of *Tristan und Isolde*. Isolde utters the line to her attendant, Brangäne, after sending Kurwenal to fetch Tristan so that he may seek Isolde's pardon: "Now farewell Brangäne / Greet the world for me, greet my father and mother" [ed.].

PART IV

CRITICISM AND
RECEPTION

On the Tone Poems of

Richard Strauss

RUDOLF LOUIS

TRANSLATED BY SUSAN GILLESPIE

Rudolf Louis (1870–1914) was both an important theorist and an influential music critic who played a significant role in Munich's musical life at the turn of the century. His *Harmonielehre* of 1907 was written in collaboration with Strauss's boyhood friend Ludwig Thuille, and for a time he served as music critic for the *Münchner neusten Nachrichten*. Louis was a rather controversial figure in Munich: unsympathetic to the classic romanticism of Brahms and—later—Reger, he greatly admired the work of Berlioz, Liszt, and Bruckner. Indeed, he wrote important essays on all three composers. The following excerpt on Strauss's tone poems is taken from chapter 3 of his *Die Deutsche Musik der Gegenwart* (revised edition), one of the most important books on contemporary German music in the first decade of the twentieth century. In that work, Louis may have been the first to use the term "emancipation of dissonance." At the time the revised edition went to press, *Der Rosenkavalier* had recently achieved great success. Thus, this retrospective glance at the tone poems was made at a time when Strauss was being hailed as the leading *opera* composer of his day.

With the exception of the *Symphonia Domestica* (a rather remarkable exception at that), Louis observes a certain artistic decline in the later tone poems. The earlier works were direct expressions of a gifted composer, but Strauss, according to Louis, ultimately allowed himself to be lured by the "trends of the moment," which he did not always fully comprehend. Ernest Newman, around the same time, made a similar observation (ironically, pointing to Louis's beloved *Symphonica Domestica*) when he asserted that the later tone poems—as well as

Salome and *Elektra*—show a composer simulating emotion rather than being emotional. Louis's essay represents an early example of this view, which has been a recurrent theme (almost to the point of cliché) in much Strauss criticism. Especially since the end of the Second World War, much of the literature on Strauss has seen a general uniformity in the composer's creative output. In this regard, Louis's essay stands out, for he finds the composer's creative path full of "sudden and unexpected turns": from confirmed classicist to ardent Wagnerian, from tone poet to stage poet. Louis concluded that, at present, "It is impossible to predict where his genius might finally lead him" [ed.].

[Source: Rudolf Louis, *Die Deutsche Musik der Gegenwart,* rev. ed. (Munich: Georg Müller, 1912), pp. 172–80]

·

The three tendencies in which we can trace the development of the post-Beethoven symphony lead directly to the three men who are the most commonly cited instrumental composers of our day: the first, program-musical, tendency leads via Berlioz and Liszt to Richard Strauss; the second, diametrically opposed direction leads via Schumann to Max Reger; and the third, which in a certain sense mediates between them, leads to Gustav Mahler.

Of the three, Richard Strauss is today a figure of worldwide fame who, while he may be judged in very contradictory terms, possesses a significance that is generally recognized, known, and cited by people far beyond the narrow circle of the true friends of music. . . .

I still consider it to be an especially fortunate accident that the first work I encountered by Richard Strauss was *Don Juan,* which along with *Till Eulenspiegel* can undoubtedly be considered his least problematic achievement in the symphonic arena. My opinion of this creation has not remained unchanged either, since the time almost twenty years ago when I first heard it played by the Vienna Philharmonic under Hans Richter and fell into a transport of delight. But I have maintained a decided preference for this piece, and at this moment it is still one of the few Straussian orchestral works that I hear again and again not only with interest but with renewed pleasure. It is easy to understand the enthusiasm of a twenty-two-year-old who hailed from Wagner and Liszt and now all at once encountered a music that seemed to incorporate all the peculiar qualities of the tonal language of these two masters, further intensified by a personal element whose carefree audacity could not help exerting its fascination over the young man—all the more so because he knew that this very audacity inspired horror in the hearts of the Philistines.

A year later I heard *Tod und Verklärung* in the same place and experienced a disappointment, a disappointment that at first I scarcely dared admit to myself, but felt no less strongly as a result. The great mass of those who consider *Tod und Verklärung* as representing the pinnacle of Strauss's creations of that period will hardly find this disappointment understandable, and it is, in fact, not self-evident. For *Tod und Verklärung* is quite clearly the more mature work, and in its formal unity, in particular, it is far superior to *Don Juan.* But I remain convinced, as I was then, that the power of musical invention is incomparably more powerful in the earlier than in the later work and that it is, above all, much more personal and reveals much more of the real, individual Richard Strauss than the symphonic death poem, whose whole concept and execution betrays the influence of Alexander Ritter[1] more clearly than any other work by Strauss (with the exception of the original plan and intention of *Guntram*). Furthermore, and above all: in *Tod und Verklärung,* for the first time, one could observe, as a decided weakness, that Straussian externality and superficiality of feeling that falls short whenever inner feeling and depth of emotional expression are called for.

Later, too, the symphonic composer Strauss always moved me the most where his splendid and—despite all (not entirely undeserved) misunderstandings—lovable *human* personality expresses itself purely in his music, where he presents himself as what he actually is, and does not allow himself to be lured by half- or completely misunderstood trends of the moment to heights where he *cannot fail* to feel out of breath. Thus the quality in Strauss that is best expressed in the word *gamin* found a very delightful expression in *Till Eulenspiegel,* which I am told most serious observers prefer above all the master's other orchestral creations. And if the baroque tendency that afflicts Strauss—as it does all musicians of our time, almost without exception—had not played a bad trick on him in the *Symphonia Domestica* by causing him to try to give adequate artistic reflection to the inner, spiritual significance of family life by intensifying the musical means of expression numerically and dynamically in a way that created a ridiculous contrast to the nature of the subject, then this work would follow immediately after *Eulenspiegel* in my affection and it might even, since it is so much more *serious,* supplant it. For if a person can only manage to overlook a priori such ludicrous and tasteless events as the marital fight fugue and similar inventions and to accept them as something about which not a word need be spoken, he will find in this score, in particular, some of the most beautiful things Strauss has written, things that—quite in contrast to the usual expression of sentiments in Strauss, with its tendency to remain all too much on the surface—are distinguished by an eminently personal and nearly profound *emotional content*. Whoever feels compelled to make a judgment about Richard Strauss's *character* would do well, at any rate, to pay attention to, among other things, the testimony given by this music: it is at least as worthy of consideration as all the unreliable gossip about the smart behavior of the businessman Strauss, which one finally does not have to find defensible in every case but which most certainly does not—as has been claimed—express Strauss's most profound striving.

Unsympathetic, on the other hand—despite the requisite admiration for the things an unbiased observer always has to admire in Richard Strauss—have always been for me *Also sprach Zarathustra* and *Heldenleben*. In the first work the composer was misled by the fashion of the times to allow himself to be inspired by a spirit with whom he had nothing in common and for whom he had not the slightest *emotional* comprehension (by which I naturally do not mean to say that such an educated and intelligent man as Strauss did not "get" Nietzsche in the sense of rational comprehension). Strauss's musical Nietzsche interpretation, as such, is a strange misunderstanding, and whatever it contains in the way of absolute musical values does not seem to me to be sufficient to compensate for this weakness of complete discrepancy between the poetic-philosophical model and the musical imitation. Almost as repellent as this discrepancy is the attempt, in *Heldenleben,* to elevate his own person, which possesses a number of excellent characteristics but certainly nothing "heroic" and in fact never actually had to struggle in life, to the height of the heroic—a process that is "aggravated" by the fact that this heroism is seen as so completely external, that is, warlike, not to say "military," and the artist, where he attempts to achieve emotional depth, namely in the romantic episode and the "resignation" of the conclusion, does not get beyond a shallow, even trivial sentimentality.

A certain ambiguous position is occupied, in my evaluation, by *Don Quixote*. In many respects it resembles *Eulenspiegel,* and one can certainly not say in this case that the composer lacked the essential thing, namely a feeling for the tragic *humor* of Cervantes' immortal character. In this regard, it was an unusually felicitious inspiration to use the form of the variation, programmatically motivated, in this tone poem (corresponding to the rondo form in *Eulenspiegel*). What prevented *Don Quixote* from becoming a masterpiece that is just as perfect, in its own way, as *Eulenspiegel,* was evidently the unfortunate cir-cumstance that the striving for the greatest possible realism in the aural depiction of the poetic events caused the *instrumentation* of *Don Quixote* to remain mired, in more than one place, in unsuccessful ex-periments. And with that I come to the point that finally had to be-come a fateful factor in the further development of the symphonic poet. No musician before now has ever advanced nearly so far in the art of letting the listener *see*, as it were, with his ears. This is the source of Strauss's unique and personal strength, that he has devel-oped the ideal, elevated gestures of the tonal language of Liszt into a gestural language of great specificity that undertakes quite seriously not only to interpret the events of an external plot in tone (by re-vealing the music that is latent in them) but to *draw* them until they are recognizable to the inner eye.

This undertaking could not possibly succeed. It led Strauss down a path along which there was much to be discovered that enriched music's expressive means but which finally turned out to be a dead end. For the "deictic" musician, whose highest ambition as an artist is to be found not in complementing the poet or painter as depicter of objective events but in *competing* with them, must necessarily arrive at the point where he recognizes that even the most cleverly developed tonal language is not capable of representing its object in an unam-biguous way, but that, on the contrary, it can be fully effective only when the events it represents are also present in the listener's mind *as such* and not merely in an aural version. This leads to the require-ment either that the listener must "keep track" of the progress of the piece of music throughout its entire length, with the help of a de-tailed "program"—an imposition that would immediately destroy the actual enjoyment of music—or else that these events must be presented to the listener as *visual* ones, so the impression of the eye accompa-nies and explicates that of the ear, and mime explains the music.

Thus it is out of inner necessity that Richard Strauss, in recent years, has turned away from symphonic music and toward the stage. People—and there are not a few of them—who believe they are obliged to assume the lowest motivation for everything Strauss does may perhaps be tempted to think that the artist pursued only one purpose with his entire symphonic opus—to make a name for him-self in the concert hall that would secure or at least facilitate his con-quest of the stage with its promise of incomparably greater booty. It would be more decent and factually correct if one were to assume, for example, that Strauss, as a symphonic musician, created the tools and forged the weapons with which he now fights for leadership of the theatrical world; that he wanted, by means of his symphonic production, to test and steel the powers that would allow him to triumph on the stage. But however highly one may rate the importance of Strauss's turn to the theater, even this interpretation of Straussian symphonic music as a kind of propaedeutics for Straussian drama does not nearly do justice to a creativity to which we owe such works as *Don Juan, Tod und Verklärung, Till Eulenspiegel,* and the *Symphonia Domestica.* One thing, at least, is clear: that Strauss, in the pursuit of his own particular direction, has now reached the point where there is greater likelihood that he will write a harmonious and, from the point of view of the listener who is sensitive to issues of taste, completely satisfactory work for the *stage* than for the *concert hall.*

Strauss, who represents the highest that can possibly be achieved without actual genius, in the sphere of talent, distinguishes himself from the majority of his composing contemporaries by the fact that his artistic development has proceeded in much less of a straight line than theirs, that the path he has followed is rich in sudden and unexpected turns. The artist, who began as a rigorous classicist and one-sided admirer of Brahms under the aegis of Hans von Bülow, who was, at the time, completely estranged from the new romanticism; who then, under the influence of Alexander Ritter, became an equally one-sided partisan of the view of art represented by the "opposition party"—and at that time the two opposing tendencies really did regard each other as strictly divided enemy camps—who, in his symphonic tone poems, then took the further step of pursuing "illustrative" tone painting to its uttermost ends, that is, to the point where it continues ad absurdum; only, having arrived at this point, to undergo the conversion from the concert hall to the stage, where he had, until then, made only one—unsuccessful—attempt, this highly skilled artist with his transformative capabilities, who has just made the transition from youth to middle age, can yet offer his epoch many surprises, and it is impossible to predict where his genius may finally lead him.

NOTE

1. Alexander Ritter (1833–98) was a composer and violinist who met Strauss in 1885 in Meiningen, where the latter served as Hans von Bülow's assistant conductor. Ritter was a guiding force behind Strauss's conversion to the aesthetics of Liszt and Wagner [ed.].

Richard Strauss and

the Viennese Critics (1896–1924):

Reviews by Gustav Schoenaich,

Robert Hirschfeld, Guido Adler,

Max Kalbeck, Julius Korngold,

and Karl Kraus

SELECTED AND INTRODUCED BY LEON BOTSTEIN

TRANSLATED BY SUSAN GILLESPIE

Vienna's place in Richard Strauss's life and work extended well beyond the role that city might ordinarily have been expected to play
in the career of any non-Viennese nineteenth- and early-twentieth-century composer or performer. For musicians from Central Europe,
Vienna was preeminent as a musical center. Few could avoid a confrontation with Viennese performing institutions, the Viennese audience, and the city's newspaper critics. Recognition in Vienna often
marked the difference between an international career and a provincial one.

For painters, writers, and musicians from Catholic Bavaria, there was
a particular affinity with Vienna. The cultural links were residues of
a shared history that dated back to the Middle Ages. The deep tradition of fluidity in relations between the Austro-German regions of the
Hapsburg Monarchy and South Germany would help make the 1938
Anschluss appear to many a natural consequence of history and culture.

However, Richard Strauss's tie to Vienna constituted a special case. From 1911 on, the image and idea of Vienna, perhaps more than the practical opportunities it afforded, became a decisive metaphor for Strauss's artistic energies. What rendered Vienna compelling to Strauss was not the fin-de-siècle ferment that has attracted subsequent generations and elevated early-twentieth-century Vienna to a crucial force in the development of twentieth-century modernist art and ideas. The Vienna of Arthur Schnitzler, Schoenberg, Alban Berg, Freud, Adolf Loos, Karl Kraus, and Egon Schiele was of little personal or intellectual interest to Strauss.

The Vienna that captured Strauss's imagination was the baroque city, the treasures of the past collected in the *Kunsthistorisches Museum*, the visible links to the city's eighteenth-century heritage and its local traditions, including the waltz. For Strauss, Vienna, especially after World War I, symbolized the context and content for a response to the radical side of an emergent aesthetic modernism. The Vienna implicit in the ideas and language of *Der Rosenkavalier* framed, for Strauss, a viable setting; an inspiration to begin the process of formulating an alternative to modernism, whose center, by 1912, had already begun to shift from Vienna to Berlin.

The alternative aesthetic strategy Strauss crafted from 1911 on was not simply reactionary, even though it flourished after 1918 in the unique retrospective cultural milieu that developed in Vienna. The shadow of Vienna was perceptible from the start, in 1911, indirectly through influence exerted by Hugo von Hofmannsthal. It was strengthened after *Der Rosenkavalier* by their collaboration on the *Ariadne*-Molière project (between 1911 and 1916), on the ballet *Josephslegende* (1914), and most of all on *Die Frau ohne Schatten* (1919). It was in these three works that the explicit segregation of essential meanings from any visible historical framework emerged, along with the free appropriation of painterly ideals from the past and the transformed use of myth. Opera, drama, and ballet became objects of a new sort of experimentation in dramatic and narrative form, which provided Strauss with the chance to confront the idea of modernity and the logic of modernism directly (and with self-critical irony). At the same time Strauss played with conceptions of tradition in the uses of speech, gesture, and music.[1]

Post–World War I Vienna was an ideal place to pursue this artistic project; the city celebrated myths about itself as history. Although such myth making about its own civic character dated from the mid–nineteenth century, after the fall of the monarchy, Vienna gave birth to the first modern project of invented nostalgia as cultural ideology.[2]

An imagined bygone Vienna came into being that mirrored a vanished Italianate grace, the civility of a romanticized eighteenth century, a colorful but extinct aristocracy, a baroque love of ornament, a premodern sense of wit, and a construct of classicism powerful enough to debunk the claims of an ascetic modern functional or rational aesthetic.

In the crucible of postwar Vienna, Strauss fashioned a strategy for writing music that was consciously detached from any perceptible link between aesthetics and historical teleology. Both the overt celebration and the critique of the potential of historical progress and the triumph of rationality were set aside. The idea that art, if unfettered, would naturally match its historical moment (an idea inscribed, poignantly, over the entrance of Joseph Olbrich's 1897 Secession Building in Vienna) in some evident or implicitly progressive manner dominated in the years from the mid-1880s until World War I. In the postwar years Strauss searched for a way around this facile parallelism. The subject matter of the 1920s, let alone the arguments, put forth by Marxists (e.g., Lukács), liberal democrats (e.g., Masaryk), and aesthetes (e.g., the Stefan George circle) about the relationships between art and social progress, failed to engage Strauss.

Paradoxically, however, the refuge provided by postwar Vienna, under a surface of cultural pessimism and detachment from the historical, permitted aesthetic innovations to develop. The evidently artificial re-creation and embrace of an imagined past blocked a replay of late-nineteenth-century historicism. Beneath a self-consciously false mask representing the seemingly historical, a nonorthodox but novel dimension within twentieth-century aesthetics took shape.

Stemming from the interwar years in Vienna, this dimension, from the perspective of the late twentieth century, bears striking similarities to late-twentieth-century postmodernism. The fragmentation and reordering of the past, the disavowal of traditional empiricism, the conscious obliteration of boundaries between fantasy and fiction, the use of quotation, self-quotation, ornament, and evident allusion to canonic art works of the past, and the appropriation of distorted historicist surfaces (including an altered use of narrative continuities) are hallmarks of late-twentieth-century postmodernism. Strauss's works from 1919 on experiment with these types of aesthetic strategies.

Strauss's innovative reaction to the more "progressive" trends in aesthetic modernism, formulated within the framework of an apolitical milieu in Vienna, had parallels in other arenas. The prose of Joseph Roth, Robert Musil, Ödön von Horvath, and even Hermann Broch, as well as Hofmannsthal's own work from the same period, are part of this peculiar and specifically Viennese postwar cultural direction. Joseph Roth's great novel *Radetzkymarsch* (1932), for example, shares common ground with Strauss's *Arabella* (1933) in style and ideas; likewise the evolution of Viennese design after 1919, visible in the work of Eduard Josef Wimmer-Wisgrill and Michael Powolny from the *Wiener Werkstätte* (as well as in some Josef Hofmann and Dagobert Peche designs and much of Viennese ceramic work from the 1920s) reflected directions comparable to those taken by Strauss in Vienna during the same period.[3]

Strauss took inspiration from the invented Vienna that fit so neatly with aspects of the actual city of the 1920s, particularly its status as an imperial capital without an empire. Conscious that their political-historical moment in world history had passed, the Viennese sought to sustain a fanciful historicist and eclectic culture and an atmosphere that evoked the lost and unrealized opportunity for modernity, which, ironically, the passage of time and history had made permanently impossible. More than any other European city, Vienna itself became a stage set in the 1920s, in terms of its cultural life, and it relished the fact. As an amalgam of the real and unreal, it seemed filled with actors assuming various stylized roles from a visible and invisible heritage.

The cultural myths of Vienna spun out in the 1920s, most crudely displayed in Strauss's *Schlagobers* (1924), were conscious deceptions whose paradoxical celebration of a false past managed to turn stylistic neoclassicism and surface historicism into a powerful critical weapon against both a confident modernism and a facile traditionalism. That weapon demanded of its user the stance of cultivated detachment. The Viennese aestheticism of the 1920s was justified not by a disdain of politics but by the confident sense of its transcendence. Strauss's and Hofmannsthal's *Die ägyptische Helena* from 1928 (a major work all too often denigrated in the critical literature) mirrors this sense of transcendence of the mundane and historical through its transformation of the distant historical into affectionate fantasy. The locus classicus of the dominant interwar Viennese cultural and aesthetic ideology was Egon Friedell's massive three-volume *Kulturgeschichte der Neuzeit,* published between 1927 and 1932. The most compelling and innovative achievement—in musical terms—written by Richard Strauss within this specifically Viennese aesthetic framework, as Arnold Schoenberg (ironically) recognized, was *Intermezzo* (1924).[4] However, the aesthetic sensibilities Strauss sharpened during his Vienna years would dominate both *Daphne* (1938) and *Die Liebe der Danae* (1944).

In view of the significance of Vienna in Richard Strauss's artistic development in the years after 1918, a brief review of his actual contact with the city is appropriate. Strauss's first encounter with Vienna took place in 1882 with his first concert tour away from home. His debut occurred on 5 December 1882 at the Bösendorfer Hall, the city's leading recital space until 1913 and a favorite of both Brahms and Hans von Bülow (who had inaugurated it in 1872 for its sponsor, Vienna's leading piano manufacturer, Ludwig Bösendorfer). Franz (Richard's father) Strauss's colleague at the Munich Opera and Richard's teacher, the violinist Benno Walter, performed with the pianist Eugenie Menter. Included in the program was the first performance of Richard Strauss's Violin Concerto, Op. 8. Menter was the sister of the more famous pianist Sophie Menter, a pupil of Liszt and von Bülow. The eighteen-year-old Strauss himself played the piano reduction for the concerto.[5]

The *Deutsche Zeitung* critic and Bruckner advocate Theodor Helm recalled that the work was "conventional" yet "rewarding" for the violin. Eduard Hanslick was generous, noting only that this work, despite the evident display of talent, was somewhat "immature." Ludwig Speidel, another powerful critic, was unimpressed. Strauss was not the only eighteen-year-old to make a debut as composer in 1882. Earlier that year the young Eugène d'Albert had appeared, playing his B-minor Piano Concerto with the Vienna Philharmonic.[6]

The young Strauss felt immediately at home in Vienna, so much so that Eugenie Menter lamented to Strauss's father that playing chaperone to Richard was proving to be no easy task.[7] To the eighteen-year-old Strauss, Vienna seemed merely a bigger version of Munich. Even the girls looked similar to him. By the time Strauss returned nearly a decade later, he had already established himself as a rising young modernist, a leader of the New German School of post-Wagnerian composers. Between 1892 and 1897 the Vienna Philharmonic performed *Don Juan, Tod und Verklärung, Till Eulenspiegel,* and *Also sprach Zarathustra* under Hans Richter. Two reviews of these performances are included in this section.

With Gustav Mahler's arrival in Vienna in 1897, a new era of opportunity opened up for Strauss in Vienna. Mahler, during the decade in which he dominated the Viennese musical scene, conducted Strauss's *Aus Italien* and excerpts from *Guntram* in orchestral concerts. He produced *Feuersnot* in 1902 at the Imperial Opera. In 1901 and 1902 Strauss himself came with visiting orchestras to conduct. Viennese performances of *Macbeth* and the *Symphonia Domestica* also took place during the first years of the century.[8]

In 1905 Mahler failed to get Strauss's *Salome* approved by the censors for the Imperial Opera. The collapse of Mahler's efforts to produce the world premiere of the work marked the beginning of the deterioration in his relations with the Viennese cultural bureaucracy. The *Salome* affair led in part to the 1907 crisis, which ended with Mahler's resignation. Ironically, in 1907 the Vienna premiere of *Salome* took place with the Breslau State Theater company conducted by Julius Prüwer. Fanchette Verhunk sang the title role. The performance, as the reviews collected in this section attest, was one of the sensations of the 1907 season. The Vienna Opera would finally present *Salome* for the first time in October 1918.[9]

The 1905 Vienna *Salome* affair, together with the poor reception Munich had given *Guntram* more than a decade earlier, helped to confirm Strauss's lifelong preference for Dresden as the site of world premieres. Nevertheless, Strauss's links to Vienna grew steadily. His fascination with Vienna and musical and pre-1848 (particularly baroque and rococo) Viennese cultural traditions, first evident in the score of *Der Rosenkavalier,* reappear in the Prologue to *Ariadne,* in *Arabella,* and in the ill-fated ballet *Schlagobers.*

Strauss conducted the Vienna production of *Elektra* (which also ran afoul of censors before its Vienna premiere in 1909) in 1910. In 1911, Franz Schalk, later Strauss's co-director at the Opera, presented *Der Rosenkavalier.* Strauss's librettist, Hugo von Hofmannsthal; the set designer, Alfred Roller (whose earlier collaboration with Mahler in Vienna revolutionized the tradition of opera set design and lighting); and the great director Max Reinhardt (who directed the 1912 *Ariadne* and *Der Bürger als Edelmann* and who worked in Vienna in the 1920s and 1930s) were personally, artistically, and intellectually tied to Vienna. In 1919, *Die Frau ohne Schatten* (with Roller's sets) was premiered in Vienna. From 1918 on, Strauss maintained intimate artistic contacts with Vienna, not only through Hofmannsthal and Roller but through Stefan Zweig, Hermann Bahr, Joseph Gregor, Maria Jeritza, Clemens Krauss, and Karl Böhm, among others.

Immediately after World War I, Vienna supplanted Munich and Berlin, which had become centers of a new politics and a new art, as the locus of Strauss's activities. Given Strauss's ideas about the apolitical nature of the aesthetic realm, his growing distaste for contemporary modernism, and his brand of German patriotism (which amounted to a mix of chauvinism and fatalism about Germany's unique dynamic cultural heritage), Vienna promised to provide the ideal new home. After the collapse of the monarchy, nostalgia and mythic but alluring constructs of the past quickly became coincident with the city's self-image. In 1919, Strauss accepted a five-year contract as co-director with Schalk of the Vienna State Opera. However, the provincialism of Vienna's cultural bureaucracy, Strauss's contempt for practical issues in times of economic hardship, and the ultimate fact that Strauss was not an Austrian doomed his five-year appointment. In 1924, Schalk outmaneuvered his co-director and Strauss resigned. Nevertheless, Strauss accepted the unusual official invitation to build a home in Vienna within the Belvedere Park. He continued to conduct the Vienna Opera and, most of all, the Vienna Philharmonic. In 1931, Strauss edited, revised, rewrote, and added to Mozart's *Idomeneo* for a new production at the Vienna Opera (which he conducted).

After Hofmannsthal's death and their last collaboration, *Arabella* (with its Viennese setting), Strauss's remaining operas retained a Viennese link. *Die schweigsame Frau* was Stefan Zweig's work. Subsequent Joseph Gregor operas contained the work of both Hofmannsthal and Zweig. *Capriccio* was written with Krauss.

In the 1930s Strauss lived primarily in Garmisch, although he continued to spend time in Vienna. Strauss's collaboration with the Nazis made him less welcome in Austria after the assassination of Engelbert Dollfuss in 1934. But given the subsequent deterioration of his relations with the German Nazis, Strauss decided in 1941 to move to Vienna. The personal support of the *Gauleiter* of Vienna, Baldur von Schirach, and the musical community of Vienna offered him a more hospitable base from which to work. The Viennese Nazis were more willing to overlook the fact that Strauss's daughter-in-law was part Jewish. The Vienna Philharmonic's 1939 celebration of Strauss's seventy-fifth birthday in Vienna had been particularly warm. Strauss participated in the scandalously Nazified Vienna Mozart anniversary festival of 1941 and in 1944 basked in Vienna's official celebration of his eightieth birthday, a milestone that was left essentially unnoticed in Germany.

After the war, Strauss did not return to Vienna. In the final years of his life, from 1945 on, Strauss lived in Switzerland. He moved home to Garmisch in 1949, just five months before his death.

The critical essays chosen for this section document three stages in Strauss's relationship with Vienna. The first two reviews from the influential Vienna-based periodical the *Neue Musikalische Presse* help to delineate Strauss's reputation in Vienna as a young modernist composer in the tradition of Liszt and Wagner. The reviews from the late 1890s by Robert Hirschfeld and Gustav Schoenaich of two tone poems grapple with the aesthetics of program music and musical form. The battle lines in Vienna were drawn in part by the familiar Brahms-

Wagner conflict and a Brahms-Bruckner rivalry. However, as the Hirschfeld review makes clear, Strauss's notoriety in the 1890s derived as much from a sense of Strauss's post-Brucknerian modernity. His use of harmony and orchestral color and his formal ambitions in terms of narration and representation through instrumental means placed him at the head of a controversial new musical movement.

The second group of reviews and the short essay by Guido Adler are Viennese responses to *Salome,* to Strauss's singular success on the operatic stage. These articles were directed at the general public and appeared in three of Vienna's daily newspapers, including the *Neue Freie Presse.* All were *feuilletons,* that specifically Viennese cultural essay that appeared "under line" of the first page of the daily newspapers. Here again, Strauss is understood as a leader of modernism, as an innovator. These feuilletons reveal the critical climate of Vienna and the particular brand of conservatism shared by critics and audiences. Despite the adverse criticism Strauss received, from the 1890s on he enjoyed a strong Viennese following that would reach its apogee in the early 1940s.

The third group of selections, which begins with Julius Korngold's remarkably negative 1911 review of the first Vienna performance of *Der Rosenkavalier,* focuses on Strauss's direct relationship to Vienna and Viennese traditions. The Kraus selections, taken from his legendary periodical, *Die Fackel* [The torch], provide an example of how Strauss was attacked not from the perspective of any facile reactionary conservatism but on the basis of a principled radicalism located, ironically, in its own form of aesthetic and ethical conservatism.

Kraus and his followers were exceptions to the sustained adulation of Strauss by Viennese critics and audiences in the 1920s. When one compares the Kraus and Hirschfeld essays, one can see a notable continuous thread of criticism in Viennese aesthetic discourse. Kraus was a great admirer of Hirschfeld's literary style and fierce independence. Hirschfeld and Kraus defined a nonphilistine position that contested the basic premises of Strauss's art and conception of the relation of musical art and audience. Too often we dismiss out of hand contemporary criticism that "failed" to recognize greatness in its own time. In these two cases, contemporary criticism reveals not only something about the vanished context of the past but also a nontrivial if not compelling critical perspective whose inherent challenges continue to maintain validity.

The authors of these selections were all leading figures in the intellectual and artistic life of Vienna.

Gustav Schoenaich (1841–1906) wrote primarily for the *Wiener Allgemeine Zeitung* and the *Wiener Tagblatt*. He was a native Viennese. A well-known Viennese Wagner advocate, he became acquainted with Richard Wagner personally through his stepfather, Joseph Standhartner, the distinguished Viennese physician, who was Wagner's close friend. Standhartner was also (together with Brahms) a long-standing member of the board of directors of the Vienna Society of the Friends of Music. A connoisseur of things Wagnerian, Schoenaich, who also was equally notorious for his prodigious appetite and wide girth, was for a time an intimate friend of Hugo Wolf.[10]

Robert Hirschfeld (1858–1914), the son of a rabbi, was born in Moravia and came to Vienna from Breslau. In Vienna he established himself as an iconoclastic critical voice. He completed a dissertation in music history under Hanslick's direction but later openly attacked Hanslick's disregard for baroque, Renaissance, and medieval music. Hirschfeld taught aesthetics at the Vienna Conservatory, wrote theater criticism (he was a great admirer of Frank Wedekind), published scholarly articles, and prepared modern performing editions of Haydn and Schubert stage works. Apparently a prickly character, he figured prominently in the campaign against Mahler in Vienna. Hirschfeld died in 1914, soon after assuming responsibility for the *Mozarteum* in Salzburg.[11]

Max Kalbeck (1850–1921) is remembered most for his magisterial biography of Johannes Brahms. As a journalist he wrote for the *Neues Wiener Tagblatt*. However, he was also known in Vienna as a poet and writer. He came to Vienna from Silesia in 1880. An admirer of the great anti-Wagnerian Viennese satirist Daniel Spitzer, Kalbeck edited Spitzer's works and wrote a short biography of him. Although he had written extensively on Wagner as a young man, he became hostile to Wagner's cause. Kalbeck devoted considerable energy to opera. He prepared German-language versions of Mozart's Italian operas and wrote a series of original libretti, including one for Johann Strauss, Jr. If Robert Hirschfeld escaped Karl Kraus's scathing criticism of journalists, Max Kalbeck (despite Kraus's own admiration for Spitzer) exemplified for Kraus the vacuousness and pretentiousness of Viennese cultural journalism.

Julius Korngold (1860–1945) succeeded Eduard Hanslick as chief music critic of Vienna's most prestigious paper, the *Neue Freie Presse*. Korngold's position as a critic was somewhat compromised by his fanatical ambition to enhance the career of his son, the child-prodigy composer Erich Wolfgang Korngold. Julius Korngold was an admirer of Mahler and Debussy, but he had little use for Schoenberg and his followers. Born in Brno, he studied both music and law in Vienna. After working in Brno as a critic, he came to Vienna in 1901. Korngold maintained a particular interest in opera, a subject on which he wrote extensively. Korngold's memoirs, written in exile in America and published for the first time in 1991 as *Die Korngolds in Wien,* are an invaluable source of information on the musical life (including Strauss's activities in Vienna) during the interwar years in Vienna.[12]

Guido Adler (1855–1941), one of the founders of modern musicology, established the Music Historical Institute at the University of Vienna, where he succeeded to Hanslick's professorial chair in 1898. An indefatigable worker, he trained generations of musicologists, edited journals and sets of monographs and manuscript editions, organized scholarly gatherings, and wrote widely, from scholarly articles to textbooks. Like Mahler and Hirschfeld, Adler was born in Moravia. He was friendly with Mahler (particularly before Mahler's marriage) and helped Schoenberg and his Viennese disciples, including Anton von Webern and Egon Wellesz. Adler concerned himself with issues of periodization, historical method, and the nature of Viennese musical classicism. A genuine Austrian patriot, Adler sought to play a constructive role in the cultural politics of both the Empire and the First Republic. Adler never functioned as a professional critic, although his occasional newspaper articles and speeches directed at lay audiences attracted substantial attention. His 1904 book on Wagner was one of the first efforts at a revisionist historical and independent scholarly assessment of Wagner. As a young man, Adler (who was born a Jew) had been an enthusiastic Wagnerian and a leader in Vienna's Academic Wagner Society. His 1916 book on Mahler was among the earliest sympathetic and comprehensive interpretations of Mahler's life and work.[13]

Karl Kraus (1874–1938) was among the greatest figures of the Viennese fin de siècle. Kraus was born in Bohemia but came to Vienna when he was two years old. His ideas—particularly his notion of language and its relation to art and ethics—exerted a decisive influence on generations of writers, artists, and thinkers, including Schoenberg, Berg, Broch, Musil, Ludwig Wittgenstein, Oskar Kokoschka, and Elias Canetti. Kraus never considered himself particularly musical. He was, however, impressed by Wagner's writings. He admired Jacques Offenbach and gave legendary one-man renditions of Offenbach's musical theater. Kraus cherished the Viennese satirical tradition of Johann Nestroy, Friedrich Kürnberger, and Spitzer and continued it in his journal, *Die Fackel.* Among Kraus's favorite targets were journalists, fellow Jews—particularly Zionists (Kraus was born Jewish but converted to Catholicism as an adult)—psychoanalysts, Secession painters and their supporters, and politicians. He was an admirer of the architect Adolf Loos. Like Loos, Kraus harbored doubts about Mahler's work and many aspects of modernist aesthetics. Nevertheless, Kraus defended Mahler vociferously against what he regarded as Vienna's philistine critical community. Kraus's influence was considerable throughout the 1920s. His monumental theater piece, *The Last Days of Mankind* (1919), and his essays (particularly on the nature of language) are among the most compelling writings in the German language from the early twentieth century.[14]

Opera and Concert Reports

GUSTAV SCHOENAICH

Vienna (Philharmonic concert).[15] The program of the Philharmonic concert that took place last Sunday seemed to have been put together with the expectation that every listener would bring a revolving chair with him in his head. There is no other way we can explain the requirement of hearing music from such rapidly changing, varied points of view. A Mozart symphony from Arcadia, Strauss's *Till Eulenspiegel* from Cayenne, Mendelssohn's *Hebrides* Overture in faultless elegance, striding by like Bulwer's *Pelham*,[16] and Bruckner's E♭-major symphony, with genuine ermine peeking out from under the Tyrolean peasant's jacket and held together by buttons crafted in part from contrapuntal twenty-cent pieces and in part from genuine diamonds! And all this at 12:30 P.M., the zenith of human sobriety.

Among the young composers, most of whom have already been crushed under the weight of the phenomenon of Richard Wagner and can only stammer out their own sounds if they bring forth anything at all, Richard Strauss occupies a prominent place. Everything of his that has come to the attention of the public until now, even the unfortunate things, reveals a personal element, unmistakable attempts at an individual language. The great confidence that Hans von Bülow, who hated every epigonal art, placed in the talent of this young man—he is now in his thirty-first year—seems entirely justified to us. Richard Strauss's musical education is profoundly thorough. Not until he had acquired quite astonishing knowledge in the center of music making, in all the technical matters, did he begin to become eccentric. But the solid connection, which he can never lose, with this good foundation prevents him from flying off completely. His newest composition, *Till Eulenspiegels lustige Streiche,* gives very good sounding and hardly controvertible evidence of this. The piece is program music only in the sense in which it always has and probably always will be considered permissible. Strauss has expressly declined to bring the events of the Eulenspiegel story into direct relationship with his score. He could have chosen the overture form and would have been no less justified than Reinecke with his *Nutcracker* Overture or innumerable others who have given [their works] whatever titles they fancied. Strauss, wittier and more distinctive, cast his piece in the form of an expanded rondo. This form, which is filled with lively content, provides the listener with a solid point of departure. We do not have to trouble ourselves with relating individual parts of the piece to specific external events, and the firm structure allows us to absorb and enjoy the underlying mood of the whole, as it is laid out in the themes and fully exploited by variations, undisturbed by programmatic suppositions. We do not know, if the piece had been sent out into the world without the title, whether the name *Eulenspiegel* would have been attached to it by someone from among the circle of listeners; but [its] fundamental character, oscillating between humor, sarcasm, and irony, radiates from every measure, here and there perhaps even too garishly. The piece is dazzlingly clever, does not break down into its individual parts, and captivates the intellect of the listener perhaps more than his sensibility—but with its convincing logic and skillfully measured length it never for a moment leaves him without stimulation. It is eminently amusing. The means that are used are, admittedly, very opulent. But when one considers that from the death of Gluck until the creation of the *Symphonie fantastique* of Berlioz[17] not even fifty years went by, one might, for a change, express a certain satisfaction with the fact that the means of musical expression have undergone so little intensification, relatively speaking, in the longer period that has elapsed since then. That a work of music whose effect aims more at the intellect than at the heart should find more willing listeners today cannot be surprising at a time when every "truth" gives birth, as though through self-generation, to the worm of the question mark. Perhaps that will change someday, when a profound but generative error once again exerts its one-sided but sufficiently powerful formative influence on the world of culture. Today's errors are too paltry for that. We are expressing our pleasure at Strauss's work not in the name of any "principle" or "tendency." When one grows old, one learns to understand the devil to mean that laws are followed best by those whose spirit has engendered them and tendencies pursued most successfully by those who have already set out upon their path. We think *Eulenspiegel* is a very personal piece and a stroke of genius. That Strauss is not someone one should take lightly is something of which anyone can convince himself with the help of the score. A cheap effect, based for example on a few cleverly thought-out tonal effects, it is not. Nevertheless, it has that drastic and plastic quality that is one of the indispensable characteristics of every significant piece of music. Let us cultivate in ourselves some of Goethe's tolerance for individual peculiarity and personality and we will recognize that nowadays we are permitted to enjoy such exotic products with complete impunity. The flaming sword of the aesthetician who would bar the way to such phenomena does not singe the person who courageously bares his breast to it—and if one examines it more closely, it has precious little to distinguish it from the schoolmaster's cane. . . .

[Source: *Neue Musikalische Presse* 2 (1 December 1896)]

.

Zarathustra

ROBERT HIRSCHFELD

"Thus" the new Zarathustra also "spake" in Vienna. Our Philharmonic players let Richard Strauss's anarchic music-bomb explode in their last concert. The fragments of the score were simply flying. The destruction was horrific. Here a C-major motive lay next to the B-minor theme from the "Great Longing";[18] there a Credo or Magnificat was sent flying.[19] The violins were divided into sixteen different parts; all the music stands were pushed away from one another; horns and trumpets were muted to the point of unrecognizability; even the double basses were toned down. A fugue with wounded limbs bore witness to the lost greatness of musical "science"; on all sides a frightful whimpering, whining, and stammering; of Zarathustra's Dance, which conquered the Spirit of Gravity, only the hacked, dislocated, torn, and cut-up pieces of motives remained, and no one was able to say where the titles "Backworldsmen," "Joys and Passions," "Grave Song," and "Night Song" belonged. Everything head over heels, heels over head; finally B major and C collided with each other so that one could take a B for a C and a C for a B, which in Strauss circles is called the "World Riddle." Among such explosions we are meant to pick out Nietzsche's *Übermensch*! Certainly there are sparks of genius that fly out in the midst of this musical blasting operation, glowing out of the delirium of the symphonic backworldsman. But this genius awakens horror; for we are at the end of music, at a music that finally seems to have been created only for the eagle and the snake of Zarathustra. We are not yet mature enough for this "dance," and if we reach maturity what good will it do us? Then another superman will come and climb on top of this superman and divide the violins into thirty-two parts, blow from sixteen horns, and make the tubas play trills. Scores that merely add sounds can be sequenced infinitely. And the same is true of the musical revaluing of philosophical ideas; one can lead them to infinity and finally bring musical composition to the point at which it plays several volumes of Kant or Hegel into our hands, with musical footnotes, and as explanations of the philosopher the motives "pure reason" or "immanent negativity" are identified in the notes. Nothing in art is accomplished by material evidence. Strauss says proudly: "That is *my* counterpoint." And no one can argue that counterpoint away from him. In a little while others will come and say, "This is *our* counterpoint," and before you know what has happened it will be the general counterpoint. The "backward" ones who cannot fly fast enough to keep up with the conductors from the New Germany will achieve nothing by their hue and cry. Warnings do no good and are laughable. Art must protect itself. If it cannot or will not, then the way is free for the rule of the street. All *Heil!*

In the execution of the musical assassination attempt, Hans Richter[20] and his Philharmonic musicians showed themselves to be the true supermen. Anyone who was capable, after such a masterful accomplishment, of hissing, as a way of taking issue with Richard Strauss, cannot count himself among either the backworldsmen or the frontworldsmen of music.

[Source: *Neue Musikalische Presse* 13 (27 March 1897), Vienna]

.

Problems of Musical Culture in Our Time

GUIDO ADLER

When we look around us at the colorful musical doings of our time, we become aware of a number of phenomena—alongside the actual art of the contemporary era, alongside the art that results in modern creations—that seem, judging by their origins, to belong to the most varied artistic periods. In the churches of the Benedictines, as in other Catholic churches, the Gregorian Latin chant, a deeply felt

artistic product from the first millennium A.D., is still being sung today. In the Protestant churches, the German chorale, as it arose during the period of the Reformation, is performed. Many sacred and
secular choral societies are devoted to polyphonic, or a cappella, singing from the era when unaccompanied vocal music was at its height,
the fifteenth and sixteenth centuries; and a whole series of musicians
have taken it upon themselves to continue to produce works in the
manner of this art form. In the Catholic church they are called
"Cecilians."[21] Here and there, one may also hear operatic arias from
the seventeenth century; and starting with the era of Bach and Handel
one may attend performances here [in Vienna] of the artistic products not only of these two musical heros but of a long series of artists that extends in unbroken succession into the present. One can
probably say that the art of Vienna's classical composers is, today, the
shared possession of all our musical circles. The question might be
asked: When, then, does modern music actually begin? Although one
must recognize in the works of Beethoven's last creative period the
signposts and milestones of the era that followed, the historian will
probably date the beginning of modern music from Schubert and
Chopin. The practicing composers of our day, however, would probably not agree with this opinion and would only regard as truly modern that music which they are creating under new conditions. As the
main representatives of this movement in German-speaking countries
one could identify Richard Strauss, Gustav Mahler, and Max Reger.

Thus the total picture of musical practice in our era shows the musical-cultural layers of earlier periods both appearing next to and overlapping each other, as geological formations at different points on the
earth's surface might lie exposed to the eye of the geologist; or at
this or that location older layers may be identified, while elsewhere
only the most recent geological stratum meets the eye. Who would
wish to prevent someone from finding individual enjoyment in a certain artistic layer or someone else from feeling more at home in another; and who, above all, would want to discourage young people,
driven by their need for activity, from finding satisfaction in whatever
appears completely new to them? Only too soon, after twenty or thirty
years, they will often become just as intolerant toward later-comers and
new phenomena as those people nowadays who call the taste of
today's youth depraved. The wheel of history advances inexorably, and
woe betide anyone who tries to put his hand in the spokes! He cannot stop it but runs the risk of injuring or losing his limbs. And it is
a joy to see that in our time there are people who are busily dedicated to continuing to create, that artists do not rest until they do

justice to themselves and consequently also to their era and build the path of the future with their works. In the sphere of purely instrumental music—especially of the symphony and the quartet—we see fresh, pulsating life. The notion that independent orchestral music reached its conclusion in the creations of Beethoven and must now necessarily be swallowed up by the drama—as Richard Wagner maintained—has not proven to be true. Along with him there were Johannes Brahms and many other composers who strove to continue the work that had been passed down to them and who continue working undaunted. This sketchy summary of what is heard today from cathedrals, churches, opera houses, concert halls, in homes and living rooms already suffices for us to recognize that despite all the reverence for what has been inherited from the past that characterizes our era, production continues unabated. Does it satisfy elevated tastes; are the artists finding the requirements that they need for their production—and if not, what should be done to make this possible?

From the great mass of those who are producing in our era three names have been selected, all of them Germans. To all appearances, it is not to be expected that German music will relinquish any of its prominence in the next period of time. The romantic music of the last century favored nationalism, that is, the emergence of national traits within the framework of the individual works of art. Although our classical composers make use of the motives and themes from other cultures in such a way that they simply utilize them as raw material for the development of their works, one can already observe in the very first works of the romantics the effort to emphasize the specific and differing [national] features of folk music, for example, in Weber's *Chinese* Overture, which he used as incidental music to Schiller's *Turandot;*[22] in Schubert's *Divertissement hongrois,* or in Chopin's mazurkas, polonaises, and krakowiaks. The national element is prominent in Chopin not only in these works, which follow popular light music and transform it through greater stylization, but also in other compositions—the impromptus, nocturnes, and études. As the individual peoples who until then had played either no role or a very subordinate role in music history appeared on the stage with new works of art, not only were actual national works of art created, using their works and forms, but such elements also found their way into the most developed form, the sonata form, and lent it an exotic character. This is evident in the chamber-music works of Grieg and Dvořák, among many others. Free forms also appear based on national motives, for example, the Hungarian rhapsodies of Franz Liszt or the symphonic cycle *Die Heimat* [*Má Vlast;* The fatherland] of Smetana.

Slavs and Scandinavians offer new works that, despite their freshness and their great advantage in being able to draw their material from still untapped treasure troves, have so far failed to reach the artistic heights embodied in the works of the Germans and the other older cultivated nations, the Italians, French, Spanish, and English. And now, in the most recent period, we can derive satisfaction from seeing how, despite all the fecundity of the newly emerging peoples in musical-cultural life, German masters are creating works that, each with its own novelty, are born of the spirit of our era.

The old contradictions that have existed since the very beginning of instrumental music can be seen here, too: on the one hand, the attempt to satisfy the demands of formal structure; on the other hand, the intention to regard poetic ideas as the center of the work of art, by which everything else in it is determined. Form and expression, which should coincide with each other in every perfect work of art, find their various forms of cultivation in various tendencies, so that in different art-historical periods one may distinguish the dominance now of formalism, now of emotionalism and the striving for expression. Fortunately practice is not doctrinaire. What is clearly distinguished in the language of words reaches an equilibrium in artistic works of a higher order. Richard Strauss tends definitely more in the programmatic direction of Berlioz or Liszt, while Max Reger wishes to speak to the listener in tones free of programmatic tendencies. Gustav Mahler takes a middle road; on the one hand, his symphonies satisfy the requirement that every instrumental creation of a higher kind should be accompanied by a poetic idea, in the sense in which Haydn once said, "Every one of my symphonies is a moral person"; on the other hand, they [Mahler's symphonies] are completely responsive at each and every movement to strict formal requirements for the construction of the various works in sonata form, even in the final movements that are written from texts. The means available to modern musicians are, it is true, much increased, and are two or three times—occasionally even four times—greater compared to the orchestra of the classical composers. This expansion cannot, in itself, be considered grounds for reproach. So long as means and expression coincide, the work of art can be considered completely justified in itself. Difficulties in performance do result: greater demands are placed not only on musicians and equipment but also on the mental and physical capabilities of the listener. This, then, makes it legitimate to raise increased expectations of what is offered; and here, admittedly, it must be said that this expectation is not always fulfilled. Here we will speak not of particular individuals but of the increase in the means that all these works have at their disposal when it comes to harmony, rhythm, and color. This increase is by no means a result of the individual preferences of these musicians; there is a whole series of other moderns who make even greater demands in one direction or another.

This phenomenon of the all-too-much is not entirely new in the history of music. The classical consummation of unaccompanied, regular four- to six-voice vocal works in the sixteenth century was followed by polyphony and the use of multiple choruses; the scores that are written in this style include up to fifty and more voices. In our era the opposition of the various voices is even bolder; sometimes they are led in such a way that it is as if they had nothing to do with one another; here the principle of opposition is pursued to excess, encouraged by the instrumental character of our music, which is incorrectly carried over into multivocal pieces. This is the source of one of the principal shortcomings of our music. The Secessionists of the old school of the end of the sixteenth century permitted themselves similar freedoms in their five- and six-voice pieces; the giant scores of modern provenance can probably also be reduced in their actual vocal lines to at most five or six, in general only three or four real voices altogether, while the others serve either as means of coloristic stimulus or as harmonic filler. Individual masters of our time make a definite abuse of the addition and insertion of vocal fragments. Vocal remnants of this kind turn up here and there, without one knowing what higher purpose they serve. Instead of adding charm to the work, which is probably what the composer intends, they confuse the listener. It is likely that the imagination creates in this way as a consequence of its own internal drive, but then this drive does not appear to us to be artistically refined. Such achievements do not correspond to the expectations we have of them, based on the examples of the most perfect artworks of the past. This is by no means mistakenly to apply standards based on these older works of art. Nothing is worse or more inappropriate than making idle comparisons. It is not permissible to attempt to measure a modern work of art against one or the other work from the past—no matter how perfect it may be. The new content requires a new form. Every artist has the right to demand of the listener or viewer that he adapt himself as much as possible to the artist's own manner; only with love is it possible truly to enjoy and appreciate a work of art. Fortunate is the artist who is able to create freely from within himself, without the influence of external forces, in intimate contact with a few listeners and friends who follow him with understanding and love. May his congregation increase! The modern expression *l'art pour l'art*, or *l'art pour les artistes* is accurate only if it is interpreted in such a fashion that the artist always regards himself as standing in the highest service of art; it should not be interpreted in the arrogant way that occurs all too of-ten—that the artist creates without any thought to the possibility and method of the work's performance, without regard for its suitability for reception by those who see or hear it or its ability to reach broader circles.

Today artists and composers have been almost entirely deprived of the opportunity to write so-called occasional works. They sit down and write whatever they like without having to consider an employer or a commission, and yet Goethe declares that the occasional poem is the first and oldest of all the types of poetry that he considers to have a higher value—"occasional" in the sense that their creation serves a particular purpose or derives from a particular cause, as, for example, the composer of sacred music must arrange his work for this or that liturgical act. Extraordinary works are then suitable for extraordinary occasions. In this regard, all kinds of blunders are made in our era, as the natural limits that exist in every branch of the art of music are arbitrarily stretched and twisted. If Beethoven, in his last quar-tets, extended the measure of tension, both in his own act of cre-ation and in what he demanded from his listeners, in comparison to the previous flowering of chamber music—a process that, by the way, took half a century to be accepted in the musical world—this does not provide justification for twisting this most extreme tension by vari-ous means or through further temporal expansion into sheer inad-equacy.

Despite various aberrations and confusions, one can see in the in-strumental music of our era discoveries of previously unknown terri-tories, and no one today can yet say to what degree such attempts, valuable as they may be in themselves, may gain broad general ac-ceptance. There is a high probability that they will; for in the spiri-tual struggle nothing is ever completely lost. Certainly the musical material of our culture has not been exhausted; the wellsprings of German folk music have been variously drawn upon but are far from being used up. Thus, if our music, too, shows symptoms of decay in a number of respects, still one can certainly not say that it is in the stage of agony or retreat; rather it is leading to new deeds that are already unearthing splendid results.

Much more difficult than the purely musical damage to our art of composition is that which is done through its relations to other arts— above all, poetry. Whereas previously every work of poetry, if it was to be woven about with music or—as we Germans say—set to music,[23] had to fulfill certain requirements in order to prove that it was suitable for musical treatment, today poetic products that have been created under quite different preconditions are simply submerged in music by the composers, whereby the drowning element is sometimes not the thing that is submerged but rather the submerger. As disconcerting as the rough outline of the libretti of the last few years may be, it has, from the beginning, an advantage over these purely literary products—namely, its ability to give consideration to certain requirements of musical treatment in its scenes and acts and in the division of the whole into parts. There are not a few people today who seem to think it possible to set every dramatic work whatsoever to music, just as it was written for the stage. These composers deprive themselves of an important advantage, for they do without the things that are most crucial for bringing out the emotions and sentiments that arise in the course of the drama. In exchange, they get reasoned exchanges and psychological analyses; but instead of music dramas what they write are symphonic works with an underlying text, in which the music assumes a more luxuriant position than it ever had even in the worst musical excesses of the Italian opera. An example of this kind is provided by the musical playlet that has recently attracted so much attention and brought the opinions pro and contra into such violent opposition: *Salome* by Richard Strauss.

The admirable technique of this work, whose tonal language is new in many respects, dazzles by means of its artistic treatment. Nonetheless, the composer falls far short of the poetic original and precisely in the most important moments fails to deliver what some of the older opera composers provided more unerringly in the traditional exercise of their musical-dramatic or—let us simply say—operatic profession. There is no doubt, in this case, that the music that programmatically reproduces the events on stage fails to accord completely with the poetic content that fills the drama, and sometimes—as in the musically most valuable part, the conclusion—it actually contradicts the original. The language of the singing falls far below the symphonic language, and the very thing that should provide the main artistic value of the musical drama, the communication of emotional content in song, is nipped in the bud.

As in the musical drama of our day, so the same thing is true of the setting of many lieder texts, in which the striving after the most intimate marriage of music and poetry brings about a *mésalliance* in which the thought content of the text remains outside the realm of the music and the words seem to be babbled into an empty barrel.

The art of the past offers us enough examples of how this striving for the intimate marriage of word and melody can be accomplished without falling into such extremes. In this regard the works of Franz Schubert—whom I have characterized as one of the first modern artists, according to our point of view—offer incomparable and unsurpassed examples, especially his latest compositions, for example, to texts by Heine. Outwardly, the technical artistic treatments of subsequent eras have advanced much farther; but sometimes it was just running and fighting without any sense or purpose. What has emerged in the area of lieder composition in the period since Schubert, with its much more copious means of modulation and rhythm, achieves this goal of the congruence of poetry and music only on those occasions when it has behaved in the manner of these last songs of Schubert, created without external form. Here again we see that form alone does not suffice. Even if in the future the form that occupies the highest place in the pure [instrumental] music of our era—namely, the sonata form—should be unable to be further developed, either because it is worn out or used up or because it proves inadequate to the content that the composer has in mind, we would not need to worry for long: new forms will be created and developed that, though they may be different in nature, will be appropriate for the purpose the composer wants to achieve. There are already indications of this. In any case, the relationship between poetry and music must be put back on the right track; the overflowing mass of the orchestra must be brought back within its banks, and the means of vocal presentation must be helped to achieve their rightful place. It is a good symptom that, in general, increased and general attention is once more being paid to vocal music. In this turn toward the vocal I see the principal task of the opera of the future.

Alongside these purely artistic problems, the social side of musical composition must also be considered. The complex of relevant questions is very considerable; it includes economic, pedagogical, didactic, and associated elements. As in every sphere, here, too, the movement of the lower strata of society into the upper ones is of particular significance for the art of our era. During the period of the Viennese classical composers, alongside the aristocracies, which cultivated music and had among their officials and servants almost no one but musicians and players from whom they could form orchestras and choruses, associations drawn from bourgeois circles and dedicated to the cultivation and encouragement of instrumental and vocal music also began to gain prominence. In the most recent period, these have been joined by workers' associations, which are sufficiently trained to perform oratorios and choral works. Today these groups are also being introduced to the classical instrumental works, which are being met with a gradually increasing clarity of comprehension and an enthusiastic reception. Good programs there, as everywhere, are a life-and-death artistic question. Today the works of classical instrumental music, and the timeless masterpieces of past periods in general, can be performed by lay associations, especially those formed from among bourgeois circles, with the result that the level of musical education as well as the general cultural level are raised. Thus the circle of those who participate in music either passively or actively is expanded. The greater this participation is, the greater is the probability of gaining real talents for music, whose products not only are the result of a freely creating and disciplined fantasy but also depend on material conditions of all kinds.

Our era, with the gigantic demands made by practicing artists on the capabilities of those who reproduce their work, demands extensive support from the broadest strata of the population, on the one hand by associations of lay persons and on the other hand by appropriate guild organizations of performing artists. Schools and teaching play an important role—not only professional musical schools but also musical activities in all other educational institutions, from primary schools to the universities. The type of support that is given to art by public bureaucracies and private associations, as well as by individuals, must be considered. All this is of significance for artistic and thus also for general cultural life. A healthy music can only flourish in ethically healthy circumstances. Proof of this is offered by the biographies of the leading intellects in the sphere of music, as in all other artistic fields. Talent and ability must be paired with the strictest sense of duty; even to the greatest genius it is given to fulfill his artistic task only in this way.

In order to awaken talent, people who do not participate professionally in music should be given the opportunity to explore the essence of music or to approach it, either by attending classes or by listening. For music, in regard to artistic education, it should only be emphasized that vocal instruction generally seems more effective than instrumental performance. In primary and secondary school, slumbering talents can be awakened and brought to remarkable musical receptivity through the proper encouragement of vocal music. In the professional schools, the masterworks of the past should be cultivated in such a way as to awaken a sense of the historical development of music. By deepening our study of history, we also learn to understand our own era better. From this starting point, the results of scientific study should be applied practically in the broadest circles. Pursued in this fashion, music will be not a luxury item but a purely cultural means of education and pleasure, and it will make everything in the human spirit and soul resound that awakens its inner music and encourages the harmonious development of all its spiritual powers and of the balance and harmony of its essential being. However much one must allow every artist the right to pursue his individuality, his artistic drive, and his inclinations, whatever the beginning and end of his strivings and accomplishments may be, in general it seems justified to demand that the artwork of the future should take as its goal not stimulating or overstimulating the nerves but rather having an elevating effect by awakening spiritual vibrations and providing balm and consolation amid the confusions of our daily struggles.

[Source: *Neue Freie Presse* (17 December 1906)]

·

Richard Strauss's *Salome:* Premiere in Vienna at the Deutsches Volkstheater on 15 May 1907 by the Opera Society of Breslau

ROBERT HIRSCHFELD

Salome as opera represents what is most annoying in art and therefore what is worst. I do not wish to be misunderstood; annoying, in art, is only what is superfluous. Art demands that the simplest and most powerful, the most delicate and severest things all arise out of inner necessity. Annoying, therefore, is every unorganic form, and annoying, too, is everything that harms our emotions without inner justification or draws them into a risky game. Things that are common or perverse, therefore, are not at all annoying if nature itself pushes in that direction, if natural drives bring them into being. What Salome experiences in the play by Oscar Wilde is grounded in her own nature, in the character of the age of decline. It is the final throes of a dying state behind which a new one is dawning. The poetic means of an inexpressibly delicately organized language serve to soften the events, and a profound historical perspective draws our gaze, in the picture created by Wilde's play, past the real events.

Annoying, because unnecessary and not generated by adequate aesthetic motives, is the musical treatment of the material, which illustrates the entire play, word for word, with music. As clever as the attempt, in its originality, may seem to uncertain viewers, it is after all only a presumptuous curiosity, a stimulating sensation that destroys every healthy feeling for art. It is not correct, as Strauss partisans imagine, that the subject of *Salome* "cries to be put to music." The music simply cried for this material.

The art of Richard Strauss bears, like *Salome,* deep traces of decay: from *Zarathustra* it drags itself lasciviously to the children's room; from the *Domestica* it staggers to the excesses of impure blood and demands the head of John the Baptist. The public stares hypnotically, like slaves of the tetrarch, at the bloodthirsty music, then throws the shield of indignation over it and, laughing sarcastically, leaves the house that has incited its curiosity. That is the true picture of the most recent opera premiere.

Why should music, which is really a reflection of the will of the world, not also seek to represent atrocity and horror? The annoying aspect of Strauss's error does not lie here. But his music has seized upon Wilde's work without aesthetic necessity, indeed contrary to artistic logic, and, far from giving form to something higher, it has merely destroyed Oscar Wilde's play. In a tragicomical misunderstanding of Richard Wagner's principles, Strauss, in order to escape from the Scylla of a miserable libretto, cast himself into the Charybdis of the erroneous notion that a "finished" work could best be adapted to music. Wagner's texts are poetry but with unique laws: in their conception, an organic connection to the music is already foreseen. Wagner's poetic works are created in such a way that the emotional language of the music can stream in broadly and powerfully, lifting up and carrying the word along on its waves. Wilde's poetry does not support this invasion. It has within it the gentlest music; it is as if it is spun out of music. The elements, the rhythms of its mobile language, the remarkable syncopation of its thoughts, the gentle melding of harmonious and dissonant words, the retards of the ideas and also the disposition of the pauses, which Richard Strauss has unnecessarily tried to stop up with orchestral music—all these, in Wilde's poetry, are intrinsically musical. It is cruel to destroy music with music. Oscar Wilde's poetry is moonlight. In this airy magic Richard Strauss installs the spotlights of his leitmotifs. The destiny of non-original inventions decrees that these motives, straying through the territory of ancient masters,—"One might think he sought dead things"—finally do not disdain the healthier fare of the *Barber of Seville*. The wonderful, much-praised transparency of Wilde's poetry must now allow the workings of an entire opera to shine through it. Into the starry shimmer of the mysterious night sky bursts the sunny brightness of the Straussian orchestra and the assembled tenors. Dreadful!

Right at the beginning the longing of the young Syrian is transformed into the immensely comical outburst of a hopeful tenor. And then—John the Baptist with the operatic gestures of a gorgeous baritone! That one is forced to be a party to such a thing! . . . The *Faust* monologue or the singing Hamlet are embarrassing enough in opera. But we are informed daily that we have now ascended the highest heights of aesthetic culture and that Richard Strauss is the leader of the musical aesthetes!

Where Oscar Wilde lets unpleasant thoughts drift off lightly or disappear into darkness, lest they cause us pain, the Straussian orchestra holds them fast and works them over with all the means afforded by harmonic and instrumental technique. Where Oscar Wilde is moved by gentle feelings, Richard Strauss is conceptually specific. Where Oscar Wilde permits the witty dialectic of a sinking culture to sparkle, Richard Strauss covers it with the emotional aspects of musical forms. So in the famous quintet of the Jews: the characteristically twisted idea content at the heart of the dispute is suddenly overwhelmed with an artificial counterpoint in which finally only the dynamic of the voices and gestures is recognizable. Does not the eternally excited Straussian orchestra, accompanying and whispering over the events with distorted harmonic images, in its restless, grotesque gestural language, play precisely the role of that group of voluble Jews in Wilde's drama? Not a word is spoken but the explicators in the orchestra must deliberate upon and develop it far and wide. In the age of illustration even the terrible event at the well, the falling and rolling of the dear head, must be demonstrated by the orchestra. O this infamous exactitude! Who, in Oscar Wilde's drama, would ever, at this decisive point, have missed the book illustration? The style of Wilde's poetry stands in opposition to this technical undertaking. And what is now the upshot of the heartbreaking moment? . . . The public cranes its neck toward the orchestra and wants to see how Richard Strauss does that. And at the end, too, Salome must remain in the kiss for as long as Richard Strauss's music—music of monstrosity—is pleased to develop it.

One will not be so backward as to demand that dramatic music, in the explication of the fearful, should offer a catharsis, a purification of the emotions, a discharge of the passions, liberation, exaltation. Music no longer follows the paths that were laid out by the masters who came before Wagner. It ceaselessly electrifies and discharges the spirit; it rattles and bangs until the emotions are worn out; it no longer wants anything but explosions, and the dynamic of these has no effect but that of dynamite. The virtuosity of the well-known

Straussian operatic experiments has been heightened to a monstrous degree. Cleverly worked-out series of tones that calculatedly resist every ordinary comprehension rob the ear of its powers of discretion: the most far-flung notes are rubbed together so that it rains sparks. Cruel harmonic jokes, which Richard Strauss once permitted himself only as exceptions, have become the rule. Trivialities, Verdi-offshoots, everyday comprehensibilities as well as incomprehensibilities are tossed into the spicy mixture: art has become nothing but a great pestle. The enormous intellectual qualities that are required to bring it into being—to pile motives that were never heard before on top of yet other unheard-of things and still give the illusion of larger cohesion to the whole—are certainly not to be underestimated. The Straussian orchestra with its limitless polyphony, with the infinite transitions in the instrumental spectrum of colors and the harmonic analysis that reminds one of chemical experiments, demonstrates in every new work the very pinnacle of what it is possible to achieve to date. And the view from this pinnacle? Again the next-higher one, and so on; the musical air becomes thinner and thinner; the vegetation of musical art disappears, and only the record of possibilities, the application of new climbing techniques, beckons afar. . . .

[Source: *Wiener Abendpost* (26 May 1907)]

·

Salome: Music Drama in One Act after Oscar Wilde, by Richard Strauss

MAX KALBECK

In the wax museums and anatomical display cabinets of speculative sideshow owners there are certain sections that are hung with curtains bearing the words "Admission for adults only" or "Customers with weak nerves are warned not to visit this room" and that contain some monstrosity as the actual main attraction of their otherwise very harmless collections. With particular refinement the mass of the curious public identifies itself adequately as to its majority or the strength of its nerves, and the owner of the booth, completely unconcerned about the physical and moral consequences of his tidy little business, rubs his hands with satisfaction. Our great sideshows, otherwise known as theaters, are currently enjoying the strangest specialty, which is everywhere exerting an irresistibly alluring appeal on the sensation-starved public. Its novelty outstrips all other novelties; its gruesome subject tempts everyone to test and display, to whatever degree he wishes, the steadiness of his already much-tested soul and the strength and resilience of his nerves.

The music drama *Salome,* by Wilde-Strauss—for it is this that I wish to speak about—outwardly reveals its fatal similarity with the main attraction of a wax museum and curiosity cabinet in the form of the realistic imitation of a severed human head, which, dressed and presented on a gleaming silver platter, is the pièce de résistance of this voluptuously disgusting feast for the senses. To have dragged the sacred head of John the Baptist onto the stage, where it is abandoned to the unnatural desires of a degenerate, shameless, and wanton paramour before the eyes of the horrified audience, is the disreputable accomplishment of the English erotomaniac and aesthete Oscar Wilde. The story is told of the poet's mother that she gave a youthful friend of her son, who visited her when young Oscar was away, the advice that sin is the most beautiful thing in life. No wonder the son of such a mother brought upon himself, through the systematic abuse of his physical and mental gifts, the crude and foolish fate to which he succumbed in the bloom of his youth.[24] It has unfortunately become customary to cite the regrettable fate of the unfortunate artist as a defense against his aesthetic crimes or to excuse Wilde's dissolute life by reference to his even more dissolute writings. In our opinion, criticism should not act as a sister of mercy to art, which, when it reaches beyond temporal phenomena into eternity, does not need any such thing—sympathy only corrupts taste and character. No doubt Wilde, with his great poetic talents, could have produced more than the golden nuggets of grace, intelligence, and wit that are strewn among the mud of his writings. May the remainder be appreciated and used, with caution, as a valuable fertilizer for future cultures!

At least Wilde has produced more significant things than the unworthy and insignificant *Salome,* which is patched together from the debris of various literatures cloaked in elevated biblical language. It is possible that the poet wished to develop the tragic end of John the Baptist, which is found in the fourteenth chapter of the Gospel according to Matthew, into a magnificent worldview. Others before and after him have attempted this—for example, Gustave Flaubert in "Herodias," the last of his *Trois contes.*[25] But Wilde either did not feel himself equal to such a task or, in the course of carrying it out, thought worse of it. For instead of following Flaubert's lead and developing the world-historical side of the novella, he allowed himself to be enthralled by the poetical parts of the legend, which encouraged his sexual-pathological tendency; by the dance of Salome, which is described in detail by Flaubert; and by the rigid figure of the un-approachable saint. Pulled from his underground dungeon into the light of day and confronted in as sharp and crass a manner as possible by the lewd daughter of Herodias, whose senses lust for foreign charms, John the Baptist was guaranteed to produce a prickling sensation. Therefore Wilde stumbled from Flaubert to Heine.[26] In his fantastic-satirical *Atta Troll*, Heine reinterpreted the medieval cautionary tale about the tempestuous head of John the Baptist with fearful irony and used it for a wonderful, lyrical episode of his adventure in the Pyrenees. In Flaubert the disgusting love of Salome for the severed, bloody head is lacking, as, in his work, Salome, following the Gospel, is merely the unwilling tool of Herodias. She has so little interest in her victim that after the end of her dance she does not even recall his name. "Je veux que tu me donnes dans un plat la tête" [I want you to give me on a platter the head], she says to Herod, and hesitates. She had forgotten the name, writes Flaubert, but she continued with a smile: "la tête de Jokanan." And she says all that "d'un air enfantin"—with a childlike air.

This is also how Herodias had been portrayed by the earlier visual arts—as the completely naive, ingenuous, misled, dutiful child of her repulsive mother. One of the oldest representations (in Siena) shows her turning away from the head, full of horror. Titian went so far as to give the platter to his charming Lavinia to carry, and she lifts it up with the same cheerfulness as if it were a basket of fruit. Salome appears similarly in Guercino, Carlo Dolci, and others. In the masterpieces of Klinger and Klimt,[27] she appears in a symbolic light, as a lewd, cruel woman already, it seems, under the influence of the misunderstood Heine and his awkward, infamous imitator. Heine uses humor to deaden the embarrassing effect of his vision and liberate the emotions. Identifying Salome with Herod's wife, he writes:

> In her hands she always bears
> That platter, with the severed head
> Of John the Baptist, which she kisses;
> Kisses it with fiery passion.
> Once, you see, she loved the Baptist—
> That's not what the Bible says,
> But an ancient folk tale tells us
> Of Herodias's bloody passion.

Jocularly, he adds:

> Otherwise how could one fathom

> The amorous passion of that woman—
> Would a woman desire the head
> Of a man she does not love?

The singer of *Atta Troll* was not so deeply initiated into the mysteries of sexual pathology as our moderns, who are extraordinarily scientific in this regard. He knew nothing of the dreadful aberrations of a natural drive that stills its desire with blood and corpses, and if he knew about it, he did not take such abnormalities for the subjects of artistic creation but rather thought like Goethe, who demands of art that it should "not portray what is offensive." Excesses that were previously cloaked in seven veils of darkness are staggering around today free and unfettered in the light of day, having thrown off one veil after the other in their dance. First denied and persecuted, then described and discussed, then understood and excused, then beautified and imitated, they are finally praised and glorified.

Wilde's drama, in the final analysis, represents nothing but a glorification of the beast in woman. Crude and dilettantish to the point of ridiculousness in its execution, it leaves the spectator ignorant of the reasons for the John the Baptist tragedy, transforming it into the Salome affair, which can only be explained by invoking exceptional psychophysiological states. Thus he gives [his] poetic sensibility and creativity over to an intoxicated reveling in horror, to the concentration of lustful deliriums. Adultery, incest, and sexual madness are the motives; suicide, execution, and necrophilia the consequences of this drama, which spends itself in brutal effects and is so drastic that it seems to demand a palliative. Richard Strauss gave Oscar Wilde's *Salome* this kind of relief. His music should be understood as a purgative for the tragedy, and it accomplishes this cleansing of the dark and confused passions by means of colossal exaggeration, which, admittedly against the will of the composer, turns into parody. Wilde's drama would have caused the most acute embarrassment to any simpleminded composer to whom it occurred to examine the dramatic material with regard to its suitability for the musical expression of emotions and situations. How should the paralytic tetrarch Herod, tormented by compulsions, and his scolding vixen of a wife, who was jealous of her own daughter, sing? What kind of melodies should he put into the mouth of the amorous Salome, lusting after filth and blood, when she has the starving saint of the desert, covered with the refuse of his damp prison cell, brought up out of the cistern and praises the details of his doubtful male beauty before the assembled soldiery in the style of the Song of Songs? And what solemn tones should be used to accompany the oaths of the intermittent preacher at the well, the dark monologues of the occasional underground prophet who always speaks up at the wrong moment, when John the Baptist fills the gaps in the above-ground dramatic entertainment with Bible quotes?

For a Richard Strauss there were no such questions and misgivings. A stepson of music, who takes revenge for his poor powers of melodic invention by trying to reduce the gentle art of music to a soulless and heartless jumble of instrumental effects and hair-raising dissonances, this sovereign ruler of the orchestra did without the pleasing intervention of a librettist and composed the antimusical drama just as he found it, stuttering and stammering, storming and raging, shrieking and screaming, whimpering and howling, groaning and moaning, from Narraboth's first, thrice-repeated trivial exclamation to the last, brief, lethal command of Herod, which comes as if shot from a pistol. "How lovely Princess Salome looks this evening," and "Have this woman killed!" are the poles of a musical drama that far exceeds everything previously achieved in this area in regard to shameless exploitation of all the artificial material means that have been created for this purpose and ostentatious display of dazzling and deceiving inessentials, which glitter with a thousand nuances. "Vive la Bagatelle!" is the motto of the intricate score. From the thousands and thousands of tone particles that are shaken up in kaleidoscopic fashion, colorful images and bright constellations emerge as if of their own volition and attempt to condense the billowing fog into a world. But no strong tone issues from the heavenly depths of the unconscious to order and rule over the whole.

Only an eros could transform the artificially created chaos into the cosmos—but the artist's love froze in the rime of his overactive mechanics; its awakening call never sounds. The most eloquent and sensitive, the first and last organ of spiritual expression, with which no mechanical sound-producing instrument, however finely made and perfected, can compete—the human voice—has been forced to renounce its inborn right of leadership and sovereignty and relinquish its rule to the noisy chorus of the instruments, which, with its tendency to mob rule, deprives the voice of its right to speak. Ass's intestine and calf's hide, wood and reed, metal and glass are the leading spokesmen. In the giant organ of the Straussian orchestra the *vox humana* represents only one register. If only for this reason, one ought not to speak, in the case of *Salome*, of music drama.

We do not wish to be misunderstood and thought, for example, to be contemptuous of instrumental music with its splendors. No, we

too know and believe that it is destined—even more than vocal music—to communicate the most profound and lofty sense of all that is
inexpressible in the mind and heart of a human being. But in a
drama it is a matter less of the inexpressible than of the clearly spoken or sung, meaningful human word, and there it is bad when the
speaker and singer are outdone by a subordinate, purely sensual, ap-
purtenance. I want to hear not what the oboe thinks about a certain
case but rather what the person on stage who is affected by it has to
say about it. The orchestra can complement and raise the level of plot
and dialogue; it cannot replace it, no matter how many leitmotifs it
introduces as evidence. Strauss seems, through the great number of
such repeatedly recurring series of tones, to be trying to make up for
their lack of plastic form and effective impression.

With minor exceptions, these tonal phrases are so unimpressive, expressionless, and insubstantial that we hardly notice them, much less
are able to follow them in their changes and encounters. Not embry-
onic seeds of their own melodies but rather splinters of alien
thoughts, they remind one of this and that, only not the things they
are meant to represent and stand for. Often they are the rhythmic
or phonetic reproduction of a sentence, an interjection, and the
breadth of their tones exactly fits the sound of the syllables of elevated
speech; or they are coloristic in nature, tone-painterly abstractions of
some irrelevant objects or other. To create in tones a gentle still life
that contrasts with the dramatic power of the movement and to make
it resound—this is the composer's real strength. He does not allow
even the most insignificant substantive reference in the text to escape
his notice but builds it into his score, as someone taking inventory
makes note of a valuable object. How far this overconscientious painting of details goes can scarcely be calculated or measured. Much of
it is beyond our ability to determine, particularly those things that are
elevated from a material to an intellectual plane by his extraordinarily fine technique. The graceful language of Wilde, overloaded with
pictures—the Orient excuses it!—has made the sober musical muse
of the composer quite literally intoxicated. Salome's rainbow dance
with its seven veils, from which the clever seductress gradually unwinds
the pure sunlight of her alabaster body, brought the drunken muse
to a state of even greater ecstasy and even made it productive. To
us, this dramatically justified ballet scene represents the high point
of the musical drama, surpassing two other high points of the work—
the terrible illustration of the execution of John the Baptist and
Salome's infatuation with the *caput mortuum*. Here the purple sound
ocean of the painter of musical colors makes its proudest waves, and

when they close over our heads we are made blind and seeing at the same time—seeing its advantages, blind to its shortcomings. But the marvels of the palette do not last, the entrancing magic of the symphonic poem no longer holds us fast, as soon as we are reminded of the intellectual price that we have had to pay for it, and we leave the poisonous plant that has been cultivated in the greenhouse of modern hyperculture with the words of Michelangelo:

> Woe to the man who, dazzled and deluded,
> Drags beauty down into the sensual realm!
> It lifts the healthy spirit up to heaven.

[Source: *Neues Wiener Tageblatt* (28 May 1907)]

·

Richard Strauss's *Salome:* A Conversation

JULIUS KORNGOLD

"Well?"

"How beautiful *was* Princess Salome?"

"Do you mean that you have lost your enthusiasm? I saw you watching very intently."

"Would I deny 'effects'? Would I deny 'charms'?"

"I see that you are sitting in front of a mountain of printed material—actually, articles and brochures about *Salome*. For someone who does not go along with it, you are thorough."

"One wants, after all, to hear from others what *Salome* is for them. Listen: 'Salome is the defeat of Wagner and his impotent distortion, a step forward for art and its dismal decay, new musical-dramatic territory and a monument to a sick era, a triumph of the power of modern musical form and its declaration of bankruptcy, a creative deed and a mere triumph of tonal technique, a revelation and a commercial gimmick, an inspiration and a calculation, a precious fruit and a running sore.' Truly, the inner value of this work does not seem to have been entirely settled . . ."

"Yes, if you ask people who are members of the guild. But listen beyond the printed page to the public, and *Salome* is a world success."

"Certainly—if you mean that the value of her stock has gone up. Within two years the daughter of Herodias has traveled all over Europe and even America. The French received her, even though she spoke German, with a politeness that is historic. In Germany she rules as the trumpeter of Säckingen once did—and he had no vices.[28] None of the most famous opera heroines before Salome had it so good, least of all Wagner's—not even, to mention a lady who was also of some sexual interest, Bizet's Carmen."

"You won't draw any conclusions from all this?"

"Some, after all. Art that is truly original and profound generally requires a longer period to put down roots. When I see such prompt, general, and vehement effects, I hesitate and involuntarily look for sensational elements. They are not lacking, as I convinced myself yesterday. They are present in the material, in the adaptation of music to such material, and then fully in the cut of the music itself."

"The material? You don't mean to say anything against Wilde?"

"Certainly nothing against Wilde: a poet, an artist, whom I love; one who wrote the most seductive paradoxes and experienced the most terrible things. With his *Salome,* admittedly, I have a sense that it is arranged. This oppressive dream is staged, complete with its Oriental draperies. Wilde read Flaubert, then the Bible, stood in front of the numerous Salome paintings. The mysterious little princess demanded the head of the Baptist for a dance—where is the motive? The poet was looking for the most original one. He almost made his Salome gentle and chaste, as you know, and allowed Jehovah, whose enemy was to be destroyed, to endow her with the fateful talent for ballet. But then, after all, he gave her sick nerves. With that she had become very contemporary, in this time of neurasthenia, dispositions to hysteria, and sexual problems. And Richard Strauss? He always had an eye out for anything that was contemporary. A musician who is modern through and through, including keeping up with literary modernity, with all its moods and fantasies, and heeding the currents of the times. The dancing Salome could scarcely escape the notice of Strauss, the creator of the dancing Zarathustra. And you know he already paused at Elektra's blood mania."

"Allow me to say something. You have probably read Wilde's *De Profundis,* this heart-wrenching self-conversion from a proud religion of beauty to the self-lacerating one of pain? Here is the poor prisoner speaking of *Salome:* 'It is a refrain that recurs in *Salome,* by means of which she so truly resembles a musical work and is put together like a ballad.' And don't you hear the music in his language, the way it reverberates with the Song of Songs?"

"That is supposed to mean that the poetry cried out for music? No, my dear friend, only the musician cried out for poetry. Do you really believe it would ever have occurred to Wilde to make room for him in his bed? If a poet makes his own music, the last thing he needs is another one. Wilde didn't need Strauss, but Strauss needed Wilde and found in his poems something related to his art: the most daring realisms, something that occurs completely within the world of the senses and nerves, that is all mood and color, that glows and burns outwardly and remains cold inside. Wit and satanic spirit go together. Even Offenbach provides an example of this: see *Tales of Hoffmann* . . ."

"And do you consider it a weakness if the artist chooses his materials according to his individual talent? Gives form, as an opera composer, to new moods, expands the scope of its material? You smile— you are thinking about Salome's desires. Don't think I am a heretic— in this regard I can find nothing that dishonors our beloved music. Step by step we saw how, in recent years, she let go of her idealism. Now she really resembles those modern girls who are still being anxiously protected from dangers while they—already know everything. At every moment she is being told, 'That is not appropriate for you,' but she has already read the seamiest pulp novels, made her acquaintance with crime and vulgarity, befriended the whore—and without inner damage, believe me. Why should something that is human remain foreign to music, of all things? Music has never avoided coarse sensuality; it climbed out of that dark well; the sexual drives were always involved in dance music. . . . And didn't our master in Bayreuth let brother and sister unite in passionate love?"

"Don't confuse great pathos with petty psychology. In *Salome* we are talking about pathological lust. What you are saying about the subjects of opera music—no one is more in agreement with you there than I am. But there are limits, and I for my part would rather draw them all the more narrowly, the more I see music itself slide into realism. All music softens, it is said. That applies least of all to a music with the unheard-of powers of imitation we find in Richard Strauss. It outstrips its material, completely exposes it; now he rips off all seven veils. But a scene like the final scene in *Salome* refuses every kind of collaboration by music. Nothing is more characteristic than that Strauss himself vacillated here, changed his system."

"?"

"Salome has her John the Baptist head, kisses it, couples with it. Here Strauss breaks with his principle; here he *wishes* to soften, to make 'beautiful,' that means—even for him—melodic and songful music for a redeeming conclusion. And what is the result? The scene only becomes more revolting."

"How can you say such a thing! I admit that here the musician departed from the path of the poet. His art triumphed all the more splendidly. It carries out and lends credence to a psychological change in Salome, lets her have love in place of destructive lust, and now Salome feels what other women feel . . ."

"With a bloody head in her hands and with kisses for a dismembered corpse. No, my dear friend, those are phrases, artificial euphemistic constructions, and in the printed material I have in front of me there are all kinds of variations on that theme. Salome with the above-mentioned silver platter and its contents cannot turn into Isolde. Salome's *Liebestod*—there is no such thing. The more beautifully and soulfully she begins to sing, the worse. Salome turns into an opera singer too late; she should have thought about it earlier, from the beginning. It would not have been a hair more grotesque if she had sung the Vilja song at the end.[29] Here she must not sing at all. You probably notice yourself that it was not possible to set Wilde's short drama, in the completed form in which Strauss found it, to music. That kind of thing always has its unavoidable problems. In this last scene it was completely wrong: music *slows things down*."

"Don't you have a few strong comments for me about Strauss's music? What will I have to hear from you on that score!"

"I do not deny its qualities, but I judge them differently from you."

"At least you will admit what is new about this music?"

"Not entirely, my friend. It is by no means entirely new in style. To stick with Strauss himself: no leap from *Feuersnot* to *Salome* like that from *Tannhäuser* to *Tristan*. It is true that both works probably have their roots in Wagner, in his orchestral symphony, in its leitmotif."

"That's what I say too. Without Wagner's leitmotif no 'motivic polyphony for coloristic purposes' in Strauss. And thank you for being the one to bring up Strauss's symphonic poems. I need them. How often one hears theater music in *Heldenleben, Don Quixote, Domestica*! Theater music with *invisible* scenery. Now, in *Salome*, the scenery becomes *visible*. The 'program' is spoken—truly more spoken than sung—and portrayed on stage. That is the style of *Salome*. It is a symphonic poem that paints with motives, imitates realism, and goes over completely to the theater, to which it already owes so much. To recall the Wilde remark you quoted earlier, it is a great ballad, a scenically portrayed symphonic ballad."

"I accept that. And does one not, in this way, achieve a unity that was never attained in the past?"

"Certainly, and I particularly value this positive trait of *Salome*. But let us not forget that music drama needs more. So now I shall tell you how the theater adapted itself to the symphony. It became impressionistic, in two respects: first in the artist's unconstrained surrender to every nuance of mood that the scene offers; and then in the way he handles color, which is almost totally reminiscent of a painterly conception. That, too, is not entirely new; the Frenchman Debussy led the way, although without the fat of polyphony and without the impetus that is characteristic of things German. But I guess you don't recognize the result that derives from all this: a dominance by the orchestra that is quite without precedent. It reaches heights that even Wagner would never ever have attempted to scale, and for good reason. It represents a degradation of the vocal element, of dramatic singing. The singing in *Salome*—often nothing but droning, nervous speech, excited screams! And what dominates once again in the dominant orchestra? Color and instrumental mood values by far outweigh melody, motives, and themes. *Melos,* which Wagner, above all else, upheld as his highest principle, drops to second place here. *Melos* abdicates; collateral musical lines ascend the throne. A dangerous overthrow of the current hierarchy of the means of musical representation, admittedly accomplished with fabulous virtuosity."

"And if you were right, what difference does it make, if as a result the music in *Salome* has become capable of the finest differentiation of moods, the most wonderful expressive power, the likes of which have never been known before? And let me quote Oscar Wilde again: 'Color in itself is already a true mystical life of things.'"

"A saying for the most modern school of painting, with which Strauss's music admittedly has much in common. But if you will permit, we will wax enthusiastic about the painterly powers—not expressive powers—of the *Salome* orchestra later on. Above all, I miss the principal expression: that of melody."

"And would you really ignore the motives and themes of *Salome* and their polyphonic links?"

"Not their polyphonic use, for I admire its particular technique—although it, too, has to be seen as more coloristic than well drawn. But I would prefer you not to talk to me about the motives in *Salome*. These skimpy successions of notes often seem like the result of an accidental mood. How banal their core is! One is tempted to conclude that the composer feels a certain indifference toward his thematic material, since he can rely on the added weight it will gain from weaving and coloring. Can you comprehend that John the Baptist, who should rise up larger than life, compellingly ideal, has to content himself now with a weak Mendelssohnian phrase, now with a couple of fourths capriciously piled on top of each other, or with some chromatics left over from Amfortas? John the Baptist! From his cistern he already makes an impression reminiscent of the old opera.

And at the same time, what a musical ascetic!"

"All right, I will sacrifice the head of John the Baptist to you! But Salome's lyrical songs, steeped in the steamy breath of the Orient?"

"I will not bring as evidence the fact that in Paris, by giving the wrong interpretation to a few melismas, they could be considered 'Italian.' I can find these few vocal phrases neither original nor exactly distinguished. I will accept the soft final cantilena. So far as actual Salome themes are concerned, I will admit only the nervous rhythm. The temptation motive seems to have been borrowed from a military trumpet call. . . ."

"For shame! Now, as punishment, you must praise the orchestra for me!"

"With complete conviction. This is where Strauss's inventiveness is to be found, in the main; here I bow before a particular talent of genius. Strauss multiplies the musical individuals; gets up to six clarinets; finds a new, deeper oboe, the heckelphone; calls for an array of percussion with a generosity that rivals Mahler. Celesta, xylophone, harmonium, organ all chime in. This orchestra can do anything. It not only captures every aural phenomenon but mirrors everything else that occurs in the sensual world as well. One hears killing, perceives the trembling ripples of a frightened soul, senses the 'icy wind,' feels the awakening, increase, and groaning of desire. When jewels are mentioned, the orchestra sparkles like a wonderful huge diamond. It is as if it were saturated with the fumes of this dreadful *Salome* world. Vague reveries, dark rushes of feeling, brutal lust, the failure of sick nerves, delirium, paroxysms, sharp screams, bellowing, howling—everything in this orchestra. What inexhaustible mixtures, what mysterious, satanic, orgiastic, bacchantic sounds!"

"Bravo! I couldn't express my feelings any more enthusiastically. If orchestral color can do so much, then hats off to the 'color' that is so much despised!"

"Despised? Not at all. Only not valued more highly than it should be. As much as I admire it, I do not mistake the nature of these effects. You can tell from my descriptions, and your own nerves must also teach you something about it. And I am still not done with the orchestra of *Salome*. Strauss's harmonic practice, which fills out the great paint box, is also part of it."

"Here you must also confess the wealth of invention."

"No; the great harmonic discoverers brought necessities, revealed nature. In the harmonies of *Salome* you find all the laws of progression, stages, tonal relationships as if blown away. Is it possible to hold on to the concept of modulation if a chord literally lies in two keys?

At one point D minor and B major are in each other's arms like that, if an example will make you happy. Tones and sounds bump up against one another as if in chance encounters. Every other measure contains a friendly reminder to destroy all the books on harmonic technique—which, by the way, I would not regret. This frightful element of cacophony, admittedly, undergoes a transformation in the midst of the Straussian orchestra. It is often said that this orchestra disguises the discordance. More properly: it transforms it into a simple color value."

"Now take a moment to look at the progression of the work. Its divisions are so full of life! The curtain rises and at once we are surrounded by an alien world, an oppressive atmosphere of moonlit nights pregnant with disaster."

"At the same time, I find the exposition drags. In the speeches and responses of the captain [Narraboth], the mercenaries, and Salome herself too much Wilde has been retained. The composer was forced to continue the prelude for too long."

"John the Baptist appears before Salome. Her thrice-reiterated, fiery wooing, her repeated bacchantic cry 'I want to kiss your mouth, John' lead up to the first great crescendo . . ."

"You mean the first paroxysms."

". . . which concludes with a broad orchestral interlude, whose *Schwung* you will concede. This marks a kind of break in your 'symphonic ballad.' Now a necessary lessening of the suspense follows: the impotent lusting of the weak-nerved Herod after his stepdaughter. Herod is given a peculiar, bizarre scale that seems to sink swooning to the earth. And then a humoristic intermezzo delays the revival of the action even longer: the quintet of the quarreling Jews."

"Here Strauss is in his element, that of witty imitation. Nevertheless the grotesque piece suffers from rhythmic and harmonic distortions. A joke that, by the way, is quite old in music. Just between the two of us, doesn't the whole vocal score of *Salome* sound somewhat Jewish?"[30]

"Now the dramatic torrent gradually begins to swell again. In counterpoint he brings lustful Herod; rejecting, watchful Salome; poisonous Herodias. And a droning pedal point: John the Baptist in the cistern. And suddenly the event that sets off the catastrophe: Herod asks Salome to dance for him."

"The dance is too long, despite all the fine, colorful, varied lights in the orchestra that fall on this mosaic of motives. And oddly the most elemental intoxication is lacking here—that of movement."

"And the art of dramatic suspense, the gripping energy that Strauss develops in what follows, when Salome demands and receives from Herod the head of John the Baptist?"

"But don't talk to me about the execution music, about that certain howling string of the double bass."

"And now the last, powerful, simultaneously reconciling crescendo: Salome's love song."

"Here beauty appears, even if it is not in the right place. *Pulchrum est, sed non hic erat locus* . . .[31] Now let me give a short summary. *Salome* is undoubtedly the most Straussian of Strauss's works and at the same time the first unmistakable evidence of his theatrical blood, his scenic abilities. It demonstrates once more that the talents with which this admirable master of technique is endowed lie principally on one side of his art: that of colorful description, of ruthlessly realistic imitation. And one might almost say that the place occupied in Wagner by endless melody is now taken over, in Strauss, by endless color. But even endless melody was at least—melody. The more noble and mature, more long-lasting effects and powers of music, which the musical-dramatic work of art cannot do without, are knocked out of commission in *Salome*. Didn't Strauss sense that himself when he attempted to crown his work with a 'beautiful melody'?"

"Say what you want: for me the living impression is decisive. *Salome* seizes my attention and has me in its power."

"And I no longer feel the slightest thing after the curtain has fallen. The soul goes away empty. Would Wagner's new art have been victorious if it hadn't touched our feelings with new greatness, new beauty? The effects of the 'merely characteristic' don't last, and the strongest stimuli for our nerves grow dull. Believe me, dear friend, in the short or the long run you will be exclaiming with me: 'How beautiful *was* Princess Salome!'"

[Source: *Neues Wiener Tagblatt* (28 May 1907)]

·

Der Rosenkavalier: Comedy for Music by Hugo von Hofmannsthal, Music by Richard Strauss

JULIUS KORNGOLD

Although his superior talents have caused him to be designated a leading musician, no one is less suited to this role than Richard Strauss. The Germans want a priest, someone who will champion an art that serves profound ends. Strauss is driven by the ego sensibility of the modern artist, who wants, first of all, to serve himself and his sensations. Living entirely in the present, in its tendencies and interests, he smiles skeptically or storms impatiently past the solemn demands of immortality. Thus the strange opposition of the critics when the *Rosenkavalier* appeared. What Strauss had in mind was a light work for the musical stage, something with broad appeal. But German idealism expected him to provide the musical comedy that the epoch desires in its heart. And some people, then, go on to believe what they desire; compare the *Rosenkavalier* with *Figaro* or *Meistersinger*—truly, with *Figaro* or *Meistersinger*. Other people, deeply disappointed, miss finding what they had hoped for, *because* they compare the *Rosenkavalier* to *Figaro* or *Meistersinger*—truly, with *Figaro* or *Meistersinger!* Both groups seek the new style in Strauss's musical comedy. But nothing could have been further from the intent of the *Rosenkavalier* than to offer them *that* silver rose! Elements of *Feuersnot, Elektra*, singspiel, and operetta, combined, provide neither a new style nor the style of a musical comedy at all. Better to seek in the *Rosenkavalier* the old Strauss—whom one finds, admittedly, with half-weakened, half-lame powers of invention, the victim of three overlong acts, particularly *these* acts, and only occasionally their fascinating conqueror. One finds what one loves in Strauss—this or that musical idea that gives one wings, refreshing élan, the clever play of motives, beguiling sounds, rascally jokes—and also what one loves less—lack of discrimination in the basic musical substance, lack of disposition and unity, sweetish sentimentalities. One finds, also, what one should never have found: the far-reaching, demeaning "concession." "The lovely music," it is said in the opera about such things—"it makes one cry!" Indeed.

In *Salome,* in *Elektra,* the composer had forced his way into the house of the poet. Nonetheless, it proved more accommodating than the living quarters that have been furnished for him by the poet in the *Rosenkavalier.* The poet, if one may believe his assurances, hardly wanted to keep even a garret for himself, but the labyrinthine passages of the structure occasionally led the composer into the cellar . . . Let us recall the facts. Vienna; the age of Maria Theresa. A young man of good family did well even in those days. Thus the seventeen-year-old Count Octavian Rofrano is breakfasting quite cozily after a night of love in the bedroom of Princess Werdenberg, the wife of the Field Marshal; the Field Marshal is hunting in Croatia. The tête-à-tête is interrupted by Herr Ochs von Lerchenau,[32] a cousin of the Marschallin. Octavian disguises himself in women's clothes, transforming himself into the chambermaid Mariandl. Herr von Lerchenau has left his turnip fields in order to announce to the Marschallin his engagement to Sophie, the daughter of the recently ennobled merchant Faninal, and to ask her advice about the bridegroom's assistant, who, according to a custom of the high nobility whose origins are obscure, is to present his fiancée with a silver rose—which does not prevent the noble fiancée from immediately beginning to flirt with the cute young thing, the supposed Mariandl. Discovered by the Marschallin, he goes into great detail about his countrified sex life. The Horacian *ne tibi sit amor ancillae pudori*[33] becomes the cynical confession of this lewd gentleman. Let us describe him plainly: he is a Falstaff of the manure pile, a Don Juan of the cesspool. A figure of such unconsidered remarks, manners, and mentality as has seldom set foot on the stage. Evidently he could only do so to music. As we expect, the Marschallin recommends Count Octavian to her cousin as Rosenkavalier, or Knight of the Rose. Now the "antechamber" joins the *levée*:[34] a broadly developed burlesque episode with a colorful crew of secondary characters. The notary and the chef appear, and the *marchande de modes*, a scholar, an animal peddler, a high-born mother with three daughters, a tenor, a flutist; also an Italian pair—Valzacchi, the schemer, and Annina, his companion. When the other *bagagi* have left the stage, to vanish permanently from the plot, this Latin pair makes itself useful by spying, denouncing, and generally aiding and abetting. The disreputable Lerchenau *livrée*[35] also turns up to make the picture even more refined, among them his favorite lackey, "a stupid, fresh lout" whom Lerchenau introduces as the child of an amorous hour. This Lerchenau rabble, for its part, brings all kinds of boorishness and uncleanness to the action. Like master, like servant. Finally the Marschallin tells the pack to leave. And now, when she is alone with her "boy," comes the melancholy that follows pleasure. She is getting old; how long will the young men from good families still come to visit her when the Field Marshal is hunting in Croatia? To sympathize more deeply with the amorous lady will be possible only for people who are able to see things from the erotic perspective of today's young Viennese. But when the curtain has descended for the third time, we know of this first act that it has the happiest conclusion and is ultimately the best.

At the beginning of the second act, we are also greeted with a silver ray of poetry, in the form of the silver rose that Octavian Rofrano brings the fiancée. A drop of Persian rose oil has been placed in the rose; but its perfume is soon driven away by the smell that Herr von

Lerchenau and his followers bring into the house. He approaches his fiancée with the gestures of a faun, and his servants are also forced by a stage direction, "almost knocking Sophie down" and "drunk with cognac," to throw themselves at the female servants. One can only grasp one's forehead. Must the two seventeen-year-olds find each other in the midst of disgust, including our own? The poet, in any case, gives us even more to think about in the means by which he develops his plot from here on. Octavian and Sophie are in each other's arms. Then Valzacchi and Annina, the Italians, slip out of the chimneys(!). "Annina grabs Sophie, Valzacchi takes hold of Octavian." And shout for Baron Lerchenau, who, even now, is unshaken in his distinguished way of seeing things. He has seen nothing and will hear nothing, not Sophie's refusal, not the challenging insults of Octavian. Forced to draw his sword, he receives a cut on the arm. Ochs, the ox, bellows. Tumult; grotesque attempts to help him; the Lerchenau *livrée* gloriously in ascendancy, as it attempts to tear the shirts from the backs of the younger and prettier maids in order to make bandages. "Abominable! To a nunnery!" rages the newly ennobled Faninal; "Frenchified dog!" storms the son of the old nobility. And Lerchenau's faithful servants do themselves proud with verses like the following: "If I ever catch you; / you're under the stool; / Just see what I'll do, / You Frenchified fool!" Interminable fuss; chatter.—Until Annina sneaks up and gives the wounded man a letter. It is from the chambermaid Mariandl: Octavian is baiting his trap. Cheered at once, the Baron forgets all his aches and pains along with the tip for the messenger. This kind of thing brings its revenge in Vienna. Herr von Lerchenau will experience it in the third act.

The two Italians have completely gone over to Octavian's side. They arrange the little joke that the poet has invented to amuse us. The Baron, with his willing Mariandl, has found a room at an inn, with alcoves and a bed. The feminine coquetry of a man disguised as a woman must, by itself, already provide a source of inexhaustible operetta-style amusement. When the Baron wants to turn tender, there are apparitions. From trap doors, alcoves, and the wall, faces stare out and startle the love-starved Baron. The poet thinks this is comical. A blind window springs open suddenly; a woman in mourning—Annina—appears and identifies the man as her husband. Also four children, who burst in and scream "Papa! Papa! Papa!" The poet thinks this is comical. Furious, the Baron calls the police and loses his wig, like the oldest *buffo* bass in the oldest *opera buffa*. The poet thinks this, too, is comical. Now, with the intervention of the Commissioner, there follows another spectacle scene, as wild as it is complicated, whose comedy, at least, never seems to end. In succession we hear Faninal *père,* Sophie, the Marschallin. Octavian, in an alcove, removes the insignia of the chambermaid. Ochs, discovered, leaves the field of battle, after the most shameless attempts to defend it in the face of all that has occurred. The owner of the inn, waiters, musicians, coachmen, a servant do their best to convince him; the two Italians jeer at him insolently; the children get underfoot—"he takes a swipe at them with his hat." Thus this likeable nobleman departs from the action as he entered it. Since the coast is now clear, the Marschallin, Sophie, and Octavian have things out, and the poet does so, simultaneously, with the poetry. Frau Therese is resigned. Octavian and Sophie belong to each other. One more final pantomime: the young lady, in a state of blessed transport, has dropped her handkerchief. In comes the Marschallin's little Black Boy and trips out. Curtain.

The little Black Boy is evidently meant to interrupt the tender mood of the conclusion. Are we permitted to take the handkerchief for the symbol of sentimentality? Then one may take the little Black Boy for the spirit of grotesque play that is meant to have the last word. But that spirit has already been afforded too much space in this comedy, concerning which the Marschallin has put the malicious phrase into our mouths: "The whole thing was just a farce and nothing more." The sentimental [element] is precisely the better part of the tender, young-Viennese goings-on that dominate the libretto, and also the part that is best suited for music. We will not quarrel with the slim kernel of a plot, which Hofmannsthal, weak inventor and virtuoso reshaper of foreign material that he is, gets through by adding Figaro, Falstaff, and Fatinitza[36] motives. But we will take issue with its unmotivated leaps into nonorganic, tiresomely burlesque, or embarrassingly realistic add-ons. Things that would be experienced as shallow in a farce on the *Prater*[37] are no less tiresome when they are tolerated by a Hofmannsthal. That the playful element threatened to engulf the action, as well—that the plot, for example, wanted to take turns such as might have been taken by any miserable farce-maker of the past— may help to explain the matter but does not make it any better. In all, play and more play! Even a writer of comedies has to give form, not [just] play, especially if he wants to serve music as a librettist. Finally, Hofmannsthal's play is lacking, not least of all, in taste. He also distorts the image of the times, which, otherwise, is what is most fascinating about his libretto, and he exaggerates the sexual element, which has assumed a broad stance in the *Rosenkavalier,* following the fashion of the times, and unfortunately overpowers a fine, appealing sexual event with one that is coarse and repugnant. This "comedy for music" could only have gained if Hofmannsthal's engaging lady of a certain dangerous age had pushed aside the unclean Ochs von Lerchenau. Underneath his crust of filth, he is finally nothing but the *buffo* of the old comic opera, cheated of his reward, and seemingly expressing the work's fate in the form of its principal comic figure, who is intended to be comical and should arouse a feeling of pleasure but does only the opposite. But the *Rosenkavalier* is finally as lacking in comedy and humor as in wit or clever high spirits. Hofmannsthal's virtuoso ability to adapt to faraway times and faraway cultures, to that past with which, "for the poet, the present is inextricably intertwined," is not in question. Nevertheless, the unnatural divisions of that feudal period seem to find a no-less-unnatural reflection in the *Rosenkavalier,* when the lady of high station, the young gentleman eager to enjoy life, the clumsy country squire, the rich parvenu, and the crowd of freeloaders, adventurers, and lackeys are painted half with grim realism, half with a parodistic lack of verisimilitude. Hofmannsthal's chief means of conjuring up the past is the magic of the word, and he invents for himself an individual language, an Esperanto of Maria Theresa–Viennese rococo that occasionally modulates into *Tristan* German or Viennese-operetta German. In all: too many words in this comedy against music!

And more words than even a virtuoso the likes of Richard Strauss was able to come to grips with. Even he was unable to overcome the [work's] lack of unity, concentration, and genuine serenity. To bring order and natural flow into this boundlessly chatty dialogue, with its lack of concern for the formal requirements of the music, would have required a special style of composition, a different style, at any rate, from Richard Strauss's, drawn half from the *Meistersinger* and half from his own symphonic works. This weaving about of situations, verses, and words with motives, accompanied wherever possible by detailed individual characterizations in the recitative as well as in the orchestral parts, results in a thick flow of successive tones or a completely confused simultaneity. A quickened tempo does not help matters; the heavily laden wagon only begins to sway. This is especially evident in the busy ensemble scenes that are inserted with ponderous breadth into every act and have developed into a serious weakness of the score. This is the kind of thing that Mozart, Rossini, Nicolai bind into solid rhythms, organizing and enhancing them. In the third act, there is a situation whose basic elements are drawn from Mozart, Rossini, and Nicolai. The main figure gets into greater and greater difficulties, everything storms in on him in turbulent confusion, the police appear.

We remark here, not for the first time, that all this is not as it ought to have been provided by the writer of the libretto. But neither has the composer done his part in the manner of, for example, a modern Mozart, a modern Rossini, or even a modern Nicolai. And here the erroneous stylistic principle exerts pressure on the musical imagination. Recapitulations occur only at sentimental-lyrical junctures; they are almost never attempted in support of the spirit of light comedy. Here in *Rosenkavalier,* Strauss, who can be so gripping and witty in his rhythms, expends himself almost entirely in small change, so that the lyrical moods, because they are more unified in their presentation, assume greater weight. In this way something is lost that is essential to the style of every musical comedy. It is no accident that the form of the finale, as a musical piece that *gives form to* and sums up the progress of the plot, was invented in the vicinity of the comic opera . . . And since we are discussing questions of style, Strauss does, after all, vary his tone from time to time. The Marschallin and her Cherub are suddenly breakfasting in Mozartian style; Frau Maria Theresa suddenly becomes pensive in the style of Lortzing; Octavian and Sophie finally fall into each other's arms in the naive, folk song–like style à la "Sah' ein Knab' ein Röslein steh'n." And a flood of waltzes announces the pact that has been concluded with the operetta.

And *that* is something no unbiased assessment of the *Rosenkavalier* can ignore: the impulse toward Viennese operetta and Viennese waltz derived from the Viennese milieu. Once again: Vienna, the waltz capital, this Vienna that is, in a certain sense, also the city of Haydn, Mozart, Beethoven, and Schubert—who, by the way, also sang many a happy piece of music. But for the Vienna of Maria Theresa the waltz is not accurate. Strauss, contradicting his material, pays little attention to the period costume that is presented to us in such conscientious detail in the libretto. It is true that the archaic musical impulse in the *Meistersinger* takes its inspiration not from the sixteenth century but from the seventeenth and eighteenth centuries. But it does arouse the impression of a time that is long past. In contrast, the anachronism practically forces itself on our attention when, as in the case of the *Rosenkavalier,* it can be identified by means of Viennese waltzes of a very specific, very contemporary style. And here one may be allowed to protest a little; indeed this protest *must* come from Vienna about the *Rosenkavalier.* If Vienna is really the city of waltzes, it is by no means the city of the expressionless, paper-cutout, banal operetta waltzes that are popular at the moment. Waltzes of this type really do not stand up under the social elevation that Richard Strauss has in mind for them—in profound misapprehension, on top of everything else, of the art of Johann Strauss. A question arises not about the use of waltzes in general, for they were never entirely foreign to the music of the light opera, but rather about the use of *these* waltzes and above all about their use in such entirely improbable numbers. When the first and second waltzes turn up, one may smile agreeably, and is still smiling at the third and fourth; but when the fifth and sixth ones approach, one is disturbed and is thoroughly annoyed by the third act, when one has to sit through an endless series of in part unimaginably shallow waltzes—nearly fifty pages in the piano reduction! A cheap and deceptive musical cheerfulness that is, in addition to everything else, of quite doubtful dramatic value. No operetta composer would have dared to do anything similar. Truly pretty, its cozily swaying Viennese undisturbed by the insertion of a few more refined detours, is only Herr Ochs von Lerchenau's favorite waltz. Throughout the opera, this agreeable gentleman is flatteringly accompanied by Viennese waltz music as soon as his sensuality is aroused. Joke, satire, or deeper significance?

Not only in the waltzes does one observe the composer's impulsive, not particularly choosy selection of musical substance. As in *Salome,* or in *Elektra,* the composer seems to have contented himself with the first, superficial association of ideas, particularly in striving for "melody" by means of whatever tonal progression happened to strike his fancy, with minimal attention to content or expressive value. The invention is most powerful when it does not deny Strauss's earlier symphonic and dramatic works. Thus what is new in *Rosenkavalier* is not all that rich in significance; and what is beautiful is not all that new. That this beauty is to be sought more in the lyrical passages has already been suggested, even if the environment that surrounds these moods is freighted with questionable cantilena banality. Languishing *Tristan* sevenths "for the popular taste"; dominants wrapped in thirds and sixths; worn-out cadences. At least Strauss sings more in the *Rosenkavalier* than in his earlier operas—sings and lets his characters sing—a true advantage of this new work and one that deserves our heartfelt thanks. It contains duets and trios that successfully strive for vocal harmoniousness. But in the *Rosenkavalier,* as elsewhere, Strauss's greatest power resides in the sound of the orchestra. In a thousand refractions of color, the orchestra—a poetic, witty, and occasionally also capricious companion—is able to stand in from time to time for the comical tone that is missing on stage.

Let us add a few more details to the general picture in an effort, for the most part, to pluck the flowers. The theme of the young, happy Octavian, bubbling over with life, with which the orchestral prelude begins, is genuine Strauss: one of his venturesome E-major themes that burn upward, like a flame. Similarly, the following love scene, enlivened by Strauss's pointed motives, has the gestural quality of *Feuersnot*—full of energy and playfulness. The breakfast cocoa is already sweetened with a sugary waltz that actually has the grace of a Mozart minuet, the most well-mannered of the pieces in three-quarter time. The first appearance of Lerchenau shows us that no proper characteristic motive occurred to the composer for this character—which should actually be taken as a compliment to the musician. Lerchenau's tale, vainly seeking the appropriate brio, has the tone of *Eulenspiegel* in its orchestral coloring but without a thematic kernel worthy of note. Soon the first informal waltz melodies begin to stick to his heels. The parodistic accents that have been offered in the *levée* scene are lacking in comic power. With the Marschallin's monologue, the composer's pleasure in creation and action comes alive again. In the final scene, he becomes more affectionate and warm-hearted and takes us with him. There the poet provided him with heartwarming detail, such as the lament of the aging damsel over the passing of time, and the composer took advantage of it in equally heartwarming fashion. The scene fades away in a delicate, sated mood. A strong plus in the overall balance sheet of the work. Equally strong is the appearance of the Rosenkavalier at the beginning of the second act. A brilliant passage whose praises our valued colleague Specht[38] has sung in such beautiful words. The gentle, mystical mood is created by shimmering chords on the celesta, which give testimony to the relative nature of all "dissonance." The basic motive is surrounded by the dominant [chord] in a gently yodeling fashion. When the two female voices join in a transport reminiscent of *Meistersinger,* the result is the first of several two- and three-voice delicacies that this score contains. A similar piece follows in the duet scene between Octavian and Sophie, except that here the regularity is disrupted by a few stilted harmonic steps. When Lerchenau's servants chase after the maids, one hears an intentional *Elektra* quotation. There are also unintentional ones. To include a brief comment here concerning the harmonic scheme of the *Rosenkavalier*: it frequently has an intentional, tired quality about it. The duel scene that follows dissolves in unstructured uproar. How much intelligent, interesting detail has been wasted here without creating an overall impression! To draw out the course of events, even musical ones, is fatiguing. Finally, at his waltz, Lerchenau stops. The mood takes on a quality that is hardly more refined but at least brighter and more engaging. The attacks of the strings are desired by the composer to be "always in the sweetish

Viennese glissando." Now, in the third act, the *chambre-séparée* action, borne on waves of waltz music, begins in earnest. Fortunately it is preceded by one of the oddest little pieces in the *Rosenkavalier*, a witty, rhythmically soaring prelude in a minor key with fugal form. If only more such things were to follow! But what comes next is the musically not terribly well-ordered hubbub of the police scene. It takes a considerable, rather long time until Herr Ochs von Lerchenau is escorted out with all the honors of an operetta-waltz finale. Then the composer collects himself again to create purer, nobler tones. The trio of the three sopranos in D♭ major is heard, this reminiscence of the *Meistersinger* quintet in the same key. The concluding G-major duet of the two lovers is one we like less, but we will be genuinely pleased if its naiveté finds other adherents.

Have we made the reader impatient? Our aim here was to report with deliberate facticity about a work that from the very beginning has been surrounded by "sensation." Our feeling is that Strauss has been fortunate neither in the choice of his libretto nor always in its musical form. The brilliant, seductive individuality of its creator lifts the *Rosenkavalier*, too, above the majority of modern German operas; his popular charms—we almost said "hits"—guarantee him, here and there, public success, anchored by some instances of a more solemn beauty. That the new work of this leading musician even hints at the way to a new operatic ideal is something we have been unable to bring ourselves to admit. On the contrary: the path Strauss has taken is one we would like to warn imitators from taking by erecting a warning sign.

[Source: *Neue Freie Presse* (9 April 1911), Vienna]

·

Cultural Bankruptcy

KARL KRAUS

This is how things looked on 4 April 1924, in the *Neues Wiener Tagblatt:*

Profitable Night Business
Fantast. house w. 25 furn.
rms. in lg. Germ.-Austr.
industr. center, 1st-rate
business (gold mine),
        for sale

For sale:
Villa, 1st class, in best Salzburg
neighborhood, incl. furnished 6-rm.
apt., full comfort, move-in cond.,
1,500 mil. kronen

Aristocr. property w. castle, approx.

2,500 mil. kronen Principals only, apply to Arch. H. Naaff, Vienna, Intl. Hotel Klomser	320 acres excell. grazing land, own hunting & fishing asking 2,500 mil. kronen Profitable Night Business Fantast. house w. approx. 25 well- furn. rms. in lg. Germ.-Austr. industr. center, very profitable 1st-class venture (gold mine) for sale, asking 2,500 mil. kronen. Principals only apply Arch. H. Naaff, Vienna, Intl. Hotel Klomser, or Salzburg, Faberstrasse 13

The left side was generally noticed—but not the fact that it was repeated just to the right with minor changes in form and with the reference to Salzburg, which is revealed to be a large German-Austrian industrial center, although until now it was not even commonly known that it may be regarded as a trading center for women, since the tourist traffic has generally been diverted by the offerings of Messrs. Bahr and Reinhardt.[39] To the extent that readers were able to find their way through the "fantast. house" with its suites of rooms, which seems well adapted to the Salzburg summer, it was said that this was the most sensational advertisement with which the capitalist press had ever shown its true colors, after all the moralistic fervor of the epoch, and that an editorial staff that had turned prostitution into a gold mine had now shown its true face and been taken in by its own fool's gold. And when shortly after that the film *Madhouse of Love* was advertised, people were even more thoroughly confused, since now the identity of a madhouse of ill repute seemed to converge with a house of mad distortion of good repute. Many people were also of the opinion that the whole thing had to do with the sale of a newspaper with twenty-five (or "approx. 25") "well-furn." editorial rooms, which was available and could be had for a pittance, together with the entire inventory of its convictions—a transaction that the residents, as is well known, are accustomed to resist less strongly than the inhabitants of a brothel a change of madams. But first of all it would not be a gold mine, and second, the profitable night business of a daily that only supports the buyability of the press in specific cases would not lower itself to such an indecency. In fact it was only a perfectly harmless bordello ad—in other words the most decent thing one is likely to find in the Viennese capitalist press of today, so that one can only say, "Father

Wedekind, look at this"[40]—a humble attempt to draw conclusions from the advertising section about the whole, whereby it must be remarked that Herr Sieghart[41] completely lacks the stuff to run a brothel. What would that worthy predecessor, whose name was still Singer and who knew how to combine a tolerant cosmopolitanism with a sense of journalistic dignity, have said to this! These are anomalies that may be explained by the confusion of our times. The *Neue Freie Presse,* which has long ceased to be a gold mine, has decided to decorate its home, to make things more comfortable for its guests, since the latter have to be satisfied with the likes of Salten, Müller, and Ludwig Hirschfeld;[42] and on the anniversary of the appearance of the *Fackel,* the paper will be published with illustrations. An accidental coincidence of deeply motivated causes. When the *Fackel* was founded, not a single opera singer could have boasted that her picture had appeared in the *Neue Freie Presse,* just as it would have been unimaginable, on the other hand, for a tragic actress to appear in the Café Lurion and for public opinion to be writhing in ecstasy over a boxing champion.

Or over Richard Strauss, whose profound connection with the times is quite evident and who is quite certainly more of a stock company than a genius. But now even his famous versatility seems to have failed him, and even the Corybant critics cannot conceal the fact that there has not been a nastier desolation of the spirit even of the ballet or a more thoroughgoing degradation of theater to the level of a preschool than this *Schlagobers,*[43] in which the droll old master, ever the joker, comes to terms in his own fashion with the social question. Namely, in such a way that the fine pastry from Dehmel[44] mixes it up with the ordinary baked goods, pretzels, chips, cookies and suchlike proletariat—the latter, truly, incited by the intellectual matzohs—until those circles who sit in the opera boxes and whose capitalist consciousness this art touches as movingly as it otherwise only touches their snobbism, have been pacified—until the resolute Munich beer—that's the way!—puts a conciliatory end to the class struggle. Which purpose Munich beer fulfills especially well in the arena of the Vienna *Konditorei.* For in one of these, it appears, a candidate for confirmation has overeaten, and his nausea, which seems to provide the external plot, is subjected to a musical illustration that causes us to experience something very similar. It is just a "merry Viennese ballet." The matzohs as rabble rousers of the Revolution had been omitted at the premiere, so as not to offend anyone, even though everything ends well; instead the rabble rousing was done by simple "magicians" of no particular confessional stripe. But what an artist's dream to create a "Princess Praline," from whom it is obviously only a hop and a skip to the Sugar King. A "Don Zuckero," after all, is nothing to sneeze at, and besides that there are dancing candies and acting chiffon rolls. And what would you say to a "quince-pie bodyguard"? Critical admirers who cannot for the life of them imagine Richard Strauss sans *Weltanschauung* have wanted to see in all this a Goethe-style flight of the pure artistic being from the horrors of the social cataclysm into a children's fantasyland (albeit one in which Herr Slivovitz and Herr Vodky also make an appearance). But with all the shallowness Goethe got into on his flight from the Revolution,[45] still, it would be entirely too unappetizing to imagine his head filled with whipped cream and garnished with "Schiller locks."[46] It is undoubtedly one of the most regrettable consequences of the French Revolution that the comedies *Der Bürgergeneral* and *Die Aufgeregten*[47] were written, but even if one combines the horrors of the Sansculottes with those of the Bolsheviks, the resulting terror cannot possibly come close to even the mere plot summary of *Schlagobers*. That the blood of mankind flows away in rivers of Munich beer could be interpreted as a pessimistic witticism based on events closer to the home territory of Herr Richard Strauss, but he himself seems to be inclined to a relaxed interpretation of such revolutions, whose flame only needs to be toasted, or even to suggest in a symbolic way that he expects all political salvation to come from Munich. Be that as it may, it would seem to be a matter here less of the need for fairy tales of a genius who has turned away from the dark sides of this world than of the venture of a no longer entirely vigorous impresario of taste who can still permit himself to offer a rabble that falls for anything sensational, as a special treat for the holidays, pure idiocy (dedicated to his friend Karpath[48]). And for the theatrical production of the idea that the patisserie gets into a fist fight with the cake from the suburbs, but if I am not mistaken Mlle Chartreuse has a liaison with Herr Slivovitz—and indeed, there does exist a theatrical world that is willing to devote itself to playing alcoholic drinks and baked goods—a beggar state spends billions, while the city gives the master a piece of property on which to construct a castle in Vienna's most elegant park.[49] All this and a week-long celebration of enthusiasm in the ideal expectation that the creator of a musical world that has the Will to Tourism written all over its face should remain with us for a few months of the year in full nonconnection to the institute with which he has been entrusted. I say all this out of the most profound prejudice, for I know as little about Richard Strauss, and possess as little of the specialized knowledge required to appreciate his obviously unheard-of abilities, as of that required to understand certain technical achievements or the science of stock manipulations—scarcely more than a stage direction by Herr Hofmannsthal, who suits him perfectly, the text of which he erroneously composed;[50] his refusal to participate in the artists' support for starving humanity in Russia; and his face. But this alone, these eyes, between which is located so much worldly and pecuniary sense, this justifiably bored expression with which he waves his magic baton at the treasures of the musical archive in the Redoutensaal,[51] this well-trimmed moustache, which would suffice for all the general directors of all the other branches of industry that are required for twenty-five annual editions of the *Woche*[52] until the end of time—this face that expresses an entire new Germany of the Will to Power and Presentation, of economic recovery as a prelude to bankruptcy, on whose wall the UFA, HAPAG,[53] and other words of warning have now appeared, *Mene tekel*–like; this face that seems to contain much less of Beethoven's than of Ballin's[54] *ingenium:* to me it is all so completely revealing and convincing that compared to this kind of rider of the apocalypse with his fine paces, compared to this most powerful ringleader of our time, I would not hesitate to lay my hand in the fire for the genuineness of the appearance of a Reinhardt or Hermann Bahr. And within this world of economic booms and careers and accidents, in which only genius cannot act otherwise, but talent can do anything and has complete freedom in the choice of profession, I consider it a total fluke that Herr Richard Strauss did not become the [boxing] champion and Herr Carpentier the creator of *Schlagobers*.

I ask myself today what I ever used to have against a world whose Golden Age didn't give the faintest hint of this gigantic possibility of nonsensicalizing and in which the bourgeois newspaper neither recommended the sale of brothels nor had sold itself as a brothel. And so far as the *dernier cri* in journalism is concerned, which one hopes is the cry of a dying man, the explanation is quite simple. Humanity has already been so stultified by the text of the newspaper that it can no longer understand it without pictures. To have recognized this and seized the opportunity it offers is the deed of the younger generation. The dear departed gentleman for whom the images of language were sufficient splendor would no longer recognize "the" paper, and if he had a degenerate son who was so lacking in every sense of the paper that he finally made the *Neue Freie Presse* into an interesting publication, he would break the editorial staff over his head and make the sign of the cross.

[Source: *Die Fackel* 649–56 (June 1924): 52–56]

.

Seeigeleies

KARL KRAUS

. . . And I must admit, the master of them all, Herr Richard Strauss, has something of this note about him. I cannot say, for my part, whether he is a genius in music, I can only say that he isn't, for I am aware of the intellectual brilliance of *Schlagobers* and all the precious things that the thoughtful Frau Storch has packed in her husband's suitcase:[55] "Do you have everything for Herr Storch? The rolls, the ham, the milk bottle for ten at night? Is the cake well packed? The raspberry juice can't run out? Ten hard-boiled eggs: *very nourishing!* With such a demanding job he must nourish himself well. Do you have the pills, Anna? The *throat gargle?* The compress?"

A dialogue about which Karpath[56] remarks that it is straight out of daily life: "Then again to the husband: 'Be sure to cool off before you go out in the cold; turn your fur collar up!'"

Strauss does not spare himself in the slightest, remarks Karpath, but he doesn't mean the fur collar, he means the satire, the confession of his Simandldom,[57] which was, until now, one of the public private affairs of Vienna and has now assumed world-musical expression. Whether this is also musical, whether raw material of such simplicity and multiple indiscretion, whether this weighty burdening of the world with marital affairs, whose humor lies merely in the strain of it all— with such stressful activity he must nourish himself well—whether such foolishness can result in a work of music is something the contemporary brain, which is no longer capable of being deterred by any disgracefulness, will hardly be capable of deciding. For my part, I prefer to believe that the sentence Hofmannsthal gave the master to compose is correct, finally, in the version in which he mistakenly composed it. Herr Hofmannsthal imagined it this way: "The noble father of the bridegroom, according to propriety, must have gone out for a drive before the Knight of the Silver Rose arrives. It would not be proper for them to meet at the front door." However, this Theresan[58] nonsense from a calcified bourgeois brain that has been lingering in the vicinity of Gotha[59] was a bit too elevated for Bavarian standards, and so the master arranged it like this: "The noble father of the bridegroom says that propriety must have gone out for a drive before the Knight of the Silver Rose arrives. It would not be proper for them to meet at the front door." Propriety and the knight, that is. The former really does seem to have gone out when Herr Strauss occupies himself with the text; when Herr Hofmannsthal does it, only nature has gone out. But so far as the public is concerned, this or that version, this way or that way, and in fact anything at all is all right, and in the realm of genius it is evidently not important what is actually set to music. But what is possible under the autocracy of swindle is proven by the capacity to set to music the marital joys and sufferings, complete with skat game, of Herr Richard Strauss, and above all by the weighty literature that could be written to discover the source of the images in this world of foolishness. The intelligence and good humor with which nature has endowed the average level of musical practice is somewhat in doubt anyway, especially in times when literary production already confronts our normal mental state with things the latter would previously not have expected to find even in the lowlands of the most private philistinism. But when the hippopotamus keeper in Schoenbrunn[60] calls, "Come here, Fritzl!" and a salmon-colored gorge opens to receive a bread crumb, that is an act of intellectual heroism compared to everything we experienced in the vicinity of Herr and Frau Storch. Even Archduke Friedrich, who recognizes the two Buquoys, each identified by a medal, looks like Voltaire next to the foolishness that identifies little Franzl as the "veritable Dr. Franz Strauss" and the commercial counselor as the "merchant from the Hohenzollernstrasse in Berlin who has for years been a close friend of the master." Karpath deserves the honor of having been the first to recognize the participants in the skat game. He was also the one who was able to tell his European public that Miss Maier—a "person of easy virtue," as he calls her with justified self-assessment—was actually called Miss Mücke (or Miss Midge),[61] Berlin, Lüneburgerstrasse no. 5. So that was the girl who approached a conductor Stransky, whom an Italian in the company always called "Straussky" and who is called "Stroh" in the opera, with a request for opera tickets, from which that fateful note to Herr Richard Strauss (Storch) resulted and which led to a marital spat and unfortunately also to the libretto of *Herr and Frau Robert Storch*. A more trivial but at the same time shameless dreariness has probably seldom entered the realm of artistic creation. That the creator can bring himself to "turn the tables" on his jealous spouse, as the breathlessly watching press recounts it, in order to accuse her ("naturally more as a joke") of a "light flirtation with the young baron," is a private matter that the participants will perhaps resolve among themselves in such a way that it must be sublimated once again. But that in an opera à clef a woman who has nothing to say about the artistic decisions of Herr Strauss should be maligned is perhaps the worst thing the realm of genius has ever had to answer for. Herr Decsey[62] speaks of a "lady in quotation marks," a "fresh Berlin lip," a "female" for whom it never "even in a dream" occurred to Herr Stransky-Straussky to procure opera tickets, for it is well known that only Herr Decsey has a right to such a thing. In deciding whether a female was forward enough to remind the "three men, who were sitting contentedly and unsuspectingly over cocktails" of a promise that they had never given her, or whether a male was condescending enough to give one and then not keep it, the historian will not hesitate to assume the former. They were "males," after all, and the circumstance is as unattractively amusing as the word, but they were probably not sitting quite so unsuspectingly in a bar nor were they quite so lacking in responsibility for the approach of the "female." And all this with naming of the address, without any consideration whether "the fatal Mücke," as he terms her with good reason—for it is indeed demonic, the way the midge's body finds room here after all—without any consideration of whether she is still alive, whether she is married or in any circumstances in which her sullying by this group and the music-historical publicity might be damaging. Yes, it is probably a result of fate that I knew this midge personally, in fact at the very time that she was making trouble and consequently royalties for Herr Strauss, and I can say that she, the perfect image of a woman, was more beautiful than Herr Decsey and Herr Karpath and perhaps even than Messrs. Strauss, Storch, Stroh, Stransky, Straussky, and whatever the monikers of these multiple quid pro quos may be, one of whom has been wrestling with the experience for lo these twenty years. That I therefore also consider her more valuable is something I need not assure the reader, and what moral distinction I make between girls who love every day and gentlemen who write every day is well known. There is nothing I like to see less than unjustified professional arrogance, which assumes the moral concepts of a bourgeois world that has long deserved its patronage, and jeers at the "lady" where the gentleman should be identified. And how much more humor the "fresh Berlin lip" possessed than the skillful creator who extracted his *Intermezzo* from her and who has a comic demon around his neck the likes of which would spoil the pleasure of anyone else who might ever think of laying claim to that place. When Herr Strauss goes so far in his customs declaration of the changing moods of his marital bliss as to permit himself to be suspected by his wife of "Jewish extraction" (for which only one thing speaks—namely, an acquisitiveness that does not shrink even from the use of such a motive!), then truly he is rehabilitated by the simplicity of his wit, and there was no need for

Karpath to intervene, who, mindful of his dignity, is on the spot here, too: "I hasten to Strauss's assistance and can ascertain that no Jewish blood flows in his veins."

Ah, if Herr Strauss had ever had an inspiration that was as comical as this: the helpfulness of a Figaro who has risen from temple singer in Pressburg to government advisor in Vienna in order to carry out a blood test for the readers of the *Neues Wiener Tagblatt* and to guarantee a German man his certificate of non-objection in regard to race! Or the hearty concurrence with which he coins the pithy remark concerning the master's profound but somewhat sadistic realization that he "enjoys working with his head":

That recalls the wisdom of Hans Sachs. . . .

Or when Herr Decsey, who approaches the Israelite nature from a more provincial standpoint, waxes enthusiastic about the marital friend of the composer [that she is] "only too modest to show it," and Storch draws from this affair the moral that we should judge one another by the hidden treasures of the soul, "not by the nasty words." Or when he points to the ten-egg packet and giggles in parentheses, "(hard-boiled, very nourishing!)." God, it is all so awful. Nonetheless I would still be curious to hear the music to the exclamation of the modest one: ". . . And what am I and what was I as the wife of a composer? Ha, ha, ha, not even presentable at court!"

This and the delightful sledding scene, along with the clumsy trampling of the Grundlsee owner[63] in the score: "Not to forget that wit, intelligence, and humor also reign," remarks Karpath, who has already inherited and is now distributing Speidel's personal note.[64] But the music historians have provided us with a sense of not only how much effort was necessary to involve these co-rulers but also how much was expended on the realization of the idea before the master ever took it upon himself: "*Neither* Hermann Bahr *nor* Hugo v. Hofmannsthal *dared to take on the ticklish task* of the libretto; indeed, *after repeated attempts,* Bahr gave his friend Strauss the advice that as the head of the family he should write the text of the family opera himself."

So it should be, and the appeal to family feeling not to share the honor and the profit with anyone else was taken to heart. Even two such hard-boiled bookmakers (one of whom, it is true, has to struggle against temptation) finally had enough tact to sense that private and family life is something in which no stranger, but only each person himself should intervene; and then it depends on the father of the groom as to whether propriety must have gone out for a drive. . . .

[Source: *Die Fackel* 668–75 (December 1924): 133–38]

NOTES

1. See the Strauss-Hofmannsthal correspondence from the years 1911–19 in *Richard Strauss–Hugo von Hofmannsthal: Briefwechsel,* 5th ed., ed. Willi Schuh (Zurich: Atlantis, 1978), particularly pp. 125, 130, 131, 149, 154, 183, and 186–187.

2. See Leon Botstein, "Between Nostalgia and Modernity: Vienna 1848–1898," *Pre-Modern Art of Vienna 1848–1898,* ed. Linda Weintraub and Leon Botstein (Detroit: Wayne State University Press, 1987), pp. 10–17.

3. See Traude Hansen, *Wiener Werkstätte: Mode. Stoffe. Schmuck. Accessories* (Vienna, 1984), pp. 38–96 and 100–106; and Werner J. Schweiger, *Wiener Werkstätte: Kunst und Handwerk 1903–1932* (Vienna, 1983).

4. See Arnold Schoenberg, "On Strauss and Furtwängler" in H. H. Stuckenschmidt, *Schoenberg: His Life, World, and Work* (New York: Riverrun Press, 1977), p. 544.

5. Willi Schuh, *Richard Strauss. Jugend und frühe Meisterjahre. Lebenschronik 1864–1898* (Zurich: Atlantis, 1976), pp. 68–69.

6. Theodor Helm, *50 Jahre Wiener Musikleben. Erinnerungen eines Musikkritikers,* ed. Max Schönherr (Vienna, 1977), pp. 167–75.

7. Richard Strauss, *Briefe an die Eltern 1882–1906,* ed. Willi Schuh (Zurich: Atlantis, 1954), p. 20.

8. See Knud Martner, *Gustav Mahler im Konzertsaal* (Copenhagen, 1985) and Franz Grasberger, *Richard Strauss und die Wiener Oper* (Tutzing: Schneider, 1969).

9. Franz Willnauer, *Gustav Mahler und die Wiener Oper* (Vienna, 1979), pp. 225f.

10. See Frank Walker, *Hugo Wolf* (London: Dent, 1968) and Ernest Newman, *Richard Wagner* (Cambridge: Cambridge University Press, 1976), vol. 4, p. 396.

11. On Hirschfeld, Kalbeck, and Viennese musical criticism see Leon Botstein, *Music and Its Public: Habits of Listening and the Crisis of Musical Modernism in Vienna 1870–1914* (Ph.D. Dissertation, Harvard University, 1985).

12. See *Die Korngolds in Wien. Der Musikkritiker und das Wunderkind. Aufzeichnungen von Julius Korngold* (Zurich, 1991).

13. See Volker Kalisch, *Entwurf einer Wissenschaft von der Musik: Guido Adler* (Baden-Baden, 1988).

14. See Edward Timms, *Karl Kraus. Apocalyptic Satirist* (New Haven: Yale University Press, 1986).

15. The concert took place on 5 January 1896. The performance of *Till Eulenspiegel* was followed by the first performance of Bruckner's Fourth Symphony [Botstein].

16. The reference is to a novel by Edward George Earle Lytton-Bulwer, the first Lord Lytton (1803–73), a politician, playwright, and novelist. Bulwer, who is buried in Westminster Abbey, wrote *Pelham, or the Adventures of a Gentleman* in 1828. It was a bestseller and the first work he published under his

own name. Bulwer was popular in Germany and particularly among Wagnerians, including Schoenaich. He had published a historical novel, *Rienzi, or the Last of the Tribunes,* in 1835. Wagner tried, unsuccessfully, to visit Bulwer in 1839 in London. In any event Wagner used the Bulwer novel as the basis for his 1842 opera *Rienzi* [Botstein].

17. Hector Berlioz's *Symphonie fantastique* dates from 1830, although it was first published in its orchestral version in 1845 [Botstein].

18. This and other references are to the sections of Nietzsche's book *Also sprach Zarathustra* [trans.].

19. Hirschfeld refers to plainchant quotations in Strauss's score [ed.].

20. Hans Richter (1843–1916), the famous Wagner conductor, was the conductor of the Vienna Opera and of the Vienna Philharmonic from 1875 to 1898 [ed.].

21. Followers of St. Cecilia, the patron saint of music [trans.].

22. The reference here is to Carl Maria von Weber's 1809 incidental music to Schiller's translation of Gozzi's *Turandot* [Botstein].

23. The German expression is *in Musik setzen,* to set in music [trans.].

24. Kalbeck may be referring to Wilde's imprisonment for homosexual offenses from 1895 to 1897 [trans.].

25. Gustave Flaubert's *Trois contes* [Three tales] appeared in 1877 [trans.].

26. Heinrich Heine (1797–1856), German-Jewish poet and journalist, emigrated to France where he became acquainted with Karl Marx and supported socialist ideas. He is the author of some of Germany's most famous "folk" songs and lyric poems as well as of acerbic and ironic rhymed poems of a distinctly political nature. Among these is *Atta Troll: Ein Sommernachtstraum* (1842), written when Heine was living in Paris. This satirical epic in rhyme recounts the story of a dancing bear that escapes from its master and flees to the Pyrenees. It is a sarcastic commentary on many political and literary tendencies of the times [trans.].

27. Kalbeck's references to depictions by Gustav Klimt (1862–1918) and Max Klinger (1857–1920) are direct allusions to Secessionist aesthetics. Klimt was Vienna's leading modernist painter and first president of the Secession. The work of the German artist Max Klinger was particularly favored by the Vienna Secession. His *Christus in Olympus* was exhibited in 1899. Klinger's statue of Beethoven had been the focus of a famous 1902 Secession exhibit that included friezes by Klimt [Botstein].

28. The reference is to the three-act opera *Der Trompeter von Säckingen* from 1884 by Viktor Nessler (1841–90). This opera enjoyed wild popularity. Nessler also composed a *Pied Piper of Hamlin* opera [Botstein].

29. Korngold refers to the famous aria from Franz Lehar's *The Merry Widow* [ed.].

30. The German word *mauscheln* refers unmistakably and disparagingly to Jewish speech habits but in a commonplace racist tone without any overt philosophical or intellectual implications [trans.].

31. It is beautiful, but this was not the place for it [trans.].

32. The name means "Ox of Lark Meadow" [trans.].

33. Let the love of a servant girl not be a source of shame [trans.].

34. Reception held by a person of distinction as he or she rises from bed [trans.].

35. Servants [trans.].

36. Operetta in three acts composed in 1876 by Franz von Suppé (1819–95) [trans.].

37. The famous large public amusement park in Vienna [Botstein].

38. Richard Specht (1870–1932), a native Viennese, was a leading music critic and journalist in Vienna. In 1921 he wrote a major two-volume study of Richard Strauss. In 1909 he founded the journal *Die Merker.* Specht, who wrote a 1919 monograph on the Vienna Opera, was a staunch defender of Mahler's work [Botstein].

39. Hermann Bahr (1863–1934) was an important Austrian writer and critic. He was a key figure in fin-de-siècle Vienna and later married Mahler's first love, the great soprano Anna Mildenburg, whom Strauss admired. The Bahrs were friends of both Strauss and Hofmannsthal. After 1912 Bahr lived in Salzburg. Bahr's writings are of historical importance, but despite the fact that he was an acquaintance of everyone in fin-de-siècle Vienna he managed to gain the admiration of few. Kraus was particularly contemptuous of Bahr's fickle and thoughtless trendiness. To gain a perhaps more judicious appraisal, one might consider this comment by Hugo von Hofmannsthal in a letter to Strauss dated 26 July 1911: "The sooner you see through a giddy, insufferable renegade like Bahr, the happier I will be . . . Such individuals are not without judgment but actually are far, far worse and more dangerous." Max Reinhardt (1873–1943) was, with Hofmannsthal, the co-founder of the Salzburg Festival. He was perhaps the greatest stage director of the twentieth century in German-speaking Europe. He directed the first Strauss-Hofmannsthal *Ariadne*-Molière production of 1912. His work at the Deutsches Theater in Berlin after 1905 (which Strauss often saw, including the production of Hofmannsthal's *Elektra,* which led to his writing the opera) became the stuff of legend [Botstein].

40. Frank Wedekind (1864–1918) was a writer and man of the theater whom Kraus thoroughly admired [Botstein].

41. Rudolf Sieghart (1866–1934) was a Viennese Jewish businessman whom Kraus considered particularly powerful (especially with respect to the press) and dangerous [Botstein].

42. Felix Salten (1869–1947), a well-known Viennese-Jewish writer, was a favorite target of Kraus. He is best remembered for his book *Bambi* (oddly enough translated into English by none other than Whittaker Chambers!). Hans Müller (1882–1950) was an Austrian writer and journalist. He was another object of Kraus's ire, who actually sued Kraus for defamation of character. Müller had written a patriotic play during the First World War and represented the worst of the warmongering and ethically bankrupt press. Ludwig Hirschfeld (1882–1945) was a Viennese writer, operetta composer, and libret-

tist who was also an editor of the *Neue Freie Presse*. Among the operettas on which he worked were *A Year without Love, The Silver Dancer, Journey around the Demi-Monde in 120 Minutes,* and *Two Laughing Eyes* [Botstein].

43. The title for Strauss's 1924 ballet, in Viennese usage, means whipped cream [trans.].

44. The reference is to one of Vienna's oldest café-bakeries on the Kohlmarkt [Botstein].

45. After Goethe's move to Weimar, where he entered the employ of the duke in 1775, his political stance seemed to take on a more conservative cast [trans.].

46. A sugary pastry [trans.].

47. Goethe wrote and produced two comedies in 1793 having to do with the French Revolution: *Der Bürgergeneral* [The bourgeois general] and *Die Aufgeregten* [The agitated citizens]. *Der Bürgergeneral* concerns a barber in revolutionary uniform who attempts to con a peasant out of breakfast. The day is saved by a nobleman who points out the virtues of laughing at the uniform. *Die Aufgeregten,* which Goethe never completed, dealt with the impact of the Revolution on a German village [trans.].

48. Ludwig Karpath (1866–1936) was born in Budapest. He was a failed opera singer (who once auditioned for Gustav Mahler). He became music critic at the *Neues Wiener Tagblatt.* Karpath was hated not only by Kraus but also by Arnold Schoenberg, whom Karpath attacked. He was an inveterate intriguer and in the 1920s became friendly with Strauss, whom he tried to help keep at the Opera. Throughout his career he was active in the cultural politics of the city and was also a well-known gourmet. His self-serving book, *Begegnung mit dem Genius* [Encounter with genius] (1934), was dedicated appropriately enough to Alma Mahler. Strauss's *Schlagobers* was dedicated to Karpath [Botstein].

49. Kraus is referring here to the official offer by the city of Vienna in 1924 to permit Strauss to build a home on the grounds of the Belvedere Park [Botstein].

50. Kraus apparently refers to the mistake discussed in his article "*Seeigeleis*"; see p. 363 of this volume [trans.].

51. This space, in the old Imperial Palace in Vienna, was built in the eighteenth century and served in the early nineteenth century as Vienna's most important musical performance space as well as the most prestigious place for balls. After the fall of the monarchy in 1918 it was used periodically for opera productions and exhibitions from the collection of the Austrian National Library [Botstein].

52. A Viennese weekly [Botstein].

53. Well-known industrial firms [trans.].

54. Albert Ballin (1857–1918 [suicide]), the German shipping magnate, was head of the passenger division and later *Generaldirektor* of the German-America line. Under his leadership the fleet grew dramatically. It boasted the fastest steamship in the world. He was also an innovator in the area of tourist cruises [Botstein].

55. Kraus refers to act 1, scene 1 of *Intermezzo* (1924), in which Richard Strauss—alias Robert Storch—is about to embark on a concert tour [ed.].

56. See n. 47 [ed.].

57. Simandl is a German literary figure used by Hans Sachs and Abraham Santa Clara to describe men who are tied to their wives' apron strings. The name comes from the Hebrew of Simon, which means "one who obeys" [Botstein].

58. Kraus is referring to Hofmannsthal's allusions to Viennese etiquette in the era of Maria Theresa in *Der Rosenkavalier* [Botstein].

59. A reference to the official reference book and genealogy of German artistocracy, the Almanac of Gotha [Botstein].

60. The summer palace of the Hapsburg imperial family. Located just outside Vienna (now within the city's limits), it was begun by Fischer von Erlach in 1695. The park around it became an important place for the Viennese population. Maria Theresa rebuilt and expanded the palace in the 1740s [Botstein].

61. The word *Mücke* means mosquito or midge [trans.].

62. Ernst Decsey (1870–1941) was a critic who wrote biographies of Hugo Wolf and Anton Bruckner. He was born in Hamburg and worked until 1920 in Graz. He wrote for the *Neues Wiener Tagblatt* and taught at the Conservatory. Decsey's very readable and thoughtful memoirs were published in 1962 under the title *Musik war sein Leben*. In addition to his scholarly writings, Decsey wrote pseudohistorical novels about Vienna [Botstein].

63. Christine Storch and the young baron meet on the sledding slope. In the next scene, they are shown dancing at the Grundlsee Inn [ed.].

64. Ludwig Speidel (1830–1906) was one of Vienna's most influential and distinguished nineteenth-century cultural critics. His feuilletons on music, literature, theater, and the arts are central documents of nineteenth-century Vienna [Botstein].

Elektra: A Study by Paul Bekker

TRANSLATED BY SUSAN GILLESPIE

One of the leading writers on music in the early twentieth century, Paul Bekker (1882–1937) served as music critic in Berlin (1906–11) and Frankfurt (1911–25). Thereafter he was appointed *Intendant* in Kassel and later Wiesbaden before emigrating to the United States in 1934. He published important biographies on Beethoven, Liszt, Schreker, and Wagner, and wrote a book on Mahler's symphonies; it remains one of the most important studies of the composer's works. Bekker's various writings on German musical life in the teens and twenties are central to anyone wishing to study this period in German music history. At a time when music criticism could be quite polemical, Bekker remained a remarkably calm, independent voice.

His study (1909) of Strauss's *Elektra* was the first major article on the opera to be published (an article by Carl Meinnicke appeared later that year in the *Riemann Festschrift*), and this probing study remains one of the most important essays on the work; it has never appeared in English translation. Bekker wrote the article after having seen the Dresden and Berlin premieres of *Elektra,* and it appeared—in three installments—in the *Neue Musik-Zeitung.* Most critics, including some of Strauss's admirers, stated a preference for *Salome* in their reviews of the *Elektra* premiere. But Bekker believed *Elektra*—with its originality, dramatic concentration, and profundity—had surpassed not only any opera that Strauss had written thus far but "all [operas] that other musicians of the present have attempted." In his later book *Wandlungen der Oper* (1934; translated by Arthur Mendel in 1935 as *The Changing Opera*), Bekker tempers his opinion of Strauss's opera, observing that after *Intermezzo* (1924) the composer's road becomes "lost in artistic reflections of a speculative nature." Nonetheless, in 1909, Bekker sees no living opera composer who is Strauss's equal [ed.].

[Source: Paul Bekker, *"Elektra.* Studie," in *Neue Musik-Zeitung* 14, 16, and 18 (1909): 293–98, 333–37, and 397–91]

Seldom, I think, has the outward success of a work of art, its public reception at the moment of its performance, had less in common with its artistic value than was the case with Strauss's *Elektra*. Seldom have opinions been more confusedly contradictory, judgments more super-ficially formulated and constructed according to preconceived notions. For months mysterious rumors about the music had been circulating among the public. One heard that the score was being torn out of the composer's hands piecemeal, to be turned into piano reductions and individual orchestra parts. The dates and locations of the per-formances were announced before the singers had even got their hands on the score. The most important opera houses competed for the right to hold the premiere. The opera directorship had no sooner come to an agreement than the performers were fighting over the roles. But the impatience of the public was not to be satisfied with mere facts. Although not a single note of the score was known to any-one, its significance and quality became the subject of ever bolder speculation. Not only in trusted, more intimate circles but even in public it was felt to be acceptable, given the intense curiosity of the public, to make one judgment after another. Since no one knew any-thing specific, everyone could let his fantasy soar as high as he wished and thus successfully prepare the ground for an inappropriate recep-tion of the work. Not only artistic but also pecuniary questions be-came the subject of public discussion. Farfetched reports circulated about the size of the honorarium paid by the publisher or the amount of the expected royalties. Richard Strauss's income was calculated, and the prospects of the publishing house of Fürstner were weighed in the balance.[1] A regular set of statistics was created to tally up all this wealth, every plus and minus precisely estimated, tested as to its ac-tual value, and booked. *Elektra* was the great, exciting secret of our entire public sphere. From the moment when Strauss made known his intention to undertake the composition of Hofmannsthal's book, until the general pilgrimage to Dresden, *Elektra* was the conversation piece of the day. Every newspaper considered itself fortunate to be able to add some slight piece of new information to the already well known news about the progress of the score. And in order that the legendary veil that had been draped about the work by overzealous speculation might be drawn even tighter, no one was permitted to lay eyes on the piano reduction, even after it had been completed and printed, and no one was permitted to attend the dress rehearsal in Dresden. The premiere itself would be the first time the suspense would be lifted.

One must recall this prehistory of *Elektra* in order to assess correctly the effect of its performance. One must also bear in mind that for more than a year now there has been a movement afoot whose chief aim is to undermine Richard Strauss's reputation as an artist and which does not hesitate to stoop to the lowest, pettiest means if they seem to shorten the distance to this goal. Who among all the persons who attended the premiere in Dresden can maintain that he went without prejudice? Who would be, I would like to say, so *naive* as to think himself free of the influence of the many rumors and veiled critical remarks? Who, even with the most carefully guarded independence, could have failed to be a little bit infected and confused by the general fever of expectation that greeted this strange novelty? The general interest was not in the worth or lack of worth of the piece itself but only in the correct answer to the question, Will the extremely intense expectation of a fascinating sensation, fueled by all the preliminary excitement, be fulfilled? Almost without exception the answer was in the negative. *Elektra* did not fulfill expectations of this nature. It lacks the element of the piquant, the titillating, the sensuality torn between voluptuousness and fear found in *Salome*. It has been remarked that at the conclusion of *Salome* everything is left in a state of breathless excitement, while the end of *Elektra* produces only a feeling of grateful relief. Personally, I appreciate the contrast. For me the *Salome* conclusion, like many another significant episode of the work (particularly the scenes with John the Baptist) has never been able to arouse genuine sympathy. I always felt there was an incongruity between poetry and music, a failure of the composer to confront the full implications of the events. I always found *Salome* to be a colorful mixture of the most diverse stylistic elements, a *ragout* whose tastiness resulted precisely from its complicated combination of ingredients. And therefore I respond almost with a kind of gratification when many of the *Salome* enthusiasts are now in doubt or even turn away. For the things they valued and held in high regard were, for me, not at all what was valuable or significant about it. Thus the expectation I had of *Elektra* was always combined, for me, with hopes for a more unified, stylistically well rounded piece. The fulfillment of these hopes was for me the first, most important result of the Dresden and Berlin performances. No matter if the fanatics scream themselves hoarse or break out in hymns of praise, if the critics crack jokes or heap scorn, if the doubters and the faint of heart cloak themselves in embarrassed phrases—all that meant nothing compared to the recognition that here for the first time a living individual had succeeded in reformulating a drama as a creative musician, in eliciting from the poetic draft a style of his own, and thus bringing about a new rebirth of tragedy from the spirit of music.[2] I am by no means asserting that this new work has no weaknesses, nor do I deny that it has one or the other shortcoming. But its positive value seems to me to be so great and capable of development that particular errors, such as its unusual length, the unfavorable division of the principal roles among three women, or its enormous difficulty, particularly that of the Elektra role, seem to me to be of only secondary importance. From this work broad perspectives open up. Many a person will have been forced to change his point of view regarding Strauss. Many who were previously his supporters will now desert him—I almost believe their number will be greater, for the moment, than the number of those whom Strauss will now, for the first time, win over to his side. But what do numbers signify? And what does the term "supporter" mean for an art that asks only about works, not theories? One judges an artist not by the number of his followers but by his ability to create impressions for us. Richard Strauss, among all living artists, has understood how to develop this ability to its greatest extent. A brilliant intellect and an unlimited skill have helped him accomplish this. The most impressive demonstration of both appears to me to be *Elektra*, the most serious of almost all Strauss's works since *Guntram*, the most technically perfect, the most unified in style, the most personal and mature in plan and execution.

.

The action of the drama has a somewhat fragmentary quality. It presents a brief excerpt from a great event. Elektra wishes to punish the murderer of her father Agamemnon—Klytämnestra, her own mother—and Klytämnestra's paramour, Aegisthus. But she is incapable of carrying out her plan alone and so she awaits the return of her brother, who is growing up in a foreign land. Finally the brother, already believed dead, comes home. In a few minutes the fate that has been threatening the guilty parties for years is carried out. Elektra's mission is accomplished, and, seized with raging intoxication of victory, she dies, an orgiastic shout of joy on her lips.

That—briefly sketched—is all. With Elektra's death the action comes to an end. We know from history that this single occurrence is only an episode in a continuing chain of events and that the tragedy of Elektra and Klytämnestra is followed immediately by that of Orestes and was preceded by that of Iphigenia and Agamemnon. But the historical content of the legend of the house of Atreus was evidently not considered suitable by the poet. He was not interested in the fate of the royal house of Mycenae; what fascinated him was only the characters of the actors in the Elektra episode. What appealed to him was the portrayal of psychological problems for whose formulation and development precisely those personalities that he found in Sophocles' treatment of the material offered the most useful stuff. Would it still have interested us today to learn that there are unfathomable powers of fate that drive mankind to evil deeds and then cause them to be destroyed by the proliferating consequences of those deeds? Does the old theme of blood vengeance, in itself, still hold meaning for us? Is it not much more congenial for us to observe—instead of the power of these unfathomable, mysterious forces—the free play of the characters, the intensification, the ecstasy of the passions, the clash of temperaments? Like *Salome*, *Elektra* is a tragedy of the passions. There it was love, here it is hate that forms the basic theme of the work. Undoubtedly love is a more rewarding, productive theme. Hate contains a dangerous one-sidedness—it presses ceaselessly for destruction and it can only be portrayed musically if it is understood not in its actual activity but rather as a sweeping exaltation of feeling that numbs all other feelings in its path. Seen from this point of view, the contrast between love and hate, which seems so sharp at first, melts away. Both appear as extreme outgrowths of a *single* fiery passion, both have their roots in the same emotions, both are simply the opposite poles of the same essence. The portrayal of hatred as a boundless exaltation of feeling can have the same attraction for an artist who sees the aim of his art in the intellectual examination and illumination of characters, in the form he gives to psychological problems, as the portrayal of love. For to him, in the final analysis, what matters will not be the cause and the effect but first and foremost the emotion's power and capacity for heightened intensity. This is the test by means of which his art proves itself. Everything external—the events of the plot itself, the questions of historical or (in translations) philological faithfulness, of the characters' bourgeois morality or even the "moral of the story"—are of no concern for the artist.

Moral! Here I touch on a theme that actually has nothing to do with art and yet cannot be avoided in any discussion of the Strauss question. For shortsighted and small-minded opponents have raised the most Philistine objections precisely in regard to Strauss, and, what is more, they have been warmly supported by the majority of our worthy, bourgeois German public. A respected writer has even permitted himself to remark, "The whole thing impresses one as a sexual aberration. The blood mania appears as a terrible deformation of sexual perversity. This applies all the more because not only Elektra but all the females are sexually tainted." I am convinced that these sentences have been warmly welcomed in many a German household, for our customs are so chemically pure nowadays that it is sufficient to say the word "sexual" in order to establish a priori the inferiority of a given work. A sharp but telling remark of Heinrich von Kleist's[3] occurs to me in this connection. It is from a letter that he wrote to Tieck about *Penthesilea*.[4] Kleist refers to the possibility of performing not only *Penthesilea* but also *Kätchen*, and his opinion is that in view of the demands made on the theater nowadays by the public, there is little possibility of performing these plays on the stage. "If one considers it aright, it is finally the women who are responsible for the entire decay of the theater in our country, and either they should stay away from the theater altogether or their own stages should be created for them, separate from the men. The demands they place on decency and morality destroy the entire essence of drama, and the essence of Greek drama could never have developed if they had not been completely excluded from it." What Kleist says here about the women of his day can be applied to many *men* of the present era, who, mindful of their moral dignity, throw out their chest full of German pride and demand of the theater, above all else, that it should accord with the currently accepted moral codex.

What do the words perverse, moral, immoral mean for art? Words, empty words without content, nonsense that has absolutely nothing to do with the inner essence of art. No matter what the artist may portray, it is not the *what* but the *how* that is decisive. The way in which a given theme is developed and portrayed is the sole determinant of the quality of a work of art. And the character of the theme itself can be judged solely according to whether it truly gives the creative artist an opportunity to express his individuality fully. If this is the case, then the external plot of the piece may reach into the remotest regions—we may be left cold by the work or may even be repelled by it out of personal antipathy—but we have no right to characterize it as immoral. There is only one kind of immoral art—and that is art that is boring.

Closely related to this ridiculous hue and cry about the perversity of Strauss's content is the indignation over the supposed falsification of Sophocles' originals—except that these attacks are, if anything, even more shallow and untenable. What would remain of all of world literature if we were to question the right of later poets to rework old originals? What would happen to Goethe's *Iphigenia*, Kleist's *Amphytrion*, Grillparzer's *Medea*?[5] What would we do with Shakespeare, who, as is well known, did almost nothing but revise earlier works?

Not to mention the vast numbers of dramas that have been drawn in part from heavily revised tales or from free variations on historical events? I should almost like to assert that our entire theatrical literature would fall to pieces if we were to adopt the superficial objections of those people who protest against the modernization of Sophocles. What does Sophocles matter to us? A poet who compels our admiration as a powerful artistic phenomenon of antiquity, but to whose works we no longer feel connected by any inner sympathy. Let no one claim that the world of Sophocles was purer, holier than that of Hofmannsthal! It is unquestionably more primitive, and this primitive quality may seem to us today like loftiness. But in reality the events of that world are presented in a much crasser, more brutal manner; the characters are much more violent and bloodthirsty than in Hofmannsthal's version. The fundamental difference between the original and the new version does not at all lie in a tendency to intensify horror but rather in the exclusion of the idea—which was decisive for Sophocles—of a dark fate that grows out of the motive of blood vengeance and brings human beings inexorably under its spell. In Hofmannsthal, by contrast, the tragic nature of the occurrences is based first of all on the characters of the individuals. The development and portrayal of these characters therefore comprise the main content of the work; the few events that drive the external action forward take place behind the scenes—they are, ultimately, of secondary importance and merely serve to cast a final, glaring light on the characters, who are developed to their full extent.

.

The poet has placed two figures in the foreground: Elektra and Klytämnestra. The drama evolves between them—everything else is background. The two complement each other: the crime of the one determines the character of the other. Klytämnestra's deed turns Elektra into a vengeful fury whose fate is fulfilled the moment her victim dies. Neither woman acts on her own—Aegisthus slays Agamemnon; Orestes kills Klytämnestra. The men are the ones who serve, who carry out; the women bear responsibility for fomenting the ideas, right up to the last instant. But they are both too weak to carry out the deed itself. In order to rob Elektra of even indirect participation in the execution of the sentence, she is even prevented from handing her brother the ax; she is not even allowed to hand him the tool for executing the deed. She is merely the vehicle for the passions that lead, in an explosive outburst, to the final catastrophe. Klytämnestra, the personified guilt of the past, tortured by gloomy memories, frightened by oppressive dreams, shaken from the deathly repose in which she has attempted to drown her conscience; Elektra, the goddess of vengeance proclaiming terrible punishment, the prophetess of revenge, who incites her tortured victim again and again, filling her with ever more gloomy reflections, calling up horrible visions, dripping poison in her veins and torturing her soul to death. Elektra's lust for vengeance is played out in changing facets. Where her mother is concerned, it breaks through in the form of unbridled speech, burning with fanatical passion; toward the uncomprehending and timid sister, it shows itself as coaxing flattery or scornful contempt. Toward the brother, who has hastened to the place where the sentence is to be carried out, it is expressed as *love*. Strangely paired opposing emotions: as love, in ecstasy, can bring forth hate and in *Salome* causes the death of John the Baptist, so a related psychological process occurs in Elektra. Her hate engenders love. It is not the brother whom Elektra greets (although a certain sisterly tenderness may be heard underneath her words). But primarily she sees in him the avenger of the father, whose appearance awakens feelings in her heart that had seemed forever buried and will never appear again after this one exalted outburst. Among the group of secondary characters, Chrysothemis appears as the most significant. She is a simple character. More oppressed than indignant over what has happened, she tries to reconcile herself with the actual circumstances and has no sympathy for her older sister's insatiable lust for vengeance. Personal well-being is what means most to her; she experiences the instability and oppressiveness of her current life so powerfully only because it prevents her from freely developing her own nature. She possesses too little firmness of character to oppose the powers that be. A compromising nature, she fears conflict and longs for the joys and sorrows of ordinary life. Chrysothemis is an everyday phenomenon, and perhaps the poet emphasizes her expectations of life only in order to shed a brighter light on the contrast with Elektra. Still, the objections are completely untenable that have been raised against the scenes with Chrysothemis: that the "cry for a child" and the "cry for a man" are the only forces that motivate her. Anyone who examines Hofmannsthal's text impartially, who considers the musical characterization of Chrysothemis, which is quite free of sultry passion, must recognize that the quintessence of the wishes and desires of Elektra's younger sister: "I am a woman and desire a woman's destiny" does not differ in the slightest from the feelings of a normal young woman. Chrysothemis is a faint-hearted, weak-willed creature who is incapable of living constantly in an atmosphere so laden with tension and struggles, with the tenacious energy of unbroken instinct, toward the goals that are appropriate to her individuality. That pure sensuality as a goal in itself is quite foreign to her is shown by her second great scene with Elektra, where, despite all tempting promises, she is unable to overcome her loathing and fear of the horrible deed. The person who approaches *Elektra* looking for an opportunity for tendentious distortion or suggestive commentary may see in Chrysothemis a female who is completely controlled by sexual desire. But if he is content with factual observation of the actual material, he will take such exaggerations and distortions for what they are: the opinions of feeble natures who shrink back when confronted with a work of art that is bold and free of petit bourgeois prudery, because they recognize not what is great and characteristic in it but only their own sickliness and weakness. The defect lies not in the work of art but in the observer.

•

Besides the three women, the other characters in the piece appear only as silhouettes, to provide variety. Even Orestes remains a sketch, drawn with a few strokes, quite impersonal and presented only as the embodiment of the will to action. Strauss has pushed Orestes' attendant almost completely into the background (he is treated more fully in the original libretto); however, in the music drama, quite unnecessarily, there are three servants in place of the one who immediately recognizes Orestes. The purpose of this change is unclear. What is the aim of the operatic intensification? The effect is weakened, not strengthened by it. Retained without changes is the introduction to the piece, the scene with the five maids whose dialogue describes the strange, hate-filled goings-on in the royal household. This conversation of the maids at the well is necessary as a somber opening chord—although it seems doubtful to me whether it was necessary to retain the unabridged text at this point. Strauss later made such far-reaching cuts that I would almost think this scene would have been subjected to changes, too, had it not happened to be the beginning of the piece and of the compositional work. Other than at the beginning there is no more use of ensembles in *Elektra*. Choruses are completely lacking (as they already were in *Salome*); the servants who greet Orestes remain silent. Thus Elektra and Klytämnestra, and to a lesser degree Chrysothemis, are not only the main characters but also almost the sole actors and bearers of the plot. A great danger: three women, constantly moved by powerful emotions, continuously in the foreground of the action. I do not in any way consider this disposition of the characters to be a weakness of the work. Rather, I find that the danger of monotony is avoided so outstandingly that one could scarcely have hoped for better; that the contrasts are much too lively, the intensifications too brilliant and arousing ever to allow the need for a more varied phenomenological world to arise. And yet perhaps the fatigue that many listeners experience, the effort required to assimilate the events, would have been less great if more colorful, lively, and varied images were to appear on the stage itself. I touch here on a peculiarity of *Elektra* that I do not at all consider to be an organic defect but that nonetheless is undoubtedly one of the reasons why the broad public has shied away from the work.

The lack of attractive, dazzling colors, the predominance of a strict, simple line, the striving after monumental architectures (in contrast to the voluptuous colors of *Salome*) is thoroughly characteristic of *Elektra*. If I now turn from a consideration of the dramatic form of the work to the characterization of the music, I would like to begin by saying that nothing could be farther from my intent than to give a detailed anatomical dissection of the thematic fabric with a precise listing of all of the motives. For such a task the score, which is not available to me, would be required. Besides, Otto Röse and Julius Prüwer have already published a very detailed guide, parts of which are apparently inspired by the composer himself. It contains a detailed listing of all the motives, designated by the authors with not terribly well chosen names. Here one may also find detailed references to the specifics of the thematic structure. Only one thing bothers me about this guide: it deals too extensively with the examination and dissection of the score but pays practically no attention, on the other hand, to the musical-dramatic plan and scenic organization. To reveal these elements as far as possible and to sketch the artistic, not the technical, plan of the musical tragedy in brief strokes is what I shall attempt to do here. In the process, I shall refer to some of the same musical examples that Röse and Prüwer have selected, and I think my remarks may perhaps be understood as a complement to the above-mentioned guide in aesthetic matters.

·

The drama is divided into three great, self-contained sequences of scenes. The exposition includes the conversation among the maids, the solemn monologue of Elektra, the conversation between Elektra and Chrysothemis. In these scenes all the prerequisites of the plot are extensively laid out and established, the characters described, the previous events commented upon, the future ones suggested. The second stage of development begins with Klytämnestra's entrance. Here

the action is given new impulses; the opponents have found and recognized each other and they are both girding for the final, decisive
battle. The final dramatic climax falls into several subdivisions: the passionate attempt by Elektra to win over her sister, the decision to carry
out the deed alone, the lyrical scene with Orestes, the execution of
the sentence, Elektra's hymn of victory and death. The poet could
scarcely be more concise than this in his scenic plan and still achieve
his end. Utter concentration is the characteristic of Hofmannsthal's
tragedy. One event follows another with unheard-of force; nowhere
is a pause to be found—the only extended delay in the action, the
scene between Orestes and Elektra, was created only at the behest of
the composer.

Even in the exposition, every lengthy description is avoided. The
hearer gains an impression of the milieu by means of hints and
chance remarks. The music begins with the incisive declamatory motive

Agamemnon:

as if with a short motto characterizing the emotional leitmotif. At the
well, the maids are gossiping—talkative, careless folk who are devoted
to whoever happens to hold power and full of scorn and hatred for
the oppressed. They are talking about Elektra, who rushes by at the
very beginning like a wild animal that has been startled. "Were she
my child, my child, I'd keep her, by God! under lock and key!" Not
one of the maids still feels any awe before the daughter of their
former king and the current royal spouse. Only the youngest of them
all defends the despised girl: "I will throw myself down before her
and kiss her feet. There is nothing in this world more royal than she."
She is beaten by the others, who, egging one another on, reenter the
house. The musical framing of this scene mirrors the excited, erratic
mood of the conversation. Motives that will later unfold in significant
ways appear here in passing, without showing themselves independently in the restless flickering of the conversation. The composer
merely illustrates the text in an impressionistic manner and then
makes the transition, by means of a brief orchestral interlude, to
Elektra's entrance. The maids have left the courtyard. Elektra appears,
repellent to look at, mourning and loudly lamenting her murdered
father. Her monologue is the exact counterpart to the previous scene:
among the maids, hate-filled, petty gossip; in Elektra, gloomy, grandiose pathos. The musical style corresponds to these contrasts: the

excited movement of the first scene is followed here by a monologue
of steely repose and imposing greatness, a lament for the dead that
is shattering in its force and monumental in its conception.

Elektra is forsaken. "Alone, woe, quite alone." Her pain starts convulsively in passionate rhythms:

In her loneliness she remembers her dead father. The memory of his
lofty, kingly being is reflected in the broad triplet motive that accompanies her invocation of Agamemnon:

> "Agamemnon! Agamemnon!
> Where are you, father? Don't you have the power
> To drag your countenance up here to me?"

In a slow $\frac{4}{4}$ rhythm, the invocation of the spirit of Agamemnon begins. Elektra recalls the evildoers' murder; she buries herself deeper
and deeper in the terrible events of the past. She draws new strength
by submerging herself in times long gone. The pathos of her lamentation turns into demonic fanaticism; energetically commanding
rhythms support her invocation:

> "Agamemnon! Father!
> I want to see you, don't leave me alone today."

Until now there has been in this monologue a continual heightening of intensity, phrase for phrase, which is expressed even more powerfully and clearly in the music than in the poetry. Now the mood
slackens a little. The gloomy memories are pushed aside by a still,
plaintive melancholy. A broad melodic cantilena in A♭ major resounds
in the orchestra:

The lonely child grieves, and her longing for her father's love awakens:

> "Just show yourself again the way you did yesterday—
> for your child a fleeting shadow on the wall."

But soon the lust for vengeance gains the upper hand again:

> "Your day will come."

In prophetic foreboding of what is to come, she then proclaims the fate of the assassins and the solemn sacrificial rite that the avengers will carry out on behalf of the murder victim. Slowly, melancholy Elektra's gloomy mood lifts, her language becomes livelier, the thought of the vengeance that will finally be wreaked fills her with wild, enthusiastic ecstasy. She envisions herself and her siblings standing victorious at the grave of the father; a feeling of raging desire sweeps over her and impels her to a dance whose powerfully triumphant rhythms are already pounding in her ear:

Whether I regard this monologue of Elektra's as part of a dramatic whole or as an independent creation—I am impressed here by a demonstration of the representational power and skill of music so brilliant that this passage alone would suffice completely for me to decide the oft-debated question of Richard Strauss's dramatic abilities. The character of Elektra is sketched here in an incomparably superb fashion. Emotional expressions of various kinds are juxtaposed with one another; they are sharply differentiated but in such a way that the whole loses none of its organic unity. Where, before Strauss, could one find works of similar conception? Or where can they be found even in Strauss himself? Who among living composers, apart from him, would have the strength and power of concentration to come up with and complete anything comparable? What is left of the claims of all those people who only want to see in Strauss the master colorist, when confronted with the lapidary, magnificently dramatic lines of this monologue of Elektra? What do the couple of superficial tone paintings, which are so often reckoned against Strauss, count in comparison to the powerfully heightened emotional intensity of this scene? If this is not the ability to create dramatic forms—where else could we hope to find it?

Again a brief orchestral interlude, prolonging the dance rhythm, provides the transition to the next scene: Elektra and Chrysothemis. The younger sister appears in the palace door; her sight rouses Elektra from the intoxication of victory. Chrysothemis comes to warn her. Klytämnestra has had a bad dream; she is thinking of ways to render Elektra harmless, to get this bitter enemy out of the way. But Elektra knows nothing of slavish fear. She sees in Chrysothemis only the weak daughter of her mother, who has inherited nothing of the proud, imperious spirit of the father. The beginning of the scene consists of a short dialogue between the sisters. Mysterious harmonies sound at the mention of the mother:

They recall the terrible ghosts of Klytämnestra's dream, whose lament weighs on her like a nightmare. But the warning is only the point of departure for Chrysothemis. She wants more, she wants to convince her sister to adopt a different behavior toward their mother so that the two sisters' fate may take a friendlier turn. Chrysothemis cannot live in this stifling atmosphere: "I cannot sit and stare at the dark as you do!" Desire for freedom impels her. The musical characterization of Chrysothemis is kept very simple, as befits the essence of her personality. A songlike melody, with clear periodicity, accompanies her wish for an existence filled with light and joy.

As Chrysothemis expresses her longing for the common lot and fate of women, one of the typical Straussian triplet melodies resounds in almost arialike form:

Abruptly Chrysothemis's passionate expression of feeling is interrupted by Elektra. Scornfully the older sister sends the younger back into the house:

> "In tears? Go on! Into the house! Where you belong!
> They're making noise! Perhaps they're making
> ready for your wedding?"

From the hallways of the palace noise is heard. A ritual procession draws near, which the queen has ordered in order to appease the gods. Chrysothemis flees, attempting to take Elektra with her:

> "Go away and hide! Don't let her see you, today you mustn't cross her path; she hurls death from her every look. She had a dream.——Here they come. She's driving all the maids before her with torches. They carry sacrificial beasts and knives. Sister, when she trembles she is most terrible! Today, today of all days, this moment you must keep out of her way."

But Elektra rises proudly to her feet. She feels no fear of Klytämnestra, she feels that she is her equal, even her superior. The safety of her own life means little to her; she wishes only to look her hated enemy in the eye and revel in her fear: "I have but one desire: to address my mother as I never did before." Chrysothemis runs out. In choking, dragging rhythms the procession draws closer, out of the palace interior, noisily passing the lone figure standing outside:

The last to appear is Klytämnestra, accompanied by two servant girls, her confidante and her train-bearer. She pauses by the open window and looks down into the courtyard, where Elektra rises to confront her in demonic majesty. The exposition is complete; the two mortal enemies face each other eye to eye. The contradictions of the plot have been developed and explained. In the three introductory scenes the activity in the royal household, the character of Elektra and—in Chrysothemis's speeches—also the nature of Klytämnestra herself have been clearly drawn. The plot begins. In the meeting of the two opposing principles, the conflict, which has been prepared by all the previous events, sharpens decisively.

The scene between Klytämnestra and Elektra may be divided into several parts. The entrance of the queen serves as the introduction, the brief conversation with her daughter in the presence of the servants. Then the two women are left alone. Klytämnestra describes her torments. With rising intensity, the third important segment begins: the dialogue between mother and daughter, which ends with Elektra prophesying vengeance. There is no doubt that the dramatist evidently gave his all here. The unforced transition from exposition to the decisive turning point in the plot; the solid organic construction of these scenes, in which the most deeply hidden motives of the contending characters are revealed and notes with fearful tone colors are sounded, all without any detriment to the progress of the action—these characteristics stamp precisely this Klytämnestra scene as Hofmannsthal's master achievement, dramatically and technically as well as by virtue of its sheer poetic power.

The composer faced an extraordinarily difficult task in creating this scene, the success of which would be decisive for the overall impression made by the score. If he succeeded here in heightening the expression, intensifying the effect of the spoken word, capturing in musical colors the moods that shimmered between the lines, then we would have a scene of majestic expressive power. I admit that the problem posed here does not appear to me to have been resolved with complete felicity and that toward the end of the scene I sense a distance between what was intended and what has been achieved, which—especially when the work is heard—causes a feeling of unavoidable coolness and exhaustion. However, I find the two first parts of the Klytämnestra scene significant and original in the highest sense of the word, up to Elektra's final, vengeful threat. The musical interpretation of the characters, the brilliant reflection of psychological phenomena here attains a level of surety and self-sufficiency that one can scarcely imagine being more imposing. Poetry and music are seamlessly joined. What the poetry expresses awakens in the music a resonance of magical refinement and supple expressivity. The faintest movements of the heart, veiled moods, hidden thoughts are all transmuted into tone and resound in our ears. It is precisely the juxtaposition of successful and unsuccessful elements in this scene that illustrates the greatness and uniqueness of the task, and teaches us to value the significance of what has been accomplished.

Klytämnestra speaks with two servant girls, her confidante and the train-bearer; like demons, they whisper evil thoughts in her ear and never leave her side for so much as a moment. The queen is unable to free herself from them and yet something in her rebels against the servant girls' loathsome nature. Memories of times when she had better, nobler company recur to her, when she herself was another, loftier, purer being. She hates these memories, for through them the thought of her guilt is also awakened, which has made her into a criminal. And yet there is something soothing in the recollection of years long gone, when fearful dreams did not yet fill the queen's nights with cruel tortures and stifle every joy in living. Thus Klytämnestra is torn between memories that now torture, now comfort her. The curse that pursues her makes every moment of calm immediately give way to new terrors. As a flesh-and-blood embodiment of this fate, Elektra stands before her mother, and Klytämnestra sees in this daughter the most concentrated product of her union with Agamemnon. Elektra contains within herself all the noble qualities of her parents. This is no fearful, weak female like Chrysothemis. An extraordinarily intelligent spirit dwells in her, and her actions are inspired by a manly energy. "In your head everything is strong," her mother tells her. The noble dignity of prince Agamemnon has been bequeathed to the daughter: "There is nothing in this world more royal than she," cries the young maid, who is devoted to Elektra. Elektra is not only clever, not only the genuine child of a king, but her external appearance also reflects the nobility of her nature:

> "I think I was beautiful; when I doused the lamp,
> I felt it in front of my mirror
> with modest awe. Then I sensed how
> the slender rays of the moon
> swam in my body's white nakedness
> as if in a pond, and my hair
> was such as makes men tremble."

But these gifts, the combination of all the physical and mental advantages of her parents, have subsequently been transformed into their opposites, when the mother betrayed the father. The foundations of Elektra's being were shattered, and a transformation of her entire nature occurred. Just as she once bore the most beautiful testimony to her parents' love, so she is now a forbidding monument to Klytämnestra's horrible deed. Thus she stands before her mother as a reminder of former greatness and simultaneously as a testimony to her inextinguishable guilt. Elektra does not need to speak a word to the queen. Her appearance alone is a harsher blow to the murderess than any words could be. It unleashes a storm of wild emotions in Klytämnestra's breast.

The art of the poet has made it possible to give the scene between mother and daughter a particular intensity by making Klytämnestra's character relive once more, before our eyes, all the stages of a development that has in reality taken many years to unfold. For a brief period, Klytämnestra regains her former independence. The servant girls, who have long since become indispensable to her and are compelled to remain with her day and night, suddenly arouse in her a feeling of disgust. She is like a dying woman from whose eyes the scales suddenly fall. She recognizes the servants' hypocritical, dishonest nature; she feels the "breath of Aegisthus." A purer gust of air wafts toward her from her own daughter, air in which, after her long sufferings, she is able to breathe freely once more. She does not notice that Elektra's calm is only pretended; she feels only that Elektra knows the means to bring about her redemption, and she wants to learn it from her, since all other attempts have been in vain. Thus she extricates herself for a short time from the servant girls and now stands free of them facing her daughter—desirous, for the first time in a long while, of speaking with Agamemnon's and her child and filled, for the first time in a long time, not with hatred but with a spirit of reconciliation and the hope of being able to forget the past.

As a nature that is basically not self-reliant but dominated by foreign, external influences, Klytämnestra is not characterized musically by a particular motive that marks her individuality. Rather, her speeches reveal a series of themes, each of which serves more to reflect the mood of the moment than to describe the queen's individuality. The musical portrayal of Klytämnestra thus resembles that of Herod in *Salome*. The Wagnerian principle of the leitmotif is reinterpreted here as a tool of impressionistic technique. While in Wagner the characterization of personality forms the basis, and the musical mood of the scene emerges indirectly from the dissection and explication of the motives, here in Strauss the opposite occurs. The personalities of the actors are deemphasized; the external sense impressions of their words appear as sound in the music, with the characters hovering behind them, only suggested in bare outlines. A necessary consequence of this type of musical-dramatic portrayal is the marked increase in tone painting. Opponents of Strauss's art, based on a superficial reading of the score, have raised the objection, because of the presence of tone painting, of externality. In reality, however, what we find in Strauss is not at all an isolated cinematographic technique but merely the logical extension of a means of expression that the most important masters before him employed without scruple and in rich abundance. Tone painting by no means deserves to be treated with the disdain to which it has been condemned by ascetic aesthetes, so long as it is applied in the right place and does not thrust itself into the foreground but rather reveals its meaning in the context of, and sheds a clearer light upon, the situation. Consider the extensive use that Haydn, and to an even greater extent Bach, made of tone painting, or compare the role of effects achieved by tone painting in the works of Mozart, Beethoven, Weber, and Wagner, and one will be forced to recognize that whoever condemns in principle the use of purely illustrative effects in music is making an error that derives from a thoroughly one-sided position. Tone painting lifts the spoken word out of its everyday meaning into a pure, indefinable emotional sphere that is nevertheless identified with unmistakable clarity. Only the means through which these effects are achieved vary according to the poetic subject matter. Sometimes a heightened artistic effect can be achieved by giving a more definite, plastic form to the verbal image; in other cases it will be a matter of avoiding every reminder of the material significance of the word itself. Both methods have their justification, and only the sensibility of the creative artist is capable of choosing between them. For the critic who is making a judgment after the fact, all that matters is to determine whether the desired artistic effect is achieved. If the tone painting takes center stage, as coquettish virtuosity, then it should undoubtedly be rejected. But if the composer avoids every possibility of tone-painterly effects, even where these could give clearer form to the musical expression, then he is a pathetic pedant who does not know how to make the best use of the means provided by his art. On closer observation, therefore, the question of the permissibility and value of tone painting reduces itself to the "how?" that is finally always the highest court of appeal for the resolution of this and similar controversies.

If I now examine the tone paintings in *Elektra* completely without prejudice, I can find nothing that could give cause for any second thoughts whatsoever. Strauss, in this case—in comparison to *Salome*—has not only been extremely sparing in his use of illustrative materials, he has also managed to insert them into the whole with such perfect mastery that they are not even particularly noticeable at first to the listener who is following the musical-dramatic structure. They put themselves constantly and completely at the service of expression; their artistic character becomes noticeable only upon closer study of the work. I believe that for those listeners who share this impression the question of the aesthetic justification of Strauss's tone paintings no longer exists. One can no more reject a dramatic creation by Richard Strauss because it reveals his brilliant instrumental skill and ability to reflect phenomena of the external world in tones than one would object to Bach's most profound works on account of the fact that they are composed with incomparable contrapuntal artistry.

The Klytämnestra scene provides several opportunities for inspired tone painting. When Klytämnestra asks, "Have I been transformed alive into a desolate field?" and the strangely gloomy motive begins

it suggests to the hearer with gripping clarity the feeling of horrible desolation in the queen's heart. Another short motive has a similar effect:

When Klytämnestra descends the steps to the courtyard, the jewels she is draped with clink at every step:

Contrasting with these modest motives is a simple triplet theme that first appears at Elektra's words "You are no longer yourself!"—a somewhat sentimentally colored phrase, recalling earlier, happier times:

This concludes the recounting of all the most important motives of the Klytämnestra scene. One more new one appears toward the end of the scene, shortly before Elektra's question "Won't you let my brother return home, mother?" It is a memorable, hammering theme—

—the threat of death that follows Orestes as he hurries to the scene of the deed. Common to all these motives is their quite brief formulation, their characteristic rhythm, their (with the exception of the triplet theme) unusual but not at all unappealing harmonies. There is something peculiar about these apparently so arbitrary, but in reality very solidly constructed Straussian harmonies. Some busy statisticians have gone to the trouble of finding out where in the piece the apparently most clashing dissonances occur as a result of the coincidence of however many adjacent notes of the chromatic scale. One might think that it would be quite irrelevant whether this or that modification is made here or there. And yet—at the first attempt to make a change, the tonal image already takes on a different cast. Despite all the apparent arbitrariness and unscrupulousness, everything here is, finally, so logically organized and purposefully constructed that even the slightest interference by an outside hand is immediately noticeable. In a recently published interview, Strauss confesses that he is a devotee of the principle of tonality. As surprising as this may sound, upon close examination the score of *Elektra* confirms this statement. With relatively few exceptions, the laws of tonality assert themselves again and again. Only in isolated episodes, specifically in the characterization of Klytämnestra, does Strauss extend the boundaries farther than the most morally unassailable professors of harmony would consider permissible. In general, however, Strauss confirms as harmonist what may be said about him as an artistic phenomenon in general: that in him we may expect only a gradual intensification, not a revolutionary overthrow of the past. Where Strauss feels compelled to make innovations, it is always the particular case that drives him. If, on the other hand, existing means are sufficient to accomplish his ends, then he knows how to manage them wisely, without relinquishing any of his originality as a result of this voluntary restraint.

The final segment of Klytämnestra's appearance begins with the mention of Orestes—a part of the score to which I still remain distant, despite detailed study and repeated hearings. Elektra suddenly asks after her brother (in the original the transition is more extended). Klytämnestra attempts to sidestep the question. But in her mother's shy formulations Elektra recognizes her guilty conscience, and she paints the return of the avenger in the most garish colors. As gripping as the musical cloak is that surrounds Elektra's words, forced from her mouth in convulsions of rage, I have nevertheless not been able to form a coherent musical picture of it. I am not even thinking of so-called purely musical effects, in the sense of the professional melody-hunters. All I expect is a heightening of the spoken word through the music, and here I fail to find it. I sense at this point such a significant domination by intellectual concerns that the music leaves me emotionally uninvolved. A chilling feeling of monotony takes over, and dominates all the more since the extended text only offers a play on images that are all grouped around the same basic motive. The intended impression of horror does not make itself felt; rather, there is a sense of unstimulating monotony. Not until the end of the extensive description of the avenging deed is there a rise in the intensity of the musical expression (the performance of which, however, only the rare singer will be able to master).

The situation the poet has created here is replete with suspense. Elektra, filled with the premonition of her victory, stands triumphant before her mother. The latter, practically paralyzed with horror, has fled to a corner of the courtyard and can remain standing only with difficulty, barely in command of her senses. Elektra's ascendancy seems unquestionable. She has fantasized herself so effectively into her plan of revenge, she believes in it with such unshakable certainty, that what lies in the future, undecided, has already become definite, a conviction so strong that it can affect others. The mother is completely under the crushing thrall of this elementary outburst of feeling. The action seems to have ended—Klytämnestra has heard her sentence spoken; she suffers it without resistance. Agamemnon has been avenged, for whether the murderess lives or not is of secondary importance compared to the emotional suffering she has had to endure at the hands of her daughter.

Then suddenly the picture changes. Servant girls appear. They whisper a new message into the queen's ear. At first Klytämnestra does not understand them; she has been numbed by Elektra's terrible prophecy and cannot yet gather her thoughts. Only gradually does she revive. She wants to be surrounded by light; the demons of darkness that she believes have encircled her must be driven away. Not until a growing number of torches lights up the dark courtyard does Klytämnestra rouse herself and hear the news of Orestes' death. All at once she has regained control of herself. She casts a scornful glance at her opponent, who stands before her so certain of her victory and has, as yet, no idea that the hope she has been counting on is long since destroyed! A wordless pantomime full of significance begins. Each woman believes in the defeat of the other. But Klytämnestra is not only filled with thirst for revenge, like Elektra; she is at the same time both cowardly and cruel. She does not shout out the news of Orestes' death to Elektra's face; she leaves Elektra in her deluded— as Klytämnestra must assume—belief that Orestes will return, in order to be able to strike an even more painful blow against her later. In the rapid reversal of her mood, she lacks words that could express her sentiments. Only in her gestures are her thoughts revealed. In a nameless wild joy, "drinking her fill of it," she raises her hands as if to curse Elektra and then rushes back into the house followed by all the servants.

The musical elaboration of this scene is one of those fascinating images of a moment in time that Strauss is able to paint with such incomparable skill. The twitching motions of the two main characters, the sudden flash of the lights, the servant girls rushing in, the gradual brightening of the gloomy courtyard in which Klytämnestra and Elektra stand facing each other like furies unleashed—all this is mirrored with such astonishing clarity in the sounds of the orchestra that the technical virtuosity with which the motives of the previous scene are elaborated here becomes noticeable only upon careful examination. In addition to the first Klytämnestra motive that had already appeared in the Chrysothemis scene

the following motive also reappears as the servant girls enter:

The theme that preceded Klytämnestra's recitation of her dream also turns up, rhythmically condensed:

They are accompanied by a third, new motive of scornful triumph:

In quick, powerfully expanding sequence, these themes lead to the conclusion on the pedal point G: "What are they telling her? She's overjoyed! My head! I cannot think. What fills her with such joy?" whispers Elektra, unable to comprehend the mother's behavior.

The next scene begins with a passionately lamenting theme—the first of the final group:

Chrysothemis hurries to join Elektra, lamenting over the death of her brother, which the servants are talking about:

"Orestes is dead!
I came out, everyone already knew! They all
stood around and everyone knew,
but you and I!"

Elektra doesn't want to believe it: "No one can know it, for it is not true." But more than by Chrysothemis's wailing, she is convinced by the brief conversation between a young servant and one of the older ones, telling him to harness a team of horses to carry the news to Aegisthus, who is still out in the field. Now Elektra believes the words of her sister, who has sunk, despairing, to the ground at her side. A terrible decision gradually takes shape in her: "Now it must happen here and by our hand!" In the orchestra, shortly before Elektra speaks these words, an energetic, characteristic theme appears:

Little by little, Chrysothemis comprehends what her sister means. Horrified, she turns away from Elektra. But the latter tries to win Chrysothemis over to her plan by appealing in a flattering way to her secret wishes. The musical elaboration of this scene is based primarily on the material that has been provided and developed in the first Chrysothemis scene. This time, however, in contrast to the arialike character of the exposition, it takes on a very dramatic coloring and leads to a thrilling buildup. With a broadly held six-four chord in G minor, this scene is brought to a close with the powerfully rising Agamemnon motive. Chrysothemis tears herself away from her sister, who wants to convince her to murder Aegisthus and Klytämnestra, and flees into the house. In spite of her passionate nature and fresh youthful strength, she is too cowardly and indecisive to comprehend, much less carry out a deed like the one planned by Elektra.

Elektra sees herself robbed of her last hope. Only one possibility remains to her: to do what must be done without help from anyone, by herself. Her decision is clear: "Well then—alone!"

A brief, extremely gripping transition scene begins. Elektra, driven by wild lust, digs up the ax that is hidden in a corner of the court-yard—the very one with which Klytämnestra and Aegisthus have carried out the crime against Agamemnon. The murderers are to fall by the same weapon—Elektra has saved it until the hour of reprisal. Dark, wildly excited bass figures in the orchestra accompany the action, as Elektra, cowering on the ground in a dark corner, unearths her gruesome treasure. Several times she stops suddenly, listening suspiciously to hear whether anyone is watching her. Then, accompanied by the restless agitation of the basses, she goes back to her work. In the orchestra, after a brief prefiguration, there appears a new theme with an elegiac coloration. With its tired and dragging, regular rhythm and its downwardly moving chromaticism, it is an expression of solemn, restrained grief:

At the same time Orestes becomes visible among the chorus, costumed as a messenger, staring pensively at the apparently empty courtyard. Elektra, who is crouching on the ground, scraping and digging without cease, does not notice his arrival until she chances to look up from her work for a moment. Under the mysterious tremolo on D the theme of the decision to act appears in a new formulation:

It accompanies Elektra's shy question:

> "What do you seek here, stranger? What brings you here
> in a dark hour, observing
> what others do?
> I have some business here. What's it to you?
> Leave me in peace."

An inexplicable horror befalls her. She does not know the stranger, does not know what he brings, whether he is intruding here intentionally or unintentionally, whether he is a friend or a foe. But an intuition dawns on her that with the entrance of this man her fate has taken a new turn. Her question about the origins of the newcomer forms the beginning of the scene that represents perhaps the most perfect portion of the score of *Elektra*. The stage version has the same immediate effect as the piano reduction. I am thinking here not so much of the A♭-major episode that gained such quick fame but of the whole plan and execution of this scene as a musical-dramatic creation.

Slowly and solemnly, broad, soft chords from the wind instruments sound in accompaniment of Orestes' reply, brief and laden with meaning: "I must wait here." The same mystical harmonies, only more broadly developed, are heard again when Orestes, after exchanging a few words with Elektra, repeats his response once again. This is one of the most moving moments in the entire work. A mood of ghastly expectation makes itself felt. It is as if, in the midst of the most extreme excitement, all the wildly aroused passions suddenly fell silent, paralyzed by the terrible thought of the destruction that is inevitable. In this mood there is more than a mere presentiment of death; there is the horror of the suicide faced with the terrible step he is about to take, the bottomless void that will swallow him up. This awareness of immediately impending, self-inflicted destruction accompanies Orestes wherever he turns. It is so powerful that in his own eyes he already seems like a dead man, whose physical body is allowed to walk the earth only until such time as the deed that fate and his own will have thrust upon him has been carried out. He speaks of himself as of someone who already belongs to the realm of shadows, not merely to conceal his identity from Elektra, who is not supposed to know his name, but because every personal wish has been extinguished in him and he sees himself only as the instrument of a judgment that has long since been meted out. The ambivalent words with which he answers Elektra's pain-filled, passionate lament must be understood in this sense:

> "Forget Orestes. He felt too much joy
> in living. The gods on high
> don't like to hear such bright and joyful
> cries, and thus he had to die."

Orestes is no more. Only his ghost remains on earth, a majestic, gloomy shadow, insensitive to the joys and sorrows of this world. Thus he stands before his sister, who is overcome by trembling horror at the sight of his steely, gloomy stillness. But just as, in the world of myth, disembodied inhabitants of Hades may come back to life, regaining speech and sensation for brief periods, so Orestes' awareness of himself revives when he recognizes in the disreputable maid, whom he had taken for one of the lowest of the servant girls, his sister Elektra. His rigid, deathly quietude deserts him; he is horror-stricken; he feels that he is still alive and must continue to live in order to repay his sister for her self-sacrifice. Elektra, at first, can scarcely grasp his message. She asks her brother several times, "Who are you then?" and only the mute reverence of the servants is able to convince her that what seems incredible is actually true.

Woven through this entire scene is the tired, monotonous chromatic motive of the mourners. In contrast, Orestes' muffled harmonies are heard:

until gradually the expression becomes livelier and during Elektra's lament for Orestes the connection with the triplet theme of the first monologue—now modulated into minor—appears as a new, warmly felt theme.

"To lie there and
to know that the child [Orestes] will never return—"

Gradually motives from the Klytämnestra scene appear side by side with Elektra's sharply delineated theme, until at Elektra's outburst "Orestes!" a chaos of tones builds up, corresponding to the storm of feelings that rages in Elektra as she begins to be convinced of Orestes' return. As Elektra's excitement gradually subsides and she now fixes tender regards on the brother who has been returned to her, the uneasy waves in the orchestra are also calmed and this burst of elemental, unconstrained wildness is followed by one of the most externally effective episodes—Elektra's greeting of Orestes—which was added to the libretto by Hofmannsthal at Strauss's request.

Many critics place particular emphasis upon the lyrical beauty of this Ab-major episode and wish there were more intermezzi of this sort. I do not share this opinion; on the contrary, I find that Strauss is not at all especially felicitous when it comes to the invention and elaboration of large-scale operatic melodies that are meant to be beautiful but easily border on banality. Then his expression, which is otherwise so gripping and intelligent, frequently takes on an aspect of Philistine cheerfulness. At these moments he lacks the greatness and power that banishes every trace of ordinary feelings or emotional self-indulgence. Emotional events, when he is not able to grasp them in a primarily intellectual way, are what he succeeds at least. He appears more superficial; his language sounds insufficiently distinguished. The fact that passages of this kind make the strongest impression on the

public cannot mislead more serious observers as to their lack of originality. I have no hesitation in judging the much-lauded A♭-major passage—for many listeners the single refreshing moment of the
evening—to be one of the weaker parts of the work. I do not even
believe in the artistic-aesthetic necessity of this last-minute insertion.
The lyrical pause that he desired to create following the preceding
agitated scenes could also have been achieved without textual additions, although this would not have afforded the composer the opportunity for such a broad development. Was it really necessary? Is it
not possible that here the composer was caught short by the memory
of the conditions under which opera formerly used to operate? May
Strauss not have felt—consciously or unconsciously—a secret wish to
offer something to those listeners who were inclined to indulge their
ears? It is hardly possible to say with certainty. From a critical point
of view, this scene, up to the appearance of C major ("No, you must
not embrace me"), does not seem terribly valuable to me, even if it
is not nearly so undistinguished as the comparable passages in *Salome*.
I almost wish that Hofmannsthal had not agreed to this alteration.
The score of Elektra would be deprived of one of its most sure-fire
effects, but its unity would not have been interrupted by this lyrical
flourish.

More interesting is the second part of Elektra's song, in which the
once-proud princess talks about her own beauty, and her nature,
which is otherwise so rough, appears as if bathed in a mild, transcendent light by the memory of the past. Here the orchestral accompaniment, which is clothed in fine, airy tones, is shot through with
gentle motives. In addition to the familiar Elektra themes a new,
emotional chromatic motive appears (for the first time during
Elektra's outburst—"I am the blood of the king Agamemnon, spilt like
a dog's!"

A painfully lamenting motive accompanies Elektra's description of
her past nature:

"You are horrified
at me, and yet was a king's daughter!
I think that I was beautiful."

Elektra's question introduces the conclusion of this scene:

> "But you are trembling all over?"
> ORESTES: "Then let this body tremble!
>   It suspects where I am leading it."

The two siblings, now determined to carry out the deed, sing a brief duet based on an energetic theme from the second Chrysothemis scene:

It reaches its climax in Elektra's cry "Glad is the one who comes to do his deed":

and then closes in the most exalted ecstasy:

> "Glad is she who longed for him
> Glad the one who saw him first
> Glad the one who recognized him
> Glad the one who touched his hand.
> Glad the one who digs his ax from the earth,
> Glad the one who holds the torch,
> Glad she who opens the door for him."

This is immediately followed by several short scenes, in which the long-awaited, most important events of the external plot take place: Klytämnestra's and Aegisthus's murder, and the punishment of the servants who have remained faithful to the two rulers. Strauss cut the scene with the attendant, which had originally separated them, down to a few words, so that Orestes' entrance into the house almost immediately follows Elektra's fanatical exaltation of the act of vengeance. A strangely colored tone painting appears as Orestes takes his first step into the palace. Once again, there are extended, strange, mysterious harmonies; they create the impression of gazing into a gloomy abyss of unfathomable depth. With fearful, penetrating insistence, the following orchestral interlude paints the terrible suspense in which Elektra is left behind in the courtyard. Dark runs in the basses chase each other softly up and down, until a sudden stillness falls, as if

Elektra's blood stood still at the despairing thought:

> "I was not able to give him the ax!
> They have gone, and I was not able
> to give him the ax. There are no
> gods in heaven!"

Once more an interlude follows, filled with uneasy suspense. Violent accents start convulsively, seconds stretch into eternities—then Klytämnestra's scream sounds from inside the palace. "Strike her again!" cries Elektra in demonic rage. A second piercing scream, a moment of paralyzing silence. Then a rolling fortissimo begins. Like one of the furies, Elektra stands in front of the door as if rooted to the spot. The maids burst out of the side door with Chrysothemis. They have heard the cries and run out, startled. No sooner do they catch sight of the motionless Elektra than they rush up to her. But fear of Aegisthus, who is drawing near, drives them back into their rooms. The courtyard lies deserted and dark, as Aegisthus, unaware of what has happened, approaches, preceded by the thrumming motive that has appeared before when his name was mentioned:

He scolds the servants for their carelessness in not hurrying to greet him. His words rouse Elektra from her rigid repose. She had been unable to respond to the maids, out of unwillingness to profane the holy moments of the deed with ordinary chatter. But to lure the second victim to the altar with her wiles—that she is able to do. Obsequiously, she approaches Aegisthus; a scornfully flattering motive illustrates her hypocritical friendliness toward her mortal enemy:

Like a ghost, she circles Aegisthus as he strides unknowingly toward the slaughtering block. The light of the torches plays strangely about her figure as she staggers with joy at her victory. Aegisthus enters the house, the doors close behind him—only a brief moment is vouchsafed him, then the hands of the avengers have him in their grip. His repeated cries for help ring out unheard—only Elektra replies, "Agamemnon hears you." He, too, sinks to the ground—the drama of Klytämnestra is over.

Once more, the maids run out of the house with Chrysothemis. They know what has happened; they hear the noise of the servants struggling inside. Joyfully Chrysothemis calls out the news of Orestes' return to her sister. But Elektra does not hear. She no longer perceives anything of earthly events. For her, this world no longer exists. She has been destroyed in the instant when Klytämnestra's and Aegisthus's fate was sealed. Elektra is no longer conscious of her heritage, her sister, her brother. As other women find in love the whole meaning of life, so Elektra was completely consumed with the longing for vengeance. This has now come to fulfillment—Elektra's life's goal has been reached—and her own fate is accomplished. Her spirit rises to one more dithyrambic hymn of victory, then she sinks lifelessly to the ground, a human being who casts out life not as a result of discontent or despair but rather because it has given her everything she dreamed of as its highest good: "We doers of deeds are one with the gods."

.

The composition of this conclusion presented the composer with a most rewarding challenge. Here much more was required than illustrating the Dance of the Seven Veils. Here the dance is not a sensually titillating means of seduction but the most extreme expression of a nameless celebration that surpasses all rational comprehension and can only express itself in ecstatically rhythmic gestures. Strauss found an eminently felicitous form for this in powerfully swelling, broad $\frac{6}{4}$ rhythms with a simple, nobly drawn melodic line rising above them. That his skill in combining motives finds brilliant expression here need hardly be emphasized. Details may be found in the abovementioned guide by Röse and Prüwer. For me it was not Richard Strauss's technique but the artistic plan and execution of his work that claimed my primary interest. Arguing about his skill is scarcely worthwhile—despite Georg Göhler's well-known defamatory article in *Zukunft*.[6] As for the people who have been busy criticizing him for some time, Strauss could not have given them a more brilliant response than the score of *Elektra*. It was the artist's answer to the attacks of petty fault-finders and malicious grudges. For what is so unsympathetic about the anti-Strauss movement of the recent past is precisely this: it disdains artistic criticism and, speculating on the public's hunger for gossip and lust for sensation, attempts to press the attack into the arena of personal and private affairs. That is the noble tactic of the Göhlers, Brandes, and Co., who take particular pride in their resistance to a supposedly fashionable trend, in the correctness of their views and in their independence of public opinion. Far removed from this bunch with their reliance on journalistic half-truths is that criticism which sets as its goal the analysis and characterization of an artistic individuality. Such critics, too, will be compelled from time to time to point out blemishes, reveal weaknesses—but they will not do so with the sneering self-satisfaction of those criticasters who feel more pleasure at discovering a single blot on the artist's character than at all the merits his work contains. Rather, they will attempt to explain these errors as necessary consequences of a particular artistic sensibility. Still, if we compare what is good in the *Elektra* score with what is less successful, the weaknesses of the work will be barely perceptible compared to the wealth of its great, new ideas. This much is certain: Strauss has given us other creations that appear more well-rounded, smoother. But in none of them has he aimed so far, set his goal so high, as in *Elektra*. What he has given us in all parts of this work far surpasses, in formative powers of originality and stylistic individuality, dramatic greatness, and power of concentration, everything that other contemporary musicians have accomplished. And even from the weaker passages there speaks such a brilliant intention, such a bold spirit of enterprise, that scarcely an artist of our era will fail to recognize the signs of genius. Admittedly: it must be artists whom one asks for their opinion. For only equals can be the judge of equal quality.

NOTES

1. Strauss sold *Elektra* to Fürstner for a reported one hundred thousand marks [ed.].

2. Nietzsche's *Geburt der Tragödie aus dem Geiste der Musik* appeared in 1872 [trans.].

3. Heinrich von Kleist (1777–1811), Prussian dramatist and early modern prose writer, whose desire to be Germany's greatest theatrical writer earned him the scorn and opposition of Goethe and others. Only three of Kleist's plays were performed during his life, which ended with his suicide at the age of thirty-four. His most important dramatic works include *Penthesilea* (written in 1806–08, first performed in 1876) and its pendant *Das Kätchen von Heilbronn ·oder die Feuerprobe* (written in 1808, first performed in 1810 in Vienna), and *Prinz Friedrich von Homburg* (written in 1809–11, first performed in 1821). His works were rediscovered in the 1860s and 1870s [trans.].

4. Bekker refers to Ludwig Tieck (1773–1853), a German poet, dramatist, and editor. His literary works attracted such composers as Brahms, Mendelssohn, Schumann, Spohr, and others [ed.].

5. Johann Wolfgang von Goethe (1749–1832). *Iphigenia,* written and performed in 1779, is based on Euripides. Kleist's comedy *Amphytrion* (written in 1807, first performed in 1898) is based on Molière. Franz Grillparzer (1791–1872), was a prolific Viennese dramatist whose work represents the cultural high point of Biedermeier Austria. *Medea,* the third part of his trilogy *Das Goldene Vliess,* was completed in 1820 and first performed in 1821 in Vienna. It is based on Euripides [trans.].

6. Karl Georg Göhler (1874–1954) was not only a conductor and composer but a music critic for various newspapers and music journals, such as *Zukunft* [ed.].

Richard Strauss at Sixty

THEODOR W. ADORNO

TRANSLATED BY SUSAN GILLESPIE

Theodor Adorno (1903–69) was one of the most eminent Western Marxist intellectuals of the twentieth century. He was a prominent member of the so-called Frankfurt School, part of the Frankfurt-based Institute for Social Research that included such figures as Max Horkheimer, Leo Löwenthal, Herbert Marcuse, and Friedrich Pollock. Adorno's polemical writings have strongly informed the discourse on twentieth-century music over the past decades. Two books—available in English translation—have been especially influential: *Philosophy of Modern Music* (1973) and *Introduction to the Sociology of Music* (1976); the latter is a collection of essays and lectures.

Although Adorno's primary work involved philosophy, sociology, and aesthetics, he had extensive musical training, having studied composition with Alban Berg and piano with Edward Steuermann. Adorno admired the work of Berg's teacher, Arnold Schoenberg, and he made a number of close ties with members of that circle. Adorno was impressed with Schoenberg's "insistence on the truth content" in music, but—as the following essay (1924) on Strauss suggests—such an insistence was already an integral part of Adorno's worldview. His style of writing is complex and often seems to resist translation. Biographer Martin Jay suggests that such complicated prose "was deliberately designed to thwart an effortless reception by passive readers."[1] Adorno, no doubt, believed that the act of reading his work—with all its challenges—was part of the philosophical process.

Adorno's best-known and most-quoted essay on Strauss was written in 1964, to commemorate the one-hundredth anniversary of Strauss's birth. By then Adorno was sixty-one—only five years away from his death. Less well known, and previously unavailable in English, is his essay on Strauss, written when the philosopher was only twenty-one years old. More cogent and concise than the later essay, this sixtieth-birthday commemoration for the *Zeitschrift für Musik* represents the essential core of Adorno's critique of the composer's music, which is that "its form is appearance." Strauss's work, according to Adorno, is devoid of objectivity and, ultimately, artistic truth—the very truth demanded by someone like Schoenberg. In a typically dialectical way, Adorno declared that in order for art to be truthful it must first confess its fictitiousness. But, as a recent study suggests, by pursuing "the purpose of depicting Strauss as the absolute antagonist to his own aesthetical ideas, Adorno failed to comprehend fully Strauss's narrative-structural procedures and strategies"[2] [ed.].

[Source: Theodor Adorno, "Richard Strauss. Zum 60. Geburtstag: 11. Juni 1924," in *Zeitschrift für Musik* 91 (1924): 289–95]

.

For Richard Strauss, the sixtieth birthday is perhaps less appropriate as a symbol than for any other living musician. As a symbol, this occasion would seem to bespeak a stasis, a conclusion; and even if there has been polemical talk, for more than a decade, of Strauss's rigidification, still the intention of his works seems to be against all rigidity—in fact, the objection raised to the later Strauss is grounded essentially in the assumption that he is incapable of creating otherwise than in a constantly changed mode. The subject of his music is *life*: life in the specific sense that was given conceptual form in the philosophy of Nietzsche, Simmel, and Bergson.[3] Corresponding examples exist in art in the paintings of Slevogt and Corinth, for example, or the sculptures of Rodin, or the novels of Anatole France and Thomas Mann.[4] In all these, life, in itself still devoid of meaning, is supposed to be the ultimate meaning; in all of them life plays itself out fully in a time that unfolds meaninglessly; in all of them man does not conceive himself as a created being that knows itself dependent on God but posits himself as the highest measure of all things. As this immanent life is the subject of Strauss's music, so the vehicle of his music is the human being whose soul, fallen away from the relation to God, is fully satisfied in itself: the psychological "I."[5] The music of the psychological subject has no given, obligatory forms, forms that could be lawfully received only in the context of a relationship; it points back to man as the representative—by chance, as it were—of detached functions of the soul, among which it rests without actually ever being able to come to rest. If, in Strauss's music, some of the contents can be shown to derive from this kind of purely life-oriented artistic practice, this should nevertheless not be construed as reducing his figure to a simple formula.

·

The music of the psychological subject corresponds to that subject. The world it designates is the creation of the subject, and its content derives from the relationless "I." Thus the music of the psychological subject is not capable of breaking out of its sphere directly upward at any point. In the nineteenth century, as this phenomenon was taking shape, Mendelssohn's shivering classicism and Chopin's dazzling play, Schumann's blind repetition of the sonata, and Bruckner's congregationless chorale are all equally tragic attempts to conjure up once more the power of forms. But to all of them was given a share of real participation in lasting forms, for the collapse of the "I" is not yet complete, and Beethoven's mastery beckons from a not-unreachable distance. Beethoven is all person; he achieves this by wrestling with forms that extend challengingly into his world. In Strauss the reality of forms has vanished for good; it continues to exist only as appearance. Strauss lives neither with the forms nor against them; he establishes the forms of the past for himself. In this Strauss differs radically from Beethoven and approaches Wagner.

The restriction of the music of the psychological "I" to the subjective sphere is the limit of what it means. The farther the situation into which the artist is born is removed from meaning, the more faintly the forms show themselves to him, the more clearly his task becomes the portrayal of his own inner life—that inner life he previously did not need to portray, since, oriented to something above him, it divested itself of its forms and images as witness to this orientation. This is inner life that has long ceased to be true inner life. Wagner's music, which delved deeply into mediocre psychologizing, attempted to retain the upward striving through the medium of the word. Then Strauss decisively reduces music to psychological portrayal, gives up the medium of the word and makes the word, even where it refers to detached soulfulness, superfluous; Liszt's symphonic music, which Wagner mistrusted, finds in him its first sensual resolution. The psychology of the detached individual is the answer of his music; its form, however, is appearance.

·

It is said that Strauss occasionally referred to himself as a Mendelssohnian. The quip, which entrusts the heritage of moderate romanticism to the instrumental adventurer, has a grain of truth in it, at least compared to the habit of reckoning Strauss unthinkingly to the Wagnerian succession. The compulsive choice between concealing his inner life in empty forms, into which it can only be pressed by dint of disencumbering itself of all its essential particularities, or delving into himself to seek, between the waves of his experiences as they stream out from him through time, his own self, which has long since slipped away—this compulsive choice, as it exists, for example, between Stravinsky's and Pfitzner's ways of proceeding, he was spared. The emotional phenomena that Strauss portrays do not penetrate down to the deepest stratum of the problems of inner life; they are of typical generality and symbolize life only in its chance connection with the individual, without, however, cruelly divesting the individual of its self. Exemplary for the psychological content of Straussian music is the level of the *erotic*: it lies clearly within the sphere of the "I" and bears within it all the particularities of the individual who relates it to life. At the same time, however, it exhibits empirical lawfulness and is located, at least in its limitation to the nervous-sensual sphere, as it appears in Strauss's works, in the outer layer of the soul. Strauss's *Schwung* means something similar, closely related to Bergson's *élan vital*; like it, it is turned toward experiential time as its inner concern; it, too, permits him to give tangible visualization to the wealth of the soul's "I" without getting to the bottom of it. Strauss's psychology proceeds from the inside out and knows why it does so: in the experiential zone in which it is content to remain, it is able to salvage at least the outer husk of the real world. The talk about Strauss's superficiality is irresponsible; the entire depth of his music consists in the fact that its whole world is nothing but surface, that it floats loose on the surface of the world instead of letting go of an admittedly fragmentary reality of external things in the fruitless chase after that inner reality which is, by itself, quite unreal. And just as Strauss, by virtue of his concrete-musical vision, escaped the fate of throwing process-without-end into the soul and winding up in lyrical form-anarchy, so he was also charmed against the temptation of empty forms, which give the appearance of objectivity and yet possess, at best, the objectivity of the machine. He did not build the symphony as a logical construction and yet he was able to maintain for it a more-than-individual validity. The *apparent nature of form*, which was his contribution, derives its specific meaning in part from the situation that surrounds it. While for the individual person or society that is other-directed, the image—like the human being who created it—has essence and form but remains open toward something higher and does not perfect itself in its form, an art that has torn itself loose from this relationship is denuded of essence that has been given form and is simultaneously damned to strive for its own form as the purportedly last thing. However, this form remains mere appearance, in the end, so long as it is not empowered and is torn by doubt from above. For *Lebensphilosophie,* and above all Simmel, the work of art, seen from the vantage point of life, is appearance; it is only because it has been elevated above the flow of real life that it has permanence and offers something stable in opposition to the movement of life. This is how Strauss's form, too, must be understood. It is not proffered within a real community; it is a mere outgrowth of life, grown from the same stalk as life, freely established by the "I." In the apparent nature of forms is revealed Strauss's relationship to the romantic; and yet, at the same time, he is quite foreign to it, for neither does he wish to build up forms as reality nor does their lack of reality, for him, become an ironic tool with which to expose the unreality of his own life. Rather, they are apparent in comparison to the motion of life; but in the sphere of art, which exists at close remove from the realm of life, they are real until life sweeps them away again. Strauss is an artist in the sense of the antithesis between life and art as posited by *Lebensphilosophie*; and it is not by accident that from his works the concept of compositional technique as self-sufficient virtuosity has been abstracted. This technique not infrequently rules over the aesthetic realm as its guiding principle. Most of Strauss's types of forms emerge indirectly from the organizational principle of technique—generally, that is, from the separating off of an isolated aesthetic sphere that surrounds life with appearance. This aesthetic sphere, although its demands are of a general nature, does not absorb the psychological "I"; rather, as soon as its generality encounters the psychological "I," in the portrayal of emotional life, it wraps itself around it, so that its own apparent nature is clear for all to see. The young Strauss, who wrote the *Don Juan* fantasy, wanted to grasp life in all its immediacy as the psychological subject of his music, and he began at a point where form followed life in a disinterested, unproblematic way—in the symphonic poem of Liszt. As he matured, he discovered that the pure formlessness of the preludelike variation of forms—to which he was, in any case, not permanently susceptible thanks to a melodic plasticity that had a disposition all its own—was the least effective means of securing that aesthetic sphere. He was unable to return to the multiple movements of his earlier works because of his *program*. This program entails a variety of overlapping intentions: first, its conceptual clarity means that the music is restricted to the portrayal of detached emotional contents; next, its sensual power further strengthens the external impulse of the music; and, finally, the program reaches beyond the emotional content–turned–musical form, just as life itself reaches beyond artistic forms, and thus it ends by calling the clarity of the emotional contents into question again. The contradiction between the technique—the essence of the isolated aesthetic sphere—and the program, which embodies the abandonment of psychological portrayal and the final incapacity of forms to grasp life—this contradiction becomes the impulse behind the development of Strauss's symphonic music. The program calls for *open* forms that can clothe any and all motives involved in psychological portrayal while remaining sufficiently appearance-like to avoid being broken apart by them. The rondo and variations accommodate this. Technique, on the other hand, requires of the program that it be broader than its conceptual objectivity; the emotional realities whose uniqueness it makes fast must be related to life if the music is to be able to dissolve them; and the life from which they spin themselves out must already contain within it the contradiction to form that engenders the musical form. Eulenspiegel, who reappears again and again, as mortal or immortal as appearance itself with its colorful role in life, falls easily into the rondo; the comical endlessness of Don Quixote's attempts to make sense of the detached world of appearances congeals into variations. In each case, only the psychological surface of the sketch is assimilated in the music; its inner nature is untouched, the distance between life and form reflected in the distance from the program; and in each case the apparent nature of both life and forms reveals and gives off *humor,* more real than the pathos of *Zarathustra,* whose claim on reality is more apparent than any appearance. The more central the relationship of form and life becomes to Strauss, the stronger his tendency becomes to contrast form with life, the more apparent is the form. From *Heldenleben* and *Symphonia Domestica,* the psychological sonnets for orchestra, it is not such a long way to *Ariadne,* with its romantic play on the baroque opera. Nevertheless, the reconciliation of technique with program, of the aesthetic compulsion toward stylization with a free-wheeling psychology, of form with life, was hardly ever achieved more effectively than precisely in *Heldenleben.* His *Schwung* never swings more deeply into the sensual than here, his thematic arcs never project him farther, shooting like fireworks from the creative "I" into the dark of his loneliness. It is as if the symphonic form has become transparent; the duality of the themes corresponds to the psychological duality of movement and stasis, the sonata form reflects the conflict of typical emotional events at the external, experiential level, and life itself shines through the entire form, bodies it forth, and devours it. Only in the final movements is the technical balance of *Heldenleben* and *Domestica* threatened: life has called the form into question, opened it up, and prevented it from reaching its conclusion; but the work of art, as appearance, demands a conclusion, to affirm its own closed nature. However, this conclusion cannot come from life and is therefore no conclusion; the music breaks off arbitrarily. The pure E♭-major cadence of *Heldenleben* leads into the reprise, flying over the resistance of the repetition; but what is repeated here, since all of existence has already been absorbed into movement, is chance, while the claim of the form to exert its power requires repetition of the exposition. The repetition is altered by the program in vain; the hollowness of musical expression in the "Hero's retirement from the world" betrays the fact that no form that derives from mere life has power over life, unless it falsifies it. Likewise, the fugue in the *Domestica* has been constructed as a sensual imitation based on the abstract demand of the form; technically unsure, it piles coda on coda, without ever reaching a stopping place. What still remained completely hidden from view here was to have fateful consequences later, in the *Alpensinfonie,* which is much less tightly imagined, as a result of the crass externality of the relationship between program and form. Nonetheless, this externality, like the externality of the psychological subject matter, must not be judged too cavalierly. Strauss submits consciously to *convention*, which warns him, as he weaves the living and the static, the real and the unreal into a single fabric, against chasing after supposedly real forms and too readily leaving behind that reality with which the mere individual still clothes itself. At the same time, however, Strauss's responsiveness to convention embraces a humane meaning that points beyond its mere situation.

.

Strauss has often been criticized for his connection with Hugo von Hofmannsthal. It is said, for example, that the son of nature teamed up with the aesthete in order to retain contact with his times; or even that he wanted to introduce fresh stimulation from the more sublime regions of neoromantic poetry into the flagging sensuality of his music. Such verdicts have not comprehended very much of Strauss's essence, and what little they comprehended they have distorted in their haste. If one selects for an artist like Hofmannsthal, who is crystallized so clearly in his work, the term *aesthete,* then this term applies to Strauss as well, for as in Hofmannsthal, so also in Strauss conclusive significance attaches to the aesthetic sphere, in which the listener re-creates life. The phrase about Strauss, the "son of nature," is quite illegitimate; however strongly Strauss's music may be rooted in the sensual, its external thrust is extremely unnaive in origin, and the defenders of Straussian naiveté should be alerted, if nothing else, by the fact that the supposed hero of the Sendlingergasse[6] fell head over heels in love with Salome and even followed the erotic metamorphoses of the pagelike Octavian with a certain familiarity. Nevertheless, Strauss's turning toward Hofmannsthal marks the caesura of his development. Although in terms of content it bound Strauss even more intimately to the art of his era, which was directed toward mere life, the encounter with Hofmannsthal defines the moment at which the artist Strauss came up against an outer threshold of life that he hesitated to push back down into it, even though he experienced it in an aesthetically veiled, mild form embedded in convention. He knew already that all human emotions are contingent on life; and this knowledge concealed, from the very beginning, the knowledge of the contingent nature of life itself. But this more profound knowledge does not become emphatic until death itself intrudes into life. This is not to assert that Strauss ever experienced death as a psychological fact; perhaps for him, as Simmel formulates it in his diaries, the mystery became definitive, the consciousness of limitation came to him without overwhelming him with tragic force. But the happily perceived surface of life begins to tremble slightly, and he feels his way hesitatingly upward. The empirical world of the emotions, in which Strauss until then believed the remainder of reality secure, becomes doubtful for him—doubtful at precisely the moment when he has subjected Salome to the most ruthless psychologizing; he seeks contact with the spirit, hopes the word, which expresses limitation, may be able to protect the sensual world of appearances from collapse. The ephemerality of man in flowing time is Hofmannsthal's theme and Strauss's secret. Shrinking back from psychologism with its emptiness of meaning, Strauss grasps at a meaning that finally resounds only out of that emptiness; but at the same time his sensual power is broken; the "here" slips away from him, and the "beyond" still eludes his grasp. This is Strauss's tragedy—that as soon as his will extended beyond the sphere of mere life, he lost what reality he possessed. It was not that Hofmannsthal robbed him of his musical vision by deceiving him with aesthetic speculations; he went to Hofmannsthal when he could no longer believe the concreteness of his musical vision. In *Elektra* psychologist met psychologist; but in *Rosenkavalier* the flowing time in which the psychic events are embedded has itself become a subject, and Hofmannsthal's comment that in *Rosenkavalier* the music is *between* the characters characterizes well the defense against psychologism that inspired both poet and composer to conjure up the dancing melancholy of the Viennese atmosphere. When Strauss, transformed, now reverts to sensuality once more, he draws close to romanticism for the first time: his belief in the reality of the external has deserted him, psychology has divested itself of its form-giving rights; the music, ironic, doubts the reality of even the psychological subject that is its vehicle; ironically, it turns the break between form and life, now fully visible, into its stylistic principle. *Rosenkavalier* is criticized for being sentimental, as a music in which the decision of existential man has become impossible; but this sentimentalism is its honesty. For Strauss, at the outer limits of psychology, surveying but not overcoming it, renouncing in the face of flowing time, can give nothing but sentimental form to the sacrifice of the "here" for the "beyond." Once more he bows to convention: no longer to salvage aesthetically the reality of the external world but to expose the reality of the psychological inner world as appearance. The Straussian "concessions" of the later period—for example, the conclusion of the *Rosenkavalier*—are not concessions to the public but his admission of the inadequacy of the self-creating individual, overshadowed by melancholy; his admission, too, that the isolated aesthetic sphere is not all that serious, that it dissolves in the light of day. In the gentle atmosphere of renunciation that envelopes all these crepuscular contours in its golden mist, the music of the Marschallin, Strauss's best and most tender, was vouchsafed to him. In *Ariadne,* Strauss's most profoundly conceived work, the renunciation of the individual was meant, once again, to be intensified above and beyond itself, symbolizing the way in which life reaches beyond forms; as a metaphor for this process, the work of art itself becomes the theme of the work of art; but Strauss's powers fail him—fail him for good reason: Zerbinetta, namely, is finally right about her new god, since the world of Bacchus as a world of mere sensual ecstasy is just as much appearance as the *buffo* world above which it wishes to elevate itself. It is easy to follow Bloch in exposing the apparent nature of even this profundity; but it would be more productive to affirm the profundity of this appearance, which refers back to its rightful sphere a life that desires to be more than forms.

·

After all that, we may be permitted to celebrate Strauss's birthday without sinning against his spirit. The unconditional nature of life has long since found its limits in his works: he paid the highest price for it that he could. He has collected all the brilliance of temporal life and makes it shine forth out of the mirror of his music; he has perfected appearance in music and made music transparent as glass; with his works the end of appearance may also be meant.

NOTES

1. Martin Jay, *Adorno* (Cambridge: Harvard University Press, 1984), p. 11.

2. Anette Unger, "'Truth' and 'Illusion'—'More than Life' and 'Arranged for Life': Applying Adorno's Philosophy of Art to the Works of Richard Strauss and Gustav Mahler," a paper read at the Duke University International Conference on Richard Strauss (April 1990) [ed.].

3. Friedrich Nietzsche (1844–1900), German philosopher, philologist, and poet; Georg Simmel (1858–1918), German philosopher and sociologist; Henri Bergson (1859–1941), French philosopher [ed.].

4. Max Slevogt (1868–1932), German painter and graphic artist; Lovis Corinth (1858–1925), German painter and lithographer; Auguste Rodin (1840–1917), French sculptor and painter; Anatole France (1844–1924), French novelist and critic; Thomas Mann (1875–1955), German novelist and essayist [ed.].

5. Adorno utilizes Freudian terminology here; a more habitual translation would be "ego." However, the Freudian term conveys a technical sense in English, and since Adorno's reflections here are more general and philosophical, the "I" of the original German is retained throughout [trans.].

6. Probably a reference to the autobiographical Kunrad of Strauss's *Feuersnot* (1901) [ed.].

Index of

Names and Compositions

· 417 ·

List of Contributors

Leon Botstein is President of Bard College, where he is also Professor of History and Music History. He is the author of *Judentum und Modernität* (Vienna, 1991) and *Music and Its Public: Habits of Listening and the Crisis of Modernism in Vienna, 1870–1914* (Chicago, forthcoming) as well as Music Director of the American Symphony Orchestra. He has recently been named Editor of *Musical Quarterly*.

Susan Gillespie is Vice President for Public Affairs and Development at Bard College, where she has also taught German poetry. Her published translations of German works include several that appeared in *Brahms and His World*, edited by Walter Frisch (Princeton, 1990) and *Mendelssohn and His World*, edited by R. Larry Todd (Princeton, 1991).

Bryan Gilliam is Assistant Professor of Music at Duke University. He is the author of *Richard Strauss's "Elektra"* (Oxford, 1991) and editor of *Richard Strauss: New Perspectives on the Composer and His Work* (Durham, N.C., 1992). He has written articles on Anton Bruckner, Richard Strauss, and Kurt Weill.

James Hepokoski is Professor of Music at the University of Minnesota and is the author of *Giuseppe Verdi: "Falstaff"* (Cambridge, 1984) and *Giuseppe Verdi: "Otello"* (Cambridge, 1987). He has published articles on Claude Debussy, Richard Strauss, and Verdi and is Associate Editor of *19th-Century Music*.

Timothy L. Jackson is Assistant Professor of Music at Connecticut College. He is the author of articles on the works of Bruckner, Gabriel Fauré, Mozart, Schoenberg, Schubert, and Richard Strauss.

Derrick Puffett serves as Lecturer on the music faculty of the University of Cambridge and Fellow of St. John's College, Cambridge, and has also taught at Oxford. He is the editor of *Richard Strauss: "Salome"* (Cambridge, 1989) and *Richard Strauss: "Elektra"* (Cambridge, 1989) as well as Editor of *Music Analysis*.

Michael P. Steinberg is Assistant Professor of History at Cornell University. He is the author of *The Meaning of the Salzburg Festival: Austria as Theater and Ideology, 1890–1938* (Ithaca, 1990) and has recently been named Associate Editor of *Musical Quarterly*.